TEACHER'S EDITION

Spelling Workout

Phillip K. Trocki

Modern Curriculum Press
is an imprint of

SAVVAS
LEARNING COMPANY

COVER DESIGN: Pronk & Associates

ILLUSTRATIONS: Jim Steck

Acknowledgments
ZB Font Method Copyright © 1996 Zaner-Bloser.

Some content in this product is based upon *Webster's New World Dictionary for Young Adults*.
© 2001 Hungry Minds, Inc. All rights reserved. Webster's New World is a trademark or registered
trademark of Hungry Minds, Inc.

ISBN-13: 978-0-7652-2491-0
ISBN-10:   0-7652-2491-7
35 2021

Table of Contents

Spelling Workout–Our Philosophy

Integration of Spelling with Reading and Writing

In each core lesson for *Spelling Workout*, students read spelling words in context in a variety of fiction and nonfiction selections. The reading selections provide opportunities for reading across the curriculum, focusing on the subject areas of science, social studies, health, language arts, music, and art.

After students read the selection and practice writing their spelling words, they use list words to help them write about a related topic in a variety of forms such as descriptive paragraphs, stories, news articles, poems, letters, advertisements, and posters. A proofreading exercise is also provided for each lesson to help students apply the writing process to their own writing and reinforce the use of spelling words in context.

The study of spelling should not be limited to a specific time in the school day. Use opportunities throughout the day to reinforce and maintain spelling skills by integrating spelling with other curriculum areas. Point out spelling words in books, texts, and the student's own writing. Encourage students to write, as they practice spelling through writing. Provide opportunities for writing with a purpose.

Phonics-Based Instructional Design

Spelling Workout takes a solid phonic and structural analysis approach to encoding. The close tie between spelling and phonics allows each to reinforce the other. *Spelling Workout* correlates closely to *MCP Phonics*, although both programs are complete within themselves and can be used independently.

Research-Based Teaching Strategies

Spelling Workout utilizes a test-study-test method of teaching spelling. The student first takes a pretest of words that have not yet been introduced. Under the direction of the teacher, the student then self-corrects the test, rewriting correctly any word that has been missed. This approach not only provides an opportunity to determine how many words a student can already spell but also allows students to analyze spelling mistakes. In the process students also discover patterns that make it easier to spell list words. Students study the words as they work through practice exercises, and then reassess their spelling by taking a final test.

High-Utility List Words

The words used in *Spelling Workout* have been chosen for their frequency in students' written and oral vocabularies, their relationships to subject areas, and for structural as well as phonetic generalizations. Each list word has been cross-referenced with one or more of the following:

Carroll, Davies, and Richman. *The American Heritage Word Frequency Book*

Dale and O'Rourke. *The Living Word Vocabulary*

Dolch. *220 Basic Sight Words*

Fry, Polk, and Fountoukidis. *Spelling Demons—197 Words Frequently Misspelled by Elementary Students*

Green and Loomer. *The New Iowa Spelling Scale*

Hanna. *Phoneme Grapheme Correspondences as Cues to Spelling Improvement*

Harris and Jacobson. *Basic Elementary Reading Vocabularies*

Hillerich. *A Written Vocabulary of Elementary Children*

Kucera and Francis. *Computational Analysis of Present-Day American English*

Rinsland. *A Basic Vocabulary of Elementary Children*

Sakiey and Fry. *3000 Instant Words*

Thomas. *3000 Words Most Frequently Written*

Thomas. *200 Words Most Frequently Misspelled*

A Format That Results in Success

Spelling Workout treats spelling as a developmental process. Students progress in stages, much as they learn to speak and read. In *Spelling Workout*, they move gradually from simple sound/letter relationships to strategies involving more complex word-structure patterns.

Sample Core Lesson

• **Spelling Words in Action** presents an engaging and informative reading selection in each lesson that illustrates the spelling words in context.

• The activity in the box at the end of the reading selection helps students focus on the spelling patterns of the list words presented in the lesson.

• The **Tip** explains the spelling patterns, providing a focus for the lesson.

• The **List Words** box contains the spelling words for each lesson.

• **Spelling Practice** exercises give students an opportunity to practice writing new words while reinforcing the spelling patterns.

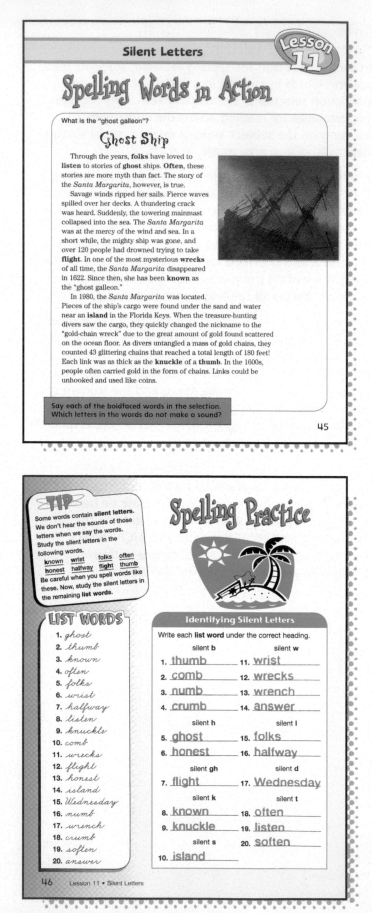

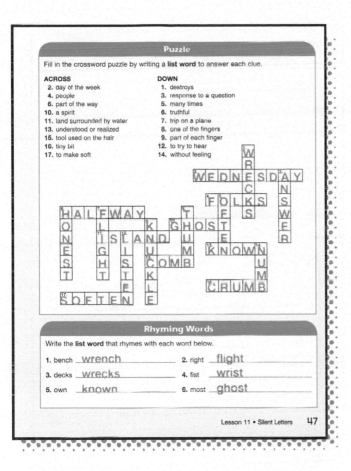

Puzzle

Fill in the crossword puzzle by writing a **list word** to answer each clue.

ACROSS
2. day of the week
4. people
6. part of the way
10. a spirit
11. land surrounded by water
13. understood or realized
15. tool used on the hair
16. tiny bit
17. to make soft

DOWN
1. destroys
3. response to a question
5. many times
6. truthful
7. trip on a plane
8. one of the fingers
9. part of each finger
12. to try to hear
14. without feeling

Rhyming Words

Write the **list word** that rhymes with each word below.

1. bench wrench
2. right flight
3. decks wrecks
4. fist wrist
5. own known
6. most ghost

- Word meaning activities provide opportunities to practice list words while helping students develop their vocabularies.

- Activities such as crossword puzzles, riddles, and games help motivate students by making learning fun.

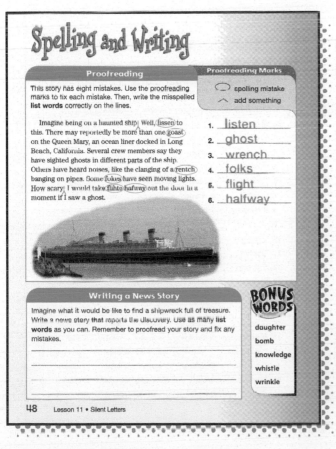

Spelling and Writing

Proofreading

This story has eight mistakes. Use the proofreading marks to fix each mistake. Then, write the misspelled **list words** correctly on the lines.

Proofreading Marks
◯ spelling mistake
⌄ add something

Imagine being on a haunted ship! Well, lissen to this. There may reportedly be more than one goast on the Queen Mary, an ocean liner docked in Long Beach, California. Several crew members say they have sighted ghosts in different parts of the ship. Others have heard noises, like the clanging of a rentch banging on pipes. Some fokes have seen moving lights. How scary! I would take flihto hafway out the door in a moment if I saw a ghost.

1. listen
2. ghost
3. wrench
4. folks
5. flight
6. halfway

Writing a News Story

Imagine what it would be like to find a shipwreck full of treasure. Write a news story that reports the discovery. Use as many list words as you can. Remember to proofread your story and fix any mistakes.

BONUS WORDS
daughter
bomb
knowledge
whistle
wrinkle

- **Spelling and Writing** reinforces the connection between spelling and everyday writing, and encourages students to apply the list words in different contexts.

- **Proofreading** practice builds proofreading proficiency and encourages students to check their own writing.

- **Writing** activities provide opportunities for students to use their spelling words in a variety of writing forms and genres. Write-on lines are provided. Students may also wish to use separate sheets of paper.

- **Bonus Words** offer more challenging words with similar spelling patterns. Activities in the *Teacher's Edition* give students the opportunity to practice the words with a partner.

Sample Review Lesson

- The **Review** lesson allows students to practice what they've learned.

- The spelling patterns used in the previous five lessons are reviewed at the beginning of the lesson.

- **Check Your Spelling Notebook** suggests that students look at their spelling notebooks to review any words that give them trouble. A partner activity provides practice for those words in a variety of learning modalities—kinesthetic, visual, and auditory.

- A variety of activities provides practice and review of selected list words from the previous lessons.

- **Show What You Know** is a cumulative review of the words in the five previous lessons using a standardized-test format.

Lessons 7–11 · Review

Lesson 12

In lessons 7–11, you learned how to spell words with consonant blends and digraphs, vowels with r, silent letters, and the sound of f.

Check Your Spelling Notebook

Look at the words in your spelling notebook. Which words in lessons 7 through 11 did you have the most trouble with? Write them here.

_____

Practice writing your troublesome words with a partner. Try writing the letters for each word in a tray of sand, salt, or sugar. Your partner can check your spelling as you write.

Lesson 7

TIP In a consonant blend, you can hear the sound of each letter. A blend may be found anywhere in a word, such as **tw** in twister, **ld** in colder, and **nds** in sounds.

Write a **list word** to complete each sentence. Not all of the **list words** will be used.

List Words

crept
crunch
dusk
refund
skunk
unfold
milk
halt
twister
stretch
blended
product

1. Bob ___blended___ the ingredients.
2. A ___skunk___ is black and white.
3. The sky begins to darken at ___dusk___.
4. The store would not ___refund___ my money.
5. Thin the batter with a cup of ___milk___.
6. Bike riders must ___halt___ at stop signs.
7. The rabbit ___crept___ into my garden.
8. Try to ___stretch___ the hat to fit.
9. My report was the ___product___ of hard work.
10. I heard the ___crunch___ of snow under my boots.

49

Show What You Know

Lessons 7–11 · Review

One word is misspelled in each set of **list words**. Fill in the circle next to the **list word** that is spelled incorrectly.

1.	○ crunch	● durty	○ bother	○ listen	○ laughs
2.	● gerafe	○ folks	○ leash	○ error	○ absent
3.	○ refund	○ organ	○ awhile	● nuckle	○ after
4.	● foto	○ ghost	○ thunder	○ carton	○ crept
5.	○ printing	○ journal	○ chimney	○ honest	● elefants
6.	○ nephew	○ comb	○ gather	● kurb	○ milk
7.	○ halt	● sherbert	○ feathers	○ wrecks	○ stiff
8.	● geografy	○ thumb	○ reaches	○ sports	○ twister
9.	○ sounds	○ heart	○ wheat	○ flight	● enuf
10.	○ alphabet	● Wenesday	○ farther	○ artist	○ dusk
11.	○ unfold	○ fair	○ foolish	● wriss	○ phony
12.	○ dolphin	● rench	○ crush	○ sparks	○ risk
13.	○ colder	○ boards	● sharpley	○ island	○ graphs
14.	● trofhy	○ numb	○ charge	○ fearless	○ stretch
15.	● diffrent	○ shore	○ shovel	○ crumb	○ phase
16.	○ cough	● sofen	○ chicken	○ spare	○ product
17.	● independant	○ garbage	○ shipment	○ halfway	○ shelf
18.	○ autograph	○ answer	○ whiskers	● cheerfuly	○ protesting
19.	○ blended	● parfume	○ brother	○ known	○ roughly
20.	○ orphan	● ofen	○ Thursday	○ harbor	○ skunk

52   Lesson 12 • Review

Spelling Workout in the Classroom

Classroom Management

Spelling Workout is designed as a flexible instructional program. The following plans are two ways the program can be taught.

The 5-day Plan
Day 1 – Spelling Words in Action and Warm-Up Test
Days 2 and 3 – Spelling Practice
Day 4 – Spelling and Writing
Day 5 – Final Test

The 3-day Plan
Day 1 – Spelling Words in Action and Warm-Up Test/Spelling Practice
Day 2 – Spelling Practice/Spelling and Writing
Day 3 – Final Test

Testing

Testing is accomplished in several ways. A **Warm-Up Test** is administered after reading the **Spelling Words in Action** selection and a **Final Test** is given at the end of each lesson. Dictation sentences for each **Warm-Up Test** and **Final Test** are provided.

Research suggests that students benefit from correcting their own **Warm-Up Tests**. After the test has been administered, have students self-correct their tests by checking the words against the list words. You may also want to guide students by reading each letter of the word, asking students to point to each letter and circle any incorrect letters. Then, have students rewrite each word correctly.

Tests for review lessons are provided in the *Teacher's Edition* as reproducibles following each lesson. These tests provide not only an evaluation tool for teachers, but also added practice in taking standardized tests for students.

Individualizing Instruction

Bonus Words are included in every core lesson as a challenge for better spellers and to provide extension and enrichment for all students.

Review lessons reinforce correct spelling of difficult words from previous lessons.

Spelling Notebook allows each student to analyze spelling errors and practice writing troublesome words independently. Notebook pages appear as reproducibles in the *Teacher's Edition* and as pages at the back of the student book.

A reproducible individual **Student Record Chart** provided in the *Teacher's Edition* allows students to record their test scores.

Ideas for meeting the needs of ESL students are provided.

Dictionary

In the back of each student book is a comprehensive dictionary with definitions of all list words and bonus words. Students will have this resource at their fingertips for any assignment.

The Teacher's Edition —Everything You Need!

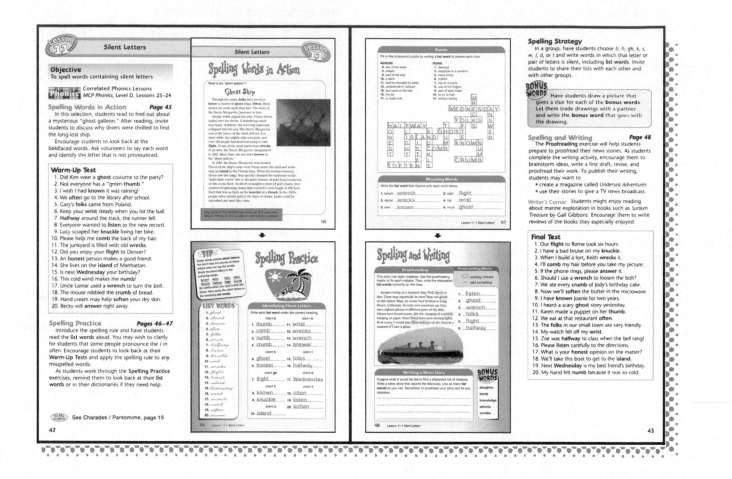

- The **Objective** clearly states the goals of each core lesson.

- Spelling lessons are correlated to *MCP Phonics*.

- Ideas for introducing and setting a purpose for reading are given for each reading selection.

- A **Warm-Up Test**, or pretest, is administered before the start of each lesson. Dictation sentences are provided.

- Concise teaching notes give guidance for working through the lesson.

- Ideas for meeting the needs of ESL students are highlighted.

- **Spelling Strategy** activities provide additional support for reinforcing and analyzing spelling patterns.

- Activities for using the **Bonus Words** listed in the student books are provided.

- **Spelling and Writing** includes suggestions for helping students use proofreading marks to correct their work. Suggestions for using the writing process to complete the writing activity are also offered.

- **Writer's Corner** extends the content of each reading selection by suggesting ways in which students can explore real-world writing.

- A **Final Test** is administered at the end of the lesson. Dictation sentences are provided.

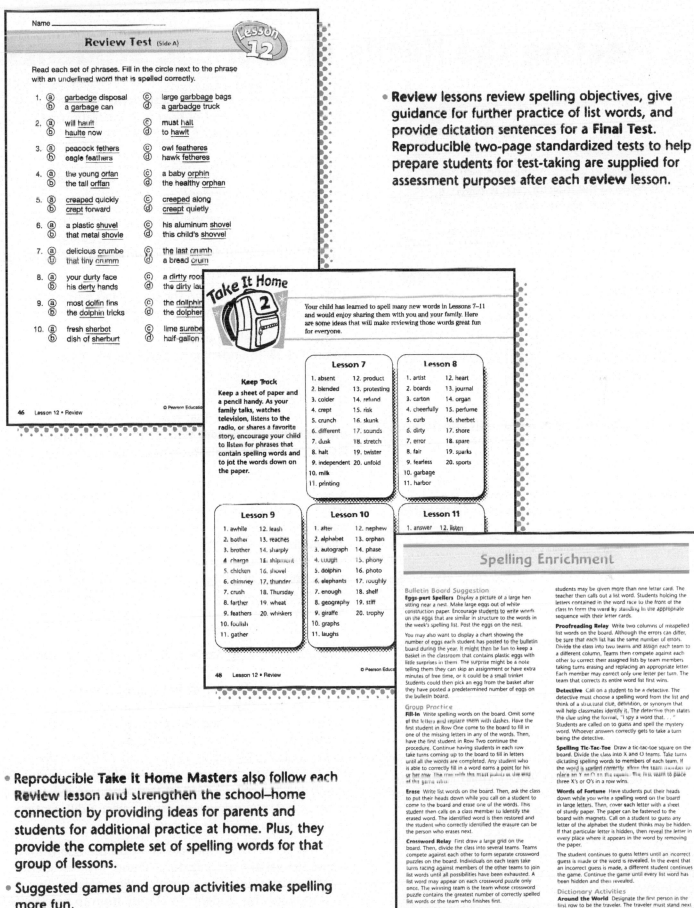

Review Test (Side A)

Lesson 12

Name _____

Read each set of phrases. Fill in the circle next to the phrase with an underlined word that is spelled correctly.

1. (a) garbedge disposal (c) large garbbage bags
   (b) a garbage can (d) a garbadge truck

2. (a) will hault (c) must hall
   (b) haulte now (d) to hawlt

3. (a) peacock fethers (c) owl featheres
   (b) eagle feathers (d) hawk fetheres

4. (a) the young orfan (c) a baby orphin
   (b) the tall orffan (d) the healthy orphan

5. (a) creaped quickly (c) creeped along
   (b) crept forward (d) creept quietly

6. (a) a plastic shuvel (c) his aluminum shovel
   (b) that metal shovle (d) this child's shovvel

7. (a) delicious crumbe (c) the last crumh
   (b) that tiny crumm (d) a bread crum

8. (a) your durty face (c) a dirty room
   (b) his derty hands (d) the dirty lau...

9. (a) most dolfin fins (c) the dollphin...
   (b) the dolphin tricks (d) the dolpher...

10. (a) fresh sherbet (c) lime surebe...
    (b) dish of sherburt (d) half-gallon...

46 Lesson 12 • Review   © Pearson Educat...

Take It Home 2

Your child has learned to spell many new words in Lessons 7–11 and would enjoy sharing them with you and your family. Here are some ideas that will make reviewing those words great fun for everyone.

Keep Track

Keep a sheet of paper and a pencil handy. As your family talks, watches television, listens to the radio, or shares a favorite story, encourage your child to listen for phrases that contain spelling words and to jot the words down on the paper.

Lesson 7
1. absent   12. product
2. blended   13. protesting
3. colder   14. refund
4. crept   15. risk
5. crunch   16. skunk
6. different   17. sounds
7. dusk   18. stretch
8. halt   19. twister
9. independent 20. unfold
10. milk
11. printing

Lesson 8
1. artist   12. heart
2. boards   13. journal
3. carton   14. organ
4. cheerfully 15. perfume
5. curb   16. sherbet
6. dirty   17. shore
7. error   18. spare
8. fair   19. sparks
9. fearless   20. sports
10. garbage
11. harbor

Lesson 9
1. awhile   12. leash
2. bother   13. reaches
3. brother   14. sharply
4. charge   15. shipment
5. chicken   16. shovel
6. chimney   17. thunder
7. crush   18. Thursday
8. farther   19. wheat
9. feathers   20. whiskers
10. foolish
11. gather

Lesson 10
1. after   12. nephew
2. alphabet   13. orphan
3. autograph   14. phase
4. cough   15. phony
5. dolphin   16. photo
6. elephants   17. roughly
7. enough   18. shelf
8. geography   19. stiff
9. giraffe   20. trophy
10. graphs
11. laughs

Lesson 11
1. answer   12. listen

48 Lesson 12 • Review   © Pearson Educa...

Spelling Enrichment

Bulletin Board Suggestion

Eggs-pert Spellers Display a picture of a large hen sitting near a nest. Make large eggs out of white construction paper. Encourage students to write words on the eggs that are similar in structure to the words in the week's spelling list. Post the eggs on the nest.

You may also want to display a chart showing the number of eggs each student has posted to the bulletin board during the year. It might then be fun to keep a basket in the classroom that contains plastic eggs with little surprises in them. The surprise might be a note telling students they can skip an assignment or have extra minutes of free time, or it could be a small trinket. Students could then pick an egg from the basket after they have posted a predetermined number of eggs on the bulletin board.

Group Practice

Fill-In Write spelling words on the board. Omit some of the letters and replace them with dashes. Have the first student in Row One come to the board to fill in one of the missing letters in any of the words. Then, have the first student in Row Two continue the procedure. Continue having students in each row take turns coming up to the board to fill in letters until all the words are completed. Any student who is able to correctly fill in a word earns a point for his or her row. The row with the most points at the end of the game wins.

Erase Write list words on the board. Then, ask the class to put their heads down while you call on a student to come to the board and erase one of the words. This student then calls on a class member to identify the erased word. The identified word is then restored and the student who correctly identified the erasure can be the person who erases next.

Crossword Relay First draw a large grid on the board. Then, divide the class into several teams. Teams compete against each other to form separate crossword puzzles on the board. Individuals on each team take turns racing against members of the other teams to join list words until all possibilities have been exhausted. A list word may appear on each crossword puzzle only once. The winning team is the team whose crossword puzzle contains the greatest number of correctly spelled list words or the team who finishes first.

Scramble Prepare letter cards sufficient to spell all the list words. Distribute letter cards to all students. Some

students may be given more than one letter card. The teacher then calls out a list word. Students holding the letters contained in the word race to the front of the class to form the word by standing in the appropriate sequence with their letter cards.

Proofreading Relay Write two columns of misspelled list words on the board. Although the errors can differ, be sure that each list has the same number of errors. Divide the class into two teams and assign each team to a different column. Teams then compete against each other to correct their assigned lists by team members taking turns erasing and replacing an appropriate letter. Each member may correct only one letter per turn. The team that corrects its entire word list first wins.

Detective Call on a student to be a detective. The detective must choose a spelling word from the list and think of a structural clue, definition, or synonym that will help classmates identify it. The detective then states the clue using the format, "I spy a word that . . ." Students are called on to guess and spell the mystery word. Whoever answers correctly gets to take a turn being the detective.

Spelling Tic-Tac-Toe Draw a tic-tac-toe square on the board. Divide the class into X and O teams. Take turns dictating spelling words to members of each team. If the word is spelled correctly, allow the team member to place an X or O in the square. The first team to place three X's or O's in a row wins.

Words of Fortune Have students put their heads down while you write a spelling word on the board in large letters. Then, cover each letter with a sheet of sturdy paper. The paper can be fastened to the board with magnets. Call on a student to guess any letter of the alphabet the student thinks may be hidden. If that particular letter is hidden, then reveal the letter in every place where it appears in the word by removing the paper.

The student continues to guess letters until an incorrect guess is made or the word is revealed. In the event that an incorrect guess is made, a different student continues the game. Continue the game until every list word has been hidden and then revealed.

Dictionary Activities

Around the World Designate the first person in the first row to be the traveler. The traveler must stand next to the student seated behind him or her. Then, dictate

162

• **Review** lessons review spelling objectives, give guidance for further practice of list words, and provide dictation sentences for a **Final Test**. Reproducible two-page standardized tests to help prepare students for test-taking are supplied for assessment purposes after each **review** lesson.

• Reproducible **Take It Home Masters** also follow each **Review** lesson and strengthen the school–home connection by providing ideas for parents and students for additional practice at home. Plus, they provide the complete set of spelling words for that group of lessons.

• Suggested games and group activities make spelling more fun.

Meeting the Needs of Your ESL Students

Spelling Strategies for Your ESL Students

You may want to try some of these suggestions to help you promote successful language learning for ESL students.

* Prompt use of spelling words by showing pictures or objects that relate to the topic of each selection. Invite students to discuss the picture or object.

* Demonstrate actions or act out words. Encourage students to do the same.

* Read each selection aloud before asking students to read it independently.

* Define words in context and allow students to offer their own meanings of words.

* Make the meanings of words concrete by naming objects or pictures, role-playing, or pantomiming.

Spelling is the relationship between sounds and letters. Learning to spell words in English is an interesting challenge for English First Language speakers as well as English as a Second Language speakers. You may want to adapt some of the following activities to accommodate the needs of your students—both native and non-English speakers.

Rhymes and Songs

Use rhymes, songs, poems, or chants to introduce new letter sounds and spelling words. Repeat the rhyme or song several times during the day or week, having students listen to you first, then repeat back to you line by line. To enhance learning for visual learners in your classroom and provide opportunities for pointing out letter combinations and their sounds, you may want to write the rhyme, song, poem, or chant on the board. As you examine the words, students can easily see similarities and differences among them. Encourage volunteers to select and recite a rhyme or sing a song for the class. Students may enjoy some of the selections in *Miss Mary Mack and Other Children's Street Rhymes* by Joanna Cole and Stephanie Calmenson or *And the Green Grass Grew All Around* by Alvin Schwartz.

Student Dictation

To take advantage of individual students' known vocabulary, suggest that students build their own sentences incorporating the list words. For example:

Mary ran.

Mary ran away.

Mary ran away quickly.

Sentence building can expand students' knowledge of how to spell words and of how to notice language patterns, learn descriptive words, and so on.

Words in Context

Using words in context sentences will aid students' mastery of new vocabulary.

* Say several sentences using the list words in context and have students repeat after you. Encourage more proficient students to make up sentences using list words that you suggest.

* Write cloze sentences on the board and have students help you complete them with the list words.

Point out the spelling patterns in the words, using colored chalk to underline or circle the elements.

Oral Drills

Use oral drills to help students make associations among sounds and the letters that represent them. You might use oral drills at listening stations to reinforce the language, allowing ESL students to listen to the drills at their own pace.

Spelling Aloud Say each list word and have students repeat the word. Next, write it on the board as you name each letter, then say the word again as you track the letters and sound by sweeping your hand under the word. Call attention to spelling changes for words to which endings or suffixes were added. For words with more than one syllable, emphasize each syllable as you write, encouraging students to clap out the syllables. Ask volunteers to repeat the procedure.

Variant Spellings For a group of words that contain the same vowel sound, but variant spellings, write an example on the board, say the word, and then present other words in that word family (*cake: rake, bake, lake*). Point out the sound and the letter(s) that stand for the sound. Then, add words to the list that have the same vowel sound (*play, say, day*). Say pairs of words (*cake, play*) as you point to them, and identify the vowel sound and the different letters that represent the sound (long *a: a_e, ay*). Ask volunteers to select a different pair of words and repeat the procedure.

Vary this activity by drawing a chart on the board that shows the variant spellings for a sound. Invite students to add words under the correct spelling pattern. Provide a list of words for students to choose from to help those ESL students with limited vocabularies.

Categorizing To help students discriminate among consonant sounds and spellings, have them help you categorize words with single consonant sounds and consonant blends or digraphs. For example, ask students to close their eyes so that they may focus solely on the sounds in the words, and then pronounce *smart, smile, spend,* and *special.* Next, pronounce the words as you write them on the board. After spelling each word, create two columns—one for *sm*, one for *sp*. Have volunteers pronounce each word, decide which column it fits under, and then write the word in the correct column. Encourage students to add to the columns any other words they know that have those consonant blends.

To focus on initial, medial, or final consonant sounds, point out the position of the consonant blends or digraphs in the list words. Have students find and list the words under columns labeled *Beginning, Middle,* and *End.*

Tape Recording Encourage students to work with a partner or their group to practice their spelling words. If a tape recorder is available, students can practice at their own pace by taking turns recording the words, playing back the tape, and writing each word they hear. Students can then help each other check their spelling against their *Spelling Workout* books. Observe as needed to be sure students are spelling the words correctly.

Comparing/Contrasting To help students focus on word parts, write list words with prefixes or suffixes on the board and have volunteers circle, underline, or draw a line between the prefix or suffix and its base word. Review the meaning of each base word, then invite students to work with their group to write two sentences: one using just the base word; the other using the base word with its prefix or suffix. For example: *My favorite mystery was due at the library Monday afternoon. By Tuesday afternoon the book was overdue!* Or, *You can depend on Jen to arrive for softball practice on time. She is dependable.* Have students contrast the two sentences, encouraging them to tell how the prefix or suffix changed the meaning of the base word.

Questions/Answers Write list words on the board and ask pairs of students to brainstorm questions or answers about the words, such as "Which word names more than one? How do you know?" (*foxes,* an *es* was added at the end) or, "Which word tells that something belongs to the children? How do you know?" (*children's* is spelled with an *'s*)

Games
You may want to invite students to participate in these activities.

Picture Clues Students can work with a partner to draw pictures or cut pictures out of magazines that represent the list words, then trade papers and label each other's pictures. Encourage students to check each other's spelling against their *Spelling Workout* books.

Or, you can present magazine cutouts or items that picture the list words. As you display each picture or item, say the word clearly and then write it on the board as you spell it aloud. Non-English speakers may wish to know the translation of the word in their native language so that they can mentally connect the new word with a familiar one. Students may also find similarities in the spellings of the words.

Letter Cards Have students create letter cards for vowels, vowel digraphs, consonants, consonant blends and digraphs, and so on. Then, say a list word and have students show the card that has the letters representing the sound for the vowels or consonants in that word as they repeat and spell the word after you. You may wish to have students use their cards independently as they work with their group.

Charades/Pantomime Students can use gestures and actions to act out the list words. To receive credit for a correctly guessed word, players must spell the word correctly. Such activities can be played in pairs so that beginning English speakers will not feel pressured. If necessary, translate the words into students' native languages so that they understand the meanings of the words before attempting to act them out.

Change or No Change Have students make flash cards for base words and endings. One student holds up a base word; another holds up an ending. The class says "Change" or "No Change" to describe what happens when the base word and ending are combined. Encourage students to spell the word with its ending added.

Scope and Sequence for MCP Spelling Workout

Skills	Level A	Level B	Level C	Level D	Level E	Level F	Level G	Level H
Consonants	1–12	1–2	1–2	1	1	1, 7, 9	RC	3
Short Vowels	14–18	3–5	3	2	RC	RC	RC	RC
Long Vowels	20–23	7–11, 15	4–5, 7–8	3	RC	RC	RC	RC
Consonant Blends/Clusters	26–28	13–14	9–10, 17	5, 7	RC	RC	RC	RC
y as a Vowel	30	16	11–13	RC	RC	RC	27	RC
Consonant Digraphs—th, ch, sh, wh, ck	32–33	19–21	14–16	9	RC	RC	RC	RC
Vowel Digraphs		33	6–7, 9	19–21, 23	8–10	11, 14–17	25	RC
Vowel Pairs	29		26	20, 22	7–8, 10	14	25	
r-Controlled Vowels		22, 25	19–20	8	RC	RC	RC	4
Diphthongs	24	32	31	22–23	11	17	RC	RC
Silent Consonants			8	11	4	8–9	RC	RC
Hard and Soft c and g		21	2	4	2	2	RC	
Plurals			21–22	25–27, 29	33–34	33	RC	RC
Prefixes		34	32–33	31–32	13–17	20–23, 25	7–8, 33	7–11, 19–20
Suffixes/Endings	34–35	26–28	21–23, 25, 33	13–17	25–29, 31–32	26–29, 31–32	5, 9, 13–14, 16, 26	5, 25–27
Contractions		23	34	28	20	RC	RC	RC
Possessives				28–29	20	RC	RC	RC
Compound Words				33	19	RC	34	RC
Synonyms/Antonyms				34	RC	RC	RC	RC
Homonyms		35	35	35	RC	34	RC	RC
Spellings of /f/: f, ff, ph, gh				10	3	3	RC	RC
Syllables					21–23	RC	RC	1
Commonly Misspelled Words					35	34	17, 35	17, 29, 35
Abbreviations						35	RC	RC
Latin Roots							11, 15, 31	13–16

Skills	Level A	Level B	Level C	Level D	Level E	Level F	Level G	Level H
Words with French or Spanish Derivations							10, 29	RC 28
Words of Latin/French/Greek Origin								21–23, 28
List Words Related to Specific Curriculum Areas							31–34, 28, 32	
Vocabulary Development	•	•	•	•	•	•	•	•
Dictionary	•	•	•	•	•	•	•	•
Writing	•	•	•	•	•	•	•	•
Proofreading	•	•	•	•	•	•	•	•
Reading Selections	•	•	•	•	•	•	•	•
Bonus Words	•	•	•	•	•	•	•	•
Review Tests in Standardized Format	•	•	•	•	•	•	•	•
Spelling Through Writing								
Poetry	•	•	•	•	•	•	•	•
Narrative Writings	•	•	•	•	•	•	•	•
Descriptive Writings	•	•	•	•	•	•	•	•
Expository Writings	•	•	•	•	•	•	•	•
Persuasive Writings			•	•	•	•	•	•
Notes/Letters	•	•	•		•	•	•	•
Riddles/Jokes	•	•	•					
Recipes/Menus	•	•	•			•	•	
News Stories		•	•	•	•	•	•	•
Conversations/Dialogues	•	•		•	•	•		•
Stories	•	•	•	•	•	•	•	•
Interviews/Surveys		•			•	•	•	•
Logs/Journals	•	•	•	•	•	•	•	
Ads/Brochures		•	•	•	•	•	•	•
Reports					•	•	•	
Literary Devices							•	•
Scripts		•					•	•
Speeches					•	•		•
Directions/Instructions	•	•		•				•

Numbers in chart indicate lesson numbers

RC = reinforced in other contexts

• = found throughout

Consonant Sounds

Objective
To spell words with single and double consonants

Phonics Correlated Phonics Lessons
MCP Phonics, Level D, Lessons 1–2

Spelling Words in Action   *Page 5*
In this selection, students read to find out about a dangerous stunt that an adventurous woman performed about a century ago. Invite students to discuss what Anna Taylor did and what they think about it.

Encourage students to look back at the boldfaced words. Ask volunteers to say each word and identify the consonant sounds.

Warm-Up Test
1. Each Olympic team carried its country's **banner**.
2. The number after ninety-nine is one **hundred**.
3. Babe Ruth achieved **fame** as a baseball player.
4. Did the school bus arrive **later** than usual?
5. The number between six and eight is **seven**.
6. Pam used a **hammer** and nails to fix the chair.
7. Do two sixes make **twelve**?
8. The farmer stored the apples in a **barrel**.
9. There are twenty nickels in one **dollar**.
10. Two **letters** of the alphabet are *A* and *B*.
11. When the movie started, everyone was **silent**.
12. Some **wild** animals are very colorful.
13. Ken worked on homework **until** dinner time.
14. In the springtime, the river currents are **swift**.
15. Please put the **bottles** on the shelf.
16. Aunt Pat brought us a **pineapple** from Hawaii.
17. That **film** was fantastic!
18. Four quarts make a **gallon**.
19. We were late because of the **traffic** jam.
20. Are there **eleven** people on a soccer team?

Spelling Practice   *Pages 6–7*
Introduce the spelling rule and have students read the list words aloud. Encourage students to look back at their **Warm-Up Tests** and apply the spelling rule to any misspelled words.

As students work through the **Spelling Practice** exercises, remind them to look back at their **list words** or in their dictionaries if they need help.

for ESL students **See Student Dictation, page 14**

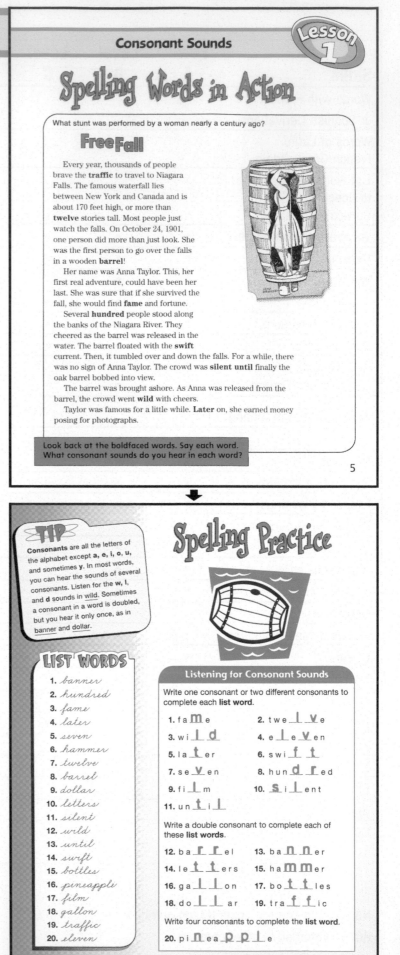

Spelling Words in Action

What stunt was performed by a woman nearly a century ago?

FreeFall

Every year, thousands of people brave the **traffic** to travel to Niagara Falls. The famous waterfall lies between New York and Canada and is about 170 feet high, or more than **twelve** stories tall. Most people just watch the falls. On October 24, 1901, one person did more than just look. She was the first person to go over the falls in a wooden **barrel**!

Her name was Anna Taylor. This, her first real adventure, could have been her last. She was sure that if she survived the fall, she would find **fame** and fortune.

Several **hundred** people stood along the banks of the Niagara River. They cheered as the barrel was released in the water. The barrel floated with the **swift** current. Then, it tumbled over and down the falls. For a while, there was no sign of Anna Taylor. The crowd was **silent until** finally the oak barrel bobbed into view.

The barrel was brought ashore. As Anna was released from the barrel, the crowd went **wild** with cheers.

Taylor was famous for a little while. **Later** on, she earned money posing for photographs.

Look back at the boldfaced words. Say each word. What consonant sounds do you hear in each word?

5

Spelling Practice

TIP
Consonants are all the letters of the alphabet except **a, e, i, o, u**, and sometimes **y**. In most words, you can hear the sounds of several consonants. Listen for the **w, l,** and **d** sounds in **wild**. Sometimes a consonant in a word is doubled, but you hear it only once, as in **banner** and **dollar**.

LIST WORDS
1. banner
2. hundred
3. fame
4. later
5. seven
6. hammer
7. twelve
8. barrel
9. dollar
10. letters
11. silent
12. wild
13. until
14. swift
15. bottles
16. pineapple
17. film
18. gallon
19. traffic
20. eleven

Listening for Consonant Sounds

Write one consonant or two different consonants to complete each **list word**.

1. fa__m__e   2. twe__l__v__e
3. wi__l__d   4. e__l__e__v__en
5. la__t__er   6. swi__f__t
7. se__v__en   8. hun__d__r__ed
9. fi__l__m   10. __s__i__l__ent
11. un__t__i__l

Write a double consonant to complete each of these **list words**.

12. ba__r__r__el   13. ba__n__n__er
14. le__t__t__ers   15. ha__m__m__er
16. ga__l__l__on   17. bo__t__t__les
18. do__l__l__ar   19. tra__f__f__ic

Write four consonants to complete the **list word**.

20. pi__n__ea__p__p__le

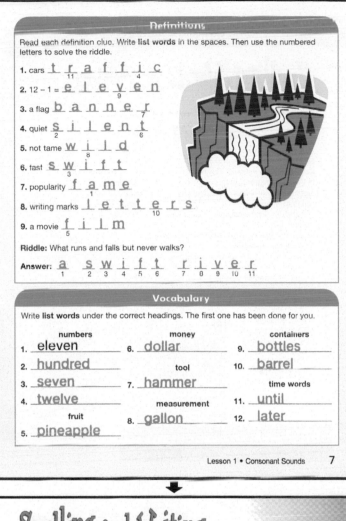

Definitions

Read each definition clue. Write **list words** in the spaces. Then use the numbered letters to solve the riddle.

1. cars t r a f f i c
2. 12 − 1 = e l e v e n
3. a flag b a n n e r
4. quiet s i l e n t
5. not tame w i l d
6. fast s w i f t
7. popularity f a m e
8. writing marks l e t t e r s
9. a movie f i l m

Riddle: What runs and falls but never walks?

Answer: a   s w i f t   r i v e r
1   2 3 4 5 6   7 8 9 10 11

Vocabulary

Write **list words** under the correct headings. The first one has been done for you.

numbers	money	containers
1. eleven	6. dollar	9. bottles
2. hundred	**tool**	10. barrel
3. seven	7. hammer	**time words**
4. twelve	**measurement**	11. until
fruit	8. gallon	12. later
5. pineapple		

Spelling and Writing

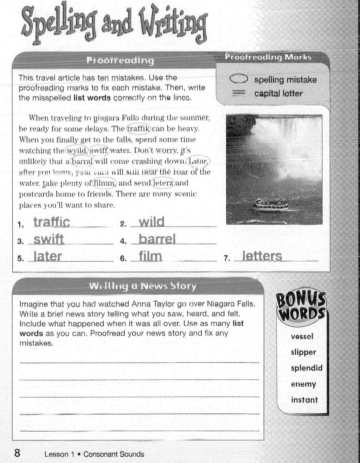

Proofreading

This travel article has ten mistakes. Use the proofreading marks to fix each mistake. Then, write the misspelled **list words** correctly on the lines.

Proofreading Marks
⬭ spelling mistake
= capital letter

When traveling to niagara Falls during the summer, be ready for some delays. The traffik can be heavy. When you finally get to the falls, spend some time watching the wyild, swift water. Don't worry, it's unlikely that a barral will come crashing down. Latar, after you leave, your ears will still hear the roar of the water. take plenty of filmm and send leterz and postcards home to friends. There are many scenic places you'll want to share.

1. traffic
2. wild
3. swift
4. barrel
5. later
6. film
7. letters

Writing a News Story

Imagine that you had watched Anna Taylor go over Niagara Falls. Write a brief news story telling what you saw, heard, and felt. Include what happened when it was all over. Use as many **list words** as you can. Proofread your news story and fix any mistakes.

_____
_____
_____
_____
_____

Spelling Strategy

To help students figure out whether to double the consonant in the middle of a two-syllable word, point out that double consonants usually follow short-vowel sounds. Ask students to say *traffic/trader* and *hammer/tamer* and to tell if
• the *a* in each word is long or short
• one or two consonants follow *a*.

BONUS WORDS Have partners brainstorm topics that relate to all the **bonus words** and then each write a paragraph using the words. They then trade papers to see how they used the words and to discuss how the paragraphs are alike or different.

Spelling and Writing   **Page 8**

The **Proofreading** exercise will help students prepare to proofread their news stories. As students complete the writing activity, encourage them to brainstorm ideas, write a first draft, revise, and proofread their work. To publish their writing, students may want to
• read their stories as radio broadcasts
• illustrate their news stories.

Writer's Corner You may want to bring in or invite students to bring in news clippings about bungee-jumping, skydiving, or other wild stunts. Ask students to write paragraphs telling whether or not they think these activities are safe.

Final Test

1. We did not get home **until** after dark.
2. Pablo gave the soccer ball a **swift** kick.
3. Can we return these **bottles** for money?
4. Mom put **pineapple** rings on the ham.
5. We made a **banner** to welcome the visitors.
6. Can you count backward from one **hundred**?
7. The young actor dreamed of **fame** and fortune.
8. I will clean my room **later**, after Cody leaves.
9. Antonio has to put **film** in his camera.
10. Paul carried the **gallon** of paint up the ladder.
11. **Traffic** is heavy around 5:00 in the evening.
12. Karla will be **eleven** on her next birthday.
13. Beautiful flowers grow **wild** on the hillside.
14. If you are **silent**, you will hear crickets chirp.
15. There are twenty-six **letters** in the alphabet.
16. Luwanda tried to save one **dollar** every week.
17. The clown came out wearing a **barrel**.
18. There are **twelve** eggs in a dozen.
19. Stop banging that **hammer**!
20. Miss Yee's class is in room **seven**.

Objective
To spell one- and two-syllable words with short-vowel sounds

Correlated Phonics Lessons
MCP Phonics, Level D, Lessons 3–4

Spelling Words in Action   *Page 9*

In "Dig It," students read about a type of sculpture that lasts only until the tide comes in. After reading, students may enjoy telling what kind of sand sculpture they would like to make.

Encourage students to look back at the boldfaced words. Ask volunteers to say each word and identify the vowel sound or sounds.

Warm-Up Test

1. Ian's **hands** moved swiftly over the keyboard.
2. The **dentist** showed Tim how to brush his teeth.
3. Kim **lifted** the heavy sack by herself.
4. There is a small **crack** in the old teacup.
5. The **bumps** in the road make drivers go slowly.
6. Keshia will **practice** the song before the concert.
7. If the ice isn't frozen **solid**, don't walk on it!
8. Let's **clasp** hands and form a circle.
9. He rubbed two **sticks** together to start a fire.
10. Last night I **spent** two hours on my homework.
11. Daniel **locked** the chest and put the key away.
12. Mr. King decided to **adopt** the students' plan.
13. Dad was chosen to **judge** the dog show.
14. Can your team win the tug-of-war **contest**?
15. They had to **stand** in line for twenty minutes.
16. I would like **shrimp** and clams for dinner.
17. How much does a **stamp** for a postcard cost?
18. Luis can **trust** John to keep a secret.
19. I waxed the **fender**, the hood, and the door.
20. Maiko's **pencil** has her name printed on it.

Spelling Practice   *Pages 10–11*

Introduce the spelling rule and have students read the **list words** aloud. Encourage students to look back at their **Warm-Up Tests** and apply the spelling rule to any misspelled words.

As students work through the **Spelling Practice** exercises, remind them to look back at their **list words** or in their dictionaries if they need help. Point out that in two-syllable words, one syllable is stronger than the other (the *stressed* syllable).

See Letter Cards, page 15

20

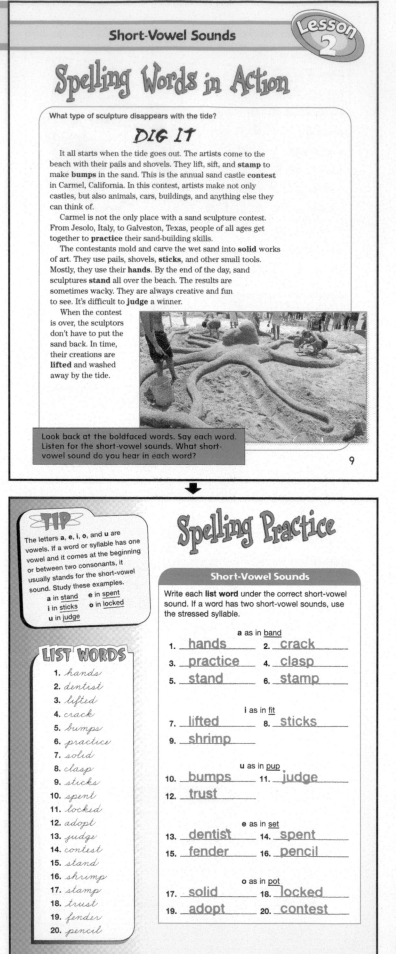

Spelling Words in Action

What type of sculpture disappears with the tide?

DIG IT

It all starts when the tide goes out. The artists come to the beach with their pails and shovels. They lift, sift, and **stamp** to make **bumps** in the sand. This is the annual sand castle **contest** in Carmel, California. In this contest, artists make not only castles, but also animals, cars, buildings, and anything else they can think of.

Carmel is not the only place with a sand sculpture contest. From Jesolo, Italy, to Galveston, Texas, people of all ages get together to **practice** their sand-building skills.

The contestants mold and carve the wet sand into **solid** works of art. They use pails, shovels, **sticks**, and other small tools. Mostly, they use their **hands**. By the end of the day, sand sculptures **stand** all over the beach. The results are sometimes wacky. They are always creative and fun to see. It's difficult to **judge** a winner.

When the contest is over, the sculptors don't have to put the sand back. In time, their creations are **lifted** and washed away by the tide.

Look back at the boldfaced words. Say each word. Listen for the short-vowel sounds. What short-vowel sound do you hear in each word?

9

Spelling Practice

TIP

The letters a, e, i, o, and u are vowels. If a word or syllable has one vowel and it comes at the beginning or between two consonants, it usually stands for the short-vowel sound. Study these examples.
a in <u>stand</u>   e in <u>spent</u>
i in <u>sticks</u>   o in <u>locked</u>
u in <u>judge</u>

Short-Vowel Sounds

Write each **list word** under the correct short-vowel sound. If a word has two short-vowel sounds, use the stressed syllable.

a as in <u>band</u>
1. hands   2. crack
3. practice   4. clasp
5. stand   6. stamp

i as in <u>fit</u>
7. lifted   8. sticks
9. shrimp

u as in <u>pup</u>
10. bumps   11. judge
12. trust

e as in <u>set</u>
13. dentist   14. spent
15. fender   16. pencil

o as in <u>pot</u>
17. solid   18. locked
19. adopt   20. contest

LIST WORDS
1. hands
2. dentist
3. lifted
4. crack
5. bumps
6. practice
7. solid
8. clasp
9. sticks
10. spent
11. locked
12. adopt
13. judge
14. contest
15. stand
16. shrimp
17. stamp
18. trust
19. fender
20. pencil

Replace the Words

Write the **list word** that goes with the underlined word or phrase in each sentence.

1. They asked him to be the <u>person to decide the winner</u>.   judge
2. The door was <u>bolted shut</u> from the inside.   locked
3. Someone always <u>knocks against</u> me while I am in line.   bumps
4. The father <u>raised</u> the box onto the counter.   lifted
5. I <u>paid out</u> a lot of money for skiing lessons.   spent
6. My brother won first prize in the spelling <u>match</u>.   contest
7. The diamond bracelet has a gold <u>fastener</u>.   clasp
8. They made a bonfire from <u>small branches and twigs</u>.   sticks
9. The team must <u>choose</u> a new method of training.   adopt
10. I can <u>rely on</u> my friend Karen to help me.   trust
11. He used his feet to <u>press</u> down the sand.   stamp

Hidden Words

Each word given is hidden in a **list word**. Write the **list word** on the line. Circle the letters that spell the hidden word.

1. rust   t**rust**
2. lid   so**lid**
3. hand   **hand**s
4. rim   sh**rim**p
5. den   **den**tist
6. tick   s**tick**s
7. pen   **pen**cil
8. end   f**end**er
9. tan   s**tan**d
10. rack   c**rack**
11. act   pr**act**ice
12. test   con**test**

Lesson 2 • Short-Vowel Sounds   11

Spelling and Writing

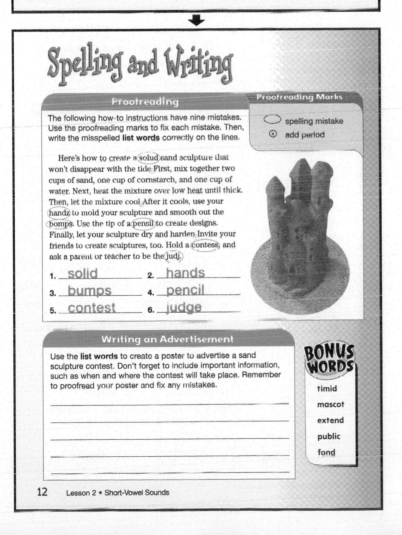

Proofreading

Proofreading Marks
- spelling mistake
- ⊙ add period

The following how-to instructions have nine mistakes. Use the proofreading marks to fix each mistake. Then, write the misspelled **list words** correctly on the lines.

Here's how to create a solid sand sculpture that won't disappear with the tide. First, mix together two cups of sand, one cup of cornstarch, and one cup of water. Next, heat the mixture over low heat until thick. Then, let the mixture cool. After it cools, use your handz to mold your sculpture and smooth out the bomps. Use the tip of a pensil to create designs. Finally, let your sculpture dry and harden. Invite your friends to create sculptures, too. Hold a contess, and ask a parent or teacher to be the judj.

1. solid
2. hands
3. bumps
4. pencil
5. contest
6. judge

Writing an Advertisement

Use the **list words** to create a poster to advertise a sand sculpture contest. Don't forget to include important information, such as when and where the contest will take place. Remember to proofread your poster and fix any mistakes.

_____

_____

_____

_____

BONUS WORDS

timid
mascot
extend
public
fond

12   Lesson 2 • Short-Vowel Sounds

Spelling Strategy

Say each **list word** and invite the class to repeat it after you. Tell students that as they say each word, they should think about how to spell it by listening to the sounds the letters stand for in each syllable. Point out that the vowel in the middle of a one-syllable word usually has a short sound.

BONUS WORDS

Review the meaning of the word *synonym*. Have students write a word or phrase that means the same or almost the same as each **bonus word**. Encourage them to check a dictionary. Then, one partner reads each synonym and the other partner names the **bonus word** it goes with.

Spelling and Writing   *Page 12*

The **Proofreading** exercise will help students prepare to proofread their advertisement posters. As students complete the writing activity, encourage them to brainstorm ideas, write a first draft, revise, and proofread their work. To publish their writing, students may want to
- display the posters in the classroom or in a hall
- use the posters to publicize real contests.

Writer's Corner Provide or ask students to bring in pictures of sandcastles. Have students choose a picture that interests them and either write a caption or a short imaginative story that tells about the picture.

Final Test

1. Let's use those **sticks** to make the kite frame.
2. Did you wash your **hands** before dinner?
3. I like a **pencil** with a good eraser.
4. Our school is having a poetry **contest**.
5. The earthquake caused the wall to **crack**.
6. I **locked** myself out of the house!
7. Please don't sit on the **fender** of the car.
8. You forgot to put a **stamp** on your letter.
9. Scott **lifted** that heavy box.
10. We **spent** two days in El Paso, Texas.
11. That was carved from a **solid** block of ice.
12. Did the **dentist** say that Julie needed braces?
13. Of course I **trust** you with my wallet!
14. **Stand** by the door and I'll take your picture.
15. It was difficult to **judge** the swimming contest.
16. I like cold **shrimp** dipped in chili sauce.
17. The **clasp** on my purse is hard to turn.
18. It takes hours of **practice** to dive well.
19. My parents said I could **adopt** a kitten!
20. The road has lots of **bumps** in it.

Objective
To spell one-, two-, and three-syllable words with long-vowel sounds

 Correlated Phonics Lessons
MCP Phonics, Level D, Lessons 5–6

Spelling Words in Action — Page 13
Students can read to learn about the tuba and how to become a tuba player. Afterward, invite the class to suggest rules for how to learn and care for other instruments.

Encourage students to look back at the boldfaced words. Ask volunteers to name the long-vowel sound or sounds in each word.

Warm-Up Test
1. I'll wear **these** boots on our hike tomorrow.
2. I can't **deny** that I missed the meeting.
3. It is important to follow bicycle safety **rules**.
4. Please see that they cross the street **safely**.
5. I can't **locate** my missing book.
6. It's a **crime** to dump garbage in the river!
7. I heated my soup on the **stove**.
8. Mother used a **scale** to weigh the vegetables.
9. Will I wear this **costume** in the play?
10. The train will **arrive** at four o'clock.
11. Jill **opened** the box of cereal.
12. The play is a **musical** called *Oklahoma.*
13. Please divide the apple into four **equal** pieces.
14. Connie has a terrific **idea** for a new game.
15. Put a **tight** cover on the container.
16. Cows like to eat **clover** out in the field.
17. Is a mouse a **rodent**?
18. The **tuba** is a heavy instrument to carry.
19. Put some ice **cubes** in the pitcher of lemonade.
20. The soldier saluted the flag with **pride**.

Spelling Practice — Pages 14–15
Introduce the spelling rule and have students read the **list words** aloud. Encourage students to look back at their **Warm-Up Tests** and apply the spelling rule to any misspelled words.

As students work through the **Spelling Practice** exercises, remind them to look back at their **list words** or in their dictionaries if they need help. For the **Word Building** exercise, you may want to write on the board *debate − deb + loc =* and model how to arrive at *locate.*

for ESL students See Tape Recording, page 15

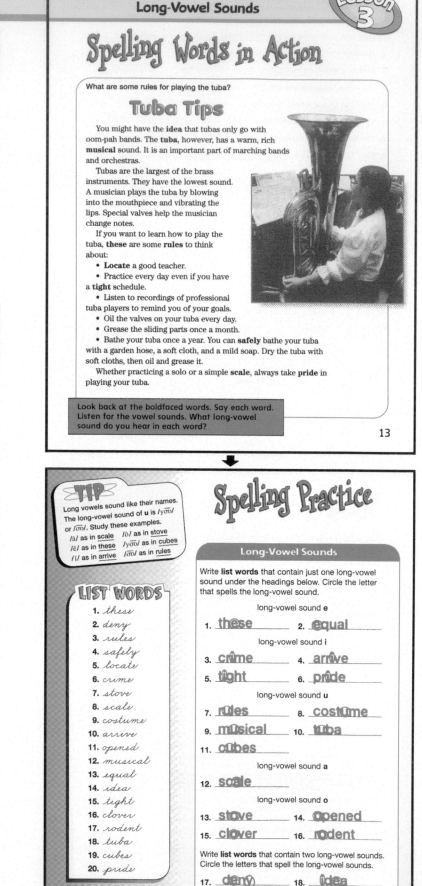

Spelling Words in Action

What are some rules for playing the tuba?

Tuba Tips

You might have the **idea** that tubas only go with oom-pah bands. The **tuba**, however, has a warm, rich **musical** sound. It is an important part of marching bands and orchestras.

Tubas are the largest of the brass instruments. They have the lowest sound. A musician plays the tuba by blowing into the mouthpiece and vibrating the lips. Special valves help the musician change notes.

If you want to learn how to play the tuba, **these** are some **rules** to think about:
• **Locate** a good teacher.
• Practice every day even if you have a **tight** schedule.
• Listen to recordings of professional tuba players to remind you of your goals.
• Oil the valves on your tuba every day.
• Grease the sliding parts once a month.
• Bathe your tuba once a year. You can **safely** bathe your tuba with a garden hose, a soft cloth, and a mild soap. Dry the tuba with soft cloths, then oil and grease it.

Whether practicing a solo or a simple **scale**, always take **pride** in playing your tuba.

Look back at the boldfaced words. Say each word. Listen for the vowel sounds. What long-vowel sound do you hear in each word?

13

Spelling Practice

TIP
Long vowels sound like their names. The long-vowel sound of **u** is /yoo/ or /oo/. Study these examples.
/ā/ as in scale   /ō/ as in stove
/ē/ as in these   /yoo/ as in cubes
/ī/ as in arrive   /oo/ as in rules

LIST WORDS
1. these
2. deny
3. rules
4. safely
5. locate
6. crime
7. stove
8. scale
9. costume
10. arrive
11. opened
12. musical
13. equal
14. idea
15. tight
16. clover
17. rodent
18. tuba
19. cubes
20. pride

Long-Vowel Sounds

Write **list words** that contain just one long-vowel sound under the headings below. Circle the letter that spells the long-vowel sound.

long-vowel sound e
1. th**e**se   2. **e**qual

long-vowel sound i
3. cr**i**me   4. arr**i**ve
5. t**i**ght   6. pr**i**de

long-vowel sound u
7. r**u**les   8. cost**u**me
9. m**u**sical   10. t**u**ba
11. c**u**bes

long-vowel sound a
12. sc**a**le

long-vowel sound o
13. st**o**ve   14. **o**pened
15. cl**o**ver   16. r**o**dent

Write **list words** that contain two long-vowel sounds. Circle the letters that spell the long-vowel sounds.

17. den**y**   18. **i**de**a**
19. s**a**fel**y**   20. l**o**c**a**te

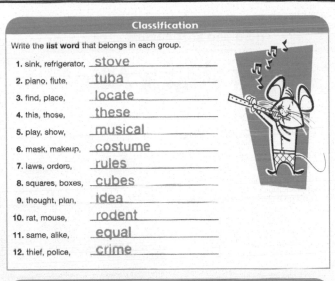

Classification

Write the **list word** that belongs in each group.

1. sink, refrigerator, _stove_
2. piano, flute, _tuba_
3. find, place, _locate_
4. this, those, _these_
5. play, show, _musical_
6. mask, makeup, _costume_
7. laws, orders, _rules_
8. squares, boxes, _cubes_
9. thought, plan, _idea_
10. rat, mouse, _rodent_
11. same, alike, _equal_
12. thief, police, _crime_

Word Building

Add and subtract letters to form **list words**.

1. right – r + t = _tight_
2. rival – riv + equ = _equal_
3. arrow – ow + Ive = _arrive_
4. rover – r + cl = _clover_
5. pale – p + sc = _scale_
6. any – a + de = _deny_
7. timely – tim + saf = _safely_
8. price – ce + de = _pride_
9. loaned – loa + ope = _opened_
10. time – t + cr = _crime_
11. drive – dri + sto = _stove_
12. moose – moo + the = _these_
13. gate – g + loc = _locate_
14. turtle – rtle + ba = _tuba_

Lesson 3 • Long-Vowel Sounds   15

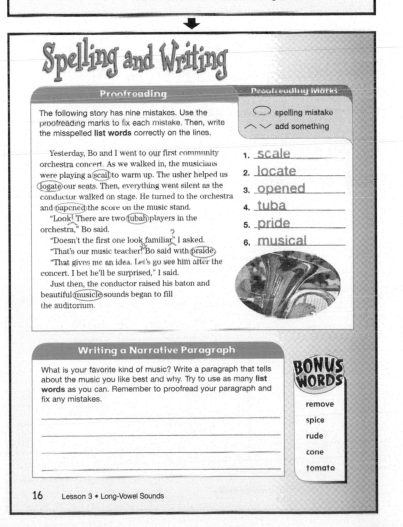

Spelling and Writing

Proofreading

The following story has nine mistakes. Use the proofreading marks to fix each mistake. Then, write the misspelled **list words** correctly on the lines.

Proofreading Marks

◯ spelling mistake
∧∨ add something

Yesterday, Bo and I went to our first community orchestra concert. As we walked in, the musicians were playing a scail to warm up. The usher helped us logate our seats. Then, everything went silent as the conductor walked on stage. He turned to the orchestra and oapcned the score on the music stand.

"Look! There are two tubah players in the orchestra," Bo said.

"Doesn't the first one look familiar" I asked.

"That's our music teacher," Bo said with praide.

"That gives me an idea. Let's go see him after the concert. I bet he'll be surprised," I said.

Just then, the conductor raised his baton and beautiful musicle sounds began to fill the auditorium.

1. _scale_
2. _locate_
3. _opened_
4. _tuba_
5. _pride_
6. _musical_

Writing a Narrative Paragraph

What is your favorite kind of music? Write a paragraph that tells about the music you like best and why. Try to use as many **list words** as you can. Remember to proofread your paragraph and fix any mistakes.

_____
_____
_____
_____

BONUS WORDS

remove
spice
rude
cone
tomato

Spelling Strategy

Write these words on the board: *crime, late, cube, pride*. Then, list: *rim, stop, cub, bad*. With a partner, students can say the words in each list and compare the spellings. Help students conclude that one-syllable words with a long vowel followed by a single consonant usually end in *e*. Ask them to name other words that follow this rule.

BONUS WORDS

You may want to invite partners to write a silly recipe using the **bonus words**. Students can swap recipes to see how other students used the words.

Spelling and Writing   Page 16

The **Proofreading** exercise will help students prepare to proofread their narrative paragraphs. Remind students that the proofreading mark ^ is used to add something, such as a word, a space, a comma, a question mark, or an exclamation mark. As students complete the writing activity, encourage them to brainstorm ideas, write a first draft, revise, and proofread their work. To publish their writing, students may want to play examples of their favorite music as they read their paragraphs.

Writer's Corner The class may want to contact a professional musician or performing group to ask if it would be possible to discuss what it's like to be a professional musician. To prepare for the discussion, students can write a list of questions to ask.

Final Test

1. Nick hopes for a role in the school **musical**.
2. Jeff's mother made him a snake **costume**.
3. Roger **opened** the envelope.
4. Will Rosa's train **arrive** at six o'clock?
5. I found a four-leaf **clover** in the yard.
6. A square has four **equal** sides.
7. Your dog's collar is too **tight**!
8. Ellen has a good **idea**.
9. Drive **safely**!
10. Each of us tries hard to follow the **rules**.
11. May I borrow **these** books for a while?
12. Cindy may **deny** that she forgot your birthday.
13. The butcher weighed the steak on the **scale**.
14. Robbing a bank is a **crime**.
15. We have a new **stove** in our kitchen.
16. We tried hard to **locate** the missing cat.
17. I take **pride** in my work.
18. Is a squirrel a **rodent**?
19. My friend Robert plays the **tuba**.
20. Mother chopped the meat into **cubes**.

Objective
To spell words with the hard and soft c and g sounds

Correlated Phonics Lessons
MCP Phonics, Level D, Lessons 7–8

Spelling Words in Action   **Page 17**

In "Cool as Ice," students read to find out what kind of sculpture never gets into a museum. Ask students whether they have ever seen an ice sculpture and why they would or would not like to try sculpting ice.

Call on volunteers to say each boldfaced word and identify the sounds made by c and g.

Warm-Up Test
1. We stood at the **edge** of the steep cliff.
2. White is a **common** color for houses.
3. The moon is in the shape of a **circle**.
4. A **cactus** plant grows well in a hot, dry region.
5. On their birthdays, Ray and Jim exchange **gifts**.
6. A **gentle** breeze swayed the leaves of the tree.
7. The clown on the **stage** made everyone laugh.
8. Did you hear a **strange** sound on the roof?
9. The cat curled up in the **corner** of the room.
10. The **graceful** dancers glided across the stage.
11. The sun is the **center** of our solar system.
12. Tom put the **baggage** in the overhead bin.
13. Put words with the hard c in one **category**.
14. It's time to feed our pet **gerbil**.
15. Don't step in the wet **cement**!
16. Does this store offer discount **prices**?
17. The **force** of the wind ripped the flag.
18. This bunch of **celery** looks fresh.
19. Please **decide** which shirt you prefer to wear.
20. It is important to conserve **energy** resources.

Spelling Practice   **Pages 18–19**

Introduce the spelling rule and have students read the **list words** aloud. Encourage students to look back at their **Warm-Up Tests** and apply the spelling rule to any misspelled words.

As students work through the **Spelling Practice** exercises, remind them to look back at their **list words** or in their dictionaries if they need help. You may also want to point out that some words, such as *circle* and *baggage*, contain both hard and soft c or g.

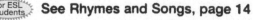
See Rhymes and Songs, page 14

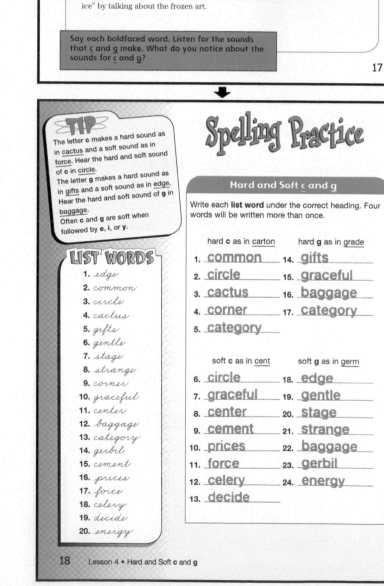

Spelling Words in Action

What kind of sculpture never gets into a museum?

Cool as Ice

If someone wore ski pants, heavy kneepads, a warm jacket, a baseball cap, and warm gloves, who could that person be? A skier? A **strange**-looking baseball player? Possibly, but that person could also be an ice sculptor. An ice sculptor carves works of art out of giant blocks of ice. Not a very **common** job, is it?

It can take an ice sculptor hours of cutting, chipping, and smoothing to complete a single carving. A good sculptor can **decide** to turn a block of ice into almost anything. The result might be an animal full of **energy**, a **gentle** mermaid, a horse-drawn chariot, or even a frozen **cactus**.

Unlike most works of art, ice sculptures are not meant to last. Once they're displayed, they melt. These **graceful** figures are often used as party decorations. They are usually placed in the **center** of a food table, in a **corner**, or on a **stage**. Talking about the sculptures puts guests at ease. They can easily "break the ice" by talking about the frozen art.

Say each boldfaced word. Listen for the sounds that c and g make. What do you notice about the sounds for c and g?

17

TIP
The letter **c** makes a hard sound as in cactus and a soft sound as in force. Hear the hard and soft sound of c in circle.
The letter **g** makes a hard sound as in gifts and a soft sound as in edge. Hear the hard and soft sound of g in baggage.
Often c and g are soft when followed by e, i, or y.

Spelling Practice

LIST WORDS
1. edge
2. common
3. circle
4. cactus
5. gifts
6. gentle
7. stage
8. strange
9. corner
10. graceful
11. center
12. baggage
13. category
14. gerbil
15. cement
16. prices
17. force
18. celery
19. decide
20. energy

Hard and Soft c and g

Write each **list word** under the correct heading. Four words will be written more than once.

hard c as in carton
1. common
2. circle
3. cactus
4. corner
5. category

hard g as in grade
14. gifts
15. graceful
16. baggage
17. category

soft c as in cent
6. circle
7. graceful
8. center
9. cement
10. prices
11. force
12. celery
13. decide

soft g as in germ
18. edge
19. gentle
20. stage
21. strange
22. baggage
23. gerbil
24. energy

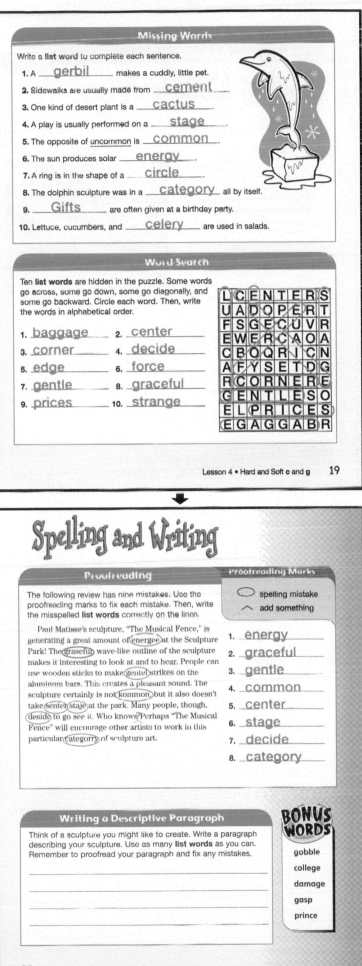

Missing Words

Write a list word to complete each sentence.

1. A __gerbil__ makes a cuddly, little pet.
2. Sidewalks are usually made from __cement__.
3. One kind of desert plant is a __cactus__.
4. A play is usually performed on a __stage__.
5. The opposite of uncommon is __common__.
6. The sun produces solar __energy__.
7. A ring is in the shape of a __circle__.
8. The dolphin sculpture was in a __category__ all by itself.
9. __Gifts__ are often given at a birthday party.
10. Lettuce, cucumbers, and __celery__ are used in salads.

Word Search

Ten **list words** are hidden in the puzzle. Some words go across, some go down, some go diagonally, and some go backward. Circle each word. Then, write the words in alphabetical order.

1. baggage 2. center
3. corner   4. decide
5. edge   6. force
7. gentle   8. graceful
9. prices   10. strange

L	C	E	N	T	E	R	S
U	A	D	O	P	E	R	T
F	S	G	E	C	U	V	R
E	W	E	R	C	A	O	A
C	B	O	Q	R	I	C	N
A	F	Y	S	E	T	D	G
R	C	O	R	N	E	R	E
G	E	N	T	L	E	S	O
E	L	P	R	I	C	E	S
E	G	A	G	G	A	B	R

Spelling and Writing

Proofreading

The following review has nine mistakes. Use the proofreading marks to fix each mistake. Then, write the misspelled **list words** correctly on the lines.

Paul Matisse's sculpture, "The Musical Fence," is generating a great amount of energee at the Sculpture Park! The graceful wave-like outline of the sculpture makes it interesting to look at and to hear. People can use wooden sticks to make gentel strikes on the aluminum bars. This creates a pleasant sound. The sculpture certainly is not kommon but it also doesn't take senter staje at the park. Many people, though, deside to go see it. Who knows? Perhaps "The Musical Fence" will encourage other artists to work in this particular categorry of sculpture art.

Proofreading Marks
◯ spelling mistake
∧ add something

1. energy
2. graceful
3. gentle
4. common
5. center
6. stage
7. decide
8. category

Writing a Descriptive Paragraph

Think of a sculpture you might like to create. Write a paragraph describing your sculpture. Use as many **list words** as you can. Remember to proofread your paragraph and fix any mistakes.

BONUS WORDS
gobble
college
damage
gasp
prince

Spelling Strategy

To help students figure out whether a *c* or *g* is hard or soft, write **list words** containing *c* on the board and invite the class to
• identify the letter that follows the *c*
• say the word and tell if the *c* is hard or soft.
Follow the same procedure with **list words** that contain *g*. Help students conclude that *c* and *g* are usually soft before *i*, *e*, and *y*.

BONUS WORDS
Have students write a sentence for **each bonus word**, then read each sentence aloud to a partner, saying "blank" in place of the bonus word. Partners can complete each sentence with the correct word.

Spelling and Writing   Page 20

The **Proofreading** exercise will help students prepare to proofread their descriptive paragraphs. As students complete the writing activity, encourage them to brainstorm ideas, write a first draft, revise, and proofread their work. To publish their writing, students may want to
• illustrate their paragraphs
• make a speech about their sculpture.

Writer's Corner Invite students to use an encyclopedia or a library card catalog to help them gather information about sculpture. Have them write a summary of the information they found the most interesting. Then, they can illustrate their writing and create a classroom display.

Final Test
1. The source of solar **energy** is the sun.
2. The **graceful** skater glided across the ice.
3. Leo couldn't **decide** between the two jackets.
4. Don't stand so close to the **edge**!
5. Write your name in the **center** of the page.
6. Draw a **circle** around your name.
7. **Celery** is a crunchy green vegetable.
8. The train porter helped us with our **baggage**.
9. Is Lee a **common** name in the United States?
10. Thank you for all these lovely **gifts**.
11. Dad had to **force** the cabin door open.
12. Ruby got nervous when she walked on **stage**.
13. The **prices** in this store are outrageous!
14. Corey fed my pet **gerbil** while I was away.
15. Look at the orange flower on that **cactus** plant.
16. Lisa had a **strange** feeling about the visitor.
17. Doesn't Jason's uncle drive a **cement** truck?
18. Apples and pears belong in the fruit **category**.
19. Ed decided the lamp looked best in the **corner**.
20. Although our dog is huge, she is very **gentle**.

Objective
To spell words with two- and three-letter consonant blends

 Correlated Phonics Lessons
MCP Phonics, Level D, Lessons 9–12

Spelling Words in Action   *Page 21*
Students may enjoy reading to find out which sport used to be called *baggataway* or *tekwaarathon*. Afterward, ask students whether they have ever played lacrosse, and invite them to tell what they know about the histories of other sports.

Call on volunteers to name the beginning consonant sounds in each boldfaced word.

Warm-Up Test
1. Did Juan buy a pair of woolen **gloves**?
2. A jet flies at great **speed**.
3. Taking photographs requires a lot of **skill**.
4. **Screens** on the windows will keep the flies out.
5. **Protect** yourself by driving defensively.
6. We planted flowers in **front** of the house.
7. The man's **craft** is making leather belts.
8. The **brains** of birds are very small.
9. I was **scared** when the dog barked!
10. Please put everything back in its **proper** place.
11. **Trace** the picture carefully.
12. I had a pleasant **dream** last night.
13. The students formed a **straight** line.
14. I got a **splinter** from that broken pencil.
15. We all heard the **screech** of the owl.
16. Write your answers in the **spaces**.
17. We will **stuff** the pillow with feathers.
18. The **greedy** dog ate the food in the cat's dish.
19. **Sprinkle** cheese on the pizza.
20. Do you think the rules are too **strict**?

Spelling Practice   *Pages 22–23*
Introduce the spelling rule and have students read the **list words** aloud. If desired, point out that some words, such as *screech*, sound like the sound they are associated with. Then, encourage students to look back at their **Warm-Up Tests** and apply the spelling rule to any misspelled words.

As students work through the **Spelling Practice** exercises, remind them to look back at their **list words** or in their dictionaries if they need help.

for ESL students **See Categorizing, page 15**

Spelling Words in Action

What sport was once called "baggataway" or "tekwaarathon"?

Lacrosse

Historians can **trace** the game of lacrosse back to Indians living in Canada. These North American Indians called it "baggataway" or "tekwaarathon." The game was played with as many as a thousand warriors. There were very few **strict** rules. Later, French settlers adopted the game and gave it the name *lacrosse*. They added a few rules to make it safer to play.

In 1867, lacrosse was made the national game of Canada. It was first played in the Olympic Games in 1904. Today, it is a popular sport in such faraway places as Australia.

A **proper** game of lacrosse requires both **speed** and **skill** as well as **brains**. Today, lacrosse is played by two teams on a grassy area a little larger than a football field. Each team usually has ten players. They wear heavy **gloves**, helmets, and shoulder pads to **protect** themselves. Each player carries a **straight** stick called a *crosse*. It is usually made of wood and has a small pocket at one end. The pockets are made with **screens** of loose net. A player uses the crosse to catch and throw the ball. Only the goalkeepers can touch the ball with their hands. The object of the game is to score goals. The team scoring the most goals wins.

Say each of the boldfaced words. How many consonant sounds do you hear at the beginning of each word?

21

TIP
A **consonant blend** is two or more consonants that come together in a word. Their sounds blend together, but each sound is heard. Listen to the sounds of these consonant blends:

gl as in <u>gl</u>oves
dr as in <u>dr</u>eam
str as in <u>str</u>aight
scr as in <u>scr</u>eens

Spelling Practice

LIST WORDS
1. gloves
2. speed
3. skill
4. screens
5. protect
6. front
7. craft
8. brains
9. scared
10. proper
11. trace
12. dream
13. straight
14. splinter
15. screech
16. spaces
17. stuff
18. greedy
19. sprinkle
20. strict

Beginning Consonant Blends

Add the **sc**, **sk**, **sp**, or **st** consonant blend to each group of letters to form a **list word**.
1. stuff
2. skill
3. scared
4. speed
5. spaces

Add the **br**, **cr**, **dr**, **fr**, **gl**, **gr**, **pr**, or **tr** consonant blend to each group of letters to form a **list word**.
6. proper
7. protect
8. dream
9. brains
10. greedy
11. trace
12. craft
13. front
14. gloves

Add the **scr**, **spl**, **spr**, or **str** consonant blend to each group of letters to form a **list word**.
15. strict
16. splinter
17. screens
18. screech
19. sprinkle
20. straight

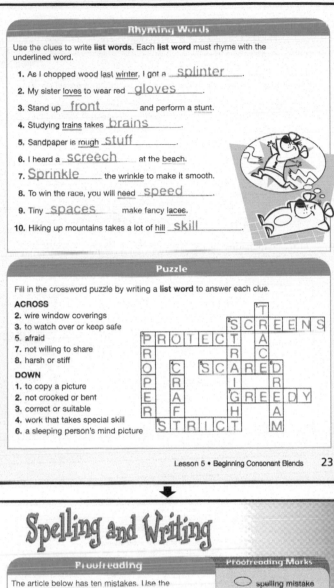

Rhyming Words

Use the clues to write **list words**. Each **list word** must rhyme with the underlined word.

1. As I chopped wood last <u>winter</u>, I got a _splinter_.
2. My sister <u>loves</u> to wear red _gloves_.
3. Stand up _front_ and perform a <u>stunt</u>.
4. Studying <u>trains</u> takes _brains_.
5. Sandpaper is <u>rough</u> _stuff_.
6. I heard a _screech_ at the <u>beach</u>.
7. _Sprinkle_ the <u>wrinkle</u> to make it smooth.
8. To win the race, you will <u>need</u> _speed_.
9. Tiny _spaces_ make fancy <u>laces</u>.
10. Hiking up mountains takes a lot of <u>hill</u> _skill_.

Puzzle

Fill in the crossword puzzle by writing a **list word** to answer each clue.

ACROSS
2. wire window coverings
3. to watch over or keep safe
5. afraid
7. not willing to share
8. harsh or stiff

DOWN
1. to copy a picture
2. not crooked or bent
3. correct or suitable
4. work that takes special skill
6. a sleeping person's mind picture

Crossword answers:
- S C R E E N S (2 across)
- P R O T E C T (3 across)
- T R A C E (1 down)
- S C A R E D (5 across)
- P R O P E R (2 down)
- C R A F T (4 down)
- G R E E D Y (7 across)
- S T R I C T (8 across)
- D R E A M (6 down)

Spelling and Writing

Proofreading

The article below has ten mistakes. Use the proofreading marks to fix each mistake. Then, write the misspelled **list words** correctly on the lines.

Proofreading Marks
- ◯ spelling mistake
- ≡ capital letter

Kickball races are popular among many native peoples in mexico, especially the Tarahumara. in a race, two teams of players kick a ball made of wood for many miles. The race can last for several hours or even days. Some tarahumara players race barefoot with nothing to protekt their feet. They move the ball in frunt of them with great skil and spead they have to keep the ball going as strayht as possible in order to win. Sometimes, they kick the ball across flat spases to gain more ground and move ahead.

1. _protect_
2. _front_
3. _skill_
4. _speed_
5. _straight_
6. _spaces_

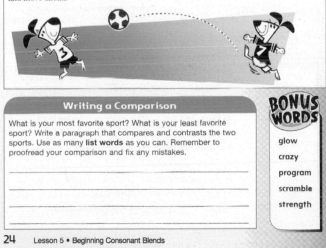

Writing a Comparison

What is your most favorite sport? What is your least favorite sport? Write a paragraph that compares and contrasts the two sports. Use as many **list words** as you can. Remember to proofread your comparison and fix any mistakes.

_____
_____
_____
_____

BONUS WORDS

glow
crazy
program
scramble
strength

Spelling Strategy

With a partner, students can take turns saying the **list words** aloud to each other. The listening partner repeats the word and spells it, snapping a finger or tapping a foot when he or she says the letters for the consonant blend. Remind students that the sound of *k* in some of the **list words** (for example, *screens*, *craft*) is spelled with the letter *c*.

BONUS WORDS You may want to suggest that students write a clue for each **bonus word**. Partners can read each clue aloud. The other partner then supplies the **bonus word** that goes with the clue.

Spelling and Writing   Page 24

The **Proofreading** exercise will help students prepare to proofread their comparisons. As students complete the writing activity, encourage them to brainstorm ideas, write a first draft, revise, and proofread their work. To publish their writing, students may want to

- use their paragraphs to hold a debate on the best and worst sports
- create a class book about sports.

Writer's Corner Students may enjoy writing fan letters to sports figures they admire. A reference librarian can help locate appropriate addresses. Point out that although some celebrities send publicity materials to fans, not all will respond.

Final Test

1. I **dream** of becoming a great scientist one day.
2. Please use **proper** manners at the table!
3. Children **trace** letters to learn how to print.
4. Is your little brother **scared** of the dark?
5. There were no **spaces** left on the card.
6. The nurse removed a **splinter** from my foot.
7. Max went **straight** home after school.
8. We heard the **screech** of the tires.
9. The rules were **strict** but fair.
10. Dad will **stuff** the turkey with bread crumbs.
11. Please **sprinkle** some water on the plants.
12. The **greedy** child refused to share his popcorn.
13. Every spring we put **screens** in our windows.
14. The horse galloped at a frightening **speed**.
15. Use my **gloves** to keep your hands warm.
16. Joanna has enormous **skill** as a carpenter.
17. Dinosaurs were huge animals with tiny **brains**.
18. Mother lions will fight to **protect** their young.
19. Is the **front** of the building painted?
20. Robin learned the **craft** of shoeing horses.

Lessons 1–5 · Review

Objectives
To review spelling words with consonant sounds, short- and long-vowel sounds, the hard and soft sounds of c and g, and beginning consonant blends

Check Your Spelling Notebook
Pages 25–28

Based on students' lists and your observations, note which words are giving students the most difficulty and offer assistance for spelling them correctly. Here are some frequently misspelled words to watch for: *straight, category, pencil, dollar,* and *cactus.*

To give students extra help and practice in taking standardized tests, you may want to have them take the **Review Test** for this lesson on pages 30–31. After scoring the tests, return them to students so that they can record their misspelled words in their spelling notebooks.

After practicing their troublesome words, students can work through the exercises for Lessons 1–5. Before students begin each exercise, you may want to go over the spelling rule.

Take It Home

Invite students to locate the **list words** in Lessons 1–5 at home—on television, on the Internet, on the radio, in conversations, and in books and magazines. Students can use **Take It Home** Master 1 on pages 32–33 to help them do the activity. (A complete list of the spelling words is included on page 32 of the **Take It Home** Master.) Students can total the number of words found and bring in their lists to share with the class.

 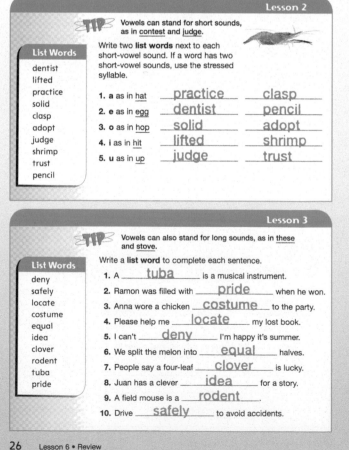

In lessons 1–5, you learned about consonant sounds, short- and long-vowel sounds, the hard and soft sounds of c and g, and beginning consonant blends.

Check Your Spelling Notebook

Look at the words in your spelling notebook. Which words for lessons 1 through 5 did you have the most trouble with? Write them here.

_____

_____

Practice writing your troublesome words with a partner. Try writing the letters of each word in the air. Your partner can spell the word aloud as you write.

Lesson 1

TIP In most words, you can hear the sound of each consonant, as in <u>later</u>. Some words have double consonants that stand for one sound, as in <u>letters</u>.

List Words
banner
hammer
twelve
dollar
silent
wild
swift
bottles
pineapple
film
traffic

Write a **list word** that belongs in each group. Not all of the **list words** will be used.

1. nickel, quarter, __dollar__
2. quiet, hushed, __silent__
3. wrench, pliers, __hammer__
4. apple, peach, __pineapple__
5. quick, fast, __swift__
6. jars, packages, __bottles__
7. free, untamed, __wild__
8. camera, movie, __film__
9. four, eight, __twelve__
10. flag, shield, __banner__

Lesson 2

TIP Vowels can stand for short sounds, as in <u>contest</u> and <u>judge</u>.

List Words
dentist
lifted
practice
solid
clasp
adopt
judge
shrimp
trust
pencil

Write two **list words** next to each short-vowel sound. If a word has two short-vowel sounds, use the stressed syllable.

1. **a** as in <u>hat</u> __practice__ __clasp__
2. **e** as in <u>egg</u> __dentist__ __pencil__
3. **o** as in <u>hop</u> __solid__ __adopt__
4. **i** as in <u>hit</u> __lifted__ __shrimp__
5. **u** as in <u>up</u> __judge__ __trust__

Lesson 3

TIP Vowels can also stand for long sounds, as in <u>these</u> and <u>stove</u>.

List Words
deny
safely
locate
costume
equal
idea
clover
rodent
tuba
pride

Write a **list word** to complete each sentence.

1. A __tuba__ is a musical instrument.
2. Ramon was filled with __pride__ when he won.
3. Anna wore a chicken __costume__ to the party.
4. Please help me __locate__ my lost book.
5. I can't __deny__ I'm happy it's summer.
6. We split the melon into __equal__ halves.
7. People say a four-leaf __clover__ is lucky.
8. Juan has a clever __idea__ for a story.
9. A field mouse is a __rodent__.
10. Drive __safely__ to avoid accidents.

TIP Listen for the hard or soft sounds of c and g in common, center, gifts, and stage.

List Words

edge
circle
cactus
gentle
graceful
baggage
gerbil
category
celery
decide
energy

Each sentence has two list words, but one is misspelled. Circle the misspelled list word and write it correctly on the line. Not all of the list words will be used.

1. Stand on the edge of the circle for this dance. __circle__
2. Decide which baggadge is yours. __baggage__
3. A deer is a gentle, gracful animal. __graceful__
4. I live on Palm Circle at the egge of town. __edge__
5. It took enargy to load the baggage. __energy__
6. Did you deside to buy the celery? __decide__
7. Be gentel and graceful with the baby. __gentle__
8. Celary is a category of vegetable. __celery__
9. Solar energy is in a catagory of its own. __category__
10. The caktus has a sharp edge. __cactus__

TIP In a consonant blend, you can hear the sound of each consonant in a word, as in sprinkle and protect.

List Words

gloves
protect
scared
proper
trace
straight
splinter
screech
greedy
strict

Write each group of list words in alphabetical order.

| greedy scared straight | trace screech strict |
| proper gloves | protect splinter |

1. __gloves__
2. __greedy__
3. __proper__
4. __scared__
5. __straight__
6. __protect__
7. __screech__
8. __splinter__
9. __strict__
10. __trace__

Show What You Know

Lessons 1–5 • Review

One word is misspelled in each set of list words. Fill in the circle next to the list word that is spelled incorrectly.

1. ○ banner ○ stamp ○ equal ○ graceful ● spead
2. ● strikt ○ decide ○ crime ○ hands ○ swift
3. ○ traffic ○ locked ○ these ○ edge ● branes
4. ○ sprinkle ○ cement ○ tight ● dentiss ○ later
5. ● hunred ○ bumps ○ scale ○ gentle ○ screech
6. ○ gloves ○ circle ○ safely ○ judge ● barral
7. ○ hammer ● stycks ○ locate ○ strange ○ skill
8. ● gready ○ common ○ opened ○ lifted ○ seven
9. ○ pineapple ○ trust ○ stove ● cactuss ○ protect
10. ● straght ○ stage ○ rules ○ contest ○ bottles
11. ○ fame ● praktice ○ deny ○ prices ○ spaces
12. ● dreem ○ center ○ cubes ○ crack ○ until
13. ○ letters ○ solid ○ costume ● cornuh ○ stuff
14. ○ front ● bagage ○ pride ○ pencil ○ film
15. ○ wild ○ stand ● tubah ○ gifts ○ screens
16. ● splintter ○ force ○ arrive ○ spent ○ silent
17. ○ eleven ○ clasp ● musicle ○ energy ○ trace
18. ○ craft ● catagory ○ clover ○ shrimp ○ dollar
19. ○ gallon ○ fender ○ idea ● cellery ○ scared
20. ○ proper ○ gerbil ○ rodent ○ adopt ● twelf

Final Test

1. Aunt Helen bought two **bottles** of orange juice.
2. We decided to **adopt** a stray puppy.
3. The cows chewed the **clover** in the meadow.
4. Our dog is **gentle** with young children.
5. The rules in this club are **strict**.
6. I saved a **dollar** by buying this shirt on sale.
7. Uncle Ken studied many years to be a **dentist**.
8. I can't **deny** that I'm thrilled to win the contest.
9. We waited at the **edge** of the road for the bus.
10. Does a triangle have three **straight** sides?
11. We heard the crowd **screech** as they ran by.
12. Luis traced a coin to make a **circle**.
13. I'm happy that your dog returned home **safely**.
14. Every afternoon I **practice** the piano.
15. Sam is making a robot **costume** for the play.
16. Let's cut the **pineapple** into slices for dessert.
17. We designed a **banner** for the soccer team.
18. We **lifted** the rug to wash the floor.
19. Please break the chalk into two equal pieces.
20. We wear **gloves** when it's cold outside.
21. That **greedy** dog ate all the food!
22. The **graceful** swans glide across the water.
23. A **tuba** is a very large instrument.
24. The **judge** wanted to ask another question.
25. I will be happy to sharpen your **pencil** for you.
26. We watched an old **silent** movie.
27. Lions and tigers are **wild** animals.
28. We tried to **locate** the train station on our map.
29. A **rodent** has made a nest in the attic.
30. Write each word in the correct **category**.
31. It takes **energy** and training to run a marathon.
32. **Cactus** plants grow in desert regions.
33. The puppy was **scared** by the loud thunder.
34. Will you show me how to **trace** a design?
35. Tony chopped the **celery** for the salad.
36. **Twelve** people attended the meeting last night.
37. Deer are **swift** runners.
38. Barbara will stir-fry the **shrimp** and broccoli.
39. Karen turned her clever **idea** into a cartoon.
40. The **baggage** was loaded into the plane.
41. Can you **decide** which sport is your favorite?
42. Grandma removed the **splinter** from my finger.
43. A mother bear will fight to protect her baby.
44. We learned the **proper** way to use chopsticks.
45. Al felt great **pride** when he solved the problem.
46. I **trust** you to take good care of my cat.
47. The old coin was made of **solid** gold!
48. The **clasp** on the necklace is broken.
49. Did you buy **film** for the camera?
50. Use a **hammer** to pound the nail into the wood.

Name _____

Review Test (Side A)

Read each set of words. Fill in the circle next to the word that is spelled correctly.

1. (a) soled   (c) solud
   (b) saulid   (d) solid

2. (a) decied   (c) decide
   (b) desied   (d) deside

3. (a) wild   (c) whild
   (b) wiled   (d) whilde

4. (a) stricked   (c) strick
   (b) strickt   (d) strict

5. (a) ekwual   (c) equel
   (b) equal   (d) equall

6. (a) strate   (c) straght
   (b) straight   (d) streight

7. (a) sielent   (c) silent
   (b) sighlent   (d) silant

8. (a) baggage   (c) bagage
   (b) baggadge   (d) bagedge

9. (a) sircle   (c) surcle
   (b) circkle   (d) circle

10. (a) pencil   (c) pensle
    (b) pencill   (d) pensil

Name _____

Read each set of words. Fill in the circle next to the word that is spelled correctly.

11. ⓐ safeley   ⓒ safely
    ⓑ safly   ⓓ saifly

12. ⓐ pinapple   ⓒ pineappel
    ⓑ pineapple ⓓ pienapple

13. ⓐ pracktice ⓒ practice
    ⓑ practiss   ⓓ practise

14. ⓐ costume   ⓒ costuem
    ⓑ costoom   ⓓ costewm

15. ⓐ judje   ⓒ judg
    ⓑ juge   ⓓ judge

16. ⓐ screach   ⓒ skreech
    ⓑ screech   ⓓ schreech

17. ⓐ roadent   ⓒ roedent
    ⓑ rodant   ⓓ rodent

18. ⓐ category   ⓒ cadegory
    ⓑ catagory   ⓓ categorey

19. ⓐ doller   ⓒ dollor
    ⓑ dollar   ⓓ dolar

20. ⓐ gready   ⓒ greedy
    ⓑ gredey   ⓓ greedey

Take It Home 1

Your child has learned to spell many new words and would like to share them with you and your family. Here are some great activities that will help your child review the words in Lessons 1–5 as your family has fun, too!

What Did You Say?

Have a sheet of paper and a pencil handy in several rooms of your home. That way, your child can listen for and record spelling words that are spoken in family conversations. Encourage your child to keep note of the number of times each spelling word is used.

Lesson 1

1. banner	12. letters
2. barrel	13. pineapple
3. bottles	14. seven
4. dollar	15. silent
5. eleven	16. swift
6. fame	17. traffic
7. film	18. twelve
8. gallon	19. until
9. hammer	20. wild
10. hundred	
11. later	

Lesson 2

1. adopt	12. pencil
2. bumps	13. practice
3. clasp	14. shrimp
4. contest	15. solid
5. crack	16. spent
6. dentist	17. stamp
7. fender	18. stand
8. hands	19. sticks
9. judge	20. trust
10. lifted	
11. locked	

Lesson 3

1. arrive	12. pride
2. clover	13. rodent
3. costume	14. rules
4. crime	15. safely
5. cubes	16. scale
6. deny	17. stove
7. equal	18. these
8. idea	19. tight
9. locate	20. tuba
10. musical	
11. opened	

Lesson 4

1. baggage	12. energy
2. cactus	13. force
3. category	14. gentle
4. celery	15. gerbil
5. cement	16. gifts
6. center	17. graceful
7. circle	18. prices
8. common	19. stage
9. corner	20. strange
10. decide	
11. edge	

Lesson 5

1. brains	12. skill
2. craft	13. spaces
3. dream	14. speed
4. front	15. splinter
5. gloves	16. sprinkle
6. greedy	17. straight
7. proper	18. strict
8. protect	19. stuff
9. scared	20. trace
10. screech	
11. screens	

Word Search

How many words can you and your child find in this puzzle? Remember to read across and down.

musical	opened	deny	decide	stamp
banner	celery	dream	later	adopt

HAPPY BIRTHDAY

```
A D R E A M A K L R
M U O R D L C Q E X
U X K T O P E N E D
S T A M P Z L B X E
I A F E T A E E M C
C I H B O U R F T I
A Z K A O O Y O O D
L B R N W Q A S R E
T D U N E L N A K F
L A T E R Z O R E Q
S E H R P X D E N Y
```

Consonant Blends

Objective
To spell words with consonant blends in an initial, medial, or final position

 Correlated Phonics Lesson
MCP Phonics, Level D, Lesson 7

Spelling Words in Action   **Page 29**
In this selection, students read to find out about a two-headed animal. After reading, invite students to discuss which part of "Double Header" they liked the best.

Encourage students to look back at the boldfaced words. Ask volunteers to say each word and identify the consonant blends and their locations in the words.

Warm-Up Test
1. The cat slowly **crept** around the corner.
2. I could hear the snow **crunch** under my feet.
3. Jill awoke at dawn to the **sounds** of birds.
4. Streetlights turn on automatically at **dusk**.
5. José will get a **refund** on his game tickets.
6. The **colder** days show that winter is coming.
7. The dog ran away when it saw the **skunk**.
8. Who will **unfold** the flag?
9. You take a **risk** riding your bike at night.
10. May I have a glass of **milk** with my lunch?
11. The soldiers came to a **halt** outside the castle.
12. Is that program on at a **different** time?
13. People are **protesting** the cuts in bus service.
14. The weather report said a **twister** is coming!
15. An **independent** person will do things alone.
16. I haven't been **absent** from school this year.
17. This material will **stretch** to fit the chair.
18. We are **printing** the newspaper tomorrow.
19. Eileen **blended** yellow and red to make orange.
20. Does this **product** come with a battery?

Spelling Practice   **Pages 30–31**
Introduce the spelling rule and have students read the **list words** aloud. Then, encourage students to look back at their **Warm-Up Tests** and apply the spelling rule to any misspelled words.

As students work through the **Spelling Practice** exercises, remind them to look back at their **list words** or in their dictionaries if they need help.

 **for ESL students** **See Charades / Pantomime, page 15**

34

Spelling Words in Action

What problems might a two-headed snake have?

Double Header

A snake **crept** along the forest floor at **dusk**, but there was something very unusual about it. It had two heads! There is a saying that "two heads are better than one." This is definitely not true when it comes to snakes. **Different** kinds of animals have been born with two heads, but no one knows for sure why a large number of them have been snakes.

One might think that there are advantages in being a two-headed snake. For instance, a snake with two heads might perhaps have better hearing. This, though, doesn't apply, because a snake can't hear **sounds** since it has no ears. As a result, a snake cannot hear the **crunch** of a footstep. A snake can, however, feel the vibrations of a footstep. Two heads would not help the snake to make sounds either. A snake has no vocal cords and therefore can only make hissing noises.

There is also a **risk** that comes with having two heads. Each head might decide to be **independent** of the other. What would happen if one head wanted to **stretch** out and the other head wanted to coil up? Everything would grind to a **halt**. The heads would fritter away all their time **protesting**, and the snake wouldn't move at all.

Say each boldfaced word in the selection. Listen for the consonant blends. What do you notice about where the blends are in the words?

29

Spelling Practice

TIP
Remember that when two or more consonants come together in a word, their sounds may blend together. In a **consonant blend**, you hear each letter. A blend may be found anywhere in a word.
sk in risk	**cr** and **pt** in crept
ld in colder	**sk** and **nk** in skunk
lk in milk	**tw** and **st** in twister

LIST WORDS
1. crept
2. crunch
3. sounds
4. dusk
5. refund
6. colder
7. skunk
8. unfold
9. risk
10. milk
11. halt
12. different
13. protesting
14. twister
15. independent
16. absent
17. stretch
18. printing
19. blended
20. product

Writing Consonant Blends

Add one or two consonant blends to each group of letters to form a **list word**.

1. differe **n t**
2. **s t r** etch
3. refu **n d**
4. twi **s t** er
5. du **s k**
6. prote **s t** ing
7. unfo **l d**
8. **p r** oduct
9. sou **n d s**
10. indepe **n d** ent
11. **s k** unk
12. abse **n t**
13. **c r** unch
14. ha **l t**
15. ble **n d** ed
16. mi **l k**
17. **p r** inting
18. co **l d** er
19. **c r** ept
20. ri **s k**

Word Meaning

Write the **list word** that relates to the word or phrase given.

1. chance or gamble	risk	2. extend	stretch
3. white drink	milk	4. stop	halt
5. return of money paid	refund	6. unusual	different
7. mixed	blended	8. tornado	twister
9. complaining	protesting	10. writing	printing
11. self-governed	independent	12. chillier	colder
13. open up	unfold	14. missing	absent
15. tones or noises	sounds	16. nightfall	dusk
17. crush or chew	crunch	18. crawled	crept
19. something made	product		

Word Building

Add and subtract letters to form **list words**.

1. grounds – gr + s =	sounds	2. duty – ty + sk =	dusk
3. bunch – b + cr =	crunch	4. about – ou + sen =	absent
5. hunk – h + sk =	skunk	6. mind – nd + l k =	milk
7. deduct – de + pro =	product	8. cooler – ol + ld =	colder
9. sound – so + ref =	refund	10. retold – ret + unf =	unfold

Lesson 7 • Consonant Blends   31

Spelling and Writing

Proofreading

The following paragraph has ten mistakes. Use the proofreading marks to fix each mistake. Then, write the misspelled **list words** correctly on the lines.

When dusc falls, the spotted scunk looks for food. Its an indepedant animal that might take over another animal's home If a dog krept up on a spotted skunk, it would be taking a risc. You'd hear some prootesting howls when the skunk sprayed the dog with a terrible smelling liquid.

Proofreading Marks
- ⬯ spelling mistake
- ⊙ add period
- ⌄ add apostrophe

1. dusk
2. skunk
3. independent
4. crept
5. risk
6. protesting

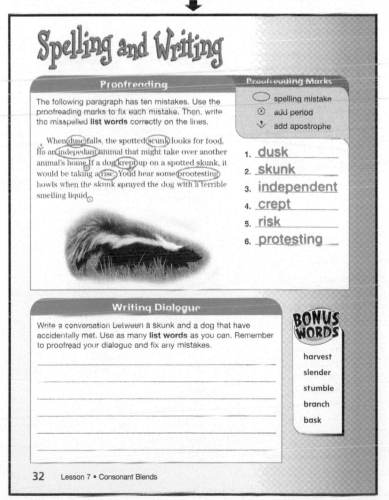

Writing Dialogue

Write a conversation between a skunk and a dog that have accidentally met. Use as many **list words** as you can. Remember to proofread your dialogue and fix any mistakes.

_____

_____

_____

_____

_____

_____

BONUS WORDS
harvest
slender
stumble
branch
bask

Spelling Strategy

You may want to write words on the board that contain consonant blends found in the **list words** (for example, *list, cream, bent, soldier,* and *landing*). Say the words and have the class listen for the consonant blends. Then, ask volunteers to come to the board, circle the consonant blend in each word, and write a **list word** that contains the same consonant blend.

BONUS WORDS
Have students say each **bonus word** to partners. The partner writes down the word and circles the consonant blends. Then, partners switch roles and repeat the activity.

Spelling and Writing   Page 32

The **Proofreading** exercise will help students prepare to proofread their dialogues. As students complete the writing activity, encourage them to brainstorm ideas, write a first draft, revise, and proofread their work. To publish their writing, students may want to
- create a cartoon strip
- perform their dialogues with a partner.

Writer's Corner Have students do additional research on snakes in their local or school library or on the Internet. Invite them to write a paragraph about the snake they found most interesting.

Final Test

1. The company said it would **refund** my money.
2. It is an **independent** station.
3. I was **absent** from school last week.
4. This **product** will make your dishes sparkle!
5. I love to **crunch** on cold carrot sticks.
6. Can you **unfold** the map completely?
7. There is little **risk** of injury when you walk.
8. Listen to the croaking **sounds** of all the frogs.
9. Please do not **stretch** my new sweatshirt.
10. The cat **crept** out of the room.
11. The two voices **blended** together beautifully.
12. We must try to **halt** the spread of air pollution.
13. Cars should turn on their headlights at **dusk**.
14. Today is much **colder** than yesterday.
15. Is there more **milk** in the refrigerator?
16. If there's a **twister**, you'll hear an alarm.
17. The store is **printing** new advertisements.
18. The citizens were **protesting** unfair taxes.
19. I knew I smelled a **skunk** nearby!
20. Here is a **different** book by the same writer.

Objective
To spell words with *r*-controlled vowels

 Correlated Phonics Lessons
MCP Phonics, Level D, Lessons 14–18

Spelling Words in Action   *Page 33*
Students may enjoy reading about transforming garbage into art. Afterward, invite them to suggest ideas for creating art from discarded objects or from trash.

Encourage students to look back at the boldfaced words. Ask volunteers to say each word and identify the sound that the vowel or vowels and *r* stand for.

Warm-Up Test
1. Keli bought a **carton** of milk at the store.
2. Is the **heart** one of the body's largest muscles?
3. Ted's school has won many **sports** awards.
4. Alwanda wants to be an **artist**.
5. Allan has a **spare** pencil if you need one.
6. This room is really **dirty**!
7. Chi and Anna went down to the **shore**.
8. Park the bicycles next to the **curb**.
9. The band is performing at the county **fair**.
10. Will there be enough **sherbet** for dessert?
11. Sherry will be using those **boards** for shelves.
12. That little dog seems **fearless**.
13. I have been keeping a **journal** for years.
14. The bus driver spoke **cheerfully** to everyone.
15. The **garbage** will be picked up tomorrow.
16. The liver is an important body **organ**.
17. There was one **error** on your spelling test.
18. **Sparks** flew when the pipe hit the sidewalk.
19. The **harbor** in Baltimore was important in 1812.
20. My father sneezes when I wear **perfume**.

Spelling Practice   *Pages 34–35*
Introduce the spelling rule and have students read the **list words** aloud. Encourage students to look back at their **Warm-Up Tests** and apply the spelling rule to any misspelled words.

As students work through the **Spelling Practice** exercises, remind them to look back at their **list words** or in their dictionaries if they need help.

for ESL students   See Student Dictation, page 14

Spelling Words in Action

How can you turn garbage into art?

Recycling for Art

Before you toss out that milk **carton** or pair of **dirty** old shoes, take **heart**. Think about keeping them. Why? You'd keep them for art, of course!

Believe it or not, **garbage** can change you into an **artist**. With a little imagination, you can turn discarded materials into artistic treasures. The best part is that you are also recycling! So, don't make the **error** of setting that trash by the **curb**. Use it creatively.

Recycling for art is not a new idea. Sculptors have used everything from broken teacups to **spare** tires. Painters have created masterpieces on everything from old **boards** to discarded clothing. Some very famous paintings have been painted on top of other paintings. Very often, artists could not afford the price of a new canvas, so they simply painted over an old one.

The challenge for you is to find objects that no one wants, then make them into something someone would love to have. If the idea of turning junk into art bothers you, don't think of it as art. **Cheerfully** think of it as just another way to clean up!

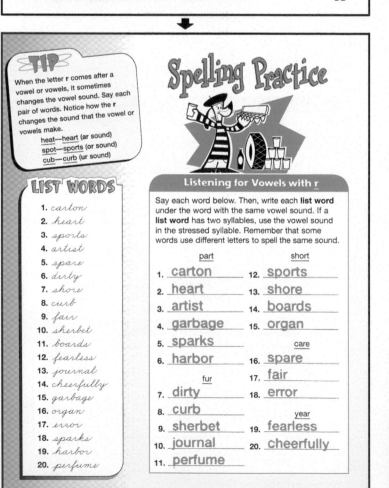

Look back at the boldfaced words. Say each word. What do you notice about the way the vowels sound in each word?

33

TIP
When the letter **r** comes after a vowel or vowels, it sometimes changes the vowel sound. Say each pair of words. Notice how the **r** changes the sound that the vowel or vowels make.

heat—heart (ar sound)
spot—sports (or sound)
cub—curb (ur sound)

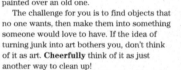

Spelling Practice

LIST WORDS
1. carton
2. heart
3. sports
4. artist
5. spare
6. dirty
7. shore
8. curb
9. fair
10. sherbet
11. boards
12. fearless
13. journal
14. cheerfully
15. garbage
16. organ
17. error
18. sparks
19. harbor
20. perfume

Listening for Vowels with r
Say each word below. Then, write each **list word** under the word with the same vowel sound. If a **list word** has two syllables, use the vowel sound in the stressed syllable. Remember that some words use different letters to spell the same sound.

part	short
1. carton	12. sports
2. heart	13. shore
3. artist	14. boards
4. garbage	15. organ
5. sparks	**care**
6. harbor	16. spare
fur	17. fair
7. dirty	18. error
8. curb	**year**
9. sherbet	19. fearless
10. journal	20. cheerfully
11. perfume	

Definitions

Write the list word that matches each definition.

1. something extra
   spare

2. edge of the street
   curb

3. festival
   fair

4. not afraid
   fearless

5. trash
   garbage

6. a dessert like ice cream
   sherbet

7. a musical instrument
   organ

8. mistake
   error

9. not clean
   dirty

10. land at the edge of the sea
    shore

11. a person who draws or paints
    artist

12. diary
    journal

Hidden Words

Each word below is hidden in a **list word**. Write the **list word** on the line. Circle the letters that spell the hidden word.

1. ports _sports_
2. cart _carton_
3. fume _perfume_
4. park _sparks_
5. air _fair_
6. full _cheerfully_
7. hear _heart_
8. oar _boards_
9. less _fearless_
10. arbor _harbor_
11. ore _shore_
12. our _journal_

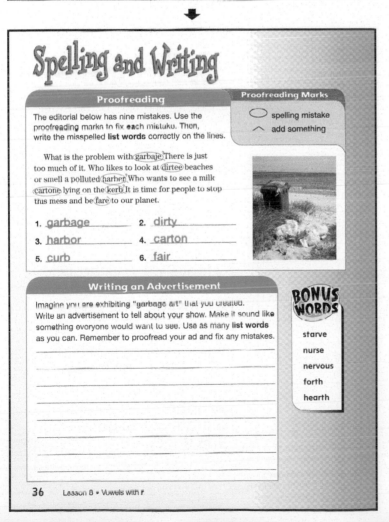

Spelling and Writing

Proofreading

Proofreading Marks
⬯ spelling mistake
∧ add something

The editorial below has nine mistakes. Use the proofreading marks to fix each mistake. Then, write the misspelled **list words** correctly on the lines.

What is the problem with garbaje? There is just too much of it. Who likes to look at dirtee beaches or smell a polluted harber? Who wants to see a milk cartone lying on the kerb? It is time for people to stop this mess and be fare to our planet.

1. _garbage_
2. _dirty_
3. _harbor_
4. _carton_
5. _curb_
6. _fair_

Writing an Advertisement

Imagine you are exhibiting "garbage art" that you created. Write an advertisement to tell about your show. Make it sound like something everyone would want to see. Use as many **list words** as you can. Remember to proofread your ad and fix any mistakes.

_____
_____
_____
_____
_____
_____
_____

BONUS WORDS

starve
nurse
nervous
forth
hearth

Spelling Strategy

To help students remember how to spell *sherbet*, write it in large letters on the board. Then, suggest that students close their eyes and picture the word. After students open their eyes, have them spell *sherbet* aloud several times.

BONUS WORDS

With a partner, have students write a story using words or phrases that mean the same or almost the same as the **bonus words**. Have students trade stories with other students and replace the words and phrases with the **bonus words**. Ask students which story sounds the best.

Spelling and Writing   Page 36

The **Proofreading** exercise will help students prepare to proofread their advertisements. As students complete the writing activity, encourage them to brainstorm ideas, write a first draft, revise, and proofread their work. To publish their writing, students may want to

• create a bulletin-board display
• take a vote on which advertisement is the best.

Writer's Corner Suggest students bring in sculptures they have created out of recycled household items. Invite them to write positive reviews of each other's work.

Final Test

1. Do you like the smell of this **perfume**?
2. The wind fanned the **sparks** from the fire.
3. The patient needed an **organ** transplant.
4. Paul whistled **cheerfully** as he did his chores.
5. The **fearless** police officer saved the child.
6. The **sherbet** is made with fresh lemons.
7. The child sat on the **curb**.
8. Wash those **dirty** hands!
9. The **artist** donated one of her paintings.
10. The **heart** is a symbol of love.
11. The **carton** of juice tipped and spilled.
12. Many boys and girls play on **sports** teams.
13. Dad had to put the **spare** tire on the car.
14. Waves were crashing on the **shore**.
15. The judges at the **fair** selected the winner.
16. The carpenter laid out the **boards** to dry.
17. Luis kept a **journal** of the events.
18. By mistake, I threw the shirt in the **garbage**.
19. Do you think I made an **error**?
20. Let's go down to the **harbor** to see the boats.

Objective
To spell words with consonant digraphs

 Correlated Phonics Lessons
MCP Phonics, Level D, Lessons 9–10

Spelling Words in Action   *Page 37*

In "Flash!" students read to find out what to do if lightning strikes. After reading, ask students whether they have ever been in a storm with lightning and, if so, what it was like.

Call on volunteers to say each boldfaced word and name the consonants that make one sound.

Warm-Up Test
1. Listen to the loud **thunder**!
2. Jed lives **farther** from school than Ann does.
3. If the batter **reaches** first base, he will be safe.
4. Susan would like a **chicken** sandwich for lunch.
5. In some states, **wheat** fields stretch for miles.
6. Will we have our party next **Thursday**?
7. David felt **foolish** when he missed the bus.
8. In winter, we all **gather** around the fireplace.
9. Is Sarah's **brother** in the class play?
10. I'd like to rest **awhile** before the next race.
11. Clean the **chimney** before using the fireplace.
12. Crease the paper **sharply** before you tear it.
13. The dog's **leash** is hanging by the door.
14. Don't **bother** your sister while she's reading.
15. The store expects a new **shipment** of shoes.
16. I am allergic to pillows made with real **feathers**.
17. Please **charge** the call to this phone number.
18. Pat will **shovel** the snow off the porch.
19. Watch the cat clean its **whiskers**.
20. **Crush** the empty cans so they take up less space.

Spelling Practice   *Pages 38–39*

Introduce the spelling rule and have students read the **list words** aloud. Point out the two different *th* sounds in the **list words**—as in *thunder, Thursday* and as in *gather, brother,* and *feathers*. Encourage students to look back at their **Warm-Up Tests** and apply the spelling rule to any misspelled words.

As students work through the **Spelling Practice** exercises, remind them to look back at their **list words** or in their dictionaries if they need help.

 for ESL students   See Categorizing, page 15

Spelling Words in Action

What should you do if lightning strikes?

Flash!

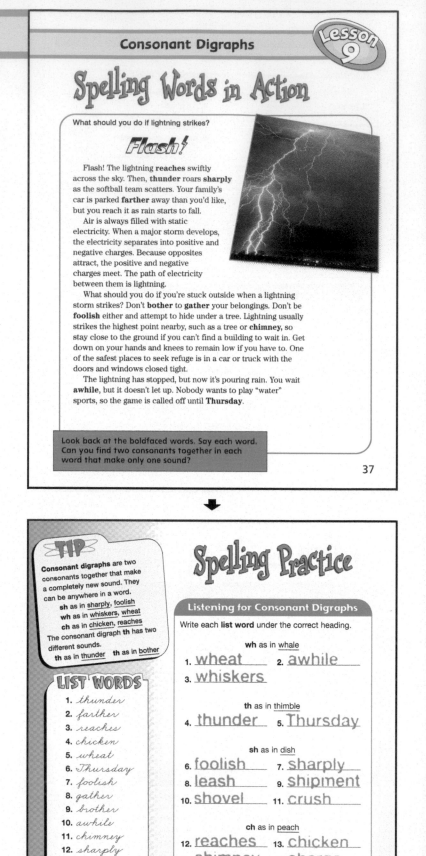

Flash! The lightning **reaches** swiftly across the sky. Then, **thunder** roars **sharply** as the softball team scatters. Your family's car is parked **farther** away than you'd like, but you reach it as rain starts to fall.

Air is always filled with static electricity. When a major storm develops, the electricity separates into positive and negative charges. Because opposites attract, the positive and negative charges meet. The path of electricity between them is lightning.

What should you do if you're stuck outside when a lightning storm strikes? Don't **bother** to **gather** your belongings. Don't be **foolish** either and attempt to hide under a tree. Lightning usually strikes the highest point nearby, such as a tree or **chimney**, so stay close to the ground if you can't find a building to wait in. Get down on your hands and knees to remain low if you have to. One of the safest places to seek refuge is in a car or truck with the doors and windows closed tight.

The lightning has stopped, but now it's pouring rain. You wait **awhile**, but it doesn't let up. Nobody wants to play "water" sports, so the game is called off until **Thursday**.

Look back at the boldfaced words. Say each word. Can you find two consonants together in each word that make only one sound?

37

TIP

Consonant digraphs are two consonants together that make a completely new sound. They can be anywhere in a word.
sh as in <u>sharply</u>, <u>foolish</u>
wh as in <u>whiskers</u>, <u>wheat</u>
ch as in <u>chicken</u>, <u>reaches</u>
The consonant digraph **th** has two different sounds.
th as in <u>thunder</u>   **th** as in <u>bother</u>

LIST WORDS
1. thunder
2. farther
3. reaches
4. chicken
5. wheat
6. Thursday
7. foolish
8. gather
9. brother
10. awhile
11. chimney
12. sharply
13. leash
14. bother
15. shipment
16. feathers
17. charge
18. shovel
19. whiskers
20. crush

Spelling Practice

Listening for Consonant Digraphs
Write each **list word** under the correct heading.

wh as in <u>whale</u>
1. wheat   2. awhile
3. whiskers

th as in <u>thimble</u>
4. thunder   5. Thursday

sh as in <u>dish</u>
6. foolish   7. sharply
8. leash   9. shipment
10. shovel   11. crush

ch as in <u>peach</u>
12. reaches   13. chicken
14. chimney   15. charge

th as in <u>mother</u>
16. farther   17. gather
18. brother   19. bother
20. feathers

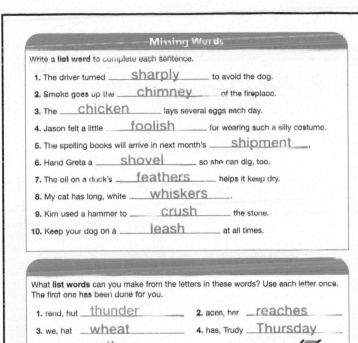

Missing Words

Write a list word to complete each sentence.

1. The driver turned _____sharply_____ to avoid the dog.
2. Smoke goes up the _____chimney_____ of the fireplace.
3. The _____chicken_____ lays several eggs each day.
4. Jason felt a little _____foolish_____ for wearing such a silly costume.
5. The spelling books will arrive in next month's _____shipment_____.
6. Hand Greta a _____shovel_____ so she can dig, too.
7. The oil on a duck's _____feathers_____ helps it keep dry.
8. My cat has long, white _____whiskers_____.
9. Kim used a hammer to _____crush_____ the stone.
10. Keep your dog on a _____leash_____ at all times.

What **list words** can you make from the letters in these words? Use each letter once. The first one has been done for you.

1. rend, hut _____thunder_____
2. aces, her _____reaches_____
3. we, hat _____wheat_____
4. has, Trudy _____Thursday_____
5. her, tag _____gather_____
6. both, err _____brother_____
7. hail, we _____awhile_____
8. the, rob _____bother_____
9. he, crag _____charge_____
10. her, raft _____farther_____

Lesson 9 • Consonant Digraphs   39

Spelling and Writing

Proofreading

The news report below has ten mistakes. Use the proofreading marks to fix each mistake. Then, write the misspelled **list words** correctly on the lines.

Proofreading Marks
- ◯ spelling mistake
- ≡ capital letter
- ℯ take out something

Strange weather hit our our area last Thurzday. The day was was warm until noon, when dark clouds began to gathur heavy rain fell awile until there was a loud crash of thundur. Suddenly, the rain turned to hail! this was the first hail storm our area has seen since 1963. The the hail came down so hard that one woman said it knocked the fithers off her prize chikin!

1. _____Thursday_____   2. _____gather_____
3. _____awhile_____   4. _____thunder_____
5. _____feathers_____   6. _____chicken_____

Writing a Descriptive Paragraph

A thunder and lightning storm can be exciting and scary. Write a description of a storm you have experienced. Use as many **list words** as you can. Remember to proofread your description and fix any mistakes.

_____
_____
_____
_____
_____
_____

BONUS WORDS
whether
arithmetic
thankful
champion
shelter

Spelling Strategy

To give students practice with consonant digraphs, invite them to get together with a partner and take turns pronouncing each **list word**. As students say the words, they can stress the consonant digraphs (*wheat*, *chicken*) and identify the letters that stand for the sounds they hear.

BONUS WORDS
Invite students to write a sentence for each **bonus word** but leave a blank where the word would be written. Have them trade papers with a partner, and see if they can complete each other's sentences.

Spelling and Writing   Page 40

The **Proofreading** exercise will help students prepare to proofread their descriptions. As they complete the writing activity, encourage students to brainstorm ideas, write a first draft, revise, and proofread their work. To publish their writing, students may want to
- illustrate their descriptions for a class book
- record them with sound effects of a storm.

Writer's Corner Invite students to research a weather hazard that threatens your region. Have them prepare a poster that gives tips for staying safe at home or at school when bad weather strikes. Give students copies to take home.

Final Test

1. The nest was lined with soft **feathers**.
2. That's a rooster, not a **chicken**.
3. Most flour is made from **wheat**.
4. On **Thursday** nights the stores stay open late.
5. The mechanic will **charge** the dead battery.
6. This machine can **crush** rocks.
7. I will help you dig if you give me a **shovel**.
8. Father shaved his **whiskers**.
9. I felt **foolish** in my silly costume.
10. Please help me **gather** the beads that spilled.
11. The bus stop is **farther** than I thought.
12. This dress **reaches** almost to the floor.
13. Is your **brother** in high school now?
14. The sound of **thunder** scares many dogs.
15. After they had walked **awhile**, they grew tired.
16. You can see the **chimney** from here.
17. Knock **sharply** on the door.
18. I keep my dog on a **leash** when we're outside.
19. If my radio starts to **bother** you, let me know.
20. When will the **shipment** of new cars arrive?

Words with the Sound of f

Objective
To spell words with the /f/ sound represented by *f*, *ff*, *ph*, and *gh*

Correlated Phonics Lesson
MCP Phonics, Level D, Lesson 21

Spelling Words in Action   *Page 41*
In this selection, students learn about photo safaris. After reading, ask students where they would like to go and what they would like to see on a photo safari.

Encourage students to look back at the boldfaced words. Ask volunteers to say each word and identify the letter or letters that make the sound of *f*.

Warm-Up Test
1. Nancy has a **photo** of her new sister.
2. We made **graphs** to show the plants' growth.
3. Bob **laughs** whenever he sees that movie.
4. The smoke made everyone **cough**.
5. Did the girls' basketball team win a **trophy**?
6. Jim **roughly** pushed us aside.
7. Bruce decided that he'd had **enough** popcorn.
8. The English **alphabet** has twenty-six letters.
9. The book you want is on the top **shelf**.
10. We will go home right **after** the movie.
11. It's so cold I feel as if I'm frozen **stiff**!
12. **Elephants** are intelligent animals.
13. A **giraffe** can stand twelve feet high!
14. **Geography** is Leon's favorite subject.
15. My brother's son is my **nephew**.
16. We studied each **phase** of the animal's life.
17. Since the kitten was an **orphan**, we adopted it.
18. A **dolphin** swam alongside the ship.
19. The museum knew the statue was a **phony**.
20. Is an **autograph** of a president valuable?

Spelling Practice   *Pages 42–43*
Introduce the spelling rule and have students read the **list words** aloud. Encourage students to look back at their **Warm-Up Tests** and apply the spelling rule to any misspelled words.

As students work through the **Spelling Practice** exercises, remind them to look back at their **list words** or in their dictionaries if they need help.

for ESL students   See Variant Spellings, page 14

Spelling Words in Action

What do you do on a photo safari?

Photo Opportunities

Once a safari meant hunting animals with guns. Today, a safari is more likely to involve cameras. The **trophy** is not an animal head hanging on a wall or sitting on a **shelf**. Instead, it is a picture of a living animal in its natural environment.

Every year, people travel to Africa to go on **photo** safaris. Africa's wildlife and **geography** provide **enough** opportunities for almost any photographer. There's nothing **phony** here. **Elephants** can be seen in their natural environment. A camera may capture a **giraffe** lumbering across the plains. The safari van may have to stop as a pride of lions crosses the road. An untimely **cough** may set a herd of zebras stampeding. Such photo opportunities are priceless.

After visiting Africa, people could go on safari to India or Australia. Both countries possess many wildlife sites.

If a destination close to home is desired, a photo safari to the countryside nearby, a local park or zoo, or a wildlife rehabilitation center might be possible.

Look back at the boldfaced words. Listen for the sound of f in each word. How many different spellings for the sound of f do you find?

41

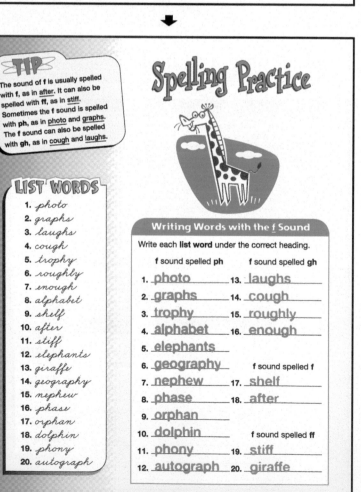

TIP
The sound of **f** is usually spelled with **f**, as in after. It can also be spelled with **ff**, as in stiff. Sometimes the **f** sound is spelled with **ph**, as in photo and graphs. The **f** sound can also be spelled with **gh**, as in cough and laughs.

Spelling Practice

LIST WORDS
1. photo
2. graphs
3. laughs
4. cough
5. trophy
6. roughly
7. enough
8. alphabet
9. shelf
10. after
11. stiff
12. elephants
13. giraffe
14. geography
15. nephew
16. phase
17. orphan
18. dolphin
19. phony
20. autograph

Writing Words with the f Sound
Write each **list word** under the correct heading.

f sound spelled ph	f sound spelled gh
1. photo	13. laughs
2. graphs	14. cough
3. trophy	15. roughly
4. alphabet	16. enough
5. elephants	
6. geography	f sound spelled f
7. nephew	17. shelf
8. phase	18. after
9. orphan	
10. dolphin	f sound spelled ff
11. phony	19. stiff
12. autograph	20. giraffe

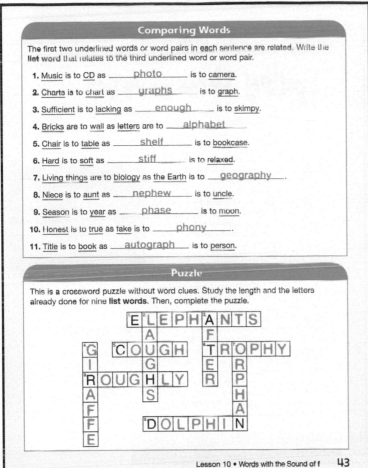

Comparing Words

The first two underlined words or word pairs in each sentence are related. Write the list word that relates to the third underlined word or word pair.

1. Music is to CD as **photo** is to camera.
2. Charts is to chart as **graphs** is to graph.
3. Sufficient is to lacking as **enough** is to skimpy.
4. Bricks are to wall as letters are to **alphabet**.
5. Chair is to table as **shelf** is to bookcase.
6. Hard is to soft as **stiff** is to relaxed.
7. Living things are to biology as the Earth is to **geography**.
8. Niece is to aunt as **nephew** is to uncle.
9. Season is to year as **phase** is to moon.
10. Honest is to true as take is to **phony**.
11. Title is to book as **autograph** is to person.

Puzzle

This is a crossword puzzle without word clues. Study the length and the letters already done for nine **list words**. Then, complete the puzzle.

```
E L E P H A N T S
A            F
G   C O U G H   T R O P H Y
I   U        E   R
R O U G H L Y   E   P
A   G        R   H
F   S            A
F        D O L P H I N
E                N
```

Spelling and Writing

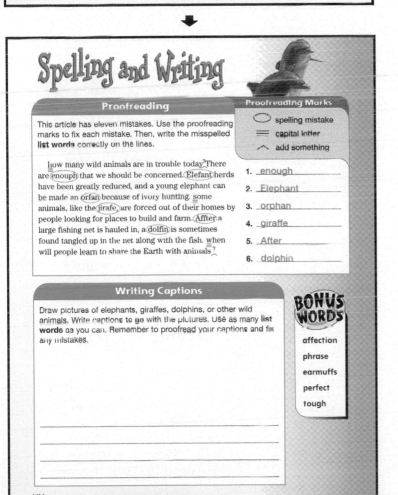

Proofreading

This article has eleven mistakes. Use the proofreading marks to fix each mistake. Then, write the misspelled **list words** correctly on the lines.

Proofreading Marks
◯ spelling mistake
≡ capital letter
∧ add something

how many wild animals are in trouble today? There are enouph that we should be concerned. Elefant herds have been greatly reduced, and a young elephant can be made an orfan because of ivory hunting. some animals, like the jirafe, are forced out of their homes by people looking for places to build and farm. After a large fishing net is hauled in, a dolfin is sometimes found tangled up in the net along with the fish. when will people learn to share the Earth with animals?

1. enough
2. Elephant
3. orphan
4. giraffe
5. After
6. dolphin

Writing Captions

Draw pictures of elephants, giraffes, dolphins, or other wild animals. Write captions to go with the pictures. Use as many list words as you can. Remember to proofread your captions and fix any mistakes.

BONUS WORDS
affection
phrase
earmuffs
perfect
tough

Spelling Strategy

Find out how many students know the sentence, "George Edward's Old Grandfather Rode a Pig Home Yesterday" as a mnemonic aid for spelling *geography*. Encourage students to make up their own sentences to help them spell difficult **list words**. You might want to prepare a handout so that students can share their work.

BONUS WORDS
Have students write a paragraph using the **bonus words**, but tell them to leave three or four letters out of each word. Then, have them trade papers with a partner and fill in the missing letters.

Spelling and Writing   Page 44

The **Proofreading** exercise will help students prepare to proofread their captions. As students complete the writing activity, encourage them to brainstorm ideas, write a first draft, revise, and proofread their captions. To publish their writing, students may want to
• make a class wildlife book
• create a bulletin-board display.

Writer's Corner Have students find a wildlife photography book or magazine at the library. Ask them to bring the book or magazine in to share with the class. Tell them to write a short paragraph on what they liked about the photographs.

Final Test
1. My brother always **laughs** at my jokes.
2. The engine ran **roughly** until it warmed up.
3. There is **enough** room in my car for one box.
4. A **dolphin** is a very intelligent animal.
5. What **phase** is the moon in?
6. Quick, let's take a **photo**!
7. We learned how to make **graphs** in math class.
8. I asked the senator for her **autograph**.
9. Not every **alphabet** has twenty-six letters.
10. The doctor gave me something for my **cough**.
11. The dictionary is on the top **shelf**.
12. The farmer fed the calf, who was an **orphan**.
13. Save the cookies until **after** dinner.
14. These pearls are **phony**, but they are still pretty.
15. In **geography** we are studying the earth.
16. The **stiff** leather gets softer as you use it.
17. Our team won a **trophy** in the state finals.
18. Those **elephants** certainly eat a lot of hay.
19. My **nephew** Peter has a birthday this week.
20. Each **giraffe** has a different pattern of spots.

Lesson 11 — Silent Letters

Objective
To spell words containing silent letters

 Correlated Phonics Lessons
MCP Phonics, Level D, Lessons 23–24

Spelling Words in Action   *Page 45*
In this selection, students read to find out about a mysterious "ghost galleon." After reading, invite students to discuss why divers were thrilled to find the long-lost ship.

Encourage students to look back at the boldfaced words. Ask volunteers to say each word and identify the letter that is not pronounced.

Warm-Up Test
1. Did Kim wear a **ghost** costume to the party?
2. Not everyone has a "green **thumb**."
3. I wish I had **known** it was raining!
4. We **often** go to the library after school.
5. Gary's **folks** came from Poland.
6. Keep your **wrist** steady when you hit the ball.
7. **Halfway** around the track, the runner fell.
8. Everyone wanted to **listen** to the new record.
9. Lucy scraped her **knuckle** fixing her bike.
10. Please help me **comb** the back of my hair.
11. The junkyard is filled with old **wrecks**.
12. Did you enjoy your **flight** to Denver?
13. An **honest** person makes a good friend.
14. She lives on the **island** of Manhattan.
15. Is next **Wednesday** your birthday?
16. This cold wind makes me **numb**!
17. Uncle Lamar used a **wrench** to turn the bolt.
18. The mouse nibbled the **crumb** of bread.
19. Hand cream may help **soften** your dry skin.
20. Becky will **answer** right away.

Spelling Practice   *Pages 46–47*
Introduce the spelling rule and have students read the **list words** aloud. You may wish to clarify for students that some people pronounce the *t* in *often*. Encourage students to look back at their **Warm-Up Tests** and apply the spelling rule to any misspelled words.

As students work through the **Spelling Practice** exercises, remind them to look back at their **list words** or in their dictionaries if they need help.

 See Charades / Pantomime, page 15

42

Silent Letters — Lesson 11

Spelling Words in Action

What is the "ghost galleon"?

Ghost Ship

Through the years, **folks** have loved to **listen** to stories of **ghost** ships. **Often**, these stories are more myth than fact. The story of the *Santa Margarita*, however, is true.

Savage winds ripped her sails. Fierce waves spilled over her decks. A thundering crack was heard. Suddenly, the towering mainmast collapsed into the sea. The *Santa Margarita* was at the mercy of the wind and sea. In a short while, the mighty ship was gone, and over 120 people had drowned trying to take **flight**. In one of the most mysterious **wrecks** of all time, the *Santa Margarita* disappeared in 1622. Since then, she has been **known** as the "ghost galleon."

In 1980, the *Santa Margarita* was located. Pieces of the ship's cargo were found under the sand and water near an **island** in the Florida Keys. When the treasure-hunting divers saw the cargo, they quickly changed the nickname to the "gold-chain wreck" due to the great amount of gold found scattered on the ocean floor. As divers untangled a mass of gold chains, they counted 43 glittering chains that reached a total length of 180 feet! Each link was as thick as the **knuckle** of a **thumb**. In the 1600s, people often carried gold in the form of chains. Links could be unhooked and used like coins.

> Say each of the boldfaced words in the selection. Which letters in the words do not make a sound?

45

> **TIP**
> Some words contain **silent letters**. We don't hear the sounds of those letters when we say the words. Study the silent letters in the following words.
>
> | known | wrist | folks | often |
> |---|---|---|---|
> | honest | halfway | flight | thumb |
>
> Be careful when you spell words like these. Now, study the silent letters in the remaining **list words**.

Spelling Practice

LIST WORDS
1. ghost
2. thumb
3. known
4. often
5. folks
6. wrist
7. halfway
8. listen
9. knuckle
10. comb
11. wrecks
12. flight
13. honest
14. island
15. Wednesday
16. numb
17. wrench
18. crumb
19. soften
20. answer

Identifying Silent Letters
Write each **list word** under the correct heading.

silent b	silent w
1. thumb	11. wrist
2. comb	12. wrecks
3. numb	13. wrench
4. crumb	14. answer

silent h	silent l
5. ghost	15. folks
6. honest	16. halfway

silent gh	silent d
7. flight	17. Wednesday

silent k	silent t
8. known	18. often
9. knuckle	19. listen

silent s	
10. island	20. soften

46   Lesson 11 • Silent Letters

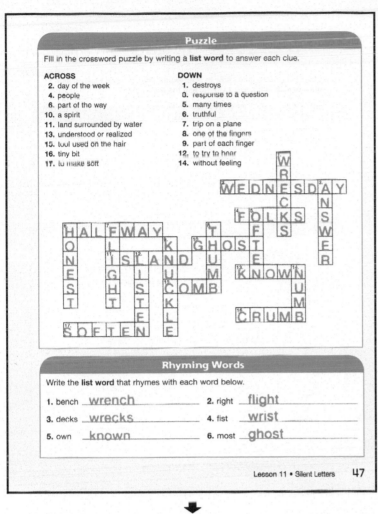

Puzzle

Fill in the crossword puzzle by writing a **list word** to answer each clue.

ACROSS
2. day of the week
4. people
6. part of the way
10. a spirit
11. land surrounded by water
13. understood or realized
15. tool used on the hair
16. tiny bit
17. to make soft

DOWN
1. destroys
0. response to a question
5. many times
6. truthful
7. trip on a plane
8. one of the fingers
9. part of each finger
12. to try to hear
14. without feeling

(Crossword answers visible: WEDNESDAY, FOLKS, HALFWAY, GHOST, ISLAND, KNOWN, COMB, CRUMB, SOFTEN, ANSWER, WRECKS, HONEST, FLIGHT, KNUCKLE, THUMB, NUMB, OFTEN, LISTEN, etc.)

Rhyming Words

Write the **list word** that rhymes with each word below.

1. bench   wrench
2. right   flight
3. decks   wrecks
4. fist   wrist
5. own   known
6. most   ghost

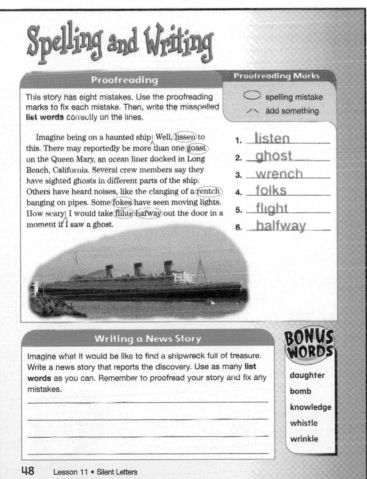

Spelling and Writing

Proofreading

This story has eight mistakes. Use the proofreading marks to fix each mistake. Then, write the misspelled **list words** correctly on the lines.

Imagine being on a haunted ship! Well, lissen to this. There may reportedly be more than one goast on the Queen Mary, an ocean liner docked in Long Beach, California. Several crew members say they have sighted ghosts in different parts of the ship. Others have heard noises, like the clanging of a rentch banging on pipes. Some fokes have seen moving lights. How scary! I would take fliht halfway out the door in a moment if I saw a ghost.

Proofreading Marks
⬭ spelling mistake
⌃ add something

1. listen
2. ghost
3. wrench
4. folks
5. flight
6. halfway

Writing a News Story

Imagine what it would be like to find a shipwreck full of treasure. Write a news story that reports the discovery. Use as many **list words** as you can. Remember to proofread your story and fix any mistakes.

_____
_____
_____

BONUS WORDS
daughter
bomb
knowledge
whistle
wrinkle

Spelling Strategy

In a group, have students choose *b, h, gh, k, s, w, l, d,* or *t* and write words in which that letter or pair of letters is silent, including **list words**. Invite students to share their lists with each other and with other groups.

BONUS WORDS
Have students draw a picture that gives a clue for each of the **bonus words**. Let them trade drawings with a partner and write the **bonus word** that goes with the drawing.

Spelling and Writing   *Page 48*

The **Proofreading** exercise will help students prepare to proofread their news stories. As students complete the writing activity, encourage them to brainstorm ideas, write a first draft, revise, and proofread their work. To publish their writing, students may want to
- create a magazine called *Undersea Adventures*
- use their stories to give a TV news broadcast.

Writer's Corner Students might enjoy reading about marine exploration in books such as *Sunken Treasure* by Gail Gibbons. Encourage them to write reviews of the books they especially enjoyed.

Final Test
1. Our **flight** to Rome took six hours.
2. I have a bad bruise on my **knuckle**.
3. When I build a fort, Keith **wrecks** it.
4. I'll **comb** my hair before you take my picture.
5. If the phone rings, please **answer** it.
6. Should I use a **wrench** to loosen the bolt?
7. We ate every **crumb** of Jody's birthday cake.
8. Now we'll **soften** the butter in the microwave.
9. I have **known** Joanie for two years.
10. I heard a scary **ghost** story yesterday.
11. Karen made a puppet on her **thumb**.
12. We eat at that restaurant **often**.
13. The **folks** in our small town are very friendly.
14. My watch fell off my **wrist**.
15. Zoe was **halfway** to class when the bell rang!
16. Please **listen** carefully to the directions.
17. What is your **honest** opinion on the matter?
18. We'll take this boat to get to the **island**.
19. Next **Wednesday** is my best friend's birthday.
20. My hand felt **numb** because it was so cold.

Lessons 7–11 · Review

Objectives
To review spelling words with consonant blends, vowels with *r*, consonant digraphs, the sound of *f*, and silent letters

Check Your Spelling Notebook
Pages 49–52

Based on students' lists and your observations, note which words are giving students the most difficulty and offer assistance for spelling them correctly. Here are some frequently misspelled words to watch for: *stretch, sherbet, chimney, garbage, answer, known, nephew,* and *cough.*

To give students extra help and practice in taking standardized tests, you may want to have them take the **Review Test** for this lesson on pages 46–47. After scoring the tests, return them to students so that they can record their misspelled words in their spelling notebooks.

After practicing their troublesome words, students can work through the exercises for Lessons 7–11. Before students begin each exercise, you may want to go over the spelling rule.

Take It Home

Invite students to locate the **list words** in Lessons 7–11 at home—on television, on the Internet, on the radio, in conversations, and in books and newspapers. Students can use **Take It Home** Master 2 on pages 48–49 to help them do the activity. (A complete list of the spelling words is included on page 48 of the **Take It Home** Master.) Students can total the number of words found and bring in their lists to share with the class.

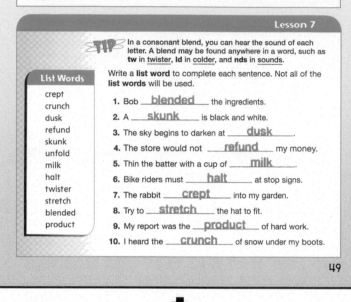

Lessons 7–11 · Review

In lessons 7–11, you learned how to spell words with consonant blends and digraphs, vowels with **r**, silent letters, and the sound of **f**.

Check Your Spelling Notebook

Look at the words in your spelling notebook. Which words in lessons 7 through 11 did you have the most trouble with? Write them here.

_____

_____

Practice writing your troublesome words with a partner. Try writing the letters for each word in a tray of sand, salt, or sugar. Your partner can check your spelling as you write.

Lesson 7

TIP In a consonant blend, you can hear the sound of each letter. A blend may be found anywhere in a word, such as **tw** in twister, **ld** in colder, and **nds** in sounds.

List Words
crept
crunch
dusk
refund
skunk
unfold
milk
halt
twister
stretch
blended
product

Write a **list word** to complete each sentence. Not all of the **list words** will be used.

1. Bob **blended** the ingredients.
2. A **skunk** is black and white.
3. The sky begins to darken at **dusk**.
4. The store would not **refund** my money.
5. Thin the batter with a cup of **milk**.
6. Bike riders must **halt** at stop signs.
7. The rabbit **crept** into my garden.
8. Try to **stretch** the hat to fit.
9. My report was the **product** of hard work.
10. I heard the **crunch** of snow under my boots.

49

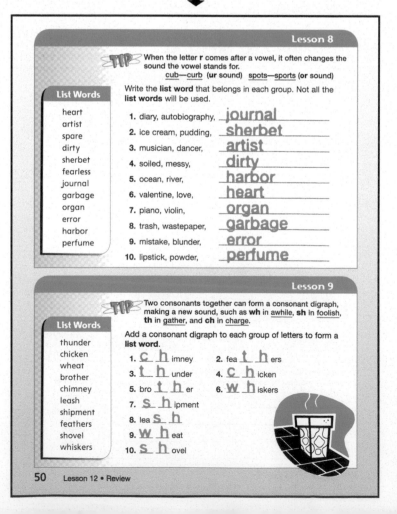

Lesson 8

TIP When the letter **r** comes after a vowel, it often changes the sound the vowel stands for.
cub—curb (**ur** sound)   spots—sports (**or** sound)

List Words
heart
artist
spare
dirty
sherbet
fearless
journal
garbage
organ
error
harbor
perfume

Write the **list word** that belongs in each group. Not all the **list words** will be used.

1. diary, autobiography, **journal**
2. ice cream, pudding, **sherbet**
3. musician, dancer, **artist**
4. soiled, messy, **dirty**
5. ocean, river, **harbor**
6. valentine, love, **heart**
7. piano, violin, **organ**
8. trash, wastepaper, **garbage**
9. mistake, blunder, **error**
10. lipstick, powder, **perfume**

Lesson 9

TIP Two consonants together can form a consonant digraph, making a new sound, such as **wh** in awhile, **sh** in foolish, **th** in gather, and **ch** in charge.

List Words
thunder
chicken
wheat
brother
chimney
leash
shipment
feathers
shovel
whiskers

Add a consonant digraph to each group of letters to form a **list word**.

1. **c h** imney
2. fea **t h** ers
3. **t h** under
4. **c h** icken
5. bro **t h** er
6. **w h** iskers
7. **s h** ipment
8. lea **s h**
9. **w h** eat
10. **s h** ovel

Lesson 10

TIP The sound f can be spelled with f, ff, ph, or gh. Find it in *after*, *stiff*, *phony*, and *laughs*.

List Words

cough
trophy
roughly
enough
shelf
after
stiff
giraffe
nephew
phase
orphan
dolphin

Build **list words** by adding or subtracting letters. Not all of the **list words** will be used.

1. knew – kn + neph   nephew
2. tough – t + c   cough
3. stick – ck + ff   stiff
4. though – th + en   enough
5. than – t + orp   orphan
6. girl – l + affe   giraffe
7. thin – th + dolph   dolphin
8. shed – d + lf   shelf
9. tropical – pical + phy   trophy
10. route – te + ghly   roughly

Lesson 11

TIP Some words contain silent letters, such as **h**, **b**, and **d**. Look for the silent letters in *ghost*, *numb*, and *Wednesday*.

List Words

known
folks
wrist
knuckle
comb
flight
wrench
crumb
soften
answer

Write each group of **list words** in alphabetical order.

wrist	flight	soften
wrench	folks	

known	crumb	comb
knuckle	answer	

1. flight
2. folks
3. soften
4. wrench
5. wrist
6. answer
7. comb
8. crumb
9. known
10. knuckle

Lesson 12 • Review   51

Show What You Know

Lessons 7–11 • Review

One word is misspelled in each set of **list words**. Fill in the circle next to the **list word** that is spelled incorrectly.

1. ○ crunch ● durty ○ bother ○ listen ○ laughs
2. ● gerafe ○ folks ○ leash ○ error ○ absent
3. ○ refund ○ organ ○ awhile ● nuckle ○ after
4. ● foto ○ ghost ○ thundor ○ carton ○ crept
5. ○ printing ○ journal ○ chimney ○ honest ● elefants
6. ○ nephew ○ comb ○ gather ● kurb ○ milk
7. ○ halt ● sherbert ○ feathers ○ wrecks ○ stiff
8. ● geografy ○ thumb ○ reaches ○ sports ○ twister
9. ○ sounds ○ heart ○ wheat ○ flight ● enuf
10. ○ alphabet ● Wenesday ○ farther ○ artist ○ dusk
11. ○ unfold ○ fair ○ foolish ● wriss ○ phony
12. ○ dolphin ● rench ○ crush ○ sparks ○ risk
13. ○ colder ○ boards ● sharpley ○ island ○ graphs
14. ● trofhy ○ numb ○ charge ○ fearless ○ stretch
15. ● diffrent ○ shore ○ shovel ○ crumb ○ phase
16. ○ cough ● sofen ○ chicken ○ spare ○ product
17. ● independant ○ garbage ○ shipment ○ halfway ○ shelf
18. ○ autograph ○ answer ○ whiskers ● cheerfuly ○ protesting
19. ○ blended ● parfume ○ brother ○ known ○ roughly
20. ○ orphan ● ofen ○ Thursday ○ harbor ○ skunk

Final Test

1. A **skunk** uses its scent to defend itself.
2. We **blended** the milkshake ingredients.
3. Your **heart** pumps blood throughout your body.
4. Three large ships were anchored in the **harbor**.
5. **Thunder** told us a storm was coming.
6. The cat cleaned its **whiskers**.
7. Each summer, my **folks** have a huge picnic.
8. Carlos guessed the right **answer**.
9. Scientists recorded the voice of the **dolphin**.
10. Karen's cold gave her a **cough**.
11. Beat the egg whites until they are **stiff**.
12. I hope I made **enough** sandwiches.
13. I wear my watch on my left **wrist**.
14. Only a **crumb** of bread was left on the plate.
15. Did you put the dog's **leash** back in the closet?
16. The store is expecting a **shipment** of dresses.
17. Pablo Picasso was a famous modern **artist**.
18. The **garbage** truck collected our trash.
19. We **crept** upstairs as quietly as we could.
20. I like to eat cereal with **milk** and fruit.
21. I heard a **crunch** when I bit into the apple.
22. The guard told the visitors to **halt**.
23. Put your **dirty** clothes in the washing machine.
24. Does Uncle Bert play the **organ**?
25. Grandma made rice and **chicken**.
26. The **chimney** on the old house needed repairs.
27. I scraped my **knuckle** when I fell.
28. This cream may **soften** your dry skin.
29. Don't play **roughly** with the puppy!
30. Ms. Manuelo took her **nephew** to the game.
31. The **giraffe** is the tallest animal of all.
32. The character Oliver Twist is an **orphan**.
33. Who made the first airplane **flight**?
34. I have **known** my friend Elaine for many years.
35. **Wheat**, oats, and barley are nutritious grains.
36. Jen's **brother** is our baseball team's pitcher.
37. Dad made homemade **sherbet** for dessert.
38. Don't make an **error** when you spell this word.
39. Every night, just at **dusk**, the nightingale sings.
40. This exercise will **stretch** your muscles.
41. We returned the bike for a full **refund**.
42. This **product** will remove stains easily.
43. Tim kept a daily **journal** throughout his trip.
44. This **perfume** smells wonderful!
45. Blue jays have beautiful **feathers**.
46. I offered to help Uncle Pete **shovel** the snow.
47. Loosen the bolt with a **wrench**.
48. I have to **comb** the tangles out of my hair.
49. The librarian put the book back on the **shelf**.
50. My dog won a **trophy** at the dog show.

Name _____

Read each set of phrases. Fill in the circle next to the phrase with an underlined word that is spelled correctly.

1. ⓐ garbedge disposal   ⓒ large garbbage bags
   ⓑ a garbage can   ⓓ a garbadge truck

2. ⓐ will hault   ⓒ must halt
   ⓑ haulte now   ⓓ to hawlt

3. ⓐ peacock fethers   ⓒ owl featheres
   ⓑ eagle feathers   ⓓ hawk fetheres

4. ⓐ the young orfan   ⓒ a baby orphin
   ⓑ the tall orffan   ⓓ the healthy orphan

5. ⓐ creaped quickly   ⓒ creeped along
   ⓑ crept forward   ⓓ creept quietly

6. ⓐ a plastic shuvel   ⓒ his aluminum shovel
   ⓑ that metal shovle   ⓓ this child's shovvel

7. ⓐ delicious crumbe   ⓒ the last crumb
   ⓑ that tiny crumm   ⓓ a bread crum

8. ⓐ your durty face   ⓒ a dirtty room
   ⓑ his derty hands   ⓓ the dirty laundry

9. ⓐ most dolfin fins   ⓒ the dollphin pool
   ⓑ the dolphin tricks   ⓓ the dolphen pups

10. ⓐ fresh sherbet   ⓒ lime surebet
    ⓑ dish of sherburt   ⓓ half-gallon of shurbet

Review Test (Side B)

Lesson 12

Read each set of phrases. Fill in the circle next to the phrase with an underlined word that is spelled correctly.

11. (a) a tall <u>chimeny</u> (c) that stone <u>chimney</u>
    (b) the brick <u>chimny</u> (d) smoke from the <u>chimeney</u>

12. (a) its <u>flight</u> south (c) an airplane <u>flighte</u>
    (b) a smooth <u>fligt</u> (d) the <u>fliet</u> home

13. (a) a hungry <u>girraffe</u> (c) the tallest <u>giraph</u>
    (b) the exhausted <u>girafe</u> (d) a newborn <u>giraffe</u>

14. (a) this new <u>product</u> (c) an effective <u>produckt</u>
    (b) an improved <u>prodduct</u> (d) a cleaning <u>producked</u>

15. (a) first place <u>trophey</u> (c) a team <u>trofey</u>
    (b) the shiny <u>troughy</u> (d) the bronze <u>trophy</u>

16. (a) an immediate <u>refunnd</u> (c) a mail-in <u>refund</u>
    (b) an instant <u>refunned</u> (d) will <u>refunde</u>

17. (a) your youngest <u>brothur</u> (c) his older <u>bruther</u>
    (b) my twin <u>brother</u> (d) my other <u>brotherr</u>

18. (a) farm <u>folkes</u> (c) adult <u>fokes</u>
    (b) young <u>foakls</u> (d) city <u>folks</u>

19. (a) your swollen <u>nuckle</u> (c) my thumb <u>knuckel</u>
    (b) his tiny <u>knukle</u> (d) her scraped <u>knuckle</u>

20. (a) a trip <u>journal</u> (c) my private <u>jornal</u>
    (b) his daily <u>jurnal</u> (d) a <u>journel</u> entry

Take It Home 2

Your child has learned to spell many new words in Lessons 7–11 and would enjoy sharing them with you and your family. Here are some ideas that will make reviewing those words great fun for everyone.

Keep Track

Keep a sheet of paper and a pencil handy. As your family talks, watches television, listens to the radio, or shares a favorite story, encourage your child to listen for phrases that contain spelling words and to jot the words down on the paper.

Lesson 7

1. absent
2. blended
3. colder
4. crept
5. crunch
6. different
7. dusk
8. halt
9. independent
10. milk
11. printing
12. product
13. protesting
14. refund
15. risk
16. skunk
17. sounds
18. stretch
19. twister
20. unfold

Lesson 8

1. artist
2. boards
3. carton
4. cheerfully
5. curb
6. dirty
7. error
8. fair
9. fearless
10. garbage
11. harbor
12. heart
13. journal
14. organ
15. perfume
16. sherbet
17. shore
18. spare
19. sparks
20. sports

Lesson 9

1. awhile
2. bother
3. brother
4. charge
5. chicken
6. chimney
7. crush
8. farther
9. feathers
10. foolish
11. gather
12. leash
13. reaches
14. sharply
15. shipment
16. shovel
17. thunder
18. Thursday
19. wheat
20. whiskers

Lesson 10

1. after
2. alphabet
3. autograph
4. cough
5. dolphin
6. elephants
7. enough
8. geography
9. giraffe
10. graphs
11. laughs
12. nephew
13. orphan
14. phase
15. phony
16. photo
17. roughly
18. shelf
19. stiff
20. trophy

Lesson 11

1. answer
2. comb
3. crumb
4. flight
5. folks
6. ghost
7. halfway
8. honest
9. island
10. known
11. knuckle
12. listen
13. numb
14. often
15. soften
16. thumb
17. Wednesday
18. wrecks
19. wrench
20. wrist

Alphabet Soup

Can you and your child make a spelling word by unscrambling the letters floating in each bowl of alphabet soup?

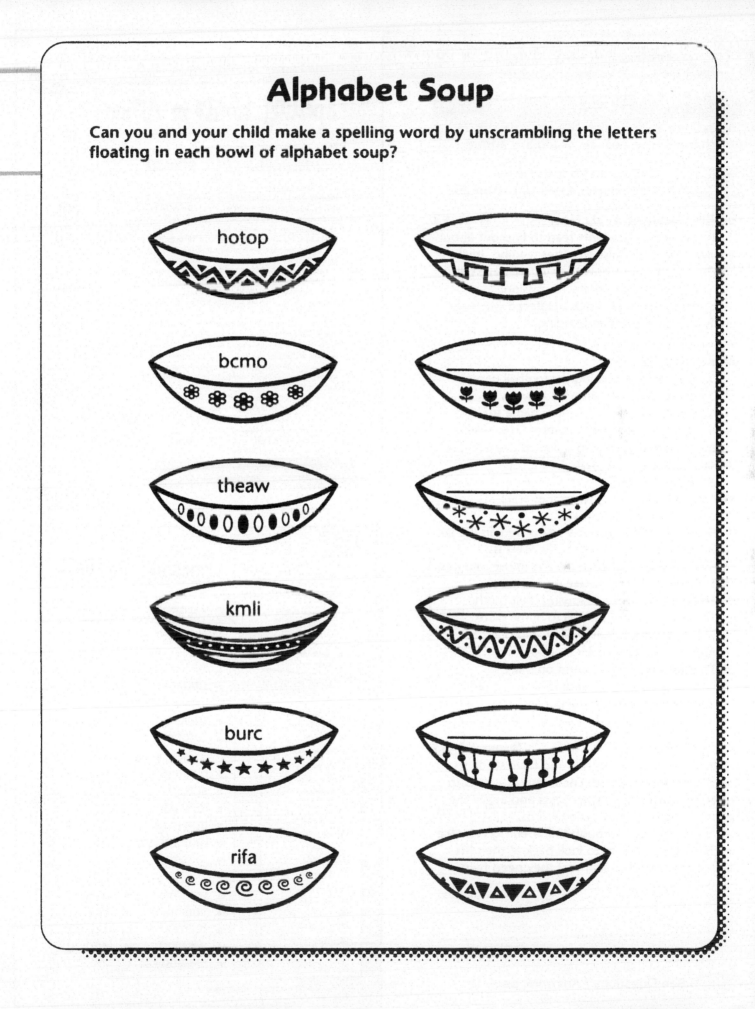

hotop

bcmo

theaw

kmli

burc

rifa

Objective
To spell words in which the base words do not change when *ed*, *er*, or *ing* are added

Phonics Correlated Phonics Lesson
MCP Phonics, Level D, Lesson 28

Spelling Words in Action   Page 53
In this selection, students read to find out about the failed Apollo 13 mission. After reading, invite students to talk about how they would have felt if they had been on the Apollo 13 mission.

Ask volunteers to say each boldfaced word and identify the base word and ending.

Warm-Up Test
1. Did you enjoy **watching** the football game?
2. Daryl was busy **checking** his answers.
3. After **finishing** her work, Rosa had a snack.
4. To be a good **learner**, you must listen well.
5. **Bending** and stretching is one way to exercise.
6. Rachel **cleaned** her desk.
7. Blake **sorted** the socks.
8. I **missed** my parents when they were in Peru.
9. Who's your favorite **singer**?
10. Brian **guessed** how many beans were in the jar.
11. What an excellent **teacher** Mr. West is!
12. A fast **walker** can reach the zoo in five minutes.
13. Tim **remembered** to take his books.
14. The ducklings were **following** their mother.
15. The fielder **tossed** the ball to home plate.
16. The leaves are **turning** yellow and orange.
17. Are you still **wishing** for a puppy?
18. The spaceship was **landing** on Mars.
19. The runner who was **leading** won the race.
20. The **catcher** spoke to the pitcher.

Spelling Practice   Pages 54–55
Introduce the spelling rule and have students read the **list words** aloud. Encourage students to look back at their **Warm-Up Tests** and apply the spelling rule to any misspelled words.

As students work through the **Spelling Practice** exercises, remind them to look back at their **list words** or in their dictionaries if they need help.

 for ESL students   See Questions / Answers, page 15

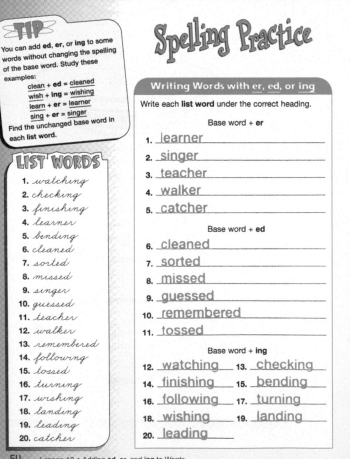

Spelling Words in Action

What happened on the Apollo 13 mission?

MISSION: CUT SHORT

Fra Mauro Hill seemed the ideal place for the next lunar **landing**. The crew of the Apollo 13 mission were ready and well trained, but something would go terribly wrong before they ever got to the moon. They would be lucky to get back to Earth at all.

Apollo 13 was launched on April 11, 1970. For the first two and a half days, the mission went smoothly. Then, on the 13th, the astronauts **remembered** hearing a big bang. They quickly set about **checking** what had happened. **Following** the bang, they discovered that a faulty switch had caught fire, **leading** to the explosion of two oxygen tanks. Without oxygen, there would be no power, water, or air to breathe. The astronauts **guessed** they would never make it back to Earth. The mission was **turning** into a nightmare.

Back on Earth, the mission control people were **watching** the drama unfold. They anxiously tried to figure out what to do. They knew the Lunar Module aboard the spacecraft had extra power supplies. It also had stores of water and oxygen. **Bending** all the rules, scientists worked hastily to design a way of connecting the two systems. Finally, they had a solution, **finishing** just in time.

The astronauts returned to Earth, tired, hungry, cold, and thirsty. In one way, though, they were fortunate. If the accident had happened after landing on the moon, supplies in the Lunar Module would have been used up. The ending would have been very different.

Look back at the boldfaced words. Did the base words change when **ing** or **ed** was added?

53

Spelling Practice

TIP
You can add **ed**, **er**, or **ing** to some words without changing the spelling of the base word. Study these examples:

clean + **ed** = <u>cleaned</u>
wish + **ing** = <u>wishing</u>
learn + **er** = <u>learner</u>
sing + **er** = <u>singer</u>

Find the unchanged base word in each list word.

LIST WORDS
1. watching
2. checking
3. finishing
4. learner
5. bending
6. cleaned
7. sorted
8. missed
9. singer
10. guessed
11. teacher
12. walker
13. remembered
14. following
15. tossed
16. turning
17. wishing
18. landing
19. leading
20. catcher

Writing Words with er, ed, or ing
Write each **list word** under the correct heading.

Base word + **er**
1. learner
2. singer
3. teacher
4. walker
5. catcher

Base word + **ed**
6. cleaned
7. sorted
8. missed
9. guessed
10. remembered
11. tossed

Base word + **ing**
12. watching   13. checking
14. finishing   15. bending
16. following   17. turning
18. wishing   19. landing
20. leading

Classification

Write the **list word** that belongs in each group.

1. pitcher, batter, <u>catcher</u>
2. hoping, wanting, <u>wishing</u>
3. supposed, imagined, <u>guessed</u>
4. runner, jogger, <u>walker</u>
5. seeing, looking, <u>watching</u>
6. dancer, actor, <u>singer</u>
7. threw, pitched, <u>tossed</u>
8. divided, grouped, <u>sorted</u>
9. thought of, recalled, <u>remembered</u>
10. curving, stooping, <u>bending</u>
11. pupil, student, <u>learner</u>
12. avoided, escaped, <u>missed</u>

Riddles

Use **list words** to answer these riddles.

1. I'm not beginning. I'm just ending. What am I doing? <u>finishing</u>
2. You can usually find me in the classroom. What am I? <u>teacher</u>
3. I'm looking. I'm just making sure. What am I doing? <u>checking</u>
4. I rhyme with <u>leaned</u> and <u>screened</u>. What am I? <u>cleaned</u>
5. I'm not leading. I'm behind. What am I doing? <u>following</u>
6. I do this when I'm going around a corner. What am I doing? <u>turning</u>
7. After descending, airplanes do this on a runway. What are they doing? <u>landing</u>
8. I'm the first. I'm not following. What am I doing? <u>leading</u>

Spelling and Writing

Proofreading

The paragraph below has ten mistakes. Use the proofreading marks to fix each mistake. Then, write the misspelled **list words** correctly on the lines.

Proofreading Marks
- ◯ spelling mistake
- ≡ capital letter
- ⌐ take out something

Yesterday, I went to an air show with my friend david and his mother, who is a teachr. We were waching six jets jets streak across the sky, one olowing the other. Suddenly, the plane that was eeding began to turn. The others followed. we stared in amazement as the jets did loops and dips. When the pilots came in for the landng, the crowd cheered! We wouldn't have mised that that show for anything!

1. <u>teacher</u>   2. <u>watching</u>
3. <u>following</u>   4. <u>leading</u>
5. <u>landing</u>   6. <u>missed</u>

Writing a Journal Entry

Imagine that you are the first astronaut to land on an unknown planet. Write a journal entry to describe what you see and hear. Use as many **list words** as you can. Remember to proofread your writing and fix any mistakes.

BONUS WORDS
gulped
performer
mending
sinking
soared

Spelling Strategy

Write two columns on the board, one containing base words for three of the **list words** and the other containing *ing, ed,* and *er.* Invite student pairs to
- copy the columns
- draw connecting lines to make **list words**
- write each **list word** and use it in an oral sentence.

Continue with the remaining **list words.**

BONUS WORDS Have students write a paragraph using all the **bonus words**, but tell them to leave a blank for each word's ending or suffix. Then, have students trade papers with partners to finish each other's words.

Spelling and Writing   **Page 56**

The **Proofreading** exercise will help students prepare to proofread their journal entries. As students complete the writing activity, encourage them to brainstorm ideas, write a first draft, revise, and proofread their work. To publish their writing, students may want to
- create a captain's log
- use their journal entries to make a postcard.

Writer's Corner Suggest students visit NASA's Web site: www.nasa.gov. Invite them to read an article that interests them, and then write a summary of the article to share with the class.

Final Test

1. Hiroshi is the **catcher** for our baseball team.
2. The tadpole was slowly **turning** into a frog.
3. Sue **missed** her friend who had moved away.
4. What a quick **learner** you are!
5. The **walker** stopped to enjoy the view.
6. I hope John **remembered** to take his umbrella.
7. When the **singer** bowed, everyone clapped.
8. We were **wishing** that the storm would end.
9. Sam was **watching** the storm approach.
10. **Bending** the metal bar took great strength.
11. He **cleaned** the stains in the sink.
12. Watching the moon **landing** was very exciting!
13. Keshia **guessed** what was in the box.
14. The little chicks were **following** the hen.
15. Is Dan **checking** the address?
16. I **tossed** the trash into the wastebasket.
17. At halftime, the Jets were **leading** the Giants.
18. Our **teacher** took us on a field trip.
19. Maria **sorted** the papers into two neat piles.
20. The students were **finishing** their spelling test.

Objective
To spell words in which the base word drops its final _e_ to add _ed_, _er_, or _ing_

 Correlated Phonics Lesson
MCP Phonics, Level D, Lesson 30

Spelling Words in Action   **Page 57**
Students may enjoy reading about a snack that has been popular for hundreds of years. Afterward, invite students to share what their favorite nutritious snacks are.

Ask volunteers to say each boldfaced word and tell how the spelling of the base word changed when _ed_, _er_, or _ing_ was added.

Warm-Up Test
1. Glenn is **coming** home in time for dinner.
2. Shannon **loved** the scary monster movie.
3. Will you help by **raking** the lawn?
4. The waiter **served** the salads first.
5. Columbus **proved** that the earth is round.
6. Megan is good at **sharing** with others.
7. Alanna and Nick **traded** baseball cards.
8. The **mover** loaded the chair into the big fan.
9. Cam **saved** his sister a seat in the theater.
10. Will Mr. Cass be **giving** swimming lessons?
11. Amanda is a careful bike **rider**.
12. The audience applauded the graceful **dancer**.
13. Max **promised** to clean his room on Saturday.
14. What a **surprising** ending that story had!
15. The gymnast is **bouncing** on the trampoline.
16. Mike is **writing** an article for our school paper.
17. Mom **sliced** the pizza while it was still hot.
18. The price of this car has been **reduced**.
19. The lake does not look the way I **pictured** it.
20. Dad is **comparing** the prices of produce.

Spelling Practice   **Pages 58–59**
Introduce the spelling rule and have students read the **list words** aloud. Encourage students to look back at their **Warm-Up Tests** and apply the spelling rule to any misspelled words.

As students work through the **Spelling Practice** exercises, remind them to look back at their **list words** or in their dictionaries if they need help.

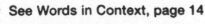 **See Words in Context, page 14**

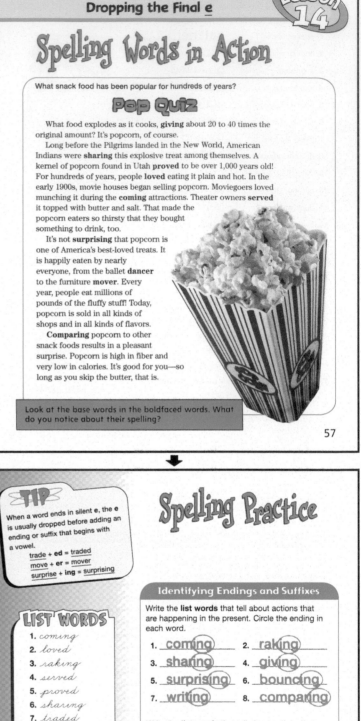

Spelling Words in Action

What snack food has been popular for hundreds of years?

Pop Quiz

What food explodes as it cooks, **giving** about 20 to 40 times the original amount? It's popcorn, of course.

Long before the Pilgrims landed in the New World, American Indians were **sharing** this explosive treat among themselves. A kernel of popcorn found in Utah **proved** to be over 1,000 years old! For hundreds of years, people **loved** eating it plain and hot. In the early 1900s, movie houses began selling popcorn. Moviegoers loved munching it during the **coming** attractions. Theater owners **served** it topped with butter and salt. That made the popcorn eaters so thirsty that they bought something to drink, too.

It's not **surprising** that popcorn is one of America's best-loved treats. It is happily eaten by nearly everyone, from the ballet **dancer** to the furniture **mover**. Every year, people eat millions of pounds of the fluffy stuff! Today, popcorn is sold in all kinds of shops and in all kinds of flavors. **Comparing** popcorn to other snack foods results in a pleasant surprise. Popcorn is high in fiber and very low in calories. It's good for you—so long as you skip the butter, that is.

Look at the base words in the boldfaced words. What do you notice about their spelling?

57

TIP
When a word ends in silent **e**, the **e** is usually dropped before adding an ending or suffix that begins with a vowel.

trade + **ed** = traded
move + **er** = mover
surprise + **ing** = surprising

Spelling Practice

LIST WORDS
1. coming
2. loved
3. raking
4. served
5. proved
6. sharing
7. traded
8. mover
9. saved
10. giving
11. rider
12. dancer
13. promised
14. surprising
15. bouncing
16. writing
17. sliced
18. reduced
19. pictured
20. comparing

Identifying Endings and Suffixes
Write the **list words** that tell about actions that are happening in the present. Circle the ending in each word.

1. coming   2. raking
3. sharing   4. giving
5. surprising   6. bouncing
7. writing   8. comparing

Write the **list words** that tell about actions that happened in the past. Circle the ending in each word.

9. loved   10. served
11. proved   12. traded
13. saved   14. promised
15. sliced   16. reduced
17. pictured

Write the **list words** that name people and what they do. Circle the suffix in each word.

18. mover   19. rider
20. dancer

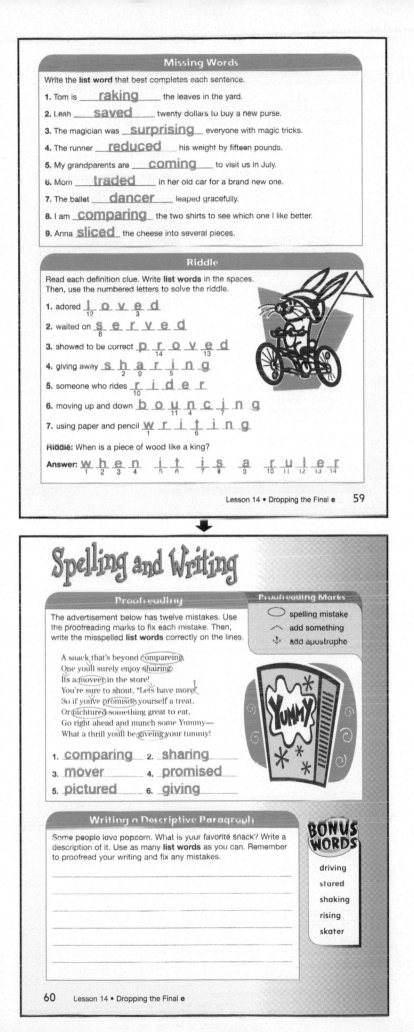

Missing Words

Write the **list word** that best completes each sentence.

1. Tom is ___raking___ the leaves in the yard.
2. Leah ___saved___ twenty dollars to buy a new purse.
3. The magician was ___surprising___ everyone with magic tricks.
4. The runner ___reduced___ his weight by fifteen pounds.
5. My grandparents are ___coming___ to visit us in July.
6. Mom ___traded___ in her old car for a brand new one.
7. The ballet ___dancer___ leaped gracefully.
8. I am ___comparing___ the two shirts to see which one I like better.
9. Anna ___sliced___ the cheese into several pieces.

Riddle

Read each definition clue. Write **list words** in the spaces. Then, use the numbered letters to solve the riddle.

1. adored l o v e d
               12   3
2. waited on s e r v e d
                      8
3. showed to be correct p r o v e d
                            14   13
4. giving away s h a r i n g
                  2   9   5
5. someone who rides r i d e r
                        10
6. moving up and down b o u n c i n g
                           11 4   7
7. using paper and pencil w r i t i n g
                             1   6

Riddle: When is a piece of wood like a king?

Answer: w h e n   i t   i s   a   r u l e r
          1 2 3 4   5 6   7 8   9   10 11 12 13 14

Spelling and Writing

Proofreading

The advertisement below has twelve mistakes. Use the proofreading marks to fix each mistake. Then, write the misspelled **list words** correctly on the lines.

Proofreading Marks
- ⬭ spelling mistake
- ⌃ add something
- ⸕ add apostrophe

A snack that's beyond comparing,
One youll surely enjoy sharing
Its a moveer in the store!
You're sure to shout, "Let's have more!"
So if youve promisd yourself a treat,
Or pictured something great to eat,
Go right ahead and munch some Yummy—
What a thrill youll be giving your tummy!

1. comparing 2. sharing
3. mover   4. promised
5. pictured   6. giving

Writing a Descriptive Paragraph

Some people love popcorn. What is your favorite snack? Write a description of it. Use as many **list words** as you can. Remember to proofread your writing and fix any mistakes.

_____
_____
_____
_____
_____
_____
_____

BONUS WORDS

driving
stared
shaking
rising
skater

Spelling Strategy

Invite students to work with a partner to write each **list word** as a word equation (*share – e + ing = sharing, dance – e + er = dancer*). Encourage students to tell whether the ending or suffix indicates the present tense (*ing*), the past tense (*ed*), or a noun that names a kind of person (*er*).

BONUS WORDS

Have students write a sentence using each **bonus word**, but ask them to draw a picture clue where the word would be written. Then, let students trade papers with partners and guess each other's words.

Spelling and Writing   Page 60

The **Proofreading** exercise will help students prepare to proofread their descriptions. As students complete the writing activity, encourage them to brainstorm ideas, write a first draft, revise, and proofread their work. To publish their writing, students may want to

- create a "tasty treats" catalog
- read their descriptions aloud as TV advertisements.

Writer's Corner Students can learn more facts about popcorn at: www.popcorn.org. You may want to have a class popcorn party at which students share what they learned about this popular food.

Final Test

1. The comedian **loved** to make people laugh.
2. The waiter **served** us dinner and dessert.
3. Peter is **sharing** his ideas with the class.
4. Has the **mover** rolled up the carpet yet?
5. The professor is **giving** a science lecture.
6. What a fantastic **dancer** Mario is!
7. It was **surprising** to find them in the gym.
8. **Writing** is my favorite classroom activity.
9. The manager of the store **reduced** the prices.
10. The lawyers were **comparing** notes.
11. I **pictured** Kyla as an astronaut or a doctor.
12. The baker **sliced** the loaf of bread.
13. Logan was **bouncing** the ball down the court.
14. The mechanic **promised** to fix the car today.
15. Did the **rider** fall off the horse?
16. The accountant **saved** us hundreds of dollars.
17. Ryan **traded** his baseball cards for a camera.
18. The bus driver **proved** she could drive well.
19. The children are **raking** leaves in the yard.
20. The doctor is **coming** to examine the injury.

Objective
To spell words in which the final consonant of the base word is doubled when *ed, er,* or *ing* is added

 Correlated Phonics Lesson
MCP Phonics, Level D, Lesson 31

Spelling Words in Action   **Page 61**

In "Culture and Canoes," students read about a race in Hawaii that involves giant canoes. Suggest that students compare these canoes to other types of boats they may be familiar with.

Encourage students to look back at the boldfaced words. Ask volunteers to say each word and tell how the spelling of the base word changed when *ed, er/ers,* or *ing* was added.

Warm-Up Test
1. As I hiked, I was **beginning** to feel tired.
2. Did I hear you **humming** a tune?
3. The second baseman **dropped** the ball.
4. The puppy was **sitting** near the door.
5. A skater was **slipping** and sliding on the ice.
6. She yelled "Watch out!" to the **joggers**.
7. After **grabbing** his coat, Dan ran out the door.
8. The cork was **bobbing** in the waves.
9. Laurie **tripped** over the box.
10. A Chinese jacket is **padded** with cotton.
11. Try **skimming** the page to find the answer.
12. I was **scrubbing** the tub to get it clean.
13. All three **winners** walked on stage.
14. The hikers were **outfitted** with new boots.
15. Tony **wrapped** the present in colorful paper.
16. The audience would not stop **clapping**.
17. John is **dragging** the trash can to the street.
18. The two neighbors are **chatting** in the yard.
19. Tara will finish because she's not a **quitter**.
20. Did Stacie use a **trimmer** to cut the hedges?

Spelling Practice   **Pages 62–63**

Introduce the spelling rule and have students read the **list words** aloud. Review the meanings of words that may be unfamiliar to students: *bobbing, skimming,* and *outfitted*. Then, encourage students to look back at their **Warm-Up Tests** and apply the spelling rule to any misspelled words.

As students work through the **Spelling Practice** exercises, remind them to look back at their **list words** or in their dictionaries if they need help.

for ESL students See Spelling Aloud, page 14

54

Spelling Words in Action

What kind of race uses giant canoes?

Culture and Canoes

The sky is bright and sunny. Light winds ripple the water. Six anxious competitors are **sitting** inside a giant canoe. Each one is **grabbing** onto a paddle, waiting for the signal. Other canoes are **bobbing** in the water. They are also waiting. Suddenly, the sound of an airhorn pierces the silence.

The sound marks the **beginning** of a 41-mile race from the Hawaiian island of Molokai to the island of Oahu. In moments, the canoes are **skimming** across the water. Onlookers are yelling and **chatting** as they watch the canoes **slipping** off into the distance.

The Molokai Outrigger Canoe Race is not just a race. It has historical importance as well. Many years ago, giant canoes were the only way to travel among the Hawaiian Islands. Each boat was usually carved from a single tree—mainly the Koa tree. The canoes were **outfitted** to be used as fishing boats, warships, and even ferries. Over time, these giant boats were replaced by more efficient means of transportation.

The tradition of the outrigger canoe hasn't been **dropped**, though. It continues today with the annual Molokai Race. The competitors who win the race aren't the only **winners**. Everyone wins, because the race preserves an important part of Hawaiian culture.

Look back at the boldfaced words. What do you notice about the spelling of the base words?

61

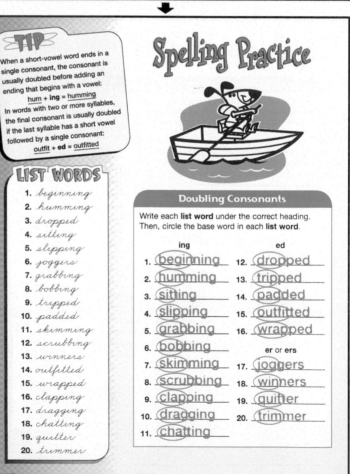

TIP

When a short-vowel word ends in a single consonant, the consonant is usually doubled before adding an ending that begins with a vowel:
hum + ing = humming
In words with two or more syllables, the final consonant is usually doubled if the last syllable has a short vowel followed by a single consonant:
outfit + ed = outfitted

Spelling Practice

LIST WORDS
1. beginning
2. humming
3. dropped
4. sitting
5. slipping
6. joggers
7. grabbing
8. bobbing
9. tripped
10. padded
11. skimming
12. scrubbing
13. winners
14. outfitted
15. wrapped
16. clapping
17. dragging
18. chatting
19. quitter
20. trimmer

Doubling Consonants

Write each **list word** under the correct heading. Then, circle the base word in each **list word**.

ing	ed
1. beginning	12. dropped
2. humming	13. tripped
3. sitting	14. padded
4. slipping	15. outfitted
5. grabbing	16. wrapped
6. bobbing	**er or ers**
7. skimming	17. joggers
8. scrubbing	18. winners
9. clapping	19. quitter
10. dragging	20. trimmer
11. chatting	

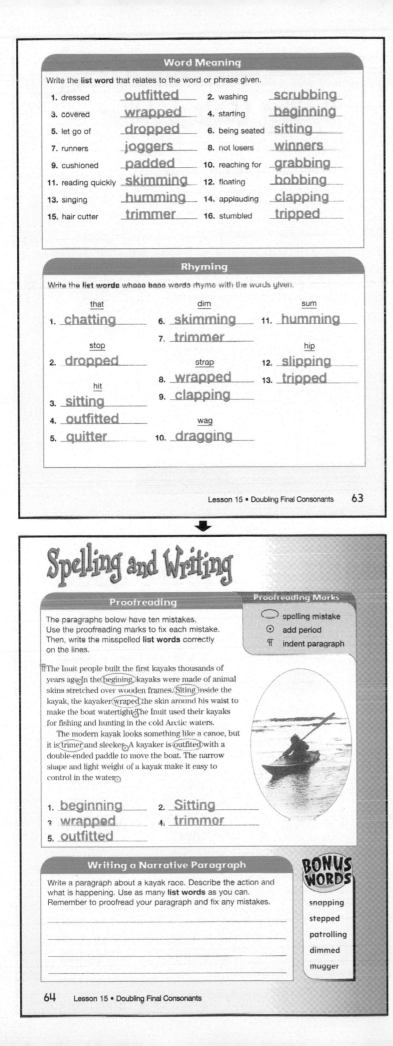

Word Meaning

Write the **list word** that relates to the word or phrase given.

1. dressed — outfitted
2. washing — scrubbing
3. covered — wrapped
4. starting — beginning
5. let go of — dropped
6. being seated — sitting
7. runners — joggers
8. not losers — winners
9. cushioned — padded
10. reaching for — grabbing
11. reading quickly — skimming
12. floating — bobbing
13. singing — humming
14. applauding — clapping
15. hair cutter — trimmer
16. stumbled — tripped

Rhyming

Write the **list words** whose base words rhyme with the words given.

that
1. chatting

dim
6. skimming
7. trimmer

sum
11. humming

stop
2. dropped

strap
8. wrapped

hip
12. slipping
13. tripped

hit
3. sitting

4. outfitted

9. clapping

5. quitter

wag
10. dragging

Lesson 15 • Doubling Final Consonants   63

Spelling and Writing

Proofreading

The paragraphs below have ten mistakes. Use the proofreading marks to fix each mistake. Then, write the misspelled **list words** correctly on the lines.

Proofreading Marks
- ◯ spelling mistake
- ⊙ add period
- ¶ indent paragraph

¶The Inuit people built the first kayaks thousands of years ago. In the begining, kayaks were made of animal skins stretched over wooden frames. Sitting inside the kayak, the kayaker wraped the skin around his waist to make the boat watertight. The Inuit used their kayaks for fishing and hunting in the cold Arctic waters.

The modern kayak looks something like a canoe, but it is trimer and sleeker. A kayaker is outfited with a double-ended paddle to move the boat. The narrow shape and light weight of a kayak make it easy to control in the water.

1. beginning   2. Sitting
3. wrapped   4. trimmer
5. outfitted

Writing a Narrative Paragraph

Write a paragraph about a kayak race. Describe the action and what is happening. Use as many **list words** as you can. Remember to proofread your paragraph and fix any mistakes.

_____
_____
_____
_____

BONUS WORDS
snapping
stepped
patrolling
dimmed
mugger

64   Lesson 15 • Doubling Final Consonants

Spelling Strategy

Write **list words** on the board (*beginning, padded, scrubbing, quitter*). Then, write short-vowel words with two final consonants and *ed, er/ers,* or *ing* added at the end: *gasped, adjusted, twisting, walker.* Have students identify the base words in each list and compare their spellings when *ed, er/ers,* or *ing* is added. Conclude that when a short-vowel word ends in a single consonant, the consonant doubles when *ed, er/ers,* or *ing* is added.

BONUS WORDS
Have partners identify the base word in each **bonus word**, then look up the base words in a dictionary. They can use the definitions to write a sentence for each **bonus word**.

Spelling and Writing   Page 64

The **Proofreading** exercise will help students prepare to proofread their paragraphs. As students complete the writing activity, encourage them to brainstorm ideas, write a first draft, revise, and proofread their work. To publish their writing, students may want to
- combine their paragraphs into a class newspaper
- read their paragraphs aloud as news broadcasts.

Writer's Corner Suggest that students research other Hawaiian traditions in the library or on the Internet. Then, have them write a paragraph about their favorite tradition and create an illustration to go with it.

Final Test

1. Uncle Jack used the hedge **trimmer**.
2. The **beginning** of the movie was boring.
3. The girls don't want a **quitter** on their team.
4. We left the show **humming** the songs.
5. "Quit **chatting**!" ordered the teacher.
6. Dana **dropped** one of her books.
7. The dog is **dragging** its leash behind it.
8. Shane enjoys **sitting** in the sand.
9. The audience is **clapping** for the play.
10. The puppy was **slipping** on the waxed floor.
11. The packages are **wrapped** and ready to mail.
12. The **joggers** stopped to drink at the fountain.
13. The band was **outfitted** in their new uniforms.
14. Rob and I were **grabbing** for the last sandwich.
15. The boat was **bobbing** in the harbor.
16. Who are the **winners** of the art contest?
17. The dancer **tripped** and lost her balance.
18. Adam is **skimming** the sports page.
19. Did you try **scrubbing** the pot with cleanser?
20. The goalie's pants were thickly **padded**.

Words Ending with y:
Adding ed, es, and ing

Objective
To spell words in which the base words that end in y change when adding ed, es, or ing

 Correlated Phonics Lesson
MCP Phonics, Level D, Lesson 33

Spelling Words in Action   **Page 65**
In this selection, students read to learn about Benjamin Franklin's many discoveries. After reading, invite students to discuss which of Franklin's discoveries they think is most important.

Encourage students to look back at the boldfaced words. Ask volunteers to say each word, identify the base word, and tell how it has changed.

Warm-Up Test
1. A champion always **tries** to excel.
2. Paula **carried** the grocery bags for her neighbor.
3. What a lot of **worries** you have!
4. Why are you **buying** two dozen eggs?
5. We're **satisfied** with the results we got.
6. "I am **relying** on you to be on time," said Dad.
7. If he **denies** what I said, I can prove it.
8. Ken carefully **copied** the words from the board.
9. The thirsty guests **emptied** the pitcher of juice.
10. Berta was **hurrying** to catch the bus.
11. The wolves' **cries** could be heard from far away.
12. No one knows where my dog **buries** her bones.
13. When 5 is **multiplied** by 4, the product is 20.
14. Joel always **replies** to my letters.
15. The supermarket **supplied** the fruit we ate.
16. While the paint is **drying**, clean the brushes.
17. **Petrified** wood is as hard as stone.
18. Please hand me the big **frying** pan.
19. Have you **applied** for that summer job?
20. All the gerbils are **scurrying** around the cage.

Spelling Practice   **Pages 66–67**
Introduce the spelling rule and have students read the **list words** aloud. Encourage students to look back at their **Warm-Up Tests** and apply the spelling rule to any misspelled words.

As students work through the **Spelling Practice** exercises, remind them to look back at their **list words** or in their dictionaries if they need help.

 See Change or No Change, page 15

Spelling Words in Action

Why would a scientist want to fly a kite during a lightning storm?

A Man of Many Talents

Benjamin Franklin **applied** his talents in many ways. He was a printer, writer, civic leader, and scientist. **Relying** on his famous **replies** and clever sayings, he often convinced people of his ideas. Today, no one **denies** Franklin's genius.

Almost 250 years ago, Benjamin Franklin conducted his most famous experiment. He proved that lightning is electricity. The exact details of his experiment are not known. Some people think Franklin may have flown a kite at the beginning of an electrical storm. Lightning may have struck a wire **carried** by the kite. It then might have traveled down the hairs of the kite string to a key. There, it created a spark. The experiment **supplied** information Franklin needed to invent the lightning rod.

Franklin also invented the Franklin stove. It produced twice as much heat as a fireplace and used much less fuel. He invented bifocal glasses, which had both reading and distance lenses. Franklin discovered that disease **multiplied** in stuffy rooms. He was the first to show that a rough sea could be calmed by pouring oil on it. He also thought up daylight-saving time, **buying** people more daylight in the summer.

Many people **copied** Franklin's ideas. Franklin, though, refused to make a profit from any of his inventions. He was **satisfied** if his inventions gave people a better life.

Look back at each boldfaced word. Identify the base word. Did it change when an ending was added?

65

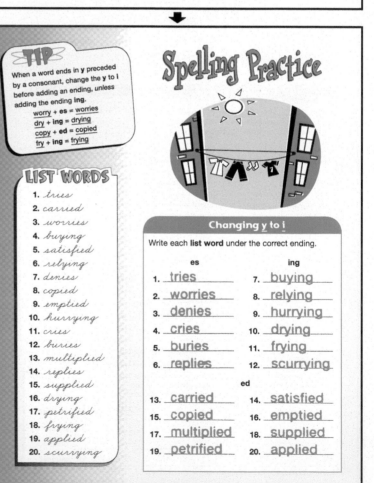

Spelling Practice

TIP
When a word ends in **y** preceded by a consonant, change the **y** to **i** before adding an ending, *unless* adding the ending **ing**.
worry + **es** = worries
dry + **ing** = drying
copy + **ed** = copied
fry + **ing** = frying

LIST WORDS
1. tries
2. carried
3. worries
4. buying
5. satisfied
6. relying
7. denies
8. copied
9. emptied
10. hurrying
11. cries
12. buries
13. multiplied
14. replies
15. supplied
16. drying
17. petrified
18. frying
19. applied
20. scurrying

Changing y to i
Write each **list word** under the correct ending.

es
1. tries
2. worries
3. denies
4. cries
5. buries
6. replies

ing
7. buying
8. relying
9. hurrying
10. drying
11. frying
12. scurrying

ed
13. carried
14. satisfied
15. copied
16. emptied
17. multiplied
18. supplied
19. petrified
20. applied

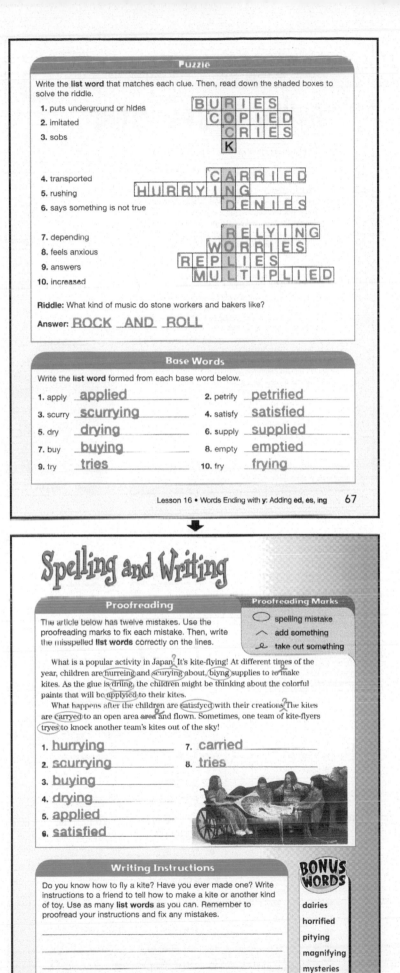

Puzzle

Write the **list word** that matches each clue. Then, read down the shaded boxes to solve the riddle.

1. puts underground or hides — B U R I E S
2. imitated — C O P I E D
3. sobs — C R I E S
   K

4. transported — C A R R I E D
5. rushing — H U R R Y I N G
6. says something is not true — D E N I E S

7. depending — R E L Y I N G
8. feels anxious — W O R R I E S
9. answers — R E P L I E S
10. increased — M U L T I P L I E D

Riddle: What kind of music do stone workers and bakers like?

Answer: ROCK AND ROLL

Base Words

Write the **list word** formed from each base word below.

1. apply — applied
2. petrify — petrified
3. scurry — scurrying
4. satisfy — satisfied
5. dry — drying
6. supply — supplied
7. buy — buying
8. empty — emptied
9. try — tries
10. fry — frying

Lesson 16 • Words Ending with y: Adding ed, es, ing   67

Spelling and Writing

Proofreading

The article below has twelve mistakes. Use the proofreading marks to fix each mistake. Then, write the misspelled **list words** correctly on the lines.

Proofreading Marks

⬭ spelling mistake
⌃ add something
⌒ take out something

What is a popular activity in Japan? It's kite-flying! At different times of the year, children are hurreing and scurying about, biyng supplies to make kites. As the glue is driing, the children might be thinking about the colorful paints that will be applyied to their kites.

What happens after the children are satisfyed with their creations? The kites are carryed to an open area area and flown. Sometimes, one team of kite-flyers tryes to knock another team's kites out of the sky!

1. hurrying
2. scurrying
3. buying
4. drying
5. applied
6. satisfied
7. carried
8. tries

Writing Instructions

Do you know how to fly a kite? Have you ever made one? Write instructions to a friend to tell how to make a kite or another kind of toy. Use as many **list words** as you can. Remember to proofread your instructions and fix any mistakes.

_____

_____

BONUS WORDS

dairies
horrified
pitying
magnifying
mysteries

68   Lesson 16 • Words Ending with y: Adding ed, es, ing

Spelling Strategy

Invite students to get together with a partner and take turns writing each **list word**. The partner who writes the word

- circles the ending
- points to the y or i
- explains why the y was or was not changed to i.

BONUS WORDS Have students pair up to write a mystery story using all five **bonus words**. Then, have partners work with other partners to compare stories. You may want to point out that the **bonus words** follow the spelling rule and discuss possible storylines for a mystery.

Spelling and Writing   Page 66

The **Proofreading** exercise will help students prepare to proofread their instructions. As students complete the writing activity, encourage them to brainstorm ideas, write a first draft, revise, and proofread their work. To publish their writing, students may want to create a class book titled *Great Things to Make for Fun.*

Writer's Corner You may want to bring in directions for making different kinds of kites and have students follow the instructions to make their own kites. Suggest they think of interesting names, such as High Flyer or Wind Sailor, to paint or write on their kites.

Final Test

1. Manuela **applied** for the manager's job.
2. The baby **tries** to talk, but she just babbles.
3. Our class is **buying** a gift for the custodian.
4. I'm **hurrying** as fast as I can!
5. Susan **multiplied** the numbers in her head.
6. I am **frying** the fish in a heavy skillet.
7. The pack mules **carried** the heaviest loads.
8. Jamie was **relying** on her mother to wake her up.
9. The coach **supplied** the players with team shirts.
10. Could you tell if the wood was **petrified**?
11. Mice were **scurrying** through the attic.
12. My dad **worries** when I am late and don't call.
13. He **denies** that he owes the teacher homework.
14. My dog **buries** his bones in the backyard.
15. I washed my clothes and am **drying** them now.
16. Our curiosity was **satisfied** by Tim's letter.
17. We **emptied** the dishwasher before we left.
18. Will you pick the baby up if she **cries**?
19. Cynthia **copied** the instructions neatly.
20. I received ten **replies** to my invitations.

Words Ending with y: Adding er, est

Objective
To spell words with comparative endings *er* and *est*, changing base words ending in *y*

 Correlated Phonics Lesson
MCP Phonics, Level D, Lesson 33

Spelling Words in Action — Page 69

In this selection, students discover which fruit is more than just a delicious food. After reading, invite students to suggest new dishes or recipes that apples could be used in.

Encourage students to look back at the boldfaced words. Ask volunteers to say each word and tell which letter in the base word was changed.

Warm-Up Test
1. My explanation just made Mom **angrier**.
2. Those were the **angriest** words he ever spoke.
3. Elena was **happier** when her cat came home.
4. That was the **happiest** time Paul had known.
5. Eric finds multiplication **easier** than division.
6. Was the last test problem the **easiest**?
7. Inez arrived **earlier** than the other guests.
8. The **earliest** bus left at 5:00 in the morning.
9. This comic is **funnier** than the first one.
10. What's the **funniest** joke you ever heard?
11. I think tulips are **prettier** than roses.
12. The **prettiest** view of town is from the hilltop.
13. It's **lonelier** on the beach than in the city.
14. My **loneliest** night was when I camped by myself.
15. Last year's snowfall was **heavier** than usual.
16. This bag of groceries is the **heaviest** of all.
17. The gold lace made the costume look **fancier**.
18. Grandpa made the **fanciest** birthday cake ever!
19. A watermelon is **juicier** than an apple.
20. The ripest pear will be the **juiciest**.

Spelling Practice — Pages 70–71

Introduce the spelling rule and have students read the **list words** aloud. Encourage students to look back at their **Warm-Up Tests** and apply the spelling rule to any misspelled words.

As students work through the **Spelling Practice** exercises, remind them to look back at their **list words** or in their dictionaries if they need help.

for ESL students **See Words in Context, page 14**

58

Spelling Words in Action

Which fruit is more than just a delicious food?

An Apple a Day

What do McIntosh, Granny Smith, and Cortland have in common? They're all apples. Some fruits may be **fancier** and others **prettier**, but few can be enjoyed in more ways than the apple. Apples can be made into apple pie, applesauce, and apple butter. The **juiciest** ones can be squeezed into apple juice or apple cider. Of course, the **easiest** way to enjoy an apple is to eat it raw.

Apples are more than just a delicious food. They're part of our language. Someone special can be described as "the apple of my eye." New York City is called "The Big Apple." The lump in a person's throat is called the "Adam's apple."

There are some interesting facts about apples. The **heaviest** apple weighed three pounds, two ounces. That's **heavier** than a bunch of eight or nine bananas! In **earlier** times, George Washington and Thomas Jefferson both grew apples. The **earliest** mention of apples in ancient writing was about 6,000 years ago. Today, about 300 different kinds of apples are grown in the United States. Some of the **funnier** names include Winter Banana, Summer Rambo, and Kidd's Orange Red.

About 200 years ago, a man named John Chapman traveled across the United States planting apple seeds. A **happier** or friendlier person would have been hard to find. People called him Johnny Appleseed. Thanks to John, apple growing is one of America's largest farm industries.

Look back at the base word in each boldfaced word. How did each base word change?

69

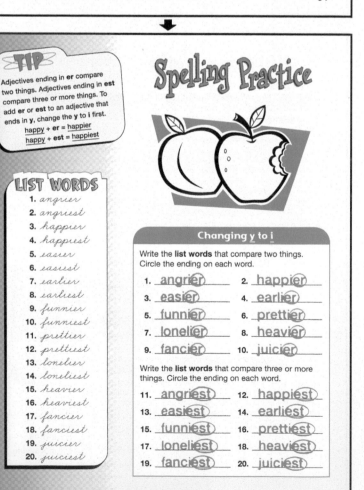

TIP
Adjectives ending in **er** compare two things. Adjectives ending in **est** compare three or more things. To add **er** or **est** to an adjective that ends in **y**, change the **y** to **i** first.
happy + er = happier
happy + est = happiest

Spelling Practice

LIST WORDS
1. angrier
2. angriest
3. happier
4. happiest
5. easier
6. easiest
7. earlier
8. earliest
9. funnier
10. funniest
11. prettier
12. prettiest
13. lonelier
14. loneliest
15. heavier
16. heaviest
17. fancier
18. fanciest
19. juicier
20. juiciest

Changing y to i

Write the **list words** that compare two things. Circle the ending on each word.

1. angri(er) 2. happi(er)
3. easi(er) 4. earli(er)
5. funni(er) 6. petti(er)
7. loneli(er) 8. heavi(er)
9. fanci(er) 10. juici(er)

Write the **list words** that compare three or more things. Circle the ending on each word.

11. angri(est) 12. happi(est)
13. easi(est) 14. earli(est)
15. funni(est) 16. petti(est)
17. loneli(est) 18. heavi(est)
19. fanci(est) 20. juici(est)

Replace the Words

Write the **list word** that best replaces the underlined word or phrase.

1. Joe was the <u>first</u> person to arrive at the party. — earliest
2. That was the <u>most humorous</u> joke I ever heard. — funniest
3. I think roses are <u>more beautiful</u> than tulips. — prettier
4. Mary was <u>madder</u> at the insult than I was. — angrier
5. The test was simpler than I thought it would be. — easier
6. I felt <u>more alone</u> than ever before. — lonelier
7. The costumes were <u>showier</u> than before. — fancier
8. Marge was the <u>most pleased</u> I had ever seen her. — happiest
9. The peaches were <u>more filled with juice</u> this year than last year. — juicier
10. This suitcase is <u>of greater weight</u> than that one. — heavier
11. Lisa was <u>the maddest</u> of all about the accident. — angriest
12. This is <u>the simplest</u> way to make a book. — easiest

Scrambled Words

What **list words** can you make from the letters in these words? Use each letter once.

1. its, juice — juiciest
2. tease, is — easiest
3. rare, lie — earlier
4. fine, run — funnier
5. tin, faces — fanciest
6. pear, hip — happier
7. pretest, lt — prettiest
8. eel, in, slot — loneliest
9. have, site — heaviest
10. are, sting — angriest
11. shape, tip — happiest
12. reel, lion — lonelier
13. let, raise — earliest
14. ten, if, sun — funniest

Lesson 17 • Words Ending with y: Adding er, est   71

Spelling and Writing

Proofreading

The paragraph below has nine mistakes. Use the proofreading marks to fix each mistake. Then, write the misspelled **list words** correctly on the lines.

Proofreading Marks
- ◯ spelling mistake
- ≡ capital letter
- / make small letter

The best apple pies are made with the firmest apples, not with watery or mushy ones. making an apple pie will he easyer if the crust is prepared ahead of time. A top crust can be made fansier and prettyer with cutouts. Remember though—the more flour in a crust or the longer you work with the crust, the heaver and tougher it will be. tough crusts make cooks the angryest Flaky crusts make cooks—and pie-eaters—happyer

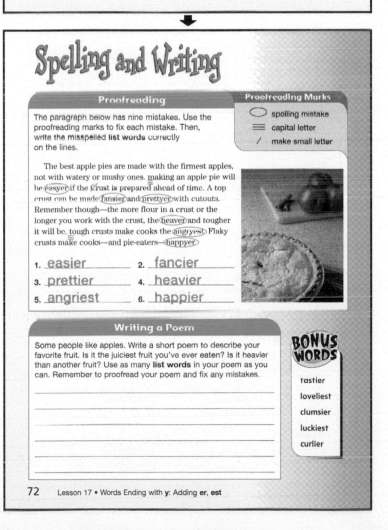

1. easier
2. fancier
3. prettier
4. heavier
5. angriest
6. happier

Writing a Poem

Some people like apples. Write a short poem to describe your favorite fruit. Is it the juiciest fruit you've ever eaten? Is it heavier than another fruit? Use as many **list words** in your poem as you can. Remember to proofread your poem and fix any mistakes.

BONUS WORDS
- tastier
- loveliest
- clumsier
- luckiest
- curlier

72   Lesson 17 • Words Ending with y: Adding er, est

Spelling Strategy

Make two columns on the board, one labeled *er* and one *est*, and ask a volunteer to come to the front of the class. Tell the volunteer a base word contained in a **list word** and have the student add *er* or *est* to the base, writing the complete word in the appropriate column. Invite other students to come to the board. Continue this procedure until all the **list words** have been written.

BONUS WORDS
Have students write each **bonus word** and a clue to go with it. Then, invite students to pair up with partners and read their clues aloud to each other. Ask them to guess the **bonus word** that goes with each clue.

Spelling and Writing   *Page 72*

The **Proofreading** exercise will help students prepare to proofread their poems. As students complete the writing activity, encourage them to brainstorm ideas, write a first draft, revise, and proofread their work. To publish their writing, students may want to
- record their poems
- create a poetry book titled *Fruitful Thoughts*.

Writer's Corner Invite students to bring in their family's favorite apple or other fruit recipe to share with the class. Suggest they write an advertisement to describe how delicious the recipe is.

Final Test

1. This play is **funnier** than the first one we read.
2. It was **easier** to ski downhill the second time.
3. That ring is Mother's **fanciest** piece of jewelry.
4. After we lost, I was **angrier** than the coach.
5. Courtney is **happiest** when she is painting.
6. The small oranges are **juicier** than the big ones.
7. I have never seen a **prettier** stage set.
8. That was the **loneliest** moment Ed had ever had.
9. Mr. Wang was the **angriest** person in the room.
10. Jermaine is **happier** about moving than I am.
11. Which peach is the **juiciest**?
12. These weights are **heavier** than they look.
13. Matt won the contest for the **funniest** costume.
14. **Earlier** in the day, I thought it would rain.
15. The **easiest** way to get there is to take the bus.
16. That is the **prettiest** garden I've ever seen!
17. The **earliest** I ever got up was 5:00 A.M.
18. Emily was **lonelier** than she expected at camp.
19. This hat is **fancier** than the feathered one.
20. The **heaviest** box is the one with all my books.

Lessons 13–17 · Review

Objectives
To review spelling words that end with *ed, er,* and *ing;* that double the final consonant or drop the final *e* when adding *ed, er,* and *ing;* that end in *y* and have *ed, er, es, est,* or *ing* added

Check Your Spelling Notebook   *Pages 73–76*
Based on students' lists and your observations, note which words are giving students the most difficulty and offer assistance for spelling them correctly. Here are some frequently misspelled words to watch for: *guessed, remembered, beginning, multiplied, tries, replies, earlier,* and *angriest.*

To give students extra help and practice in taking standardized tests, you may want to have them take the **Review Test** for this lesson on pages 62–63. After scoring the tests, return them to students so that they can record their misspelled words in their spelling notebooks.

After practicing their troublesome words, students can work through the exercises for Lessons 13–17. Before students begin each exercise, you may want to go over the spelling rule.

Take It Home
Invite students to locate the **list words** in Lessons 13–17 at home—on television, on the Internet, on the radio, in conversations, and in books and magazines. Students can also use **Take It Home** Master 3 on pages 64–65 to help them do the activity. (A complete list of the spelling words is included on page 64 of the **Take It Home** Master.) Students can total the number of words found and bring in their lists to share with the class.

In lessons 13–17, you learned how to add *ed, er, es, est,* and *ing* to the ends of words, including words that end with *y* or silent *e.*

Check Your Spelling Notebook
Look at the words in your spelling notebook. Which words for lessons 13 through 17 did you have the most trouble with? Write them here.

_____

_____

Practice spelling your troublesome words with a partner. Take turns writing a word equation for each word.

apply - y + i + **ed** = applied

Lesson 13

TIP You can add **ed, er,** or **ing** to some words without changing the spelling of the base word, as in <u>sorted</u>, <u>learner</u>, and <u>checking</u>.

List Words
- watching
- finishing
- cleaned
- singer
- guessed
- teacher
- walker
- remembered
- tossed
- wishing
- landing
- catcher

Write a **list word** that means the same or almost the same as each word or phrase. Not all of the **list words** will be used.

1. vocalist — singer
2. threw — tossed
3. touch down — landing
4. recalled — remembered
5. viewing — watching
6. ending — finishing
7. figured out — guessed
8. hoping — wishing
9. instructor — teacher
10. jogger — walker

Lesson 14

TIP When a word ends in silent *e*, the *e* is usually dropped before adding an ending that begins with a vowel, as in <u>sharing</u> and <u>served</u>.

List Words
- loved
- proved
- saved
- dancer
- promised
- surprising
- bouncing
- sliced
- pictured
- comparing

Write each **list word** under the correct category.

One Syllable
1. loved
2. proved
3. saved
4. sliced

Two Syllables
5. dancer
6. promised
7. bouncing
8. pictured

Three Syllables
9. surprising
10. comparing

Lesson 15

TIP When a short-vowel word or final syllable ends in a single consonant, the consonant is usually doubled when an ending that begins with a vowel is added, as in <u>slipping</u> and <u>quitter</u>.

List Words
- beginning
- humming
- joggers
- tripped
- scrubbing
- outfitted
- wrapped
- clapping
- dragging
- chatting

Write the **list word** that belongs in each group.

1. talking, speaking, — chatting
2. stumbled, fell, — tripped
3. runners, racers, — joggers
4. opening, starting, — beginning
5. covered, sealed, — wrapped
6. pulling, towing, — dragging
7. dressed, equipped, — outfitted
8. cheering, applauding, — clapping
9. singing, whistling, — humming
10. washing, cleaning, — scrubbing

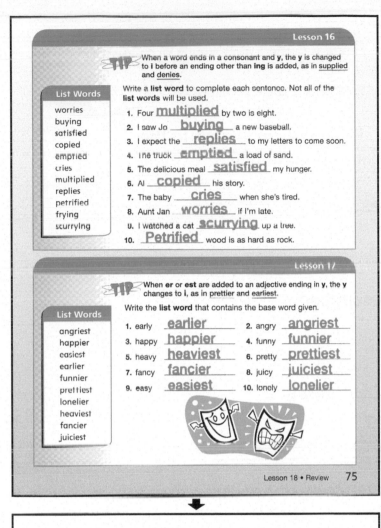

Lesson 16

TIP When a word ends in a consonant and **y**, the **y** is changed to **i** before an ending other than **ing** is added, as in **supplied** and **denies**.

List Words

worries
buying
satisfied
copied
emptied
cries
multiplied
replies
petrified
frying
scurrying

Write a **list word** to complete each sentence. Not all of the **list words** will be used.

1. Four **multiplied** by two is eight.
2. I saw Jo **buying** a new baseball.
3. I expect the **replies** to my letters to come soon.
4. The truck **emptied** a load of sand.
5. The delicious meal **satisfied** my hunger.
6. Al **copied** his story.
7. The baby **cries** when she's tired.
8. Aunt Jan **worries** if I'm late.
9. I watched a cat **scurrying** up a tree.
10. **Petrified** wood is as hard as rock.

Lesson 17

TIP When **er** or **est** are added to an adjective ending in **y**, the **y** changes to **i**, as in **prettier** and **earliest**.

List Words

angriest
happier
easiest
earlier
funnier
prettiest
lonelier
heaviest
fancier
juiciest

Write the **list word** that contains the base word given.

1. early **earlier**
2. angry **angriest**
3. happy **happier**
4. funny **funnier**
5. heavy **heaviest**
6. pretty **prettiest**
7. fancy **fancier**
8. juicy **juiciest**
9. easy **easiest**
10. lonely **lonelier**

Lesson 18 • Review   75

Show What You Know

Lessons 13–17 • Review

One word is misspelled in each set of **list words**. Fill in the circle next to the **list word** that is spelled incorrectly.

1. ○ tossed ○ padded ● rakeing ○ drying ○ earlier
2. ● angier ○ frying ○ proved ○ joggers ○ watching
3. ○ checking ○ humming ● ridder ○ replies ○ lonelier
4. ○ happiest ○ buying ○ giving ● chating ○ teacher
5. ○ bending ○ winners ● bounceing ○ hurrying ○ funnier
6. ● juicyest ○ scurrying ○ promised ○ dropped ○ catcher
7. ○ singer ○ sitting ○ reduced ● petryfed ○ prettier
8. ● heavyest ○ tries ○ sharing ○ slipping ○ turning
9. ○ landing ● triped ○ saved ○ buries ○ fancier
10. ○ denies ● happyer ○ traded ○ outfitted ○ missed
11. ○ sorted ● begining ○ coming ○ carried ○ juicier
12. ○ quitter ○ following ● earlyest ○ crier ○ dancer
13. ○ walker ● claping ○ mover ○ heavier ○ emptied
14. ● funnyest ○ worries ○ loved ○ skimming ○ wishing
15. ○ leading ● scrubing ○ sliced ○ copied ○ easier
16. ○ relying ○ easiest ● surpriseing ○ wrapped ○ guessed
17. ○ grabbing ○ learner ● writting ○ fanciest ○ satisfied
18. ● multiplyed ○ lonelliest ○ pictured ○ cleaned ○ trimmer
19. ○ bobbing ● compareing ○ applied ○ prettiest ○ finishing
20. ○ dragging ○ remembered ● supplyed ○ angriest ○ served

76   Lesson 18 • Review

Final Test

1. That is the **angriest** person I've ever seen!
2. The big gold bow made the gift look **fancier**.
3. I thought the store opened **earlier** than that.
4. Rita **worries** about being late for supper.
5. Jamal **multiplied** the numbers and got 56.
6. The trees became **petrified** over time.
7. Grandmother **loved** to play with the girls.
8. Our class is **comparing** bacteria to viruses.
9. I plan on **surprising** Gina with a big party.
10. The story's **beginning** is set in Rome.
11. I spent an afternoon **chatting** with Grandpa.
12. The hikers were **outfitted** for bad weather.
13. Michelle **wrapped** the gift in tissue paper.
14. Drivers must watch carefully for **joggers**.
15. Joe finally **proved** his point to me.
16. A **bouncing** baseball is often difficult to catch.
17. Can you name a great American **dancer**?
18. We heard the excited **cries** of the spectators.
19. The squirrels were **scurrying** after the nuts.
20. His joke was **funnier** the first time he told it.
21. This is the **juiciest** watermelon I've ever had!
22. I feel **lonelier** now that Jason's moved away.
23. Are you **satisfied** with the meal you ordered?
24. The **replies** to our survey came in quickly.
25. Mom **sliced** tomatoes for the salad.
26. Chris **promised** to send me a photograph.
27. Muriel is **humming** my favorite song.
28. We began **clapping** for the talented dancer.
29. He felt sorry when the clown **tripped**!
30. I finally **remembered** the wildflower's name.
31. The plane will be **landing** at four o'clock.
32. Amy earns money as a dog **walker**.
33. We'll be **finishing** the story tomorrow.
34. The workers were **dragging** the wood away.
35. Dad is **scrubbing** the dirty floors with a brush.
36. Would you like to be a **singer** in the choir?
37. Wayne **tossed** his dirty shirt into the washer.
38. The contestant **guessed** the right answer.
39. Debby **saved** money to buy a new bicycle.
40. The city looks just as I **pictured** it would.
41. We'll be **buying** a new house next year.
42. Mark **emptied** the ice cubes into a pitcher.
43. I **copied** the movements of the dance teacher.
44. This is the **prettiest** flower in the garden.
45. The baby seemed **happier** after her nap.
46. I was **watching** a television show about owls.
47. The **teacher** corrected the spelling tests.
48. I am **wishing** for a puppy for my birthday.
49. This is the **easiest** test I've ever taken.
50. Which box is the **heaviest** one?

Name _____

Review Test (Side A)

Read each sentence and set of words. Fill in the circle next to the word that is spelled correctly to complete the sentence.

1. Skiers are often _____ with goggles.
   - (a) outfitted
   - (b) outfidded
   - (c) outffited
   - (d) outfited

2. Tina is _____ Dad a magazine subscription.
   - (a) buing
   - (b) bying
   - (c) buying
   - (d) bieing

3. The principal informed us of the _____ news.
   - (a) serrprising
   - (b) surprising
   - (c) surprizing
   - (d) surpriseing

4. Joey is _____ his homework before soccer practice.
   - (a) finishin
   - (b) finishing
   - (c) finnishing
   - (d) finiching

5. Squirrels were _____ around the oak trees.
   - (a) scurying
   - (b) schurying
   - (c) skurrying
   - (d) scurrying

6. The present was _____ with a huge, satin bow.
   - (a) wrappt
   - (b) rapped
   - (c) wrapped
   - (d) wrapt

7. This patient would prefer the _____ appointment.
   - (a) earlier
   - (b) earlyer
   - (c) erlier
   - (d) earleyer

8. We received six _____ to our invitation.
   - (a) replys
   - (b) replise
   - (c) replize
   - (d) replies

Name _____

Review Test (Side B)

Read each sentence and set of words. Fill in the circle next to the word that is spelled correctly to complete the sentence.

9. Tyrone's grandfather _____ my exact weight!
   - (a) gessed
   - (b) guesd
   - (c) guessed
   - (d) quesst

10. The audience was _____ with pleasure.
    - (a) cliaping
    - (b) clapping
    - (c) claping
    - (d) clapeing

11. This episode is _____ than the last one was.
    - (a) phunier
    - (b) funnyer
    - (c) funnier
    - (d) funier

12. The scientist _____ his theory.
    - (a) prooved
    - (b) pruved
    - (c) proved
    - (d) proovd

13. The singer _____ all six verses of the song.
    - (a) rememberd
    - (b) remembered
    - (c) remmembered
    - (d) rememberred

14. I'm unable to lift the _____ weight.
    - (a) heaviest
    - (b) heviest
    - (c) heavviest
    - (d) heavyest

15. Kim _____ all her earnings.
    - (a) saived
    - (b) savved
    - (c) sayved
    - (d) saved

Take It Home 3

Your child has learned to spell many new words and would like to share them with you and your family. Here are some engaging activities that will help your child review the spelling words in Lessons 13–17.

Ad Words

Here's another way to recycle those old magazines and newspapers. Encourage your child to cut out magazine and newspaper ads that contain spelling words. Your child may also enjoy creating a collage with the ads.

Lesson 13

1. bending
2. catcher
3. checking
4. cleaned
5. finishing
6. following
7. guessed
8. landing
9. leading
10. learner
11. missed
12. remembered
13. singer
14. sorted
15. teacher
16. tossed
17. turning
18. walker
19. watching
20. wishing

Lesson 14

1. bouncing
2. coming
3. comparing
4. dancer
5. giving
6. loved
7. mover
8. pictured
9. promised
10. proved
11. raking
12. reduced
13. rider
14. saved
15. served
16. sharing
17. sliced
18. surprising
19. traded
20. writing

Lesson 15

1. beginning
2. bobbing
3. chatting
4. clapping
5. dragging
6. dropped
7. grabbing
8. humming
9. joggers
10. outfitted
11. padded
12. quitter
13. scrubbing
14. sitting
15. skimming
16. slipping
17. trimmer
18. tripped
19. winners
20. wrapped

Lesson 16

1. applied
2. buries
3. buying
4. carried
5. copied
6. cries
7. denies
8. drying
9. emptied
10. frying
11. hurrying
12. multiplied
13. petrified
14. relying
15. replies
16. satisfied
17. scurrying
18. supplied
19. tries
20. worries

Lesson 17

1. angrier
2. angriest
3. earlier
4. earliest
5. easier
6. easiest
7. fancier
8. fanciest
9. funnier
10. funniest
11. happier
12. happiest
13. heavier
14. heaviest
15. juicier
16. juiciest
17. lonelier
18. loneliest
19. prettier
20. prettiest

Ad Game

With your child, use as many spelling words as you can to create captions or ads for the products pictured below. Remember, ads can be serious, humorous, outrageous, or just plain silly—so have some fun!

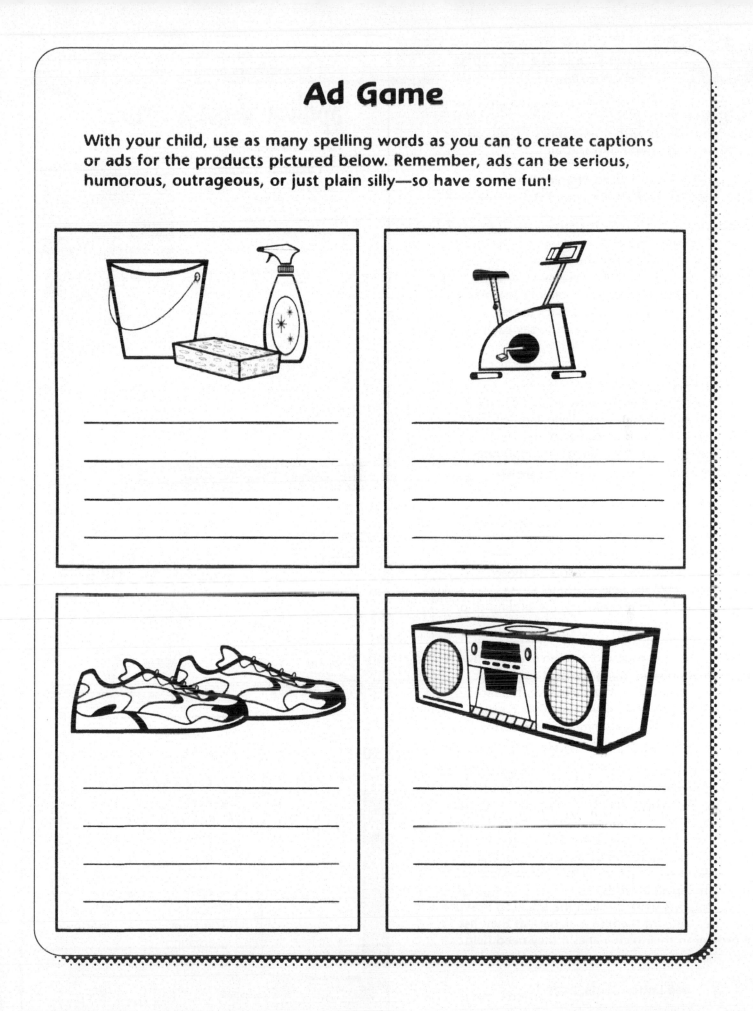

Objective
To spell words with vowel pairs *ee, ea, oa, oe,* and *ue,* and vowel digraph *ea*

 Correlated Phonics Lessons
MCP Phonics, Level D, Lessons 41–42

Spelling Words in Action   *Page 77*
In "Camping Anyone?" students discover what it can be like to experience the "Great Outdoors." Invite students to describe their own camping trips and to share their most memorable moments.

Encourage students to look back at the boldfaced words. Ask volunteers to say each word and identify the vowel sounds they hear.

Warm-Up Test
1. Please arrive **between** five and six o'clock.
2. Two **eastern** states are Maine and Vermont.
3. A cool **breeze** is welcome on a hot day.
4. The only **clues** they found were footprints.
5. Has Lisa **hoed** the weeds in the garden?
6. A dictionary will tell you a word's **meaning**.
7. Carlos **tiptoes** down the stairs.
8. Amanda had a good **reason** for being late.
9. Are you **treating** us to the movie, too?
10. The campers **roasted** corn over the fire.
11. Jefferson believed in **freedom** of speech.
12. Lisa **loaned** her new record to Teresa.
13. The jet began to **approach** the landing strip.
14. Did you **measure** two cups of flour?
15. Stephanie **glued** a label onto the package.
16. I'd like ham **instead** of chicken in my sandwich.
17. What powerful wings the bald **eagle** has!
18. Dave **boasted** that he would win the race.
19. The **fleet** of ships sailed out of the harbor.
20. The horse galloped through the **meadow**.

Spelling Practice   *Pages 78–79*
Introduce the spelling rule and have students read the **list words** aloud. At this point, you may want to point out that *fleet* can be a noun ("a group of ships or trucks") or an adjective ("swift"). Encourage students to look back at their **Warm-Up Tests** and apply the spelling rule to any misspelled words.

As students work through the **Spelling Practice** exercises, remind them to look back at their **list words** or in their dictionaries if they need help.

for ESL students **See Letter Cards, page 15**

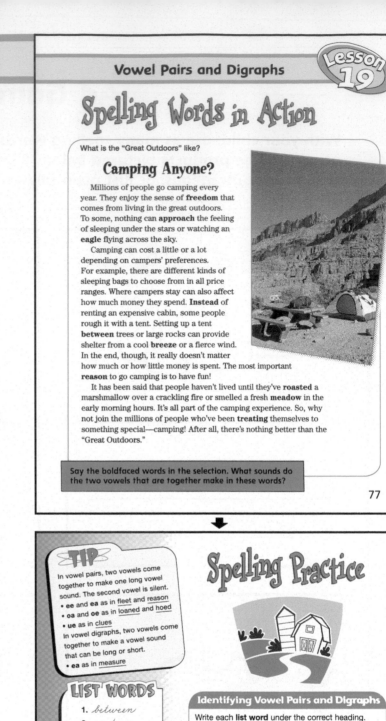

Spelling Words in Action

What is the "Great Outdoors" like?

Camping Anyone?

Millions of people go camping every year. They enjoy the sense of **freedom** that comes from living in the great outdoors. To some, nothing can **approach** the feeling of sleeping under the stars or watching an **eagle** flying across the sky.

Camping can cost a little or a lot depending on campers' preferences. For example, there are different kinds of sleeping bags to choose from in all price ranges. Where campers stay can also affect how much money they spend. **Instead** of renting an expensive cabin, some people rough it with a tent. Setting up a tent **between** trees or large rocks can provide shelter from a cool **breeze** or a fierce wind. In the end, though, it really doesn't matter how much or how little money is spent. The most important **reason** to go camping is to have fun!

It has been said that people haven't lived until they've **roasted** a marshmallow over a crackling fire or smelled a fresh **meadow** in the early morning hours. It's all part of the camping experience. So, why not join the millions of people who've been **treating** themselves to something special—camping! After all, there's nothing better than the "Great Outdoors."

Say the boldfaced words in the selection. What sounds do the two vowels that are together make in these words?

TIP
In vowel pairs, two vowels come together to make one long vowel sound. The second vowel is silent.
• **ee** and **ea** as in fleet and reason
• **oa** and **oe** as in loaned and hoed
• **ue** as in clues
In vowel digraphs, two vowels come together to make a vowel sound that can be long or short.
• **ea** as in measure

Spelling Practice

LIST WORDS
1. between
2. eastern
3. breeze
4. clues
5. hoed
6. meaning
7. tiptoes
8. reason
9. treating
10. roasted
11. freedom
12. loaned
13. approach
14. measure
15. glued
16. instead
17. eagle
18. boasted
19. fleet
20. meadow

Identifying Vowel Pairs and Digraphs
Write each **list word** under the correct heading.

ee as in see	**oa** as in boat
1. between	5. roasted
2. breeze	6. loaned
3. freedom	7. approach
4. fleet	8. boasted

ue as in blue	**oe** as in toe
9. clues	11. hoed
10. glued	12. tiptoes

ea as in beat	**ea** as in bread
13. eastern	18. measure
14. meaning	19. instead
15. reason	20. meadow
16. treating	
17. eagle	

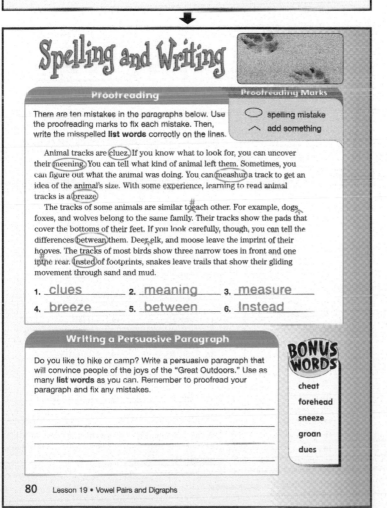

Missing Words

Write the **list word** that best completes each sentence.

1. At the school play, I sat __between__ Sue and Miguel.
2. I __loaned__ my science book to Carter on Friday.
3. Use a ruler to __measure__ the size of the photograph.
4. Mel owns a farm with a beautiful, grassy __meadow__.
5. Keep to your left as you __approach__ the school.
6. Jen __glued__ the pictures into her new scrapbook.
7. Mr. Hall __boasted__ that he was the smartest man in town.
8. The __clues__ to the crossword puzzle were not too hard.
9. A beautiful __breeze__ soared through the trees across the sky.
10. Walk on __tiptoes__ so no one will hear you when you enter.

Word Search

Ten **list words** are hidden in the puzzle below. The words go across, down, diagonally, backward, or upside down. Circle each word. Then, write the words in alphabetical order on the lines.

1. __breeze__   2. __eastern__
3. __fleet__   4. __freedom__
5. __hoed__   6. __instead__
7. __meaning__   8. __reason__
9. __roasted__   10. __treating__

```
S E A S T E R N
A O B E E T Q R
I M R O E C D O
H O E D L B A A
R D E A F X E S
O E Z D N M T T
A E E E E I S E
P R E A S O N D
L F S C L P I G
G N I T A E R T
```

Spelling and Writing

Proofreading

There are ten mistakes in the paragraphs below. Use the proofreading marks to fix each mistake. Then, write the misspelled **list words** correctly on the lines.

Proofreading Marks
◯ spelling mistake
⌃ add something

Animal tracks are cluez. If you know what to look for, you can uncover their meening. You can tell what kind of animal left them. Sometimes, you can figure out what the animal was doing. You can meashur a track to get an idea of the animal's size. With some experience, learning to read animal tracks is a breaze.

The tracks of some animals are similar to each other. For example, dogs, foxes, and wolves belong to the same family. Their tracks show the pads that cover the bottoms of their feet. If you look carefully, though, you can tell the differences betwean them. Deer, elk, and moose leave the imprint of their hooves. The tracks of most birds show three narrow toes in front and one in the rear. Insted of footprints, snakes leave trails that show their gliding movement through sand and mud.

1. __clues__   2. __meaning__   3. __measure__
4. __breeze__   5. __between__   6. __Instead__

Writing a Persuasive Paragraph

Do you like to hike or camp? Write a persuasive paragraph that will convince people of the joys of the "Great Outdoors." Use as many **list words** as you can. Remember to proofread your paragraph and fix any mistakes.

_____
_____
_____
_____

BONUS WORDS
cheat
forehead
sneeze
groan
dues

Spelling Strategy

Write cloze sentences on the board for three or four **list words** (for example, *We had a picnic in the ___*). For each sentence, provide a clue to the missing **list word** by saying the appropriate vowel sound (/ē/, /e/, /ō/, or /o͞o/) aloud (in this case, /e/ for *meadow*). After students guess the missing words, call on volunteers to write additional cloze sentences and provide the vowel-sound clues.

BONUS WORDS Invite students to use all five **bonus words** in a sentence. Have students compare their sentences with a partner's sentences.

Spelling and Writing   Page 80

The **Proofreading** exercise will help students prepare to proofread their paragraphs. As students complete the writing activity, encourage them to brainstorm ideas, write a first draft, revise, and proofread their work. To publish their writing, students may want to create a brochure about the rewards and benefits of camping.

Writer's Corner Invite students to learn more about camping by researching possible family trips at the library, on the Internet, or through magazines at a local bookstore. Suggest students bring in a paragraph about the trip they found most interesting.

Final Test

1. She lost the mittens that I **loaned** her.
2. What a silly **reason** they gave for being late!
3. Steve used the **clues** to solve the puzzle.
4. Wildflowers grow in the **meadow**.
5. Will you play baseball **instead** of soccer?
6. Sara **boasted** that her ideas were the best.
7. We **roasted** a turkey for Thanksgiving dinner.
8. Do you know the **meaning** of this word?
9. Philadelphia is a large **eastern** city.
10. Did you **measure** the length of the pool?
11. Nicole **tiptoes** around while the baby sleeps.
12. Jason gave the trapped bird its **freedom**.
13. The gentle **breeze** stirred the curtains.
14. We watched the **fleet** of ships far out at sea.
15. Has John **glued** his model plane together?
16. The shed is **between** the house and the barn.
17. The farmer **hoed** her bean field.
18. The timid deer would not let us **approach** it.
19. The **eagle** lived up on a rocky cliff.
20. Thank you for **treating** me so kindly.

Objectives

To spell words with vowel pairs *ie* and *ei*, vowel digraphs *ie* and *ei*, and to apply a spelling rule

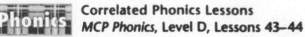

Correlated Phonics Lessons
MCP Phonics, Level D, Lessons 43–44

Spelling Words in Action   **Page 81**

In this selection, students read to find out how runners can protect their feet. After reading, ask students what kinds of exercise they like to do and how the exercises affect their bodies.

Encourage students to look back at the boldfaced words. Ask volunteers to say each word and identify the vowel sound or sounds they hear.

Warm-Up Test

1. I watered the plant, but it **died** anyway.
2. The **fields** were planted with corn.
3. Jamie had a **brief** wait before the bus arrived.
4. Does aspirin give you **relief** from headaches?
5. I jumped when I heard the siren's **shriek**!
6. Do you **weigh** more than you did last summer?
7. I **believe** that he's telling the truth.
8. The kids rode a **sleigh** through the snow.
9. Be sure you **receive** the correct change.
10. My brother is **eighteen** years old today.
11. I tried to **seize** the ball from the other player.
12. She introduced herself to her new **neighbors**.
13. A **receipt** is proof that you paid for something.
14. A loudspeaker **amplifies** sound.
15. We use the pool **chiefly** in the summertime.
16. The **freighter** carried goods from India.
17. When you lie to people, you **deceive** them.
18. Could you **perceive** anything through the fog?
19. What delicious **pies** that bakery makes!
20. A balanced **diet** is important to good health.

Spelling Practice   **Pages 82–83**

Introduce the spelling rule and have students read the **list words** aloud. Encourage students to look back at their **Warm-Up Tests** and apply the spelling rule to any misspelled words.

As students work through the **Spelling Practice** exercises, remind them to look back at their **list words** or in their dictionaries if they need help.

  See Tape Recording, page 15

Spelling Words in Action

What should runners do to take care of their feet?

Tenderfeet

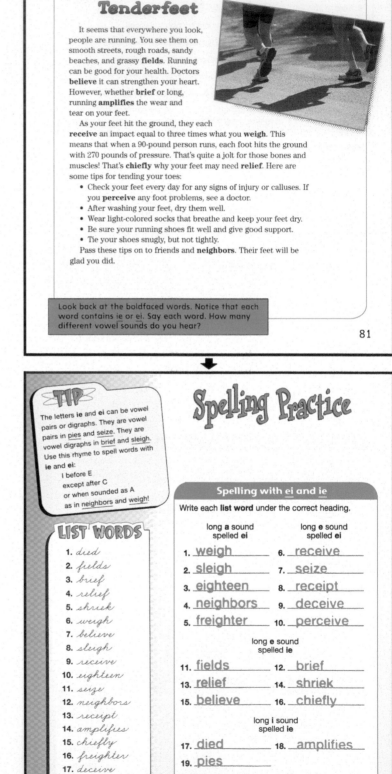

It seems that everywhere you look, people are running. You see them on smooth streets, rough roads, sandy beaches, and grassy **fields**. Running can be good for your health. Doctors **believe** it can strengthen your heart. However, whether **brief** or long, running **amplifies** the wear and tear on your feet.

As your feet hit the ground, they each **receive** an impact equal to three times what you **weigh**. This means that when a 90-pound person runs, each foot hits the ground with 270 pounds of pressure. That's quite a jolt for those bones and muscles! That's **chiefly** why your feet may need **relief**. Here are some tips for tending your toes:

- Check your feet every day for any signs of injury or calluses. If you **perceive** any foot problems, see a doctor.
- After washing your feet, dry them well.
- Wear light-colored socks that breathe and keep your feet dry.
- Be sure your running shoes fit well and give good support.
- Tie your shoes snugly, but not tightly.

Pass these tips on to friends and **neighbors**. Their feet will be glad you did.

> Look back at the boldfaced words. Notice that each word contains ie or ei. Say each word. How many different vowel sounds do you hear?

81

> **TIP**
>
> The letters **ie** and **ei** can be vowel pairs or digraphs. They are vowel pairs in pies and seize. They are vowel digraphs in brief and sleigh. Use this rhyme to spell words with **ie** and **ei**:
> I before E
> except after C
> or when sounded as A
> as in neighbors and weigh!

Spelling Practice

LIST WORDS

1. died
2. fields
3. brief
4. relief
5. shriek
6. weigh
7. believe
8. sleigh
9. receive
10. eighteen
11. seize
12. neighbors
13. receipt
14. amplifies
15. chiefly
16. freighter
17. deceive
18. perceive
19. pies
20. diet

Spelling with ei and ie

Write each **list word** under the correct heading.

long a sound spelled ei	long e sound spelled ei
1. weigh	6. receive
2. sleigh	7. seize
3. eighteen	8. receipt
4. neighbors	9. deceive
5. freighter	10. perceive

long e sound spelled ie

11. fields	12. brief
13. relief	14. shriek
15. believe	16. chiefly

long i sound spelled ie

17. died	18. amplifies
19. pies	

Write the **list word** in which the letters **ie** have two separate sounds.

20. diet

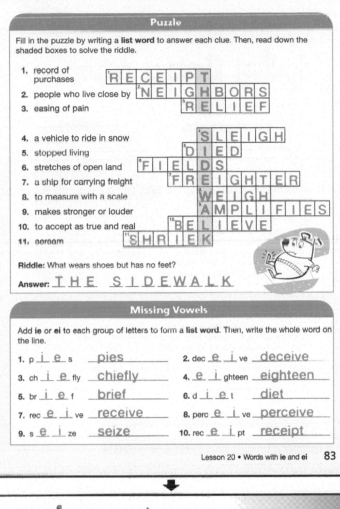

Puzzle

Fill in the puzzle by writing a **list word** to answer each clue. Then, read down the shaded boxes to solve the riddle.

1. record of purchases — R E C E I P T
2. people who live close by — N E I G H B O R S
3. easing of pain — R E L I E F
4. a vehicle to ride in snow — S L E I G H
5. stopped living — D I E D
6. stretches of open land — F I E L D S
7. a ship for carrying freight — F R E I G H T E R
8. to measure with a scale — W E I G H
9. makes stronger or louder — A M P L I F I E S
10. to accept as true and real — B E L I E V E
11. scream — S H R I E K

Riddle: What wears shoes but has no feet?

Answer: T H E   S I D E W A L K

Missing Vowels

Add **ie** or **ei** to each group of letters to form a **list word**. Then, write the whole word on the line.

1. p_ie_s — pies
2. dec_ei_ve — deceive
3. ch_ie_fly — chiefly
4. _ei_ghteen — eighteen
5. br_ie_f — brief
6. d_ie_t — diet
7. rec_ei_ve — receive
8. perc_ei_ve — perceive
9. s_ei_ze — seize
10. rec_ei_pt — receipt

Lesson 20 • Words with ie and ei   83

Spelling and Writing

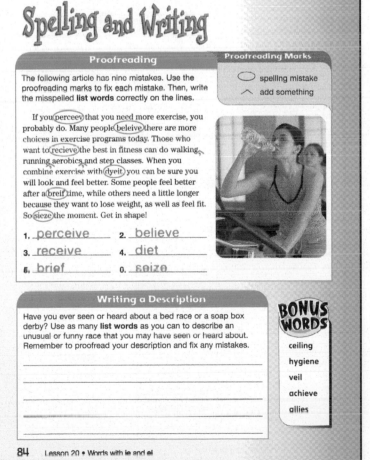

Proofreading

Proofreading Marks
- ◯ spelling mistake
- ⌃ add something

The following article has nine mistakes. Use the proofreading marks to fix each mistake. Then, write the misspelled **list words** correctly on the lines.

If you perceev that you need more exercise, you probably do. Many people believe there are more choices in exercise programs today. Those who want to recieve the best in fitness can do walking, running aerobics and step classes. When you combine exercise with dyeit you can be sure you will look and feel better. Some people feel better after a breif time, while others need a little longer because they want to lose weight, as well as feel fit. So sieze the moment. Get in shape!

1. perceive   2. believe
3. receive   4. diet
5. brief   6. seize

Writing a Description

Have you ever seen or heard about a bed race or a soap box derby? Use as many **list words** as you can to describe an unusual or funny race that you may have seen or heard about. Remember to proofread your description and fix any mistakes.

_____
_____
_____
_____

BONUS WORDS
- ceiling
- hygiene
- veil
- achieve
- allies

84   Lesson 20 • Words with ie and ei

Spelling Strategy

Say each **list word** and call on a volunteer to write it on the board. Then, have the class tell whether the word is spelled correctly. If it is, circle the letters *ie* or *ei*. If the word isn't spelled correctly, erase the incorrect letters and fill in the correct ones. Encourage students to practice the words that gave them the most difficulty until they become more proficient at spelling them.

BONUS WORDS
Have students pair up to write a definition for each **bonus word**. Then, have partners look up the words in their dictionaries. Next, ask them to confer with other students to see if their definitions match.

Spelling and Writing   *Page 84*

The **Proofreading** exercise will help students prepare to proofread their descriptions. As students complete the writing activity, encourage them to brainstorm ideas, write a first draft, revise, and proofread their work. To publish their writing, students may wish to
- read their descriptions aloud as sports broadcasts
- create a class book titled *They're Off!*

Writer's Corner Encourage students to learn more about feet by researching information in the library. Suggest they use encyclopedias and biology books and jot down information as they read. Students can use their notes to create a pamphlet on foot care.

Final Test

1. The vet put our dog on a high protein **diet**.
2. My aunt's **pies** won first prize at the fair.
3. Many young trees **died** during the cold winter.
4. The highway ran through **fields** of daisies.
5. The principal welcomed us in his **brief** speech.
6. Dogs don't **perceive** colors the way we do.
7. Some advertisements **deceive** the public.
8. What a **relief** it was to sit down at last!
9. A **freighter** carries goods to different ports.
10. The owl's **shriek** surprised us.
11. The auditorium was used **chiefly** for concerts.
12. It's easy to **believe** someone you trust.
13. This speaker **amplifies** the singers' voices.
14. One horse pulled the **sleigh** through the snow.
15. You'll need the **receipt** if you return the toy.
16. Did Joe **receive** a phone call from his mother?
17. All the **neighbors** were invited to the party.
18. You have to wait until you're **eighteen** to vote.
19. I'll **weigh** these apples before I buy them.
20. Enemies tried to **seize** the castle.

Vowel digraphs <u>au</u> and <u>aw</u>

Objective
To spell words in which *au* and *aw* spell the /ô/ sound

 Correlated Phonics Lesson
MCP Phonics, Level D, Lesson 47

Spelling Words in Action   *Page 85*

In "Little Lumberjacks," students find out which animal is a fantastic builder of dams. After reading, invite students to share additional information they might know about beavers.

Encourage students to look back at the boldfaced words. Ask volunteers to say each word and identify the vowel sound or sounds they hear.

Warm-Up Test
1. The cat sharpened its **claws** on the tree trunk.
2. It wasn't his **fault** that he was late.
3. The big snowstorm is **causing** a lot of damage.
4. It is **dawn** when daylight first appears.
5. We stuffed a scarecrow with **straw**.
6. These **drawings** are incredibly detailed!
7. Did you watch the rocket **launch** on television?
8. Dad makes a great tomato **sauce** for spaghetti.
9. The roots of your teeth are buried in your **jaw**.
10. Do you think that ghosts can **haunt** a house?
11. Kay was so sleepy that she began to **yawn**.
12. We saw a deer and her **fawns** eating in a field.
13. I felt **awkward** when I was learning to skate.
14. A beaver will **gnaw** at a tree until it falls.
15. Everyone in the **audience** loved the play.
16. Don't **scrawl** your name; print it neatly.
17. The man was a **fraud** and not a real doctor.
18. How **gaunt** he looks after his illness!
19. Which **restaurant** has the best enchiladas?
20. Sarah bought a beautiful silk **shawl**.

Spelling Practice   *Pages 86–87*

Introduce the spelling rule and have students read the **list words** aloud. You may also want to make sure students know the meanings of *awkward*, *gnaw*, *scrawl*, and *gaunt* and point out the silent *g* in *gnaw*. Then, encourage students to look back at their **Warm-Up Tests** and apply the spelling rule to any misspelled words.

As students work through the **Spelling Practice** exercises, remind them to look back at their **list words** or in their dictionaries if they need help.

 **See Picture Clues, page 15**

70

Spelling Words in Action

How can a little animal build a dam?

Little Lumberjacks

If you've ever seen **drawings** of beavers, you may think they look a little strange. Beavers have stout little bodies, small heads, tiny **claws**, and tails that look like ping-pong paddles. A beaver may look **awkward**, but in the water it is a fast, graceful, and strong swimmer.

Beavers are nature's best builders of dams. In the spring and summer, they begin their work at the break of **dawn**. They **gnaw** on trees and branches. A beaver has long teeth and a strong **jaw** that can cut through a thick tree in minutes. Once the trees and branches are cut, the beavers **launch** them into a stream. Then, they push the logs and branches into place to make a dam. The dam is packed with mud and **straw** to hold back the water.

Beavers usually make their homes in the ponds that form behind their dams. A beaver lodge has many underwater entrances. Inside, it is a warm and dry place for the beavers to live and store food.

Beavers must chew on wood even during the winter months. If they don't, their teeth keep growing and become too long, **causing** them harm. They will live in the same area for many years. Humans are usually at **fault** when beavers leave their homes.

Each boldfaced word in the selection is spelled with <u>au</u> or <u>aw</u>. Say each word. What do you notice about the sound each makes?

85

Spelling Practice

TIP
Be careful when spelling words with the /ô/ sound that you hear in fault and dawn. The vowel digraphs **au** and **aw** make the /ô/ sound, and they sound alike.

LIST WORDS
1. claws
2. fault
3. causing
4. dawn
5. straw
6. drawings
7. launch
8. sauce
9. jaw
10. haunt
11. yawn
12. fawns
13. awkward
14. gnaw
15. audience
16. scrawl
17. fraud
18. gaunt
19. restaurant
20. shawl

Writing Consonant Blends

Write each **list word** under the correct heading.

/ô/ spelled **aw**	/ô/ spelled **au**
1. claws	12. fault
2. dawn	13. causing
3. straw	14. launch
4. drawings	15. sauce
5. jaw	16. haunt
6. yawn	17. audience
7. fawns	18. fraud
8. awkward	19. gaunt
9. gnaw	20. restaurant
10. scrawl	
11. shawl	

Rhyming

Use the clues to write **list words**. Each **list word** must rhyme with the underlined word.

1. The cat's **claws** had no <u>flaws</u>.
2. I began to **yawn** at the break of <u>dawn</u>.
3. The horse chewed the <u>straw</u> with the motion of its **jaw**.
4. What's **causing** all the <u>pausing</u>?
5. It isn't my **fault** you ate the <u>salt</u>.
6. A worm writes with a <u>crawl</u> **scrawl**.
7. The creamy **sauce** lost its <u>gloss</u>.
8. The captain gave the boat a <u>staunch</u> **launch**.
9. A beaver's <u>jaw</u> helps it **gnaw** wood to keep its teeth short.
10. The lady's **shawl** was rolled up into a ball.

Word Meaning

Write the **list word** that relates to the word or phrase given.

1. sunrise **dawn**
2. thin **gaunt**
3. pictures **drawings**
4. eating place **restaurant**
5. baby deer **fawns**
6. fake **fraud**
7. listeners **audience**
8. scarf **shawl**
9. dried grass **straw**
10. chew **gnaw**
11. clumsy **awkward**
12. frighten **haunt**
13. throw **launch**
14. sharp nails **claws**
15. scribble **scrawl**
16. gravy **sauce**

Lesson 21 • Vowel Digraphs au and aw   87

Spelling and Writing

Proofreading

This description has twelve mistakes. Use the proofreading marks to fix each mistake. Then, write the misspelled **list words** correctly on the lines.

Proofreading Marks
- ◯ spelling mistake
- ≡ capital letter
- ⌃ add something

Do you know what is fun to do? Watch the otters at the High desert museum. The museum is not far from bend, Oregon. These otters love an awdience. They are up at daun playing and swimming. They lawnch themselves down hills and slide into the water, making people laugh. can you guess what happens then? They do it all over again. it's also fun to watch an otter eat. It floats, holding food in its claus. It's like a show at a restawrant.

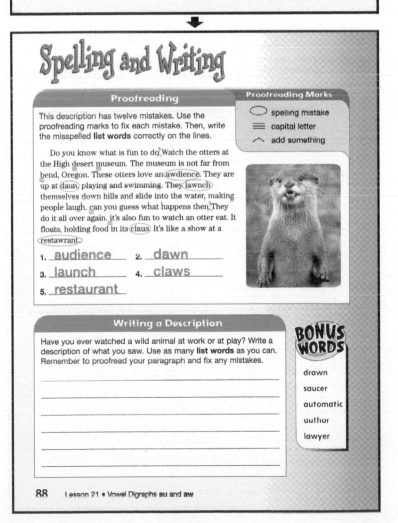

1. **audience**   2. **dawn**
3. **launch**   4. **claws**
5. **restaurant**

Writing a Description

Have you ever watched a wild animal at work or at play? Write a description of what you saw. Use as many **list words** as you can. Remember to proofread your paragraph and fix any mistakes.

_____
_____
_____
_____
_____
_____

BONUS WORDS

drawn
saucer
automatic
author
lawyer

88   Lesson 21 • Vowel Digraphs au and aw

Spelling Strategy

Write each **list word** on the board, leaving a blank for the vowel digraph au or aw (c___sing, sh___l). For each word, have the class ask, "Is it spelled with au or aw?" Then, call on a volunteer to name the missing letters and complete the word on the board. Encourage students to look in their *Spelling Workout* books to check the spelling.

BONUS WORDS Ask students to write a sentence for each **bonus word**, but leave a blank for the **bonus word** that completes the sentence. Have students trade papers with partners and complete each other's sentences.

Spelling and Writing   Page 88

The **Proofreading** exercise will help students prepare to proofread their descriptions. As students complete the writing activity, encourage them to brainstorm ideas, write a first draft, revise, and proofread their work. To publish their writing, students may want to illustrate their descriptions and use them to create a classroom display.

Writer's Corner Students might enjoy watching an informational video about beavers. Suggest that they write a paragraph about the video, detailing the most interesting facts they learned, and then share their paragraphs with one another.

Final Test

1. The museum has many old **drawings** of ships.
2. Everyone in the **audience** applauded.
3. The colt was **awkward** when it first stood.
4. Did they **launch** the new ship in the harbor?
5. Cats sharpen their **claws** on rough surfaces.
6. Did you make the **shawl** you're wearing?
7. The **scrawl** on the paper is actually a signature.
8. Abe Lincoln was a tall, **gaunt** man.
9. Do you like cheese **sauce** on your broccoli?
10. People say that ghosts **haunt** that old house.
11. The accident was no one's **fault**.
12. Rodents must **gnaw** or their teeth grow too long.
13. A leak is **causing** the cracks in the ceiling.
14. The person who sold the fake gem is a **fraud**.
15. My **straw** hat protects me from the sun.
16. Chewing this tough meat makes my **jaw** hurt.
17. What expensive food this **restaurant** has!
18. My **yawn** made everyone else **yawn**, too!
19. Let's leave at **dawn** and get an early start.
20. Look how the mother deer protects her **fawns**.

Objectives
To spell words containing the vowel pairs *ai*, *ay* and the diphthongs *oi*, *oy*

 Correlated Phonics Lessons
MCP Phonics, Level D, Lessons 40, 49

Spelling Words in Action   *Page 89*

In "End of the Trail," students learn about historic Wild West buildings and treasures preserved as a museum. After reading, invite students to discuss whether they would have enjoyed living in the Wild West.

ncourage students to look back at the boldfaced words. Ask volunteers to say e ch word and identify the letters that spell the /ā/ or /oi/ sound.

Warm-Up Test
1. The hikers' **voices** echoed in the mountains.
2. Be careful not to **sprain** your ankle.
3. What frightening **noises** those are!
4. The **disloyal** knight betrayed his king.
5. The store will **employ** Becky this summer.
6. This belt is too big for my **waist**.
7. The earthquake **destroyed** many buildings.
8. The sleeves of this jacket have begun to **fray**.
9. Is Dad **broiling** the hamburgers?
10. The sign was **swaying** in the wind.
11. The museum **displays** many famous paintings.
12. The newspaper **praised** the officers' courage.
13. Will I **disappoint** you if I don't finish in time?
14. The **railroad** tracks run through the town.
15. Some British **royalty** live in Buckingham Palace.
16. My mother was **appointed** to the city council.
17. Did you borrow this red **crayon** from Mary?
18. When the water is **boiling**, turn off the stove.
19. This bread has **soybean** flour in it.
20. Our picnic lunch became **spoiled** in the sun.

Spelling Practice   *Pages 90–91*

Introduce the spelling rule and have students read the **list words** aloud. Explain the meaning of *fray* ("to wear down so as to become ragged"), and point out that *crayon* has two pronunciations: krā′ən and krā′än. Then, encourage students to look back at their **Warm-Up Tests** and apply the spelling rule to any misspelled words.

As students work through the **Spelling Practice** exercises, remind them to look back at their **list words** or in their dictionaries if they need help.

for ESL students   **See Categorizing, page 15**

72

Spelling Words in Action

How can a town be turned into a museum?

End of the Trail

The front door of Butch Cassidy's cabin stands open, **swaying** on its hinges. A stagecoach is parked outside the general store, but no horses are restlessly pawing the gray dust. No **voices** can be heard from the well-traveled trail. In fact, the only **noises** that can be heard are whispering breezes and chirping insects.

You may think this is a ghost town, but it's really a museum called Old Trail Town. It stands outside Cody, Wyoming, and was established by Bob Edgar and his wife, Terry, in 1967. Among the **displays** are 26 buildings, 100 horse-drawn vehicles, and hundreds of treasures from the old Wild West.

Years ago, Bob noticed old cabins standing empty in the **broiling** sun of the open range. Some were falling in, and others were being **destroyed** by grazing cattle. Bob felt it was **disloyal** to let these historical relics disappear. So, the Edgars **appointed** themselves to save this part of America's history.

After working hard and sacrificing much time and money, the Edgars' dream came to life. Now, they are **praised** for preserving a long-ago way of life. Many people are interested in seeing how cowhands and pioneers really lived. A visit to Old Trail Town will not **disappoint** them.

Say each boldfaced word in the selection. How are the words with the /ā/ sound spelled? How are the words with the /oi/ sound spelled?

89

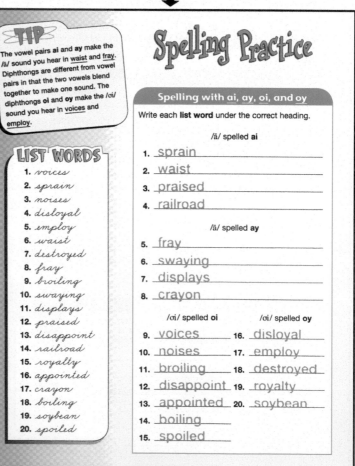

TIP

The vowel pairs **ai** and **ay** make the /ā/ sound you hear in <u>waist</u> and <u>fray</u>. Diphthongs are different from vowel pairs in that the two vowels blend together to make one sound. The diphthongs **oi** and **oy** make the /oi/ sound you hear in <u>voices</u> and <u>employ</u>.

Spelling Practice

Spelling with ai, ay, oi, and oy

Write each **list word** under the correct heading.

LIST WORDS
1. voices
2. sprain
3. noises
4. disloyal
5. employ
6. waist
7. destroyed
8. fray
9. broiling
10. swaying
11. displays
12. praised
13. disappoint
14. railroad
15. royalty
16. appointed
17. crayon
18. boiling
19. soybean
20. spoiled

/ā/ spelled ai
1. sprain
2. waist
3. praised
4. railroad

/ā/ spelled ay
5. fray
6. swaying
7. displays
8. crayon

/oi/ spelled oi
9. voices
10. noises
11. broiling
12. disappoint
13. appointed
14. boiling
15. spoiled

/oi/ spelled oy
16. disloyal
17. employ
18. destroyed
19. royalty
20. soybean

90   Lesson 22 • Vowel Pairs ai, ay; Diphthongs oi, oy

Classification

Write the **list word** that belongs in each group.

1. pen, pencil, __crayon__
2. baking, boiling, __broiling__
3. bang, crash, __noises__
4. soprano, alto, __voices__
5. dissatisfy, fail, __disappoint__
6. rice, potato, __soybean__
7. queens, kings, __royalty__
8. untrue, unfaithful, __disloyal__
9. moving, rocking, __swaying__
10. chosen, assigned, __appointed__

Move the Words

Each underlined **list word** must be moved to a different sentence to make sense. Write the correct **list word** for each sentence in the blank at the end.

1. The water in the kettle is spoiled. __boiling__
2. My sleeves are beginning to railroad. __fray__
3. Don't employ your back lifting that box. __sprain__
4. The two dogs are waist rotten. __spoiled__
5. The displays station was a landmark. __railroad__
6. The belt wouldn't go around my praised. __waist__
7. The store wants to destroyed more people. __employ__
8. The team was boiling for winning. __praised__
9. The waves sprain the sand castle. __destroyed__
10. The newly built museum fray art. __displays__

Lesson 22 • Vowel Pairs ai, ay; Diphthongs oi. oy   91

Spelling and Writing

Proofreading

The paragraph below has eleven mistakes. Use the proofreading marks to fix each mistake. Then, write the misspelled **list words** correctly on the lines.

The pioneers who came west in covered wagons are to be praysed Even with an appoynted leader, they had to use all their skills just to survive. Long days were spent riding in in the swaying wagons in boyling hot or icy cold weather. Accidents could and did happen! A wagon wheel could be destroied by the rough terrain, or someone could have a sprained ankle with with no one to treat it When the railroad came, traveling west became easier, but it was still an adventure.

Proofreading Marks
- ⟳ spelling mistake
- ⊙ add period
- ℓ take out something

1. __praised__
2. __appointed__
3. __swaying__
4. __boiling__
5. __destroyed__
6. __railroad__

Writing a Narrative Paragraph

Cowhands worked hard at herding cattle. Yet, they had fun, too. Write a paragraph telling what you think it was like to be an Old West cowhand. Use as many **list words** as you can. Remember to proofread your paragraph and fix any mistakes.

_____

_____

_____

BONUS WORDS

entertain
delay
embroider
loyal
raisin

92   Lesson 22 • Vowel Pairs ai, ay; Diphthongs oi, oy

Spelling Strategy

To help students recognize the sounds that *ai*, *ay*, *oi*, and *oy* stand for, write /ā/ and /oi/ on the board as separate column headings. Invite the class to tell which column each **list word** belongs in, and then write the word in that column. Finally, call on volunteers to come to the board, say each word aloud, and circle the letters that spell /ā/ or /oi/

BONUS WORDS

Have students write a sentence for each **bonus word**, but leave a blank in place of the **bonus word**. Ask them to write an incorrect word in the blank and then trade papers with a partner. Have partners write the correct **bonus word** in each sentence.

Spelling and Writing   Page 92

The **Proofreading** exercise will help students prepare to proofread their paragraphs. As students complete the writing activity, encourage them to brainstorm ideas, write a first draft, revise, and proofread their work. To publish their writing, students may want to
- create a bulletin board titled "Wild West Days"
- read their work aloud, role-playing a cowhand.

Writer's Corner Encourage students to learn more about the Wild West by researching people such as Buffalo Bill, Nat Love (*aka* Deadwood Dick), Calamity Jane, and Crazy Horse. Suggest they use encyclopedias, history books, and the Internet.

Final Test

1. Are some countries ruled by **royalty**?
2. The farmer **displays** his vegetables at the fair.
3. Loud **noises** came from the lion's den.
4. The drought **destroyed** many farm crops.
5. Could you hand me the **soybean** oil?
6. The baby drew on the wall with a red **crayon**.
7. The cook was **broiling** lamb chops.
8. The **voices** of my friends greeted me.
9. How many people does that factory **employ**?
10. You'll **disappoint** us if you miss the party.
11. The dancers were **swaying** to the music.
12. Tie the sash around your **waist**.
13. How painful that ankle **sprain** was!
14. My grandfather works for the **railroad**.
15. The eggs were **boiling** in a big pan.
16. The teacher **praised** us for our hard work.
17. The old shirt began to **fray** around the collar.
18. Dogs are rarely **disloyal** to their masters.
19. A sudden rainstorm **spoiled** our soccer game.
20. I have been **appointed** secretary of my class.

Words with <u>ou</u> and <u>ow</u>

Objective
To spell words in which *ou* and *ow* spell the vowel sounds /ou/, /ō/, /ô/, and /u/

Correlated Phonics Lesson
MCP Phonics, Level D, Lesson 51

Spelling Words in Action   *Page 93*

In this selection, students learn about a type of bird that can be as small as a sparrow or as large as an average-sized dog. After reading, invite students to compare owls with other kinds of birds they are familiar with.

Ask volunteers to say each boldfaced word and identify the letters that stand for the /ō/ or /ou/ sound.

Warm-Up Test

1. Do you get eight **hours** of sleep every night?
2. Janie made a birdhouse for the **sparrows**.
3. The new road goes through several **towns**.
4. **Powerful** currents pushed the canoes along.
5. The recipe calls for a small **amount** of onion.
6. Sharon solved the math problem **without** help.
7. Lin **allows** his cat to sleep on his bed.
8. A rain **shower** cooled the hot summer air.
9. The waiter **brought** the chowder to our table.
10. The mayor **sought** a solution to the problem.
11. The raccoon took a nap in a **hollow** tree trunk.
12. The runner quickly **swallowed** some water.
13. Mexico is our **southern** neighbor.
14. Ten times one hundred equals a **thousand**.
15. I sat down and **thought** about the problem.
16. Chi had **trouble** with the last part of the test.
17. Is this **bouquet** of roses for you?
18. **Although** it was nearly spring, it snowed.
19. What a great view you get from this **mountain**!
20. New England clam **chowder** is delicious.

Spelling Practice   *Pages 94–95*

Introduce the spelling rule and have students read the **list words** aloud. At this point, you may want to mention that *bouquet* has two pronunciations: bō kā′ and bōō kā′. Encourage students to look back at their **Warm-Up Tests** and apply the spelling rule to any misspelled words.

As students work through the **Spelling Practice** exercises, remind them to look back at their **list words** or in their dictionaries if they need help.

for ESL students See Rhymes and Songs, page 14

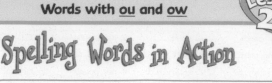
Spelling Words in Action

What bird can be as small as a sparrow or as big as a dog?

Night Prowlers

Owls aren't seen as often as other birds, but that's because they prefer the **hours** of darkness. Even if we don't see them, owls are there. In fact, owls are found throughout the world in places like **mountain** forests and dry deserts. There are more than 130 different kinds of owls. Some are as small as **sparrows**, like the elf or pygmy owls. Others are very large, such as the great horned owl. It's as big as some dogs!

Owls often live in nests left behind by other birds. Sometimes, they use **hollow** trees or logs for their homes. When they live near **towns**, owls may move into deserted buildings or barns.

Most owls sleep during the day. When dusk comes, they glide through the air **without** making a sound, looking for food. Owls can see even with a small **amount** of light and can spot food in the darkest places. Their keen eyes can't move, but an owl's long, thin neck **allows** it to turn its head in almost a complete circle so that it can easily spot prey. An owl's hearing is as **powerful** as its sight, **although** some people may not believe this. After all, if owls can hear so well, why do they always say "whoo"?

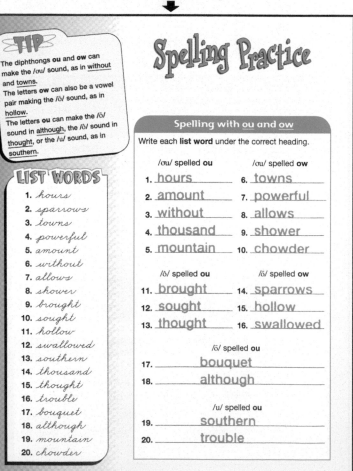

Look back at the boldfaced words. Say each word. Listen for the /ō/ and /ou/ sounds. What do you notice about the way these sounds are spelled?

93

↓

TIP
The diphthongs **ou** and **ow** can make the /ou/ sound, as in <u>without</u> and <u>towns</u>.
The letters **ow** can also be a vowel pair making the /ō/ sound, as in <u>hollow</u>.
The letters **ou** can make the /ō/ sound in <u>although</u>, the /ô/ sound in <u>thought</u>, or the /u/ sound, as in <u>southern</u>.

Spelling Practice

LIST WORDS
1. hours
2. sparrows
3. towns
4. powerful
5. amount
6. without
7. allows
8. shower
9. brought
10. sought
11. hollow
12. swallowed
13. southern
14. thousand
15. thought
16. trouble
17. bouquet
18. although
19. mountain
20. chowder

Spelling with <u>ou</u> and <u>ow</u>

Write each **list word** under the correct heading.

/ou/ spelled **ou**	/ou/ spelled **ow**
1. hours	6. towns
2. amount	7. powerful
3. without	8. allows
4. thousand	9. shower
5. mountain	10. chowder

/ô/ spelled **ou**	/ō/ spelled **ow**
11. brought	14. sparrows
12. sought	15. hollow
13. thought	16. swallowed

/ō/ spelled **ou**
17. bouquet
18. although

/u/ spelled **ou**
19. southern
20. trouble

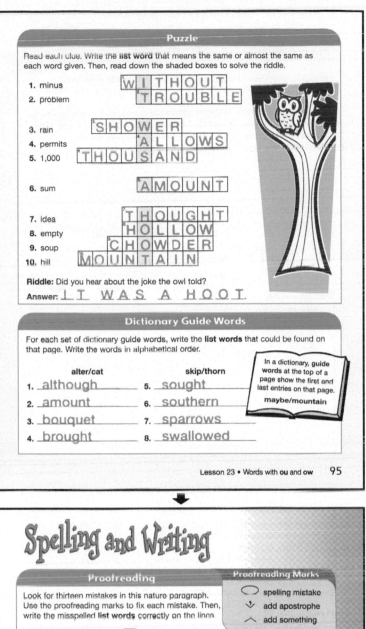

Puzzle

Read each clue. Write the **list word** that means the same or almost the same as each word given. Then, read down the shaded boxes to solve the riddle.

1. minus — W I T H O U T
2. problem — T R O U B L E

3. rain — S H O W E R
4. permits — A L L O W S
5. 1,000 — T H O U S A N D

6. sum — A M O U N T

7. idea — T H O U G H T
8. empty — H O L L O W
9. soup — C H O W D E R
10. hill — M O U N T A I N

Riddle: Did you hear about the joke the owl told?

Answer: I T   W A S   A   H O O T

Dictionary Guide Words

For each set of dictionary guide words, write the **list words** that could be found on that page. Write the words in alphabetical order.

In a dictionary, guide words at the top of a page show the first and last entries on that page.

maybe/mountain

alter/cat	skip/thorn
1. although	5. sought
2. amount	6. southern
3. bouquet	7. sparrows
4. brought	8. swallowed

Spelling and Writing

Proofreading

Look for thirteen mistakes in this nature paragraph. Use the proofreading marks to fix each mistake. Then, write the misspelled **list words** correctly on the lines.

Proofreading Marks
- ⌒ spelling mistake
- ˅ add apostrophe
- ⌃ add something

Even people who live in touns may see an eagle during daylight howrs when eagles hunt. The golden eagle is found mainly in mowntain areas. The bald eagle canbe seen in some sowthern states in the winter. Althowgh the bald eagle has been in trauble in the past, conservationlal efforts to help these powerful birds have browght some success.

1. towns	2. hours
3. mountain	4. southern
5. Although	6. trouble
7. powerful	8. brought

Writing a Journal Entry

Write a journal entry about an interesting bird you have seen recently. Don't forget to include the date you saw the bird. Use as many **list words** as you can. Remember to proofread your entry and fix any mistakes.

_____

_____

_____

_____

_____

BONUS WORDS

scouts

drowned

marshmallow

couple

fought

Spelling Strategy

To give students practice spelling the **list words**, invite partners to take turns
- writing each **list word**
- underlining the letters *ou* or *ow*
- telling the sound the letters make
- pronouncing the complete word.

BONUS WORDS   Have students work with partners to write a story using all five **bonus words**. Then, have them trade their stories with other partners. Ask students how the words were used in the different stories.

Spelling and Writing   Page 96

The **Proofreading** exercise will help students prepare to proofread their journal entries. As students complete the writing activity, encourage them to brainstorm ideas, write a first draft, revise, and proofread their work. To publish their writing, students may want to
- read aloud their writing in small groups
- create a class log of bird sightings.

Writer's Corner Encourage students to read more about owls and hawks in their school or local library or on the Internet. Invite them to draw a poster of their favorite bird and include a notecard of information to share with the class.

Final Test

1. Over thirty kinds of **sparrows** live in America.
2. What a **powerful** singing voice Tina has!
3. Sean was lonely **without** his best friend Dario.
4. He took a **shower** after exercising at the gym.
5. We **sought** shelter when it started to rain.
6. The children **swallowed** their food in a hurry.
7. The repair bill came to two **thousand** dollars.
8. I had **trouble** fitting in the last puzzle piece.
9. **Although** rain was forecast, the sun shone.
10. Mrs. Arnez puts vegetables in her **chowder**.
11. Li spends two **hours** on homework every day.
12. What picturesque little **towns** these are!
13. The **amount** you owe for the fine is one dollar.
14. He **allows** students to check their own tests.
15. All the guests **brought** birthday gifts for Cara.
16. Rabbits were living in the **hollow** log.
17. Is Australia in the **Southern** Hemisphere?
18. Chan **thought** he had written a great story.
19. **Bouquet** is a synonym for *a fragrant smell*.
20. We will hike up Shawnee **Mountain**.

Objectives
To review spelling words with vowel pairs, vowel digraphs, and diphthongs

Check Your Spelling Notebook   *Pages 97–100*

Based on students' lists and your observations, note which words are giving students the most difficulty and offer assistance for spelling them correctly. Here are some frequently misspelled words to watch for: *measure, believe, relief, restaurant, audience, awkward, voices, bouquet, hours,* and *disappoint.*

To give students extra help and practice in taking standardized tests, you may want to have them take the **Review Test** for this lesson on pages 78–79. After scoring the tests, return them to students so that they can record their misspelled words in their spelling notebooks.

After practicing their troublesome words, students can work through the exercises for Lessons 19–23. Before students begin each exercise, you may want to go over the spelling rule.

Take It Home

Invite students to locate the **list words** from Lessons 19–23 at home—on television, on the Internet, on the radio, in conversations, and in books and magazines. Students can also use **Take It Home** Master 4 on pages 80–81 to help them do the activity. (A complete list of the spelling words is included on page 80 of the **Take It Home** Master.) Encourage students to total the number of words found and bring in their lists to share with the class.

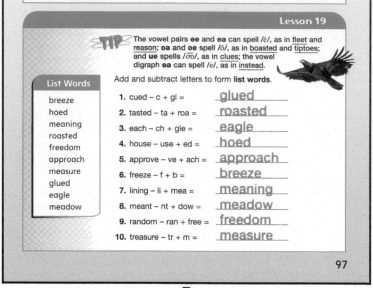

In lessons 19–23, you have learned how to spell words with vowel pairs, vowel digraphs, and diphthongs.

Check Your Spelling Notebook

Look at the words in your spelling notebook. Which words for lessons 19 through 23 did you have the most trouble with? Write them here.

_____

_____

Practice writing your troublesome words with a partner. Form the letters of each word with clay, pipe cleaners, or string while your partner spells the words aloud.

Lesson 19

TIP The vowel pairs **ee** and **ea** can spell /ē/, as in <u>fleet</u> and <u>reason</u>; **oa** and **oe** spell /ō/, as in <u>boasted</u> and <u>tiptoes</u>; and **ue** spells /o͞o/, as in clues; the vowel digraph **ea** can spell /e/, as in <u>instead</u>.

List Words: breeze, hoed, meaning, roasted, freedom, approach, measure, glued, eagle, meadow

Add and subtract letters to form list words.

1. cued – c + gl = **glued**
2. tasted – ta + roa = **roasted**
3. each – ch + gle = **eagle**
4. house – use + ed = **hoed**
5. approve – ve + ach = **approach**
6. freeze – f + b = **breeze**
7. lining – li + mea = **meaning**
8. meant – nt + dow = **meadow**
9. random – ran + free = **freedom**
10. treasure – tr + m = **measure**

97

Lesson 20

TIP The letters **ie** can spell /ī/, as in <u>died</u>, or /ē/, as in <u>fields</u>. The letters **ei** can spell /ē/, as in <u>seize</u>, or /ā/, as in <u>weigh</u>.

List Words: brief, shriek, believe, sleigh, receive, neighbors, receipt, amplifies, chiefly, freighter

Write the list word that belongs in each group.

1. canoe, sailboat, **freighter**
2. scream, yell, **shriek**
3. sled, ski, **sleigh**
4. friends, partners, **neighbors**
5. mainly, mostly, **chiefly**
6. short, small, **brief**
7. feel, think, **believe**
8. increases, boosts, **amplifies**
9. get, obtain, **receive**
10. check, ticket, **receipt**

Lesson 21

TIP The vowel digraphs **au** and **aw** both spell /ô/, as in <u>haunt</u> and <u>claws</u>.

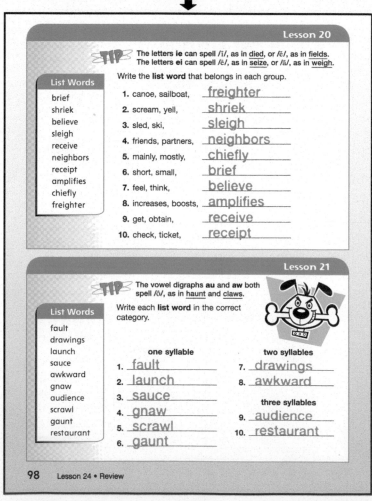

List Words: fault, drawings, launch, sauce, awkward, gnaw, audience, scrawl, gaunt, restaurant

Write each list word in the correct category.

one syllable
1. **fault**
2. **launch**
3. **sauce**
4. **gnaw**
5. **scrawl**
6. **gaunt**

two syllables
7. **drawings**
8. **awkward**

three syllables
9. **audience**
10. **restaurant**

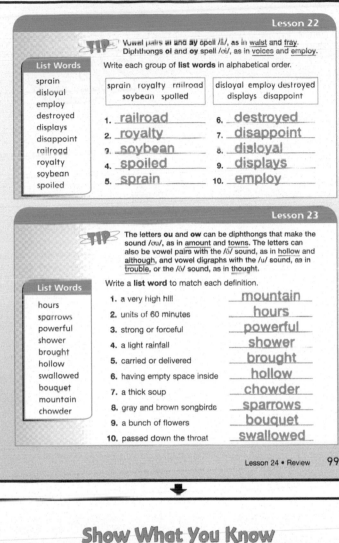

Lesson 22

TIP Vowel pairs **ai** and **ay** spell /ā/, as in *waist* and *fray*. Diphthongs **oi** and **oy** spell /oi/, as in *voices* and *employ*.

List Words

sprain
disloyal
employ
destroyed
displays
disappoint
railroad
royalty
soybean
spoiled

Write each group of **list words** in alphabetical order.

| sprain royalty railroad | disloyal employ destroyed |
| soybean spoiled | displays disappoint |

1. railroad
2. royalty
3. soybean
4. spoiled
5. sprain
6. destroyed
7. disappoint
8. disloyal
9. displays
10. employ

Lesson 23

TIP The letters **ou** and **ow** can be diphthongs that make the sound /ou/, as in *amount* and *towns*. The letters can also be vowel pairs with the /ō/ sound, as in *hollow* and *although*, and vowel digraphs with the /u/ sound, as in *trouble*, or the /ô/ sound, as in *thought*.

List Words

hours
sparrows
powerful
shower
brought
hollow
swallowed
bouquet
mountain
chowder

Write a **list word** to match each definition.

1. a very high hill — mountain
2. units of 60 minutes — hours
3. strong or forceful — powerful
4. a light rainfall — shower
5. carried or delivered — brought
6. having empty space inside — hollow
7. a thick soup — chowder
8. gray and brown songbirds — sparrows
9. a bunch of flowers — bouquet
10. passed down the throat — swallowed

Show What You Know

Lessons 19—23 • Review

One word is misspelled in each set of **list words**. Fill in the circle next to the **list word** that is spelled incorrectly.

1. ○ launch ○ royalty ○ meaning ○ powerful ● cheifly
2. ○ hours ○ sleigh ● praysed ○ reason ○ sauce
3. ○ hoed ○ towns ○ soybean ○ claws ● wiegh
4. ○ crayon ○ deceive ● between ○ sparrows ○ fault
5. ● deid ○ eagle ○ shower ○ employ ○ dawn
6. ○ boiling ● bouquay ○ meadow ○ believe ○ causing
7. ● rooasted ○ allows ○ waist ○ straw ○ eighteen
8. ○ southern ● siezo ○ jaw ○ fray ○ freedom
9. ● glewed ○ diet ○ awkward ○ sprain ○ swallowed
10. ○ amount ○ pies ● treeting ○ haunt ○ railroad
11. ● recieve ○ spoiled ○ loaned ○ hollow ○ yawn
12. ○ chowder ○ displays ● frawd ○ fields ○ clues
13. ○ broiling ○ measure ○ drawings ● sawght ○ relief
14. ○ mountain ● nieghbors ○ fawns ○ noises ○ eastern
15. ○ gnaw ○ voices ● brieze ○ without ○ brief
16. ○ tiptoes ● shreek ○ brought ○ audience ○ disloyal
17. ○ thousand ○ shawl ○ receipt ○ destroyed ● approoch
18. ● amplifyes ○ scrawl ○ swaying ○ instead ○ thought
19. ○ trouble ○ boasted ○ freighter ○ disappoint ● gawnt
20. ○ restaurant ○ appointed ● fleat ○ although ○ perceive

Final Test

1. Wildflowers bloom in the **meadow**.
2. The laws guarantee our **freedom** of speech.
3. The plane will descend and **approach** the runway.
4. Two white horses pulled the **sleigh**.
5. This **freighter** will leave tomorrow for Europe.
6. Did your **neighbors** move to Boston?
7. Beavers **gnaw** on the trunks of trees.
8. The Riverside Inn is my favorite **restaurant**.
9. My uncle was pale and **gaunt** during his illness.
10. Don't **sprain** your back moving the sofa.
11. Our plans were **spoiled** by the sudden storm.
12. Some Chinese recipes call for **soybean** oil.
13. It took two **hours** to complete my report.
14. What is the highest **mountain** in the world?
15. How delicious that **chowder** smells!
16. The **sparrows** ate seeds at our bird feeder.
17. Carmela **brought** a visitor to school today.
18. Prince Harry is a member of the British **royalty**.
19. Dogs rarely are **disloyal** to their owners.
20. Be careful crossing the **railroad** tracks!
21. Long, skinny legs make colts seem **awkward**.
22. We watched the rocket **launch** on television.
23. Do you have a recipe for spaghetti **sauce**?
24. Today I received a **brief** letter from Joan.
25. The **shriek** of the train whistle startled me.
26. When I paid for the hat, I was given a **receipt**.
27. The factory's workers are **chiefly** women.
28. Use a teaspoon to **measure** the cinnamon.
29. Yesterday a baby **eagle** was born at the zoo.
30. A strong **breeze** will make the kite fly.
31. Look in a dictionary for a word's **meaning**.
32. Mother **glued** the broken chair back together.
33. I **believe** that voting is our civic duty.
34. The **audience** waited for the curtain to rise.
35. If you **scrawl** your name, it may be hard to read.
36. The steel mills **employ** many people.
37. I'm sure that the movie won't **disappoint** you.
38. That storm in Florida was so **powerful**!
39. Tom bought a **bouquet** of roses for his wife.
40. Milk passes through a **hollow** straw.
41. Insects have **destroyed** many of the plants.
42. Chang **displays** his photographs at a gallery.
43. I'm afraid it's my **fault** that the book was lost.
44. Your **drawings** of wildflowers are beautiful.
45. A megaphone **amplifies** a person's voice.
46. You'll probably **receive** the package tomorrow.
47. Jim **hoed** the garden, then planted the corn.
48. We **roasted** the potatoes over the campfire.
49. The dog **swallowed** every bit of his food.
50. A light **shower** fell in the late afternoon.

Review Test (Side A)

Read each set of words. Fill in the circle next to the word that is spelled correctly.

1. (a) aproch   (c) approch
   (b) aproach   (d) approach

2. (a) friedom   (c) fredom
   (b) freedom   (d) freidom

3. (a) glued   (c) glueed
   (b) glud   (d) glooed

4. (a) meazure   (c) measure
   (b) mezure   (d) mesure

5. (a) beleave   (c) beleive
   (b) believe   (d) beleeve

6. (a) brief   (c) breif
   (b) brif   (d) bref

7. (a) neighbirs   (c) naybors
   (b) naybirs   (d) neighbors

8. (a) riceive   (c) receve
   (b) receive   (d) recieve

9. (a) audience   (c) audeince
   (b) awdience   (d) audiense

10. (a) aukward   (c) awkward
    (b) awkwerd   (d) aukword

Review Test (Side B)

Lesson 24

Read each set of words. Fill in the circle next to the word that is spelled correctly.

11. (a) falt   (c) fawlt
    (b) fault   (d) fallt

12. (a) resterant   (c) restaurant
    (b) restarant   (d) restawrant

13. (a) desstroyed   (c) destroied
    (b) destroyd   (d) destroyed

14. (a) railrode   (c) rallroad
    (b) raleroad   (d) railroad

15. (a) disappoint   (c) disapoint
    (b) dissapoint   (d) disapoynt

16. (a) sprane   (c) sprayne
    (b) sprain   (d) spraine

17. (a) boukay   (c) buquet
    (b) booquet   (d) bouquet

18. (a) hours   (c) howers
    (b) howrs   (d) owers

19. (a) browt   (c) brought
    (b) brout   (d) browght

20. (a) mountin   (c) mowntin
    (b) mountain   (d) mountian

Take It Home 4

Your child has learned to spell many new words and would enjoy sharing them with you and your family. These activity ideas can make sharing the words in Lessons 19–23 fun for the whole family.

Sound Bites!

Here's a "tasteful" idea! Help your child listen for and use spelling words during dinner time conversations. Start things off by using a word that interests you. (For example, "I remember the first time I met our new *neighbors*.") What spelling words hold special meanings or memories for your child? Encourage your child to use and jot down those words.

Lesson 19

1. approach
2. between
3. boasted
4. breeze
5. clues
6. eagle
7. eastern
8. fleet
9. freedom
10. glued
11. hoed
12. instead
13. loaned
14. meadow
15. meaning
16. measure
17. reason
18. roasted
19. tiptoes
20. treating

Lesson 20

1. amplifies
2. believe
3. brief
4. chiefly
5. deceive
6. died
7. diet
8. eighteen
9. fields
10. freighter
11. neighbors
12. perceive
13. pies
14. receipt
15. receive
16. relief
17. seize
18. shriek
19. sleigh
20. weigh

Lesson 21

1. audience
2. awkward
3. causing
4. claws
5. dawn
6. drawings
7. fault
8. fawns
9. fraud
10. gaunt
11. gnaw
12. haunt
13. jaw
14. launch
15. restaurant
16. sauce
17. scrawl
18. shawl
19. straw
20. yawn

Lesson 22

1. appointed
2. boiling
3. broiling
4. crayon
5. destroyed
6. disappoint
7. disloyal
8. displays
9. employ
10. fray
11. noises
12. praised
13. railroad
14. royalty
15. soybean
16. spoiled
17. sprain
18. swaying
19. voices
20. waist

Lesson 23

1. allows
2. although
3. amount
4. bouquet
5. brought
6. chowder
7. hollow
8. hours
9. mountain
10. powerful
11. shower
12. sought
13. southern
14. sparrows
15. swallowed
16. thought
17. thousand
18. towns
19. trouble
20. without

Spell-and-Step

Which words in the box complete this word ladder? Afterward, you might enjoy using some of the leftover words to build a ladder of your own.

tiptoes	weigh	launch	deceive	neighbors
diet	hoed	noises	shawl	sprain
sleigh	hours	straw	shriek	waist
loaned	mountain	meadow	disloyal	towns

Objective
To spell regular plural nouns

Correlated Phonics Lesson
MCP Phonics, Level D, Lesson 56

Spelling Words in Action   **Page 101**

Invite students to read the selection to find out how to keep a bicycle in tip-top shape. Afterward, ask them to share their favorite bicycle tips.

Encourage students to look back at the boldfaced words. Have volunteers say each word and identify the letter or letters added to make the word plural.

Warm-Up Test
1. Are the **axes** sharp enough to cut the trees?
2. Nicole wears gold **chains** around her neck.
3. The company's **bosses** work on Saturdays.
4. Bryant bought a new pair of jogging **shoes**.
5. Grandma signed her letter, "hugs and **kisses**."
6. Lisa used two different **waxes** to polish her car.
7. Three **foxes** headed toward the chicken coop.
8. Your **splashes** are getting us wet.
9. Don't leave a campfire until the **ashes** are cold.
10. We heard several loud **crashes** of thunder.
11. Keep **matches** away from young children.
12. I usually eat two **sandwiches** for lunch.
13. The dentist gave us all new **toothbrushes**.
14. My brother has blond hair and dark **eyelashes**.
15. The Girl Scouts wear badges on green **sashes**.
16. Have the workers finished digging the **ditches**?
17. The **flashes** of lightning scared me!
18. New England has many picturesque **churches**.
19. Two long **paces** cover about six feet.
20. The music has many cymbals **clashes** in it.

Spelling Practice   **Pages 102–103**

Introduce the spelling rule and invite students to read the **list words** aloud. Encourage students to look back at their **Warm-Up Tests** and apply the spelling rule to any misspelled words.

As students work through the **Spelling Practice** exercises, remind them to look back at their **list words** or in their dictionaries if they need help.

for ESL students   See Comparing / Contrasting, page 15

82

Spelling Words in Action

How do you keep a bike in tip-top shape?

Clean Machine

You have to work hard to keep a bike in tip-top shape. The best time to care for a bike is before anything goes wrong. Clean off **splashes** of dirt with soap and water, then dry your bike with soft, clean towels. Pay attention to the reflectors that give off **flashes** of light. The cleaner they are, the easier it is for the driver of a car to see you. To protect the shine, apply a coat of car or bicycle wax. Most **waxes** can be applied using a soft, clean cloth, then removed using another cloth.

To keep your bike safe, keep its chain in good condition. Old **toothbrushes** are great for removing grime. Oil the chain with bike chain oil. Don't use too much! Oily **chains** become gummy and collect dirt. If your bike has hand brakes, check the brake **shoes**. These are the rubber pads that grip the tires. Replace them if they are worn. You want the brakes to work well, so you can avoid **crashes** or riding into **ditches**.

Once your bike is in good working order, take it out for a test run and put it through its **paces**. Then, pack some **sandwiches**, bike to your favorite spot, and have a picnic.

Look back at the boldfaced words. What letter or letters are added to each word to make it plural?

101

TIP
You make most singular words plural by adding just **s** to the singular form.
shoe + s = shoes
If a singular word ends in **x, ss, sh,** or **ch,** you usually add **es** to make it mean more than one.
fox + es = foxes

Spelling Practice

LIST WORDS
1. axes
2. chains
3. bosses
4. shoes
5. kisses
6. waxes
7. foxes
8. splashes
9. ashes
10. crashes
11. matches
12. sandwiches
13. toothbrushes
14. eyelashes
15. sashes
16. ditches
17. flashes
18. churches
19. paces
20. clashes

Forming Plurals

Finish spelling each **list word**.

1. ki __sses__
2. sh __oes__
3. as __hes__
4. cr __ashes__
5. wa __xes__
6. bo __sses__
7. ax __es__
8. fl __ashes__
9. di __tches__
10. cla __shes__
11. cha __ins__
12. fo __xes__
13. ma __tches__
14. pa __ces__
15. sas __hes__
16. chu __rches__
17. sand __wiches__
18. spla __shes__
19. eye __lashes__
20. tooth __brushes__

Rhyming Words

Use the clues to write **list words** that could make sense in each sentence. Each **list word** must rhyme with the underlined word.

1. The snake <u>hisses</u> when it __kisses__.
2. If it <u>rains</u> on my __chains__, they'll rust.
3. Playing in the __ashes__ might give you <u>rashes</u>.
4. He __paces__ with loose <u>laces</u>.
5. Put the <u>batches</u> of __matches__ in a safe place.
6. Wily __foxes__ don't like <u>boxes</u>.
7. He <u>pitches</u> rocks in the __ditches__.
8. The reflectors makes <u>slashes</u> of __flashes__.
9. The tourist <u>searches</u> elaborate __churches__.
10. She <u>lashes</u> __sashes__ around her waist.

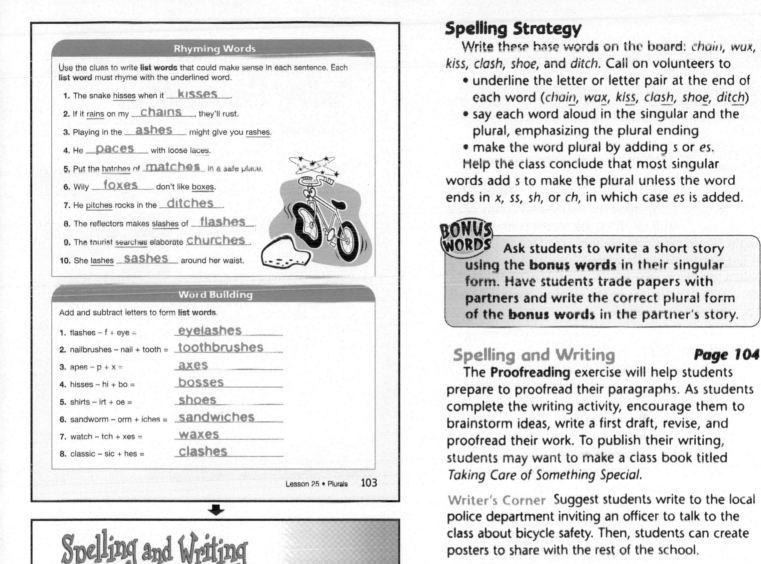

Word Building

Add and subtract letters to form **list words**.

1. flashes – f + eye = __eyelashes__
2. nailbrushes – nail + tooth = __toothbrushes__
3. apes – p + x = __axes__
4. hisses – hi + bo = __bosses__
5. shirts – irt + oe = __shoes__
6. sandworm – orm + iches = __sandwiches__
7. watch – tch + xes = __waxes__
8. classic – sic + hes = __clashes__

Spelling and Writing

Proofreading

This poem has twelve mistakes. Use the proofreading marks to fix each mistake. Then, write the misspelled **list words** correctly on the lines.

We ride bicycles on the street.
We wave to at all the friends we meet.
We hit puddles to make (splashis).
And now and then we have (krashes)
We we jump dichtes in a bunch,
And eat (sandwitches) for lunch.
Even in the the hardest rains
We always stop to fix our (chayns)

Proofreading Marks

◯ spelling mistake
︿ add something
↶ take out something

1. __splashes__
2. __crashes__
3. __ditches__
4. __sandwiches__
5. __chains__

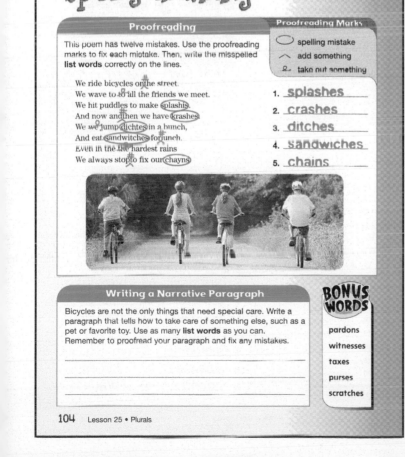

Writing a Narrative Paragraph

Bicycles are not the only things that need special care. Write a paragraph that tells how to take care of something else, such as a pet or favorite toy. Use as many **list words** as you can. Remember to proofread your paragraph and fix any mistakes.

_____

_____

_____

BONUS WORDS

pardons
witnesses
taxes
purses
scratches

Spelling Strategy

Write these base words on the board: *chain, wax, kiss, clash, shoe,* and *ditch.* Call on volunteers to
- underline the letter or letter pair at the end of each word (chai<u>n</u>, wa<u>x</u>, ki<u>ss</u>, clas<u>h</u>, sho<u>e</u>, ditc<u>h</u>)
- say each word aloud in the singular and the plural, emphasizing the plural ending
- make the word plural by adding s or es.

Help the class conclude that most singular words add *s* to make the plural unless the word ends in *x, ss, sh,* or *ch,* in which case *es* is added.

BONUS WORDS

Ask students to write a short story using the **bonus words** in their singular form. Have students trade papers with partners and write the correct plural form of the **bonus words** in the partner's story.

Spelling and Writing   **Page 104**

The **Proofreading** exercise will help students prepare to proofread their paragraphs. As students complete the writing activity, encourage them to brainstorm ideas, write a first draft, revise, and proofread their work. To publish their writing, students may want to make a class book titled *Taking Care of Something Special.*

Writer's Corner Suggest students write to the local police department inviting an officer to talk to the class about bicycle safety. Then, students can create posters to share with the rest of the school.

Final Test

1. My **shoes** gave me terrible blisters!
2. The **crashes** you heard were falling branches.
3. **Ditches** by the side of the road drain off water.
4. The pink pillow **clashes** with the orange chair.
5. Mr. Espinosa sharpens knives and **axes**.
6. Where does the family of **foxes** have its den?
7. Did you also paint the window **sashes**?
8. Mom **kisses** me goodbye every morning.
9. Keep the **toothbrushes** in the bathroom.
10. The horse's **paces** are very smooth.
11. Those **chains** keep the gate to the pen shut.
12. You can smell the old **ashes** in the fireplace.
13. Some **waxes** are self-polishing.
14. My mother's last two **bosses** praised her work.
15. Your **splashes** have made the floor wet.
16. Use long wooden **matches** to light the stove.
17. A camel's **eyelashes** protect its eyes from sand.
18. Those **flashes** of light are from a jet overhead.
19. Do you want tuna fish or ham **sandwiches**?
20. Not all **churches** have tall steeples.

Objective
To spell the plurals of nouns that end with y

 Correlated Phonics Lesson
MCP Phonics, Level D, Lesson 56

Spelling Words in Action **Page 105**

In this selection, students discover when it's okay to "pig out." After reading, ask students how they might like to celebrate National Pig Day.

Encourage students to look back at the boldfaced words. Ask volunteers to say each word, identify the final letter in the singular form, and tell how the plural is spelled.

Warm-Up Test
1. Many school **holidays** fall on Mondays.
2. On graduation day, we went to three **parties**.
3. Maricella likes to read mystery **stories**.
4. They covered the food to keep the **flies** off it.
5. They have **birthdays** on the same day.
6. Please make ten **copies** of this letter.
7. What are the class secretary's **duties**?
8. Several **ladies** are visiting my mother.
9. Each state is divided into several **counties**.
10. Have astronauts explored the moon's **valleys**?
11. Kevin helped his mother unpack **groceries**.
12. Are your **hobbies** stamp collecting and skiing?
13. The **libraries** need more money to buy books.
14. Work crews repaired the state's **highways**.
15. This flashlight needs new **batteries**.
16. There were no **injuries** from the car accident.
17. What a fancy dessert **cherries** jubilee is!
18. Some **melodies** are easy to remember.
19. Our company conducts **surveys** for stores.
20. We visited **communities** hurt by the storm.

Spelling Practice **Pages 106–107**

Introduce the spelling rule and have students read the **list words** aloud. You may also want to ask students to spell the singular form of each word and explain how the plural is formed. Encourage students to look back at their **Warm-Up Tests** and apply the spelling rule to any misspelled words.

As students work through the **Spelling Practice** exercises, remind them to look back at their **list words** or in their dictionaries if they need help.

for ESL students **See Change or No Change, page 15**

84

Spelling Words in Action

When is it okay to "pig out"?

Pig Out

Most of the time, "pigging out" is considered bad manners and unhealthy. There is one day a year, however, when *not* pigging out is impolite. That day is March 1, National Pig Day.

Most **holidays** were started to recall historic events. This one, though, was begun by two sisters from Texas and North Carolina. These **ladies** shared a childhood fascination with pigs. They brought their love for pigs to **counties** everywhere when they had their Pig Day registered as a real holiday in 1972.

Today, across the **highways** and byways of our land, National Pig Day is celebrated by pig lovers. Some **communities** have pig **parties**. Others, like Davis, California, celebrate the holiday with all-day pig festivals. People are encouraged to dress up like pigs. If needed, guests can buy fake pig snouts, ears, and tails there. Guests can visit a pig petting zoo, go on pig rides, and make pig crafts. Some people "pig out" on special food like pig-shaped cookies and cakes. There are even pig **melodies** and pig cheers.

If you want to celebrate National Pig Day, try checking out your local library. Some **libraries** observe the day with an afternoon of pig **stories** and crafts. You could also make **copies** of your favorite pig pictures and pass them out to friends.

The singular form of each boldfaced word in the selection ends with the same letter. Which letter is it? How are the plurals spelled?

105

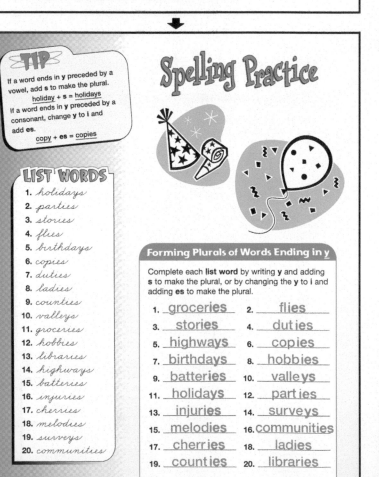

TIP

If a word ends in **y** preceded by a vowel, add **s** to make the plural.
holiday + **s** = holidays
If a word ends in **y** preceded by a consonant, change **y** to **i** and add **es**.
copy + **es** = copies

Spelling Practice

LIST WORDS
1. holidays
2. parties
3. stories
4. flies
5. birthdays
6. copies
7. duties
8. ladies
9. counties
10. valleys
11. groceries
12. hobbies
13. libraries
14. highways
15. batteries
16. injuries
17. cherries
18. melodies
19. surveys
20. communities

Forming Plurals of Words Ending in y

Complete each **list word** by writing **y** and adding **s** to make the plural, or by changing the **y** to **i** and adding **es** to make the plural.

1. groceries
2. flies
3. stories
4. duties
5. highways
6. copies
7. birthdays
8. hobbies
9. batteries
10. valleys
11. holidays
12. parties
13. injuries
14. surveys
15. melodies
16. communities
17. cherries
18. ladies
19. counties
20. libraries

Complete the Paragraphs

Write a list word on each of the lines to complete the paragraphs.

Unusual Holidays

We all have our own ___stories___ about the more usual ___holidays___. Some people even consider their ___birthdays___ to be holidays. There are probably dozens of holidays, though, that you've never heard of. In fact, there is a holiday for almost everything.

Every month has some kind of wacky holiday celebrated in ___communities___ and ___counties___ around the country. For example, did you know that the second week in January is National Pizza Week? Better include some pizza fixings in your ___groceries___ then! June 13 is National Juggling Day. Start practicing to avoid any minor ___injuries___. If you like marshmallows, you'll love National Toasted Marshmallow Day on August 30. Then, there's Miniature Golf Day on September 21. It's never too early to practice hitting that golf ball over those little hills and ___valleys___. ___Surveys___ have shown that one of the most popular holidays is September 22. That's the date to celebrate Ice Cream Cone Day. Serve those cones with ___cherries___ on top!

Scrambled Words

What list words can you make from the letters in each group of words? Use each letter once.

1. ls, elf ___flies___
2. sad, lie ___ladies___
3. side, mole ___melodies___
4. art, pies ___parties___
5. epic, so ___copies___
6. a, sigh, why ___highways___
7. bib, shoe ___hobbies___
8. us, tied ___duties___
9. rib, is, real ___libraries___
10. a, bite, rest ___batteries___

Lesson 26 • Plurals of Words That End in y   107

Spelling and Writing

Proofreading

The article below has eleven mistakes. Use the proofreading marks to fix each mistake. Then, write the misspelled list words correctly on the lines.

Proofreading Marks
- ⬭ spelling mistake
- ≡ capital letter
- ⌃ add something

have you ever heard storys about Turkey Trots? One kind of Turkey Trot is a dance. Another is a race held around one of our most popular holidays, Thanksgiving Day. Turkey Trots are held in communitees and countys around the country. They're usually planned like partees with plenty of running, food, and fun times. often, Turkey Trots are held to raise money for charities. The races are usually 5 or 10 kilometers. Afterall, we don't want any injurys. Ask around. see if there is a Turkey Trot near you.

1. ___stories___
2. ___holidays___
3. ___communities___
4. ___counties___
5. ___parties___
6. ___injuries___

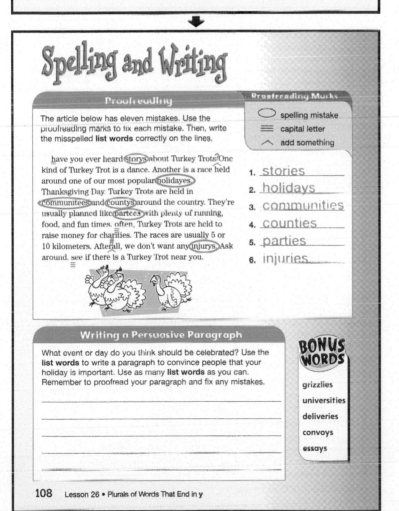

Writing a Persuasive Paragraph

What event or day do you think should be celebrated? Use the list words to write a paragraph to convince people that your holiday is important. Use as many list words as you can. Remember to proofread your paragraph and fix any mistakes.

_____
_____
_____
_____
_____

BONUS WORDS

grizzlies
universities
deliveries
convoys
essays

108   Lesson 26 • Plurals of Words That End in y

Spelling Strategy

Write these singular forms of list words on the board: *fly, valley, hobby, highway, injury,* and *community.* Have students pair up and take turns spelling the plural of each word and explaining the rule to form the plural. Encourage students to think of other words that end with *y* and to form their plurals, such as *jelly/jellies* and *company/companies.*

BONUS WORDS Have students write a sentence for **each bonus word,** but leave a blank in place of the **bonus word.** Invite partners to trade papers and write the correct word in each sentence.

Spelling and Writing   *Page 108*

The **Proofreading** exercise will help students prepare to proofread their paragraphs. As students complete the writing activity, encourage them to brainstorm ideas, write a first draft, revise, and proofread their work. To publish their writing, students may want to
- create a flyer announcing their holidays
- combine their paragraphs into a booklet titled "Holiday Happenings."

Writer's Corner Invite students to find out more about National Pig Day by looking for information in the library or on the Internet. Suggest they make notes on what they learn and bring their notes to share with the class.

Final Test

1. Ripe, sweet **cherries** are my favorite fruit.
2. I visited three **libraries** looking for that book.
3. **Flies** buzzed around my head as I tried to eat.
4. Do your relatives come to visit on **holidays**?
5. Two **communities** reported flood damage.
6. This radio uses four C **batteries.**
7. **Ladies** and gentlemen, let's welcome Ms. Ali!
8. My **hobbies** are fishing and stamp collecting.
9. James carried the **groceries** to the car.
10. We passed rivers and **valleys** going home.
11. Henry and Perry **counties** are in Ohio.
12. The singer signed both **copies** of the contract.
13. Do your new **duties** include filing?
14. Whose **birthdays** are national holidays?
15. Mother told us **stories** of her childhood.
16. Are the results of **surveys** always accurate?
17. She quit the game because of her **injuries.**
18. Some people enjoy loud music at **parties.**
19. The **highways** were choked with traffic.
20. Some **melodies** remind me of my old friends.

Objectives
To spell plural forms of irregular nouns and nouns that end in *f* or *fe*

Phonics Correlated Phonics Lesson
MCP Phonics, Level D, Lesson 57

Spelling Words in Action   Page 109

In "A Toothy Story," students find out what kind of teeth different animals have. Ask students why they think some animals don't have teeth.

Have volunteers say each boldfaced word and identify its singular form.

Warm-Up Test

1. You must brush your **teeth** every day!
2. The **mice** were afraid of the cat.
3. How many **women** work in that hospital?
4. Please put the **knives** in the drawer.
5. Let's rake the **leaves** today.
6. Cut the apples into **halves**.
7. Will we need more than two **loaves** of bread?
8. We studied the **lives** of famous inventors.
9. We saw two baby **calves** in the field.
10. What enormous animals **moose** are!
11. The farmer has a large flock of **sheep**.
12. Pioneers used **oxen** to move heavy loads.
13. Help **yourselves** to some grapes and cheese.
14. **Geese** lay larger eggs than chickens do.
15. How did the Cheyenne choose their **chiefs**?
16. **Buffaloes** used to roam across the prairies.
17. Have paper tissues replaced **handkerchiefs**?
18. They wore **scarves** to keep their necks warm.
19. Horses wear shoes to protect their **hoofs**.
20. Did you see any **bison** or other large animals?

Spelling Practice   Pages 110–111

Introduce the spelling rule and have students read the **list words** aloud, discussing the pluralization process for each word. (Note that *hooves* and *scarfs* are also acceptable plural spellings of *hoof* and *scarf*.) Then, encourage students to look back at their **Warm-Up Tests** and apply the spelling rule to any misspelled words.

As students work through the **Spelling Practice** exercises, remind them to look back at their **list words** or in their dictionaries if they need help.

 for ESL students **See Picture Clues, page 15**

Spelling Words in Action

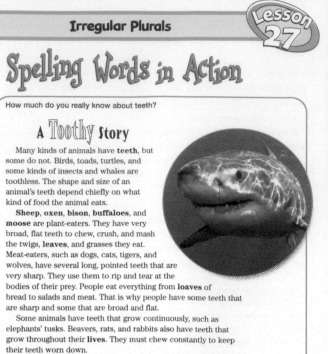

How much do you really know about teeth?

A Toothy Story

Many kinds of animals have **teeth**, but some do not. Birds, toads, turtles, and some kinds of insects and whales are toothless. The shape and size of an animal's teeth depend chiefly on what kind of food the animal eats.

Sheep, oxen, bison, buffaloes, and **moose** are plant-eaters. They have very broad, flat teeth to chew, crush, and mash the twigs, **leaves**, and grasses they eat. Meat-eaters, such as dogs, cats, tigers, and wolves, have several long, pointed teeth that are very sharp. They use them to rip and tear at the bodies of their prey. People eat everything from **loaves** of bread to salads and meat. That is why people have some teeth that are sharp and some that are broad and flat.

Some animals have teeth that grow continuously, such as elephants' tusks. Beavers, rats, and rabbits also have teeth that grow throughout their **lives**. They must chew constantly to keep their teeth worn down.

Many fish and most reptiles have teeth that are about the same size and shape and that are only used for catching prey. Sharks have teeth that are as sharp as **knives**. They have many rows of teeth. When they lose a tooth, the one in back of it takes its place.

Look back at the boldfaced words. Notice that all the words are plurals. What is the singular form of each word?

109

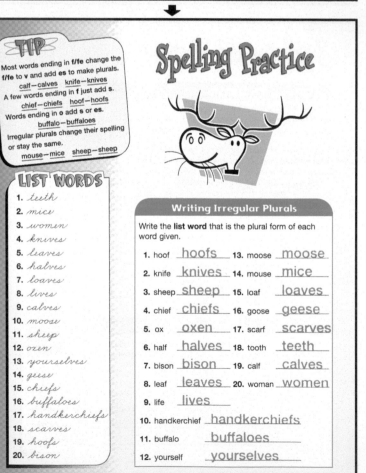

TIP
Most words ending in **f/fe** change the **f/fe** to **v** and add **es** to make plurals.
calf—calves   knife—knives
A few words ending in **f** just add **s**.
chief—chiefs   hoof—hoofs
Words ending in **o** add **s** or **es**.
buffalo—buffaloes
Irregular plurals change their spelling or stay the same.
mouse—mice   sheep—sheep

Spelling Practice

LIST WORDS

1. teeth
2. mice
3. women
4. knives
5. leaves
6. halves
7. loaves
8. lives
9. calves
10. moose
11. sheep
12. oxen
13. yourselves
14. geese
15. chiefs
16. buffaloes
17. handkerchiefs
18. scarves
19. hoofs
20. bison

Writing Irregular Plurals

Write the **list word** that is the plural form of each word given.

1. hoof __hoofs__
2. knife __knives__
3. sheep __sheep__
4. chief __chiefs__
5. ox __oxen__
6. half __halves__
7. bison __bison__
8. leaf __leaves__
9. life __lives__
10. handkerchief __handkerchiefs__
11. buffalo __buffaloes__
12. yourself __yourselves__
13. moose __moose__
14. mouse __mice__
15. loaf __loaves__
16. goose __geese__
17. scarf __scarves__
18. tooth __teeth__
19. calf __calves__
20. woman __women__

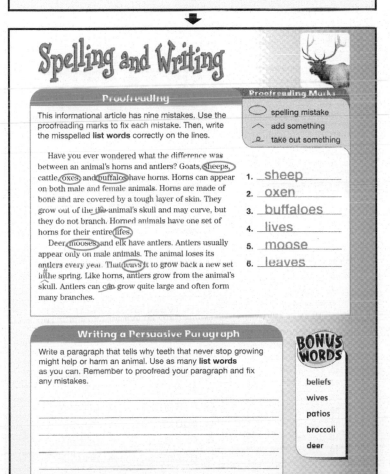

Comparing Words

The first two underlined words in each sentence are related. Write a **list word** that has the same relationship to the third underlined word.

1. Feet are to people as _hoofs_ are to horses.
2. Patties are to hamburgers as _loaves_ are to bread.
3. Walk is to legs as chew is to _teeth_.
4. Men are to boys as _women_ are to girls.
5. Scissors are to paper as _knives_ are to meat.
6. Belts are to waists as _scarves_ are to necks.
7. Hay is to horses as cheese is to _mice_.
8. Captains are to police as _chiefs_ are to firemen.
9. Napkins are to hands as _handkerchiefs_ are to noses.

Riddle

Read each definition clue. Write **list words** in the spaces. Then, use the numbered letters to solve the riddle.

1. parts of a whole   h a l v e s (8 under v)
2. young cows or bulls   c a l v e s (1 under a)
3. birds that swim   g e e s e (7 under e)
4. members of the ox family   b i s o n (5 under i, 2 under o)
5. your own selves   y o u r s e l v e s (6 under s, 9 under v)
6. animals related to deer   m o o s e (4 under o)
7. wild oxen   b u f f a l o e s (3 under f, 10 under o)

Riddle: What is most useful when it is used up?

Answer: a n _ u m b r e l l a
1 2   3 4 5 6 7 8 9 10

Spelling and Writing

Proofreading

This informational article has nine mistakes. Use the proofreading marks to fix each mistake. Then, write the misspelled **list words** correctly on the lines.

Proofreading Marks
- ⟋ spelling mistake
- ⌃ add something
- ⌿ take out something

Have you ever wondered what the difference was between an animal's horns and antlers? Goats, sheeps, cattle, oxes, and buffalos have horns. Horns can appear on both male and female animals. Horns are made of bone and are covered by a tough layer of skin. They grow out of the the animal's skull and may curve, but they do not branch. Horned animals have one set of horns for their entire lifes.

Deer, mooses, and elk have antlers. Antlers usually appear only on male animals. The animal loses its antlers every year. That leavs it to grow back a new set inthe spring. Like horns, antlers grow from the animal's skull. Antlers can can grow quite large and often form many branches.

1. _sheep_
2. _oxen_
3. _buffaloes_
4. _lives_
5. _moose_
6. _leaves_

Writing a Persuasive Paragraph

Write a paragraph that tells why teeth that never stop growing might help or harm an animal. Use as many **list words** as you can. Remember to proofread your paragraph and fix any mistakes.

_____
_____
_____
_____
_____
_____

BONUS WORDS
beliefs
wives
patios
broccoli
deer

Spelling Strategy

Write *singular* and *plural* on the board at the top of two columns. Then, write *tooth* in the appropriate column. Ask a volunteer to write the plural form of *tooth* in the *plural* column and explain the rule they used to make the word plural. Continue with the remainder of the **list words**, helping students explain the rules as necessary.

BONUS WORDS   Have students use the **bonus words** to create a crossword puzzle. Ask them to write a clue for each word, then swap papers with partners. Invite partners to fill in the puzzles with the correct **bonus words**

Spelling and Writing   Page 112

The **Proofreading** exercise will help students prepare to proofread their paragraphs. As students complete the writing activity, encourage them to brainstorm ideas, write a first draft, revise, and proofread their work. To publish their writing, students may want to make a bulletin-board display illustrating the pros and cons of teeth that grow continuously.

Writer's Corner Encourage students to learn more about one animal and its teeth by researching the animal in the local or school library. Suggest that students draw a poster of the animal and write a short description of how the animal uses its teeth.

Final Test

1. The hot **loaves** of bread burned my hands!
2. Men and **women** filled the audience.
3. Out in the meadow, the **sheep** grazed.
4. Horses wear iron shoes on their **hoofs**.
5. Were all of the Iroquois **chiefs** at the meeting?
6. **Buffaloes** have shaggy brown fur.
7. **Bison** roamed the plains.
8. **Oxen** are much larger than ordinary cows.
9. Did you put out **knives** as well as forks?
10. The **lives** of the early settlers are inspiring.
11. A large flock of **geese** flew over my house.
12. In what states are **moose** found?
13. These woolen **scarves** are soft and thick.
14. There are two **halves** in a whole.
15. The hungry **mice** nibbled the cheese.
16. The dentist cleaned my **teeth**.
17. Maple **leaves** have three points on them.
18. Mother cows take good care of their **calves**.
19. Can you finish the work by **yourselves**?
20. Do you sell lace or linen **handkerchiefs**?

Objectives
To spell singular possessive nouns and contractions

 Correlated Phonics Lessons
MCP Phonics, Level D, Lessons 59–61

Spelling Words in Action   Page 113
In this selection, students find out what a "geoglyph" is and the best way to view one. After reading, you might ask, "If people created these giant drawings, why do you think they did so?"

Encourage students to look back at the boldfaced words. Ask volunteers to say each word and tell whether it is a possessive or a contraction.

Warm-Up Test
1. Lupe said **she'll** call if she's going to be late.
2. I **wouldn't** have gone if I'd still had my cold.
3. I hope **they'll** arrive on time.
4. **How's** the state going to get more tax money?
5. After the movie, **let's** go out for a pizza.
6. Daniel asked, "**Where's** my baseball glove?"
7. If **we're** going to the show, we'd better leave.
8. Did you read about that **desert's** wildlife?
9. We found each **person's** seat at the concert.
10. My **sister's** class took a trip to the museum.
11. She painted the **bicycle's** frame a bright blue.
12. **Arizona's** capital city is Phoenix.
13. The **child's** desk held his books and pencils.
14. Did you work in your **aunt's** store in July?
15. My **cousin's** new painting is terrific!
16. **Florida's** coast has wonderful seashells.
17. I'll get to ride on my **uncle's** tractor.
18. Where is the **doctor's** telephone number?
19. Our apple tree **hasn't** blossomed yet.
20. What are each **season's** characteristics?

Spelling Practice   Pages 114–115
Introduce the spelling rules and invite students to read the **list words** aloud, discussing the placement and use of the apostrophe in each word. Then, encourage students to look back at their **Warm-Up Tests** and apply the spelling rules to any misspelled words.

As students work through the **Spelling Practice** exercises, remind them to look back at their **list words** or in their dictionaries if they need help.

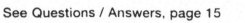 for ESL students   See Questions / Answers, page 15

88

Spelling Words in Action

What is a geoglyph?

Grand Designs

Let's imagine that we are flying high over the deserts of southern Peru. Looking toward the ground, we see giant drawings covering the desert floor. **We're** looking at what are called the Nazca Lines. The shapes these lines create can only be seen from the air. One of the largest drawings is that of a monkey that reminds us of a **child's** drawing. No child drew this, though. The monkey is 350 feet long! **How's** it possible!

These pictures in the sand, called geoglyphs, were made by the Nazca people about 1,000 to 2,000 years ago. Geoglyphs also exist in **Arizona's** deserts and in other places around the world. They are made by moving the **desert's** dark stones to reveal the lighter soil underneath. The Nazca Lines include pictures of many kinds of plants and animals. There is a 150-foot spider, a 165-foot hummingbird, and a pelican that's over 900 feet long. There are also flowers, a **person's** hand, and different geometric shapes.

Wouldn't you like to know why the Nazca made these lines? So would scientists, but **they'll** have to wait a while longer as science **hasn't** yet found the answer. There is no real evidence because there is so little left of the Nazca culture.

Look back at the boldfaced words. Notice that each word has an apostrophe. Can you identify which words are possessives and which words are contractions?

113

TIP
Use an apostrophe to show where letters have been left out in a contraction.
   she will—she'll
   how is—how's
Use an apostrophe and s to show singular ownership.
   the bike of my uncle—my uncle's bike

LIST WORDS
1. she'll
2. wouldn't
3. they'll
4. how's
5. let's
6. where's
7. we're
8. desert's
9. person's
10. sister's
11. bicycle's
12. Arizona's
13. child's
14. aunt's
15. cousin's
16. Florida's
17. uncle's
18. doctor's
19. hasn't
20. season's

Spelling Practice

Using an Apostrophe

Write the **list words** that are contractions using the word is.
1. how's   2. where's

Write the **list words** that are contractions using the word not.
3. wouldn't   4. hasn't

Write the **list words** that are contractions using the word will.
5. she'll   6. they'll

Write the **list word** that is a contraction using the word are.
7. we're

Write the **list word** that is a contraction using the word us.
8. let's

Write the **list words** that show ownership.
9. desert's   10. person's
11. sister's   12. bicycle's
13. Arizona's   14. child's
15. aunt's   16. cousin's
17. Florida's   18. uncle's
19. doctor's   20. season's

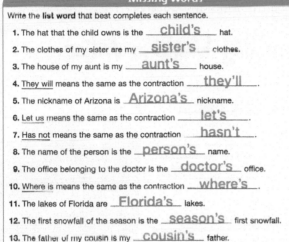

Missing Words

Write the **list word** that best completes each sentence.

1. The hat that the child owns is the __child's__ hat.
2. The clothes of my sister are my __sister's__ clothes.
3. The house of my aunt is my __aunt's__ house.
4. They will means the same as the contraction __they'll__.
5. The nickname of Arizona is __Arizona's__ nickname.
6. Let us means the same as the contraction __let's__.
7. Has not means the same as the contraction __hasn't__.
8. The name of the person is the __person's__ name.
9. The office belonging to the doctor is the __doctor's__ office.
10. Where is means the same as the contraction __where's__.
11. The lakes of Florida are __Florida's__ lakes.
12. The first snowfall of the season is the __season's__ first snowfall.
13. The father of my cousin is my __cousin's__ father.

Puzzle

Fill in the crossword puzzle by writing a **list word** to answer each clue. The apostrophes have been filled in for you.

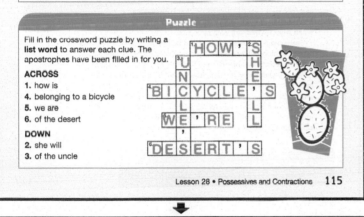

ACROSS
1. how is
4. belonging to a bicycle
5. we are
6. of the desert

DOWN
2. she will
3. of the uncle

Spelling and Writing

Proofreading

This article has eleven mistakes. Use the proofreading marks to fix each mistake. Then, write the **list words** correctly on the lines.

Proofreading Marks
- ⌄ add apostrophe
- ⌃ add something
- ≡ capital letter

Wouldnt you know it, arizona was a big surprise! I went to visit my cousins ranch near flagstaff. I asked, "Wheres the desert?" He said, "Below us. Flagstaff is too high for a desert climate. We're in forests where each seasons weather is different." What a beautiful place! It should be on every persons list of places to go. some people like Florida's palm trees. I, however, like Arizonas pine trees.

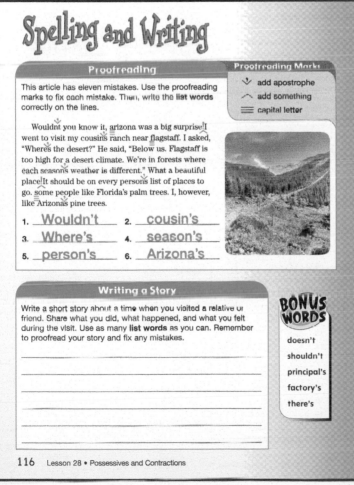

1. __Wouldn't__   2. __cousin's__
3. __Where's__   4. __season's__
5. __person's__   6. __Arizona's__

Writing a Story

Write a short story about a time when you visited a relative or friend. Share what you did, what happened, and what you felt during the visit. Use as many **list words** as you can. Remember to proofread your story and fix any mistakes.

_____
_____
_____
_____
_____
_____

BONUS WORDS

doesn't

shouldn't

principal's

factory's

there's

Spelling Strategy

To help students understand that every contraction is a short way of writing two words, invite them to get together with a partner and
- listen carefully as you say each **list word** that is a contraction
- write the two words that form the contraction
- circle the letter or letters that are left out when the contraction is formed
- write the contraction.

BONUS WORDS
Have students write a sentence for each **bonus word** but leave out the apostrophe. Partners can trade papers and add the apostrophes to the words.

Spelling and Writing   **Page 116**

The **Proofreading** exercise will help students prepare to proofread their stories. As students complete the writing activity, encourage them to brainstorm ideas, write a first draft, revise, and proofread their work. To publish their writing, students may want to
- use their stories to create a class newsletter
- perform their stories as reader's theater.

Writer's Corner Encourage students to learn more about the culture of Native Americans such as the Pueblo, the Sioux, the Nez Perce, or the Navaho. Suggest they do their research at the local or school library or on the Internet. Have them write a report to share with their classmates.

Final Test

1. I know **they'll** be very happy to see you.
2. The **doctor's** waiting room was almost empty.
3. I couldn't remember a single **person's** name.
4. Do you like this **season's** fashions?
5. When Misako sees you, **she'll** remember you.
6. Is there a leak in your **bicycle's** rear tire?
7. **Let's** all split a giant pizza!
8. The weather **hasn't** been too bad this winter.
9. **Where's** the new pool going to be built?
10. Many people enjoy **Arizona's** dry climate.
11. I **wouldn't** do that if I were you!
12. My **aunt's** husband was born in Saigon.
13. My **uncle's** hobby is fixing up old cars.
14. **How's** your family's puppy doing?
15. The **desert's** temperature drops at night.
16. My **cousin's** cat is named Mittens.
17. I think **we're** taking a bus that comes later.
18. I used my **sister's** desk when she outgrew it.
19. **Florida's** everglades teem with wildlife.
20. Is that a **child's** sleeping bag or an adult's?

Objective
To spell plural possessive nouns

Correlated Phonics Lessons
MCP Phonics, Level D, Lessons 59–60

Spelling Words in Action Page 117

In this selection, students learn about a sturdy fabric that has been popular for more than a century. After reading, invite students to discuss whether they think people will be wearing denim a hundred years from now.

Encourage students to look back at the boldfaced words. Have volunteers say each word and explain how the possessive is formed.

Warm-Up Test
1. All the **passengers'** tickets were stamped.
2. Both **armies'** supplies are running out.
3. The flood swept away two **families'** homes!
4. The police discovered the two **thieves'** loot.
5. All the **ranches'** workers went to the picnic.
6. Some **benches'** slats were broken.
7. Do you know the two **umpires'** names?
8. Most **airlines'** planes have smoke detectors.
9. Both **dresses'** hemlines were too short.
10. The **hostesses'** uniforms were red and gray.
11. Do both **banjos'** strings have to be replaced?
12. The upright **pianos'** keys need cleaning.
13. Mr. Allen joined a **men's** touch football game.
14. I bought a gift in the **children's** department.
15. Are the **bodies'** shapes similar in both cars?
16. The **daisies'** stems are quite strong.
17. The **televisions'** screens are the same size.
18. The **members'** cars are parked in the big lot.
19. Did the **governments'** leaders speak openly?
20. All the **businesses'** reports are being mailed.

Spelling Practice Pages 118–119

Introduce the spelling rule and have students read the **list words** aloud. Encourage students to look back at their **Warm-Up Tests** and apply the spelling rule to any misspelled words.

As students work through the **Spelling Practice** exercises, remind them to look back at their **list words** or in their dictionaries if they need help.

for ESL students See Word in Context, page 14

Spelling Words in Action

What fabric never goes out of style?

Durable Denim

There is a kind of fabric that never goes out of style. Almost everyone has worn it at least once. Some people wear it every day. It's denim. This sturdy cloth has been meeting **families'** clothing needs for more than a hundred years. Every family **members'** clothing can be made from it.

In 1873, Levi Strauss and Jacob Davis patented the process of using rivets in making **men's** work clothes. Strauss used denim for the fabric because it was durable, comfortable, and looked good, and then he added rivets to the pockets and other stress points. This kept the pants from ripping when worn by workers such as miners.

Jeans today are often made of denim. Denim is used not only for men's clothing, but women's and **children's** clothing as well. In fact, denim is a cloth that can be used to make almost anything. It can be used for **passengers'** luggage, **hostesses'** uniforms, **umpires'** caps, and children's shoes. **Dresses'** styles have been based on the popularity of denim. Even **governments'** highest leaders have been seen wearing this common fabric. Despite the passage of over a hundred years, denim is also still the center of Levi Strauss's **businesses'** success.

Look back at the boldfaced words. Notice that all the words are plural. How is the possessive of each word formed?

117

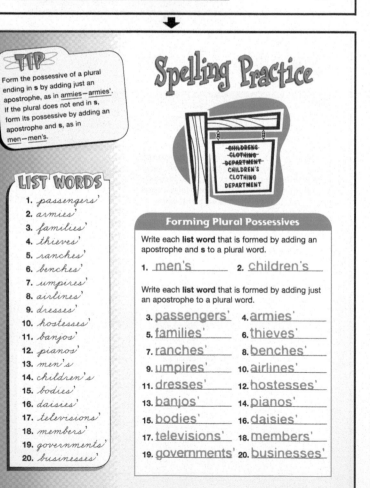

TIP
Form the possessive of a plural ending in **s** by adding just an apostrophe, as in <u>armies—armies'</u>. If the plural does not end in **s**, form its possessive by adding an apostrophe and **s**, as in <u>men—men's</u>.

Spelling Practice

LIST WORDS
1. passengers'
2. armies'
3. families'
4. thieves'
5. ranches'
6. benches'
7. umpires'
8. airlines'
9. dresses'
10. hostesses'
11. banjos'
12. pianos'
13. men's
14. children's
15. bodies'
16. daisies'
17. televisions'
18. members'
19. governments'
20. businesses'

CHILDRENS CLOTHING DEPARTMENT
CHILDREN'S CLOTHING DEPARTMENT

Forming Plural Possessives

Write each **list word** that is formed by adding an apostrophe and **s** to a plural word.

1. men's   2. children's

Write each **list word** that is formed by adding just an apostrophe to a plural word.

3. passengers'   4. armies'
5. families'   6. thieves'
7. ranches'   8. benches'
9. umpires'   10. airlines'
11. dresses'   12. hostesses'
13. banjos'   14. pianos'
15. bodies'   16. daisies'
17. televisions'   18. members'
19. governments'   20. businesses'

Possessives

The **list word** in each sentence needs an apostrophe. Circle the **list word**, and then write it correctly on the line.

1. All of the passengers meals were served hot. _passengers'_
2. Both umpires decisions are final. _umpires'_
3. Both businesses workers put in long hours. _businesses'_
4. The 50 members dues are paid every March. _members'_
5. The thieves names were in the newspaper. _thieves'_
6. The daisies petals were yellow and white. _daisies'_
7. All the benches seats had good cushions. _benches'_
8. The two ranches cattle roam the open fields. _ranches'_
9. The four hostesses uniforms are exactly alike. _hostesses'_
10. Our families homes are next to each other. _families'_

Word Search

Ten **list words** are hidden in the puzzle, but the apostrophes are missing. The words go across, up, down, backward, and diagonally. Circle each word. Then, write the words with apostrophes to show their plural possessives.

1. airlines'
2. armies'
3. banjos'
4. bodies'
5. children's
6. dresses'
7. governments'
8. men's
9. pianos'
10. televisions'

```
S O J N A B O T
T A S C U O E E
N E E H I D P L
E A S I S I I E
M I S L B E A V
N R E D O S N I
R L R R Q R O S
E I D E M A S I
V N A N U E T O
O E P S O M N N
G S A R M I E S
```

Lesson 29 • Plural Possessives   119

Spelling and Writing

Proofreading

Find the twelve mistakes in the article below. Use the proofreading marks to fix each mistake. Then, write the **list words** correctly on the lines.

Proofreading Marks

- ⌄ add apostrophe
- ⌃ add something
- / make small letter

Thousands of years ago, Only the Chinese knew that silkworms spin the silk threads needed for making silk fabric. For a long time, government members efforts to guard this secret worked. When other Countries discovered the wonderful cloth, they wanted to make it themselves. Some travelers discovered how to sneak Silkworms out of China. The thieves idea was to carry the creatures out in the hollows of bamboo canes. The idea worked! Soon, other countries could Make silk fabric and produce mens, women's, and childrens clothing. Many families wardrobes could now include this fabric.

1. members'
2. thieves'
3. men's
4. children's
5. families'

Writing an Advertisement

Imagine you are having a fashion show to exhibit the latest casual clothing. Write an ad telling people what you're showing. Use as many **list words** as you can. Remember to proofread your ad and fix any mistakes.

_____
_____
_____
_____

BONUS WORDS

diaries'
fish's
classes'
spies'
species'

120   Lesson 29 • Plural Possessives

Spelling Strategy

Write this sentence on the board, leaving out the apostrophes: *The hostesses speeches were interrupted by the mens songs.* Say the sentence aloud, circling the plurals as you do so. Then, ask the class to use context to determine which of the plurals are plural possessives (*hostesses, mens*).

Call on a volunteer to rewrite the sentence, adding the apostrophes. Ask students to think of other sentences that contain **list words** and to write them on the board.

BONUS WORDS Have students work with partners to write a short story, leaving blanks in place of the **bonus words**. Let partners trade stories with other partners and write in the correct **bonus words**.

Spelling and Writing   Page 120

The **Proofreading** exercise will help students prepare to proofread their ads. As students complete the writing activity, encourage them to brainstorm ideas, write a first draft, revise, and proofread their work. To publish their writing, students may want to

- illustrate their ads
- use their ads to role-play a fashion show.

Writer's Corner Students can learn more about denim clothing, the history of the Levi Strauss Company, and the Strauss family at www.levistrauss.com. Urge students to jot notes on interesting information to share with the class.

Final Test

1. The **bodies'** temperatures were measured.
2. Many **daisies'** colors are yellow and white.
3. Are the **hostesses'** names on the schedule?
4. The **passengers'** seats had pillows on them.
5. The **businesses'** addresses are downtown.
6. Both **armies'** doctors worked day and night.
7. The two **banjos'** tuning pegs are the same.
8. Both **televisions'** antennas can be rotated.
9. All the **families'** homes are in the same village.
10. Both **pianos'** lids have been lowered.
11. Most **members'** names are in the guest book.
12. The police found the **thieves'** hiding places.
13. The **governments'** investigation was long.
14. All the **ranches'** cattle brands are different.
15. The **men's** voices are much too loud!
16. Were the **children's** permission slips signed?
17. Four **benches'** backs have to be repaired.
18. Did you compare the three **airlines'** prices?
19. Those **dresses'** colors are the most popular.
20. All the **umpires'** uniforms are black.

Objectives
To review spelling words that are plurals; plurals of words that end in *y*; irregular plurals; plurals of words that end in *f* or *fe*; possessives and contractions; plural possessives

Check Your Spelling Notebook   *Pages 121–124*
Based on students' lists and your observations, note which words are giving students the most difficulty and offer assistance for spelling them correctly. Here are some frequently misspelled words to watch for: *sandwiches, communities, libraries, groceries, halves, buffaloes, handkerchiefs, chiefs,* and *children's.*

To give students extra help and practice in taking standardized tests, you may want to have them take the **Review Test** for this lesson on pages 94–95. After scoring the tests, return them to students so that they can record their misspelled words in their spelling notebooks.

After practicing their troublesome words, students can work through the exercises for Lessons 25–29. Before students begin each exercise, you may want to go over the spelling rule.

Take It Home
Suggest that students and their families create a crossword puzzle using **list words** from Lessons 25–29. Students can use **Take It Home** Master 5 on pages 96–97 to help them do the activity. (A complete list of the spelling words is included on page 96 of the **Take It Home** Master.) Encourage students to bring in their puzzles to share with the whole class.

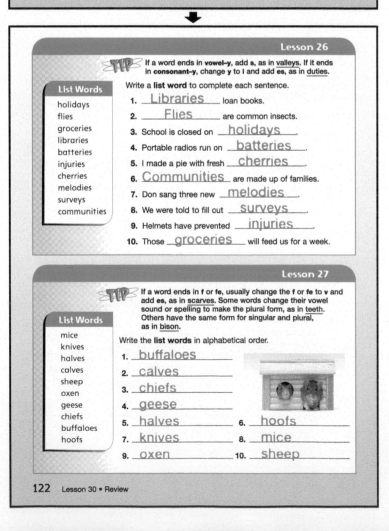

In lessons 25 through 29, you have learned how to spell plural words, irregular plurals, contractions, and possessives.

Check Your Spelling Notebook

Look at the words in your spelling notebook. Which words for lessons 25 through 29 did you have the most trouble with? Write them here.

_____

Practice writing your troublesome words with a partner. Form the letters of each word using clay. Your partner can spell the word aloud as you form the letters.

Lesson 25

TIP — Most plurals are formed by adding **s** to the singular form, as in <u>chains</u>. If a word ends in **x**, **ss**, **sh**, or **ch**, add **es** to form the plural, as in <u>foxes</u> and <u>bosses</u>.

List Words
axes
waxes
matches
sandwiches
eyelashes
sashes
ditches
flashes
churches
paces

Write a **list word** to match each definition.

1. bright bursts of light — flashes
2. cloths worn at waists — sashes
3. sticks to light a fire — matches
4. hairs on eyelids — eyelashes
5. tools to chop wood — axes
6. holes in the ground — ditches
7. meals between bread — sandwiches
8. makes surfaces shiny — waxes
9. places of worship — churches
10. steps taken — paces

121

Lesson 26

TIP — If a word ends in **vowel-y**, add **s**, as in <u>valleys</u>. If it ends in **consonant-y**, change **y** to **i** and add **es**, as in <u>duties</u>.

List Words
holidays
flies
groceries
libraries
batteries
injuries
cherries
melodies
surveys
communities

Write a **list word** to complete each sentence.

1. Libraries loan books.
2. Flies are common insects.
3. School is closed on holidays.
4. Portable radios run on batteries.
5. I made a pie with fresh cherries.
6. Communities are made up of families.
7. Don sang three new melodies.
8. We were told to fill out surveys.
9. Helmets have prevented injuries.
10. Those groceries will feed us for a week.

Lesson 27

TIP — If a word ends in **f** or **fe**, usually change the **f** or **fe** to **v** and add **es**, as in <u>scarves</u>. Some words change their vowel sound or spelling to make the plural form, as in <u>teeth</u>. Others have the same form for singular and plural, as in <u>bison</u>.

List Words
mice
knives
halves
calves
sheep
oxen
geese
chiefs
buffaloes
hoofs

Write the **list words** in alphabetical order.

1. buffaloes
2. calves
3. chiefs
4. geese
5. halves   6. hoofs
7. knives   8. mice
9. oxen   10. sheep

TIP Use apostrophes in contractions, as in where's and wouldn't. Singular possessives and those made from irregular plurals take 's, as in sister's and child's.

List Words

she'll
they'll
we're
bicycle's
Arizona's
cousin's
Florida's
uncle's
doctor's
hasn't

Write the **list word** that is part of each word given.

1. has — hasn't
2. Arizona — Arizona's
3. bicycle — bicycle's
4. cousin — cousin's
5. she — she'll
6. Florida — Florida's
7. we — we're
8. uncle — uncle's
9. doctor — doctor's
10. they — they'll

TIP Form the possessive of a plural word that ends in s by adding an apostrophe, as in dresses'. Plural words that do not end in s add 's, as in women's.

List Words

passengers'
families'
umpires'
airlines'
hostesses'
banjos'
men's
children's
members'
businesses'

Circle the correct form of the **list word** in each group. Then, write the **list word** on the line.

1. banjose' (banjos') — banjos'
2. (businesses') businesses's — businesses'
3. mens' (men's) — men's
4. hostesse's (hostesses') — hostesses'
5. umpires's (umpires') — umpires'
6. (members') members's — members'
7. (children's) childrens' — children's
8. families's (families') — families'
9. (passengers') passengers's — passengers'
10. (airlines') airlineses' — airlines'

Show What You Know

Lessons 25–29 • Review

One word is misspelled in each set of **list words**. Fill in the circle next to the **list word** that is spelled incorrectly.

1. ○ pianos' ● surveyes ○ desert's ○ sheep ○ paces
2. ○ kisses ○ uncle's ● banjoes' ○ loaves ○ hobbies
3. ○ hasn't ○ mice ○ shoes ○ ladies ● goverments'
4. ○ eyelashes ○ benches' ○ flies ● wheres ○ yourselves
5. ○ lives ○ how's ● storys ○ foxes ○ children's
6. ○ clashes ● valleyes ○ child's ○ men's ○ handkerchiefs
7. ● buffalos ○ dresses' ○ Florida's ○ ashes ○ highways
8. ○ churches ● librarys ○ oxen ○ sister's ○ armies'
9. ○ aunt's ○ waxes ● dutys ○ geese ○ businesses'
10. ○ bicycle's ○ batteries ○ chiefs ● daisys' ○ toothbrushes
11. ○ axes ○ teeth ○ we're ● chaines ○ passengers'
12. ○ leaves ○ copies ○ airlines' ○ person's ● birthdaies
13. ○ matches ○ parties ○ women ● theyll ○ televisions'
14. ○ Arizona's ○ bosses ● injurys ○ moose ○ hostesses'
15. ○ bodies' ○ ditches ● scarfes ○ she'll ○ melodies
16. ○ let's ○ counties ○ hoofs ● thiefs' ○ sandwiches
17. ● wouldnt ○ sashes ○ umpires' ○ halves ○ communities
18. ○ flashes ○ season's ● ranchs' ○ bison ○ groceries
19. ○ members' ○ crashes ● calfs ○ doctor's ○ holidays
20. ○ splashes ○ cousin's ● cherrys ○ knives ○ families'

Final Test

1. The **passengers'** tickets were collected.
2. The club built a parking lot for **members'** cars.
3. Kayla wrote a **children's** tale about a dragon.
4. My **cousin's** name is Tiffany.
5. **Arizona's** climate is hot and dry.
6. Jim **hasn't** finished cutting the grass.
7. My cat loves to play with catnip **mice**.
8. Are **buffaloes** still found in the Midwest?
9. What incredibly strong creatures **oxen** are!
10. Did he receive any **injuries** in the crash?
11. **Surveys** give facts about people's opinions.
12. Several **communities** have soccer teams.
13. Will you visit your aunt during the **holidays**?
14. I need to buy new **batteries** for my flashlight.
15. Sharp **axes** are very dangerous!
16. Some **churches** have stained-glass windows.
17. They walked twenty **paces** behind the queen.
18. The girls' dresses had bright pink **sashes**.
19. Put the **matches** in a box so they stay dry.
20. The little horse has long black **eyelashes**.
21. **Flies** buzzed against the window screen.
22. Ian washed the **cherries** before eating them.
23. At some colleges, **libraries** stay open all night.
24. A flock of wild **geese** flew over the meadow.
25. The **chiefs** of all the tribes held a conference.
26. Female **sheep** are called ewes.
27. **We're** having the dress rehearsal for our play.
28. My **uncle's** best friend is a famous author.
29. The **bicycle's** rear tire is flat.
30. Are the **banjos'** cases in the music room?
31. Many **businesses'** booths give out free samples.
32. The **airlines'** ticket prices are about the same.
33. The **hostesses'** name tags are readable.
34. The **men's** soccer team left for the Olympics.
35. **Florida's** resorts are famous the world over.
36. **She'll** be coming home for good soon.
37. Please rinse the **knives** and put them away.
38. The **calves** have soft brown coats.
39. We passed the time humming old **melodies**.
40. I carried the bags of **groceries** into the house.
41. The farmer dug irrigation **ditches** in the field.
42. **Flashes** of lightning lit up the night sky.
43. These **waxes** will restore the floor's shine.
44. Fold your paper into two equal **halves**.
45. Do you hear the clatter of horses' **hoofs**?
46. The boys said that **they'll** wash the dishes.
47. I decided to make a **doctor's** appointment.
48. Did you agree with the **umpires'** decisions?
49. The **families'** requests were read aloud.
50. Denise will serve **sandwiches** at her party.

Name _____

Review Test (Side A)

Read each set of phrases. Fill in the circle next to the phrase with an underlined word that is spelled correctly.

1. ⓐ forty paises more   ⓒ thirty pases away
   ⓑ three paces behind   ⓓ two paisses behind

2. ⓐ the school libarries   ⓒ the libaries in town
   ⓑ the city's liberries   ⓓ Internet libraries

3. ⓐ the deer's hoofs   ⓒ the horse's hoovs
   ⓑ the hard hoofes   ⓓ marks from the houfs

4. ⓐ the sharp axxes   ⓒ four axes
   ⓑ both ackses   ⓓ the dull axkes

5. ⓐ two halfs   ⓒ four halfes are not enough
   ⓑ one of the halvs   ⓓ the two halves of the garden

6. ⓐ four grown oxses   ⓒ black and white oxin
   ⓑ the brown oxen   ⓓ twin oxes

7. ⓐ two surveyes   ⓒ doctors' surveiys
   ⓑ results of survays   ⓓ companies' surveys

8. ⓐ both banjos' cases   ⓒ three banjoe's sound
   ⓑ two banjo's strings   ⓓ all the banjoes' rhythm

9. ⓐ these childrn's toys   ⓒ the children's food
   ⓑ those childrin's shoes   ⓓ the childrens' concerns

10. ⓐ hasn't slept   ⓒ haz'nt finished
    ⓑ has'nt rained   ⓓ hazn't eaten

Review Test (Side B)

Lesson 30

Read each set of phrases. Fill in the circle next to the phrase with an underlined word that is spelled correctly.

11. ⓐ that unckle's watch ⓒ this unkles' son
    ⓑ your uncle's shirt ⓓ my uncles' wife

12. ⓐ some familey's children ⓒ many familie's schedules
    ⓑ two families' businesses ⓓ three familys' apartments

13. ⓐ five more injeries ⓒ with minor injurys
    ⓑ had enough injuris ⓓ too many injuries

14. ⓐ my bicycle's wheels ⓒ his bycicles' handlebars
    ⓑ the bicycle'es seat ⓓ her bycicle's basket

15. ⓐ steeples of cherches ⓒ bells of churchs
    ⓑ beautiful churches ⓓ historic cherchs

16. ⓐ her doktors' results ⓒ the doktor's assistant
    ⓑ one doctor's equipment ⓓ his doctors office

17. ⓐ those menn's voices ⓒ three mens apartments
    ⓑ the mens' department ⓓ the men's locker room

18. ⓐ a few communities ⓒ several comunities
    ⓑ wealthy communitys ⓓ large communeties

19. ⓐ herds of bufaloes ⓒ the prairie buffallos
    ⓑ pictures of buffaloes ⓓ tracks of bufaloes

20. ⓐ tasty sandwhiches ⓒ ham sandwichs
    ⓑ grilled cheese sandwitches ⓓ crusts of sandwiches

Take It Home
5

Your child has learned to spell many new words and would enjoy sharing them with you and your family. You'll find some great ideas on these pages for helping your child review the words in Lessons 25–29.

Across and Down

Help your child create a crossword puzzle.

- Using graph paper, lightly pencil in some spelling words.
- On other paper, write definitions for the words, indicating which are Across and which are Down.
- Number each word and its definition, then erase the words on the grid.
- Invite everyone to complete the puzzle!

Lesson 25

1. ashes	12. kisses
2. axes	13. matches
3. bosses	14. paces
4. chains	15. sandwiches
5. churches	16. sashes
6. clashes	17. shoes
7. crashes	18. splashes
8. ditches	19. toothbrushes
9. eyelashes	20. waxes
10. flashes	
11. foxes	

Lesson 26

1. batteries	12. holidays
2. birthdays	13. injuries
3. cherries	14. ladies
4. communities	15. libraries
5. copies	16. melodies
6. counties	17. parties
7. duties	18. stories
8. flies	19. surveys
9. groceries	20. valleys
10. highways	
11. hobbies	

Lesson 27

1. bison	12. loaves
2. buffaloes	13. mice
3. calves	14. moose
4. chiefs	15. oxen
5. geese	16. scarves
6. halves	17. sheep
7. handkerchiefs	18. teeth
8. hoofs	19. women
9. knives	20. yourselves
10. leaves	
11. lives	

Lesson 28

1. Arizona's	12. person's
2. aunt's	13. season's
3. bicycle's	14. she'll
4. child's	15. sister's
5. cousin's	16. they'll
6. desert's	17. uncle's
7. doctor's	18. we're
8. Florida's	19. where's
9. hasn't	20. wouldn't
10. how's	
11. let's	

Lesson 29

1. airlines'	12. hostesses'
2. armies'	13. members'
3. banjos'	14. men's
4. benches'	15. passengers'
5. bodies'	16. pianos'
6. businesses'	17. ranches'
7. children's	18. televisions'
8. daisies'	19. thieves'
9. dresses'	20. umpires'
10. families'	
11. governments'	

Silly Story Titles

With your child, make up silly story titles using as many spelling words as you can. Write the titles on the blank book spines below.

Objective

To spell words with the prefixes *pre*, *re*, *im*, *non*, and *con*

Phonics Correlated Phonics Lessons
MCP Phonics, Level D, Lessons 65–69

Spelling Words in Action   Page 125

In this selection, students learn it is possible to build a community playground. After reading, suggest that students brainstorm ways they might build a playground in their community.

Ask volunteers to say each boldfaced word and identify its prefix.

Warm-Up Test

1. This **nonsense** must stop immediately!
2. She **prepaid** her airplane ticket.
3. The copilot took **control** of the plane.
4. Javier **returned** his library books on time.
5. Did their plan turn out to be **impractical**?
6. Seth took a **nonstop** flight across the country.
7. In science class, we **conduct** experiments.
8. Solomon saw a **preview** of the new movie.
9. Your book **report** is due next week.
10. The **imperfect** diamond has many cracks.
11. The **nonprofit** organization rescues animals.
12. I need to buy some **refills** for my pen.
13. Who knows how to **construct** a doghouse?
14. The heavy piano seemed totally **immovable**.
15. Fasten your seat belt as a **precaution**.
16. I **predict** that you will be very successful.
17. I tried to **convince** Megan to stay for dinner.
18. This formal business letter is too **impersonal**.
19. Is our city's air considered **impure**?
20. Dad had a bad **reaction** to the bee sting.

Spelling Practice   Pages 126–127

Introduce the spelling rule and have students read the **list words** aloud, helping them understand the meanings of the prefixes, the roots or the base words, and then the complete words. Encourage students to look back at their **Warm-Up Tests** and apply the spelling rule to any misspelled words.

As students work through the **Spelling Practice** exercises, remind them to look back at their **list words** or in their dictionaries if they need help.

for ESL students **See Spelling Aloud, page 14**

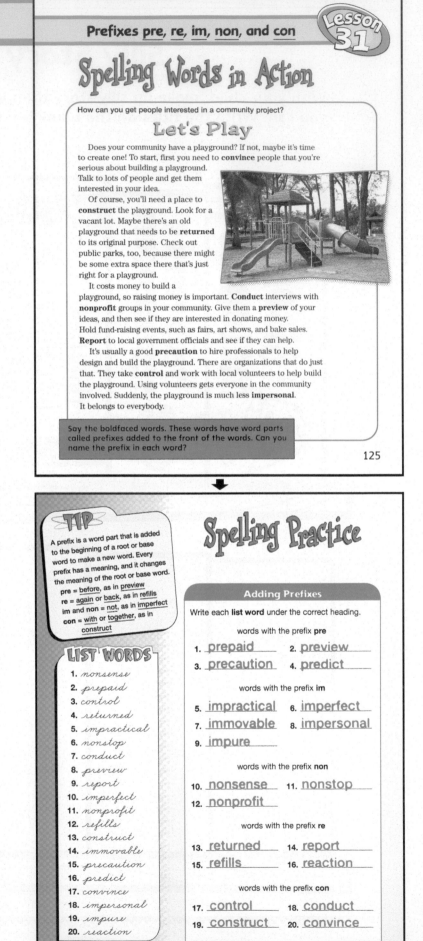

Spelling Words in Action

How can you get people interested in a community project?

Let's Play

Does your community have a playground? If not, maybe it's time to create one! To start, first you need to **convince** people that you're serious about building a playground. Talk to lots of people and get them interested in your idea.

Of course, you'll need a place to **construct** the playground. Look for a vacant lot. Maybe there's an old playground that needs to be **returned** to its original purpose. Check out public parks, too, because there might be some extra space there that's just right for a playground.

It costs money to build a playground, so raising money is important. **Conduct** interviews with **nonprofit** groups in your community. Give them a **preview** of your ideas, and then see if they are interested in donating money. Hold fund-raising events, such as fairs, art shows, and bake sales. **Report** to local government officials and see if they can help.

It's usually a good **precaution** to hire professionals to help design and build the playground. There are organizations that do just that. They take **control** and work with local volunteers to help build the playground. Using volunteers gets everyone in the community involved. Suddenly, the playground is much less **impersonal**. It belongs to everybody.

Say the boldfaced words. These words have word parts called prefixes added to the front of the words. Can you name the prefix in each word?

125

TIP

A prefix is a word part that is added to the beginning of a root or base word to make a new word. Every prefix has a meaning, and it changes the meaning of the root or base word.
pre = before, as in preview
re = again or back, as in refills
im and non = not, as in imperfect
con = with or together, as in construct

Spelling Practice

LIST WORDS

1. *nonsense*
2. *prepaid*
3. *control*
4. *returned*
5. *impractical*
6. *nonstop*
7. *conduct*
8. *preview*
9. *report*
10. *imperfect*
11. *nonprofit*
12. *refills*
13. *construct*
14. *immovable*
15. *precaution*
16. *predict*
17. *convince*
18. *impersonal*
19. *impure*
20. *reaction*

Adding Prefixes

Write each **list word** under the correct heading.

words with the prefix **pre**

1. prepaid   2. preview
3. precaution   4. predict

words with the prefix **im**

5. impractical   6. imperfect
7. immovable   8. impersonal
9. impure

words with the prefix **non**

10. nonsense   11. nonstop
12. nonprofit

words with the prefix **re**

13. returned   14. report
15. refills   16. reaction

words with the prefix **con**

17. control   18. conduct
19. construct   20. convince

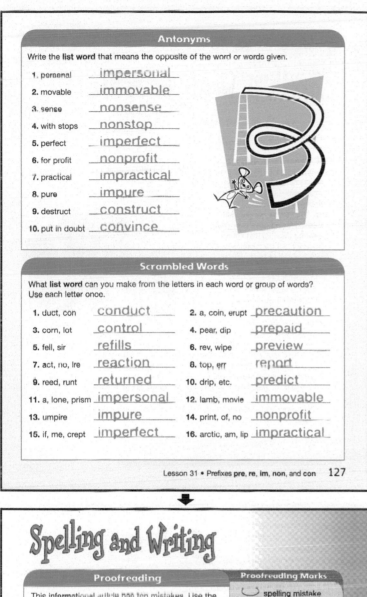

Antonyms

Write the **list word** that means the opposite of the word or words given.

1. personal   impersonal
2. movable   immovable
3. sense   nonsense
4. with stops   nonstop
5. perfect   imperfect
6. for profit   nonprofit
7. practical   impractical
8. pure   impure
9. destruct   construct
10. put in doubt   convince

Scrambled Words

What **list word** can you make from the letters in each word or group of words? Use each letter once.

1. duct, con   conduct
2. a, coin, erupt   precaution
3. corn, lot   control
4. pear, dip   prepaid
5. fell, sir   refills
6. rev, wipe   preview
7. act, no, lre   reaction
8. top, err   report
9. reed, runt   returned
10. drip, etc.   predict
11. a, lone, prism   impersonal
12. lamb, movie   immovable
13. umpire   impure
14. print, of, no   nonprofit
15. if, me, crept   imperfect
16. arctic, am, lip   impractical

Lesson 31 • Prefixes **pre, re, im, non,** and **con**   127

Spelling and Writing

Proofreading

This informational article has ten mistakes. Use the proofreading marks to fix each mistake. Then, write the misspelled **list words** correctly on the lines.

Proofreading Marks
- ⌒ spelling mistake
- ℮ take out something
- ⊙ add period

Over a hundred years ago, the the idea of a playground would have been nonsense. Children played in yards, vacant lots, or in the streets. By the 1900s, however, it was easier to convinse people that there was a need for playgrounds For one thing, playing in in the streets was becoming dangerous and impracticle due to the nonstop traffic. By 1899, the city of Boston had built a number of sandlots for small children to play in. Soon, other cities followed Boston's example. Simple sandlots gave way to a more elaborate playgrounds. Today, many cities and towns construkt community playgrounds for everyone to enjoy.

1. nonsense   2. convince
3. impractical   4. nonstop
5. construct

Writing a News Story

Imagine that your community has just opened a new community playground. Write a news story about the event. Try to use as many **list words** as you can. Remember to proofread your story and fix any mistakes.

_____

_____

_____

BONUS WORDS
- nonfiction
- contact
- preset
- recount
- impatient

128   Lesson 31 • Prefixes **pre, re, im, non,** and **con**

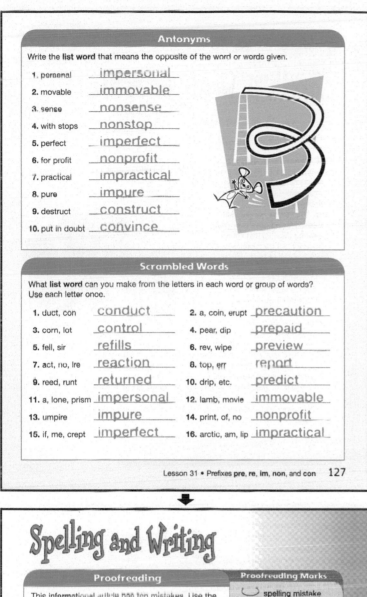

Spelling Strategy

Invite students to work with a partner to practice spelling the **list words**. One partner writes the first ten words in the **list words** box; the other partner writes the remaining words. Then, have partners trade papers and circle the prefixes in each other's words. Encourage students to get together with another set of partners to compare their work.

BONUS WORDS   Have students write a sentence for each **bonus word**, and then trade sentences with partners. Ask students to circle the prefixes in the **bonus words**.

Spelling and Writing   Page 128

The **Proofreading** exercise will help students prepare to proofread their news stories. As students complete the writing activity, encourage them to brainstorm ideas, write a first draft, revise, and proofread their work. To publish their writing, students may want to

- read their news stories as TV broadcasts
- use their stories to create a news journal.

Writer's Corner To learn more about building playgrounds, groups of students can interview the school principal or town mayor to find out how playgrounds in your area were constructed. Before the interview, you may want to brainstorm questions with students.

Final Test

1. As a **precaution**, drive slowly on icy roads.
2. How can we treat this **impure** water?
3. Manuel Ramirez will **conduct** the band tonight.
4. I donated money to a **nonprofit** organization.
5. That horse is galloping out of **control**!
6. We will **preview** the show before its opening.
7. The gardener **refills** the pot with fresh soil.
8. She **returned** from her trip at the end of June.
9. What was his **reaction** when he saw the gift?
10. We **predict** that Liz will finish the race first.
11. Her **report** said that the animals were safe.
12. Tai tried to **convince** me that I wasn't tired.
13. It is **nonsense** to want an elephant as a pet.
14. What silly, **impractical** ideas that inventor has!
15. Let's **construct** a cage for our pet rabbit.
16. He has a cold, **impersonal** way about him.
17. I have an **imperfect** knowledge of Spanish.
18. Roberto found the huge rock **immovable**.
19. Is your subscription to the magazine **prepaid**?
20. We flew **nonstop** from Boston to Paris.

99

Prefixes ex, de, dis, un, and ad

Objective
To spell words with the prefixes ex, de, dis, un, and ad

Phonics Correlated Phonics Lessons
MCP Phonics, Level D, Lessons 65, 67

Spelling Words in Action   Page 129

Students may never catch a cold again after reading "Don't Catch It!" Ask students what information they found interesting and useful.

Encourage students to look back at the boldfaced words. Ask volunteers to say the words and identify the prefixes.

Warm-Up Test

1. Poets use images to **express** their thoughts.
2. Chen will **design** the set for the school play.
3. This part of town is **unknown** to me.
4. It is often difficult to **admit** you are wrong.
5. Is any part of my explanation **unclear**?
6. Columbus was sent to **explore** distant islands.
7. Do you **disagree** with what she just said?
8. I will **defend** your right to offer an opinion.
9. Many of the story characters seem **unreal**.
10. Jose and Bob went on a grand **adventure**.
11. It's **unwise** to go without a coat on a cold day.
12. Will the detective **disclose** details of the case?
13. What good **advice** your aunt gave!
14. Mr. Patel will **excuse** us when the bell rings.
15. I was **disinterested**, but Ana was excited.
16. You cannot trust a **dishonest** person.
17. I was **unprepared** for the difficult hike.
18. The spoiled food had an **unpleasant** smell.
19. We bought our tickets well in **advance**.
20. Is this word an adjective or an **adverb**?

Spelling Practice   Pages 130–131

Introduce the spelling rule and invite students to read the **list words** aloud, discussing the meanings of the prefixes, roots or base words, and complete words. Then, encourage students to look back at their **Warm-Up Tests** and apply the spelling rule to any misspelled words.

As students work through the **Spelling Practice** exercises, remind them to look back at their **list words** or in their dictionaries if they need help. Point out that *excuse* has two pronunciations, depending on which part of speech it is.

for ESL students **See Questions / Answers, page 15**

Spelling Words in Action

How can you avoid catching a cold?

Don't Catch It!

With all the advances in medicine, doctors **admit** that they still haven't found a cure for the common cold. This **unpleasant** illness affects more people than any other disease. Each year, North Americans spend over a billion dollars to battle colds. There are ways people can **defend** themselves, though. Those who **explore** these options know in **advance** that the common cold will likely never be completely avoided.

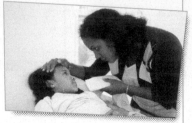

Colds are not caused by going out in the rain or getting chilled. Although many will **disagree**, people rarely catch colds just by being near someone who is sneezing or coughing. Cold viruses almost always travel from the nose of an infected person to his or her hands. From there, they go to anything the person touches. If someone else touches the same object and then touches his or her nose or eyes, the virus can infect that person.

Here's some good **advice** so you won't be **unprepared**. Wash your hands often, and try not to touch your face. It's also **unwise** to touch things people with colds have touched. The common cold will never be **unknown**. With your help, it could become a little less common!

Take a look at the boldfaced words in the selection. What prefixes do you find?

129

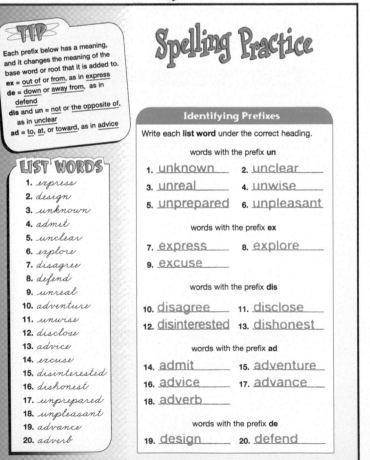

TIP

Each prefix below has a meaning, and it changes the meaning of the base word or root that it is added to.
ex = out of or from, as in express
de = down or away from, as in defend
dis and **un** = not or the opposite of, as in unclear
ad = to, at, or toward, as in advice

Spelling Practice

LIST WORDS

1. express
2. design
3. unknown
4. admit
5. unclear
6. explore
7. disagree
8. defend
9. unreal
10. adventure
11. unwise
12. disclose
13. advice
14. excuse
15. disinterested
16. dishonest
17. unprepared
18. unpleasant
19. advance
20. adverb

Identifying Prefixes

Write each **list word** under the correct heading.

words with the prefix **un**
1. unknown   2. unclear
3. unreal   4. unwise
5. unprepared   6. unpleasant

words with the prefix **ex**
7. express   8. explore
9. excuse

words with the prefix **dis**
10. disagree   11. disclose
12. disinterested   13. dishonest

words with the prefix **ad**
14. admit   15. adventure
16. advice   17. advance
18. adverb

words with the prefix **de**
19. design   20. defend

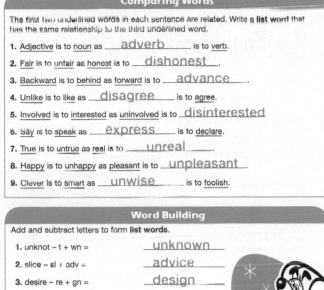

Comparing Words

The first two underlined words in each sentence are related. Write a **list word** that has the same relationship to the third underlined word.

1. Adjective is to noun as ___adverb___ is to verb.
2. Fair is to unfair as honest is to ___dishonest___.
3. Backward is to behind as forward is to ___advance___.
4. Unlike is to like as ___disagree___ is to agree.
5. Involved is to interested as uninvolved is to ___disinterested___.
6. Say is to speak as ___express___ is to declare.
7. True is to untrue as real is to ___unreal___.
8. Happy is to unhappy as pleasant is to ___unpleasant___.
9. Clever is to smart as ___unwise___ is to foolish.

Word Building

Add and subtract letters to form **list words**.

1. unknot – t + wn = ___unknown___
2. slice – sl + adv = ___advice___
3. desire – re + gn = ___design___
4. admire – re + t = ___admit___
5. amuse – am + exc = ___excuse___
6. resend – r + d – s + f = ___defend___
7. reappear – re + un – app + cl = ___unclear___
8. repose – re + dis – p + cl = ___disclose___
9. replace – re + ex – ac + or = ___explore___
10. invention – in + ad – ion + ure = ___adventure___

Lesson 32 • Prefixes **ex, de, dis, un,** and **ad**   131

Spelling and Writing

Proofreading

The article below has nine mistakes. Use the proofreading marks to fix each mistake. Then, write the misspelled **list words** correctly on the lines.

Proofreading Marks
◯ spelling mistake
¶ indent paragraph
∧ add something

Having a cold is certainly unpleasant—especially if you are unprepaired for that sudden sneeze. Here's some good advise, "Keep a handkerchief close by."

Handkerchiefs have been used for a long time. In the first century B.C., they were made from linen. Later on, in the Far East, silk was used. In the 1600s, handkerchiefs of every size, shape, and dezine could be found. Some had lace and buttons. Imagine using a handkerchief decorated with gemstones! Toward the 1800s, people became disintarested in these fancy pieces of cloth and began to use tissues.

1. ___unpleasant___   2. ___unprepared___
3. ___advice___   4. ___design___
5. ___disinterested___

Writing an Informative Paragraph

What should people do to avoid getting a cold? Write a paragraph telling people what they can do to protect themselves from catching cold viruses. Use as many **list words** as you can. Remember to proofread your paragraph and fix any mistakes.

_____
_____
_____
_____
_____

BONUS WORDS

define
unrelated
disgrace
advantage
exchange

132   Lesson 32 • Prefixes **ex, de, dis, un,** and **ad**

Spelling Strategy

Write the prefixes *ex, de, dis, un,* and *ad* on the board. Then, call out each root or base word contained in a **list word** and ask the class to name the prefix it goes with. Call on a volunteer to write the complete **list word** on the board as a word equation (*dis + interested = disinterested*).

BONUS WORDS Have students write a sentence for each **bonus word** and then erase the prefix. Ask students to trade papers with partners and add the correct prefixes so the **bonus words** make sense in the sentences.

Spelling and Writing   Page 132

The **Proofreading** exercise will help students prepare to proofread their paragraphs. As students complete the writing activity, encourage them to brainstorm ideas, write a first draft, revise, and proofread their work. To publish their writing, students may want to

• create a pamphlet called "Preventing Colds"
• use their paragraphs to make a health poster.

Writer's Corner You may want to invite the school nurse or a public health worker to talk to students about staying healthy during the cold and flu season. The class can brainstorm and write a list of questions to ask the guest speaker.

Final Test

1. We ordered a pizza in **advance**.
2. Are there still **unknown** regions of the earth?
3. We **disagree** about which game to play.
4. It's **unwise** to skip breakfast.
5. I was **disinterested** and unconcerned.
6. I **admit** that I'm not a great skier.
7. Why won't you **disclose** the hiding place?
8. Mr. Miller circled the **adverb** in the sentence.
9. **Dishonest** people do not make good friends.
10. Are you prepared to **defend** your opinions?
11. A good writer tries to **express** ideas clearly.
12. My experience seems as **unreal** as a dream.
13. Are the directions still **unclear** to you?
14. The nervous speaker was **unprepared** to talk.
15. Jason found it **unpleasant** to handle a snake.
16. Please **excuse** me for being late.
17. What a terrific **adventure** our trip was!
18. Never **explore** caves without supervision!
19. Lea will **design** her dress for the dance.
20. Many people go to Dr. Kim for **advice**.

101

Compound Words

Objective
To spell compound words

Spelling Words in Action   *Page 133*

In this selection, students learn about a frontier school. After reading, ask students to share what they thought was most interesting or most difficult about the school.

Encourage students to look back at the boldfaced words. Have volunteers say each word and identify the two words that make up the compound word.

Warm-Up Test
1. The plane flew one hundred miles **northwest**.
2. What a beautiful day to be **outdoors**!
3. **Everybody** voted in the school election.
4. Add one **teaspoon** of cinnamon to the batter.
5. We hiked as far as the **waterfall**.
6. Will this bus take us **downtown**?
7. The old **schoolhouse** is used as a museum.
8. To the **southeast** of the city is a large airport.
9. Mario works after school at a **supermarket**.
10. Their car is out front; **therefore**, they're home.
11. How much **homework** do you have tonight?
12. They planted flowers along the **sidewalk**.
13. We had scrambled eggs for **breakfast** today.
14. What an **outstanding** artist Leza has become!
15. Button up your **overcoat** to stay warm.
16. Mr. Patel put his old **typewriter** in the attic.
17. I'll teach you how to pitch **horseshoes**.
18. Did the dentist cure your **toothache**?
19. My mother works in an **aircraft** factory.
20. Bill got a new **knapsack** for his birthday.

Spelling Practice   *Pages 134–135*

Introduce the spelling rule and have students read the **list words** aloud. Encourage students to look back at their **Warm-Up Tests** and apply the spelling rule to any misspelled words.

As students work through the **Spelling Practice** exercises, remind them to look back at their **list words** or in their dictionaries if they need help. After students have completed the **Puzzle** exercise, you may wish to explain the pun involved in the word *downfall*.

for ESL students **See Charades / Pantomime, page 15**

Spelling Words in Action

What was a frontier school like?

School Days

Imagine getting up 4:00 a.m. to do chores, which might include chopping wood, carrying water, or milking cows. Then, you eat **breakfast** and get ready for school. There are no cars, buses, or even a **sidewalk**. Instead, you walk miles on a dirt trail. You take along a **knapsack**.

The **schoolhouse** is a one-room log cabin with a dirt floor. If you are lucky, there are windows. There is a cast-iron stove in the middle of the room for warmth. Wooden shelves fastened to the walls serve as desks. **Everybody** sits at the shelves on three-legged stools or on long wooden benches. Students of different ages and grades are all mixed together.

There are no blackboards, books, paper, or pencils. **Therefore**, you brought what you needed from home. When you finish one lesson, you erase your slate and start again. At recess, boys and girls play separately **outdoors**. The boys play **horseshoes** while the girls play jump rope. After school, you start the trip home. There isn't much **homework** because you have more chores to do.

Considering the hardships, though, frontier children often did an **outstanding** job of learning the three R's—reading, 'riting, and 'rithmetic.

> Take a look at the boldfaced words. What two words make up each word?

133

Spelling Practice

> **TIP**
> A compound word is made up of two or more words joined together to make a new word.
> A *sidewalk* is a place to *walk* near the *side* of the road.
> Study the **list words** to find the words that make up each compound word.

LIST WORDS
1. northwest
2. outdoors
3. everybody
4. teaspoon
5. waterfall
6. downtown
7. schoolhouse
8. southeast
9. supermarket
10. therefore
11. homework
12. sidewalk
13. breakfast
14. outstanding
15. overcoat
16. typewriter
17. horseshoes
18. toothache
19. aircraft
20. knapsack

Forming Compound Words

Add a word to each word given to write a **list word**.

1. knap   knapsack
2. out   outdoors
3. down   downtown
4. north   northwest
5. air   aircraft
6. over   overcoat
7. tea   teaspoon
8. home   homework
9. every   everybody
10. tooth   toothache
11. out   outstanding
12. type   typewriter
13. horse   horseshoes
14. break   breakfast
15. water   waterfall
16. there   therefore
17. school   schoolhouse
18. super   supermarket
19. south   southeast
20. side   sidewalk

Puzzle

Write the list word that matches each clue. Then, read down the shaded boxes to solve the riddle.

1. a walkway next to the street
2. work done at home
3. a machine that makes printed letters
4. business section of a city
5. as a result
6. a nylon, canvas, or leather bag
7. water that falls from a steep height
8. a place to learn

1. S I D E W A L K
2. H O M E W O R K
3. T Y P E W R I T E R
4. D O W N T O W N
5. T H E R E F O R E
6. K N A P S A C K
7. W A T E R F A L L
8. S C H O O L H O U S E

Riddle: What did the king find on the stairs?

Answer: His D O W N F A L L

Classification

Write the list word that belongs in each group.

1. lunch, dinner, __breakfast__
2. west, southwest, __northwest__
3. great, terrific, __outstanding__
4. cup, tablespoon, __teaspoon__
5. saddle, reins, __horseshoes__
6. store, shop, __supermarket__
7. all, everyone, __everybody__
8. jacket, parka, __overcoat__
9. east, northeast, __southeast__
10. helicopter, plane, __aircraft__
11. headache, earache, __toothache__
12. open air, outside, __outdoors__

Spelling and Writing

Proofreading

The journal entry below has twelve mistakes. Use the proofreading marks to fix each mistake. Then, write the misspelled list words correctly on the lines.

November 23rd—I got up at 4 o'clock this morning.It was my turn to carry water and collect firewood. It was really cold outdors.I'm lucky I have a warm overcote to wear. Mom made a really good Pancake breakfes.Then I left for school. Dad hooked up the horses and took me in the Carriage. The horses have special horsehoes so they don't slip in the snow.The Schoolhouse is about 4 miles northewst of here. It was still cold when I got there, but it warmed up quickly.

Proofreading Marks
- ◯ spelling mistake
- ⊙ add period
- / make a small letter

1. outdoors
2. overcoat
3. breakfast
4. horseshoes
5. schoolhouse
6. northwest

Writing a Comparison

Imagine your class was transported to frontier times. Write about how it would be the same and different from life today. Use as many list words as you can. Remember to proofread your comparison and fix any mistakes.

_____
_____
_____

BONUS WORDS
taxpayer
easygoing
sweatshirt
breakdown
westward

Spelling Strategy

Call out one of the smaller words that is part of a list word and ask the class to name the other half of the list word, referring to their *Spelling Workout* books if necessary. Then, have students say the complete word and finger-write it in the air as they spell it aloud. Call on a volunteer to write the word on the board.

BONUS WORDS
Invite students to write a sentence for each **bonus word**. Have them replace the **bonus word** with an equation that shows the two parts that make up a compound word. Then, have students trade papers with partners and solve each other's equations.

Spelling and Writing   *Page 136*

The **Proofreading** exercise will help students prepare to proofread their comparisons. As students complete the writing activity, encourage them to brainstorm ideas, write a first draft, revise, and proofread their work. To publish their writing, students may want to
- share their writing in small groups
- create a bulletin-board display titled "Then and Now."

Writer's Corner Encourage students to research life on the American frontier at the library or on the Internet. Have them write a paragraph comparing an aspect of frontier life with life today.

Final Test

1. Do you use a **typewriter** or a computer?
2. Pack your flashlight in your **knapsack**.
3. We played hopscotch on the **sidewalk**.
4. To the **southeast**, we saw huge mountains.
5. Use a **teaspoon** to measure the baking soda.
6. How nice it is to see **everyone** here on time!
7. Jake finished his **homework** after dinner.
8. Grandma went to a one-room **schoolhouse**.
9. Is your new **overcoat** waterproof?
10. I'm writing a report on the history of **aircraft**.
11. Are **horseshoes** made of iron?
12. The new **supermarket** will open tomorrow.
13. Chandra took a picture of the **waterfall**.
14. Do grizzly bears roam free in the **northwest**?
15. Eat a nutritious **breakfast** every day.
16. We went **downtown** to go shopping.
17. Carlos woke up with a painful **toothache**.
18. Do you enjoy working **outdoors**?
19. It's 5:30 p.m.; **therefore**, I have to leave.
20. Her photographs of birds are **outstanding**!

Objective
To spell and identify antonyms and synonyms

Correlated Phonics Lessons
MCP Phonics, Level D, Lessons 77–78

Spelling Words in Action   Page 137

In "The Mail Must Go Through!" students read to find out why the Pony Express lasted only a short time. Ask students, "What do you think being a Pony Express rider was like? Would you like to have been one?"

Call on volunteers to say each boldfaced word and tell which one means the same as *trip* and which one means the opposite of *easy*.

Warm-Up Test
1. Joan finds swimming easy, but diving **difficult**.
2. For dinner, they had a **tender** steak.
3. The principal gave a **lengthy** talk.
4. To reach that object, use a **sturdy** stepladder.
5. Is he saving money to buy an **expensive** bike?
6. Erin **repaired** the flat tire on her bike.
7. That dinosaur was an **enormous** creature!
8. What is the best **journey** you have taken?
9. The **weary** runners limped to the finish line.
10. Just before the race, the drivers were **tense**.
11. When crossing a busy street, be **cautious**.
12. Mei Ling felt great **sorrow** when her cat died.
13. Luis was **vague** about the date of the party.
14. Was this **ancient** ruin a Roman temple?
15. The firefighter's **courage** was admirable.
16. After a big lunch, we were **drowsy**.
17. He stared in **disbelief** at the magician's tricks.
18. I read about **current** events in the newspaper.
19. Workers **descend** into the mine in elevators.
20. The swimmer was **rapidly** taking the lead.

Spelling Practice   Pages 138–139
Introduce the spelling rule and have students read the **list words** aloud. Encourage students to look back at their **Warm-Up Tests** and apply the spelling rule to any misspelled words.

As students work through the **Spelling Practice** exercises, remind them to look back at their **list words** or in their dictionaries if they need help.

for ESL students **See Student Dictation, page 14**

Spelling Words in Action

Why was the Pony Express in business for only two years?

The Mail Must Go Through!

It's been over a hundred years since the Pony Express stopped delivering mail. The Express was started in 1860 between Missouri and California. Riders made the **difficult journey** on horseback. They had to be **cautious**, and both rider and horse often got **weary** during the long ride. To help, relay stations were set up ten to fifteen miles apart. Riders would pick up fresh horses at each station. The **lengthy** trip took eight days. Because it was so **expensive**, the Pony Express had only a brief life. Railroads could offer cheaper rates and deliver the mail more **rapidly**. As a result, after only two years, the Pony Express went out of business.

However, in 1983 in California, an **enormous** mudslide closed the road to several mountain towns. The only way mail could be delivered was by horseback, so the Express was back in business! Each morning, the postmaster gave the first rider a pouch of mail. It took up to thirteen **sturdy** riders to make the long trip. Altogether, about 62 riders helped out. Eventually, the road was **repaired**, but for a brief time the Pony Express was back!

 OREGON TRAIL
PONY EXPRESS
STAGE & FREIGHT
HICKOK / McCANLE!

Look back at the boldfaced words in the selection. Can you name the word that means almost the same as <u>trip</u>? Can you name the word that means the opposite of <u>easy</u>?

137

TIP
A synonym is a word that means the same or almost the same as another word. The word *long* is a synonym for *lengthy*.
An antonym is a word that means the opposite or almost the opposite of another word. The word *brief* is an antonym for *lengthy*.

Spelling Practice

LIST WORDS
1. difficult
2. tender
3. lengthy
4. sturdy
5. expensive
6. repaired
7. enormous
8. journey
9. weary
10. tense
11. cautious
12. sorrow
13. vague
14. ancient
15. courage
16. drowsy
17. disbelief
18. current
19. descend
20. rapidly

Writing Synonyms and Antonyms
Write the **list word** that best completes each sentence.

1. A hard problem is <u>difficult</u>
2. A long book is <u>lengthy</u>
3. A huge elephant is <u>enormous</u>
4. A sleepy baby is <u>drowsy</u>
5. A costly ring is <u>expensive</u>
6. Sadness is also <u>sorrow</u>
7. A nervous person is <u>tense</u>
8. A long trip is a <u>journey</u>
9. A brave person has <u>courage</u>
10. A fixed watch is <u>repaired</u>
11. Go slowly, not <u>rapidly</u>
12. Don't be tough, be <u>tender</u>
13. Climb up, don't <u>descend</u>
14. Be energetic, not <u>weary</u>
15. A modern desk is not <u>ancient</u>
16. A weak floor is not <u>sturdy</u>
17. A clear idea is not <u>vague</u>
18. It isn't trust, it's <u>disbelief</u>
19. Reckless people aren't <u>cautious</u>
20. A past issue is not <u>current</u>

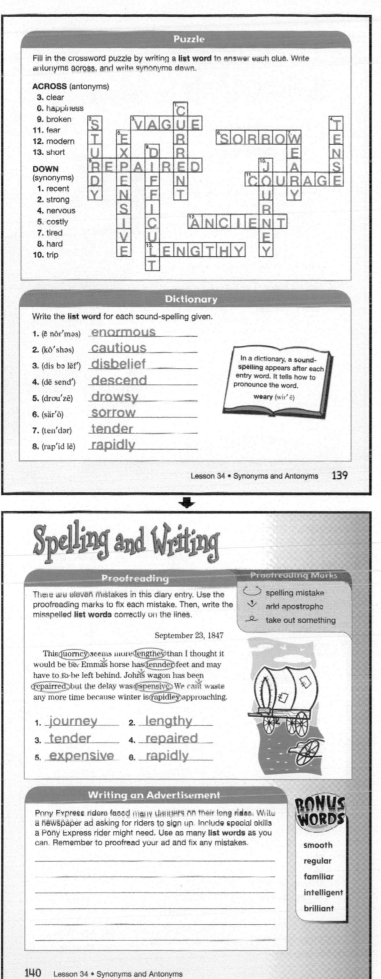

Puzzle

Fill in the crossword puzzle by writing a **list word** to answer each clue. Write antonyms across, and write synonyms down.

ACROSS (antonyms)
3. clear
6. happiness
9. broken
11. fear
12. modern
13. short

DOWN (synonyms)
1. recent
2. strong
4. nervous
5. costly
7. tired
8. hard
10. trip

Crossword answers: STURDY, VAGUE, CURRENT, SORROW, TENSE, EXPENSIVE, REPAIRED, DIFFICULT, JOURNEY, COURAGE, ANCIENT, LENGTHY

Dictionary

Write the **list word** for each sound-spelling given.

1. (ē nôr'məs) __enormous__
2. (kô'shəs) __cautious__
3. (dis bə lēf') __disbelief__
4. (dē send') __descend__
5. (drou'zē) __drowsy__
6. (sär'ō) __sorrow__
7. (ten'dər) __tender__
8. (rap'id lē) __rapidly__

In a dictionary, a sound-spelling appears after each entry word. It tells how to pronounce the word.

weary (wir'ē)

Lesson 34 • Synonyms and Antonyms 139

Spelling and Writing

Proofreading

Proofreading Marks
- ⌢ spelling mistake
- ⌄ add apostrophe
- ℓ take out something

There are eleven mistakes in this diary entry. Use the proofreading marks to fix each mistake. Then, write the misspelled **list words** correctly on the lines.

September 23, 1847

This journey seems more lengthey than I thought it would be be. Emmas horse has tennder feet and may have to to be left behind. Johns wagon has been repairred but the delay was espensive. We cant waste any more time because winter is rapidley approaching.

1. __journey__ 2. __lengthy__
3. __tender__ 4. __repaired__
5. __expensive__ 6. __rapidly__

Writing an Advertisement

Pony Express riders faced many dangers on their long rides. Write a newspaper ad asking for riders to sign up. Include special skills a Pony Express rider might need. Use as many **list words** as you can. Remember to proofread your ad and fix any mistakes.

BONUS WORDS
smooth
regular
familiar
intelligent
brilliant

140 Lesson 34 • Synonyms and Antonyms

Spelling Strategy

With a partner, students can take turns saying the **list words** aloud. The partner who is listening
- repeats the word
- writes it while spelling it aloud
- names a synonym or an antonym for it.

BONUS WORDS
With partners, have students write a paragraph using an antonym for each **bonus word**. Have them trade papers with other partner teams. Then, ask them to rewrite the paragraph, using the **bonus words**.

Spelling and Writing   Page 140

The **Proofreading** exercise will help students prepare to proofread their newspaper ads. As students complete the writing activity, encourage them to brainstorm ideas, write a first draft, revise, and proofread their work. To publish their writing, students may want to
- compile a "Help Wanted" newsletter
- create recruitment posters for Pony Express riders.

Writer's Corner Students may enjoy learning more about the Pony Express. Invite them to research in the library or on the Internet and take notes on interesting information that they can share with the class later.

Final Test

1. The temperature outside is falling **rapidly**.
2. Do you get **tense** before a big test?
3. **Current** trends indicate a hot summer.
4. We praised the **courage** of the firefighters.
5. We became **drowsy** during the long film.
6. How **weary** she was after her long hike!
7. An **enormous** clap of thunder startled me.
8. My feet are too **tender** to walk without shoes.
9. Be **cautious** whenever you ride your bike.
10. Stephanie gave a **lengthy** explanation.
11. What an **expensive** mitt this is!
12. Our grandparents built **sturdy** furniture.
13. Has the shop **repaired** your bicycle yet?
14. She could see **sorrow** on the widow's face.
15. Lana has a **vague** memory of the house.
16. What **ancient** civilization built those temples?
17. In June we will **journey** across the country.
18. How long will it take the plane to **descend**?
19. He listened to the amazing story in **disbelief**.
20. This is the most **difficult** word on the test.

Objective
To spell homonyms

 **Correlated Phonics Lesson**
MCP Phonics, Level D, Lesson 79

Spelling Words in Action   *Page 141*

In this selection, students learn fascinating facts about hair—including the person with the longest hair in the world. After reading, invite students to discuss how they would feel if their hair was 17 feet long.

Ask volunteers to identify the pairs of boldfaced words that sound the same and to suggest words that sound like *tale* and *whose.*

Warm-Up Test
1. This is a **tale** about a giant.
2. The mouse has a long, pink **tail**.
3. There's a hole in the **heel** of my sock.
4. Keep the cut clean and it will **heal** quickly.
5. After a hard day, Bill wanted **peace** and quiet.
6. Tim needed another **piece** of writing paper.
7. Do you have a **plain** white shirt to wear?
8. We boarded the **plane** to London.
9. Leave your dishes **there** by the sink.
10. They brought **their** dogs to the park.
11. Your answer showed good **sense**.
12. Of all the **scents**, I like that of roses best.
13. **Which** desk is yours?
14. The story was about a **witch** and three elves.
15. **Whose** lunch bag was left on the table?
16. We already know **who's** playing the lead role.
17. Watch out or you'll **break** something!
18. Your bike also has a **brake** on the back wheel.
19. When are you going to cut your **hair**?
20. What a large animal a Belgian **hare** is!

Spelling Practice   *Pages 142–143*

Introduce the spelling rule and have students read the **list words** aloud. Explain to students how they can tell homonym pairs apart (context, spelling). Then, encourage them to look back at their **Warm-Up Tests** and apply the spelling rule to any misspelled words.

As students work through the **Spelling Practice** exercises, remind them to look back at their **list words** or in their dictionaries if they need help.

for ESL students **See Student Dictation, page 15**

106

Spelling Words in Action

Who holds the record for the world's tallest hairstyle?

A Hairy Tale

It may seem like a tall **tale**, but **who's** to say it isn't true? According to Guinness World Records®, in 1997 Hoo Sateow became the holder of the record for the longest hair in the world. Hoo's **hair** measured almost 17 ft. long. Hoo washes it once a year with detergent and normally wears it wound up on his head. He says, "It keeps my head nice and warm."

For humans, hair is mostly decorative, but for many animals, hair can be an important tool for survival. Whiskers on animals such as cats and dogs are a kind of hair that responds to the **sense** of touch. They help the animals feel **their** way through narrow or dark places.

There are many animals **whose** hair serves as insulation, not only for the animals themselves, but also for their young. For example, the polar bear has a thick coat of fur that keeps it warm. A mother **hare** (rabbit) makes a nest of her own hair **which** shelters and protects her young. Hair is also used as protection from enemies. A porcupine's quills are a type of hair. A porcupine uses its **tail** to stick the quills into the bodies of attackers.

Look back at the boldfaced words. Which words sound the same, but have different spellings and meanings? Do you know another word that sounds the same as <u>sense</u> or <u>which</u>?

141

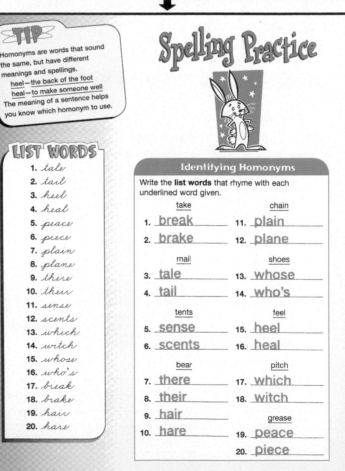

TIP
Homonyms are words that sound the same, but have different meanings and spellings.
heel—the back of the foot
heal—to make someone well
The meaning of a sentence helps you know which homonym to use.

Spelling Practice

LIST WORDS
1. tale
2. tail
3. heel
4. heal
5. peace
6. piece
7. plain
8. plane
9. there
10. their
11. sense
12. scents
13. which
14. witch
15. whose
16. who's
17. break
18. brake
19. hair
20. hare

Identifying Homonyms
Write the **list words** that rhyme with each underlined word given.

take
1. break
2. brake

chain
11. plain
12. plane

mail
3. tale
4. tail

shoes
13. whose
14. who's

tents
5. sense
6. scents

feel
15. heel
16. heal

bear
7. there
8. their
9. hair
10. hare

pitch
17. which
18. witch

grease
19. peace
20. piece

Missing Words

Write two **list words** that are homonyms to complete each sentence.

1. The white _hair_ of the _hare_ matched the color of the snow.
2. _Who's_ the lucky person _whose_ ticket won the prize?
3. The bike won't stop if you _break_ the _brake_.
4. _Their_ seats for the game are over _there_.
5. Soaking my hurt _heel_ should help it _heal_.
6. The _plane_ flew over the vast western _plain_.
7. One folk _tale_ tells how the bear lost its _tail_.
8. There was _peace_ after each child found a puzzle _piece_.

Homonym Search

There are five pairs of **list word** homonyms hidden in the puzzle. They go across, up, down, or diagonally. Circle each homonym. Then, write each homonym pair on the lines.

B	A	C	W	I	I	C	H
I	T	H	E	I	R	S	C
C	O	H	L	P	T	C	I
K	I	P	E	A	C	E	H
A	S	I	O	R	T	N	W
E	P	E	A	R	E	T	U
R	E	C	N	O	A	S	T
B	L	E	C	S	T	M	K
A	M	T	Q	A	E	S	A
T	A	B	R	A	K	E	B
R	A	C	P	S	Q	R	O

1. _break_
2. _brake_
3. _peace_
4. _piece_
5. _their_
6. _there_
7. _sense_
8. _scents_
9. _which_
10. _witch_

Spelling and Writing

Proofreading

There are ten mistakes in this article. Use the proofreading marks to fix each mistake. Then, write the correct **list words** on the lines.

Proofreading Marks
- ◯ spelling mistake
- ≡ capital letter
- ⌃ add something

This tail of the history of the beard will raise your hare did you know that at one time, all men wore beards? Then, Alexander the Great thought it made scents for soldiers to shave there beards so enemies could not grab them. Did you know that the Vandyke beard, witch was pointed, was popular in the 1600s? In the 1830s in america, most men did not wear beards. Joseph Palmer, who's beard was bushy, was jailed for wearing one.

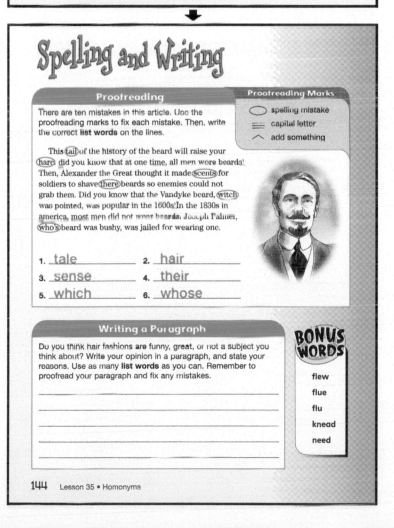

1. _tale_   2. _hair_
3. _sense_   4. _their_
5. _which_   6. _whose_

Writing a Paragraph

Do you think hair fashions are funny, great, or not a subject you think about? Write your opinion in a paragraph, and state your reasons. Use as many **list words** as you can. Remember to proofread your paragraph and fix any mistakes.

_____
_____
_____
_____
_____

BONUS WORDS
- flew
- flue
- flu
- knead
- need

Spelling Strategy

To help students distinguish between the words in a homonym pair, write cloze sentences on the board for pairs of **list words**. Next to each sentence, add letters as a clue. For example:

- "Will that wound _____ ?" (ea)
- "She broke the _____ on her shoe." (ee)
- "The answer doesn't make _____." (ens)
- "I like the different flowers' _____." (cen)

Invite the class to read each pair of sentences and decide which **list words** go in the blanks. Call on volunteers to fill in the words.

BONUS WORDS
Have students write a paragraph using each **bonus word** but in the wrong place. Let partners trade papers and rewrite each other's paragraph, using the **bonus words** correctly.

Spelling and Writing   Page 144

The **Proofreading** exercise will help students prepare to proofread their paragraphs. As students complete the writing activity, encourage them to brainstorm ideas, write a first draft, revise, and proofread their work. To publish their writing, invite students to present their paragraphs to the class as short speeches.

Writer's Corner Organize a trip to the library for students to research interesting information about animals' fur. Students can share what they learn by writing facts on a class collage.

Final Test

1. Fix your bike's **brake** so your bike will stop.
2. My shoe has a nail in the **heel**.
3. The **plane** was delayed until the fog lifted.
4. Which of these **scents** do you like best?
5. Cinderella is a fairy **tale** I have always liked.
6. Here's a fable about a tortoise and a **hare**.
7. The good **witch** granted her three wishes.
8. Ask your parents if we can use **their** radio.
9. How long will it take this wound to **heal**?
10. Your plan makes good **sense** to me.
11. I'd like my **hair** cut a little shorter in front.
12. A raccoon has stripes on his **tail**.
13. Are those your books **there** on the table?
14. Jon knew **which** street was mine.
15. Look out or you'll **break** that window!
16. Perhaps one day the world will be at **peace**.
17. Choose a partner **whose** ticket matches yours.
18. Do you want your burger **plain** or with cheese?
19. Try to find out **who's** coming to the party.
20. Yes, you may have another **piece** of toast.

Objectives

To review spelling words with the prefixes *pre, re, im, non, con, ex, de, dis, un,* and *ad;* compound words; synonyms and antonyms; homonyms

Check Your Spelling Notebook   **Pages 145–148**

Based on students' lists and your observations, note which words are giving students the most difficulty and offer assistance for spelling them correctly. Here are some frequently misspelled words to watch for: *immovable, advance, advice, design, disagree, breakfast, therefore, who's, their,* and *there.*

To give students extra help and practice in taking standardized tests, you may want to have them take the **Review Test** for this lesson on pages 110–111. After scoring the tests, return them to students so that they can record their misspelled words in their spelling notebooks.

After practicing their troublesome words, students can work through the exercises for Lessons 31–35. Before students begin each exercise, you may want to go over the spelling rule.

Take It Home

Suggest that students and their parents make up a humorous story using as many of the **list words** in Lessons 31–35 as possible. Students can use **Take It Home** Master 6 on pages 112–113 to help them do the activity. (A complete list of the spelling words is included on page 112 of the **Take It Home** Master.) Encourage students to bring their stories to class and combine them into a series of skits. After rehearsing, students may want to invite another class to a performance.

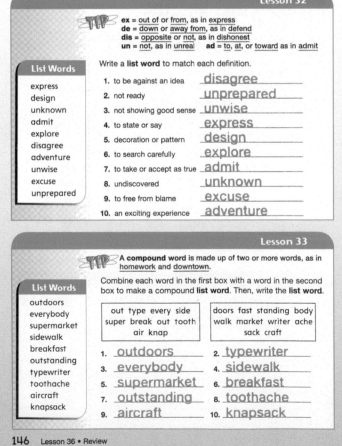

In lessons 31–35, you have learned how to spell words with prefixes, compound words, and words that are synonyms, antonyms, and homonyms.

Check Your Spelling Notebook

Look at the words in your spelling notebook. Which words in lessons 31 through 35 did you have the most trouble with? Write them here.

_____

Practice writing your troublesome words with a partner. Take turns dividing the words into syllables as your partner spells them aloud.

Lesson 31

TIP pre = before, as in preview   re = again or back, as in refills
im = not, as in impure   non = not, as in nonprofit
con = with or together, as in control

List Words

nonsense
prepaid
impractical
nonstop
nonprofit
construct
immovable
predict
convince
reaction

Add a prefix to each word or word part to make a **list word**. Then, write the **list word.**

1. im movable — immovable
2. con vince — convince
3. non sense — nonsense
4. non profit — nonprofit
5. re action — reaction
6. non stop — nonstop
7. pre paid — prepaid
8. con struct — construct
9. pre dict — predict
10. im practical — impractical

145

Lesson 32

TIP ex = out of or from, as in express
de = down or away from, as in defend
dis = opposite or not, as in dishonest
un = not, as in unreal   ad = to, at, or toward as in admit

List Words

express
design
unknown
admit
explore
disagree
adventure
unwise
excuse
unprepared

Write a **list word** to match each definition.

1. to be against an idea — disagree
2. not ready — unprepared
3. not showing good sense — unwise
4. to state or say — express
5. decoration or pattern — design
6. to search carefully — explore
7. to take or accept as true — admit
8. undiscovered — unknown
9. to free from blame — excuse
10. an exciting experience — adventure

Lesson 33

TIP A **compound** word is made up of two or more words, as in homework and downtown.

List Words

outdoors
everybody
supermarket
sidewalk
breakfast
outstanding
typewriter
toothache
aircraft
knapsack

Combine each word in the first box with a word in the second box to make a compound **list word**. Then, write the **list word.**

| out type every side super break out tooth air knap | doors fast standing body walk market writer ache sack craft |

1. outdoors   2. typewriter
3. everybody   4. sidewalk
5. supermarket   6. breakfast
7. outstanding   8. toothache
9. aircraft   10. knapsack

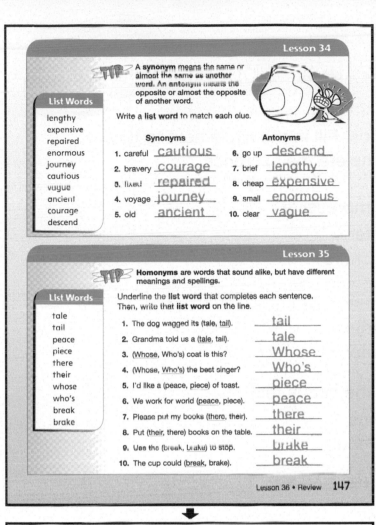

Lesson 34

TIP A **synonym** means the same or almost the same as another word. An **antonym** means the opposite or almost the opposite of another word.

List Words

lengthy
expensive
repaired
enormous
journey
cautious
vague
ancient
courage
descend

Write a **list word** to match each clue.

Synonyms

1. careful   cautious
2. bravery   courage
3. fixed   repaired
4. voyage   journey
5. old   ancient

Antonyms

6. go up   descend
7. brief   lengthy
8. cheap   expensive
9. small   enormous
10. clear   vague

Lesson 35

TIP **Homonyms** are words that sound alike, but have different meanings and spellings.

List Words

tale
tail
peace
piece
there
their
whose
who's
break
brake

Underline the **list word** that completes each sentence. Then, write that **list word** on the line.

1. The dog wagged its (tale, <u>tail</u>).   tail
2. Grandma told us a (<u>tale</u>, tail).   tale
3. (<u>Whose</u>, Who's) coat is this?   Whose
4. (Whose, <u>Who's</u>) the best singer?   Who's
5. I'd like a (peace, <u>piece</u>) of toast.   piece
6. We work for world (<u>peace</u>, piece).   peace
7. Please put my books (<u>there</u>, their).   there
8. Put (<u>their</u>, there) books on the table.   their
9. Use the (break, <u>brake</u>) to stop.   brake
10. The cup could (<u>break</u>, brake).   break

Lesson 36 • Review   **147**

Show What You Know

Lessons 31–35 • Review

One word is misspelled in each set of **list words**. Fill in the circle next to the **list word** that is spelled incorrectly.

1. ○ nonsense ○ prepaid ○ returned ● inpractical ○ control
2. ● expres ○ design ○ unknown ○ heal ○ unclear
3. ○ northwest ○ outdoors ○ everybody ● teespoon ○ waterfall
4. ○ difficult ● tendar ○ lengthy ○ expensive ○ sturdy
5. ○ tale ○ report ○ heel ● admitt ○ their
6. ○ nonstop ○ plane ○ preview ● imperfact ○ tail
7. ○ explore ○ disagree ○ defend ● advenjure ○ unreal
8. ○ downtown ○ schoolhouse ○ southeast ○ supermarket ● therefour
9. ● reparred ○ enormous ○ journey ○ weary ○ tense
10. ○ piece ○ plain ● conduckt ○ there ○ peace
11. ○ nonprofit ○ scents ○ construct ○ precaution ● imovable
12. ○ unwise ● discloze ○ advice ○ disinterested ○ excuse
13. ○ homework ○ sidewalk ● breakfest ○ outstanding ○ overcoat
14. ● cawtious ○ sorrow ○ hair ○ ancient ○ courage
15. ○ brake ● refils ○ which ○ current ○ whose
16. ○ predict ○ convince ○ impure ● impersonel ○ reaction
17. ● dishoness ○ unprepared ○ advance ○ unpleasant ○ adverb
18. ○ typewriter ○ horseshoes ● toothach ○ aircraft ○ knapsack
19. ○ drowsy ○ disbelief ○ witch ● decend ○ rapidly
20. ○ who's ● breek ○ sense ○ vague ○ hare

148   Lesson 36 • Review

Final Test

1. **Whose** dog is that?
2. Put a **piece** of cheese on the cracker.
3. The title of that **tale** is "The Little Red Hen."
4. Be careful not to **break** the glass in the frame.
5. She wrote a **lengthy** article about snakes.
6. Ben's **courage** helps him as a firefighter.
7. Did you enjoy your **journey** to Alaska?
8. Be **cautious** when you ride your skateboard.
9. For **breakfast**, Dad made blueberry pancakes.
10. Pack an extra pair of socks in your **knapsack**.
11. What an **outstanding** poem Taneesha wrote!
12. We'll buy a gallon of milk at the **supermarket**.
13. Songwriters **express** feelings through music.
14. It is **unwise** to not eat breakfast.
15. We felt **unprepared** for the difficult hike.
16. Did he **admit** to taking the candy?
17. Please **excuse** me for being late today.
18. I love to read **nonsense** poems!
19. Did she **convince** you to sign her petition?
20. The movie got a positive **reaction** from critics.
21. Uncle Bob helped me **construct** a tree house.
22. I'd like to buy a ticket on a **nonstop** flight.
23. I **predict** that Adam will enjoy his new school.
24. We had fun planning our **adventure**.
25. Will you tell us why you **disagree**?
26. The wallpaper was white with a floral **design**.
27. Let's go **outdoors** and play basketball.
28. If you have a **toothache**, see the dentist.
29. We saw a film in class about early **aircraft**.
30. The tickets for the trip are very **expensive**.
31. The **ancient** Vikings lived in Scandinavia.
32. Tonio **repaired** the broken chair with glue.
33. I have **vague** memories of my early childhood.
34. She hung **their** coats in the hall closet.
35. The rear **brake** on my bike needs to be fixed.
36. The horse has a beautiful white **tail**.
37. **There** aren't many days left until vacation.
38. Use the railing when you **descend** the stairs.
39. Nori lives in an **enormous** apartment building.
40. I **prepaid** the theater tickets months ago.
41. The heavy piano seemed **immovable**.
42. What an **impractical** plan this is!
43. I donated old clothes to a **nonprofit** agency.
44. When did Lewis and Clark **explore** this region?
45. Are any western regions still **unknown**?
46. **Everybody** in the class did well on the test.
47. Ms. Yee taught me how to use a **typewriter**.
48. A clown sold balloons on the **sidewalk**.
49. **Who's** behind that funny mask?
50. The people worked hard for **peace** and justice.

Review Test (Side A)

Read each sentence and set of words. Fill in the circle next to the word that is spelled correctly to complete the sentence.

1. Izzy's tales of _____ were very impressive.
   - (a) adventure
   - (b) advencher
   - (c) adventer
   - (d) advenchure

2. The broken keys on the _____ make typing difficult.
   - (a) typeriter
   - (b) tiperiter
   - (c) typewriter
   - (d) tipewriter

3. An _____ elephant walked into the circus tent.
   - (a) enormos
   - (b) enormous
   - (c) enormus
   - (d) enoremous

4. Let's go _____ the beach to find seashells!
   - (a) explor
   - (b) exploar
   - (c) exploare
   - (d) explore

5. The children didn't want to _____ the machine.
   - (a) brak
   - (b) braek
   - (c) breake
   - (d) break

6. It is _____ to ignore the advice of your elders.
   - (a) unwis
   - (b) unwise
   - (c) unwize
   - (d) unwaiz

7. The mayor rejected Ms. White's idea because it was _____.
   - (a) impractical
   - (b) impracticle
   - (c) impraktical
   - (d) imprectical

8. Taking a _____ vacation can be expensive.
   - (a) lengthy
   - (b) lengthie
   - (c) lenthy
   - (d) lenthie

Review Test (Side B)

Read each sentence and set of words. Fill in the circle next to the word that is spelled correctly to complete the sentence.

9. Would you like a _____ of cake before you go?
   - ⓐ peice
   - ⓒ pece
   - ⓑ peece
   - ⓓ piece

10. Please tell me _____ jacket this is.
    - ⓐ whoes
    - ⓒ whoose
    - ⓑ whose
    - ⓓ who'se

11. The _____ organization was asking for donations.
    - ⓐ nonprophet
    - ⓒ nonprofit
    - ⓑ nonprofet
    - ⓓ nonproffit

12. We might be able to _____ Emily to help.
    - ⓐ convinse
    - ⓒ convins
    - ⓑ konvince
    - ⓓ convince

13. The _____ birds refused to enter the birdhouse.
    - ⓐ cawtious
    - ⓒ caushous
    - ⓑ cautios
    - ⓓ cautious

14. He had to grab a quick _____ on his way to work.
    - ⓐ brekfast
    - ⓒ breakfast
    - ⓑ breckfast
    - ⓓ brekfest

15. This stylish _____ is well-made and comfortable.
    - ⓐ knapsak
    - ⓒ napsak
    - ⓑ knapsack
    - ⓓ napsack

Take It Home

6

Your child has learned to spell many new words and would enjoy sharing them with you and your family. Here are some ideas to help your child review the words in Lessons 31–35 and have fun, too.

And Then What Happened?

With your child, take turns using the spelling words to tell a story. Make the story funny or scary. At each turn, work one or more of the words into the story. For example, you might say, "One day I set out on an **adventure**, and the first thing I saw was a great **waterfall**. The **current** was moving very **rapidly**. Suddenly, . . ."

Lesson 31

1. conduct	12. nonstop
2. construct	13. precaution
3. control	14. predict
4. convince	15. prepaid
5. immovable	16. preview
6. imperfect	17. reaction
7. impersonal	18. refills
8. impractical	19. report
9. impure	20. returned
10. nonprofit	
11. nonsense	

Lesson 32

1. admit	12. excuse
2. advance	13. explore
3. adventure	14. express
4. adverb	15. unclear
5. advice	16. unknown
6. defend	17. unpleasant
7. design	18. unprepared
8. disagree	19. unreal
9. disclose	20. unwise
10. dishonest	
11. disinterested	

Lesson 33

1. aircraft	12. schoolhouse
2. breakfast	13. sidewalk
3. downtown	14. southeast
4. everybody	15. supermarket
5. homework	16. teaspoon
6. horseshoes	17. therefore
7. knapsack	18. toothache
8. northwest	19. typewriter
9. outdoors	20. waterfall
10. outstanding	
11. overcoat	

Lesson 34

1. ancient	12. lengthy
2. cautious	13. rapidly
3. courage	14. repaired
4. current	15. sorrow
5. descend	16. sturdy
6. difficult	17. tender
7. disbelief	18. tense
8. drowsy	19. vague
9. enormous	20. weary
10. expensive	
11. journey	

Lesson 35

1. brake	12. sense
2. break	13. tail
3. hair	14. tale
4. hare	15. their
5. heal	16. there
6. heel	17. which
7. peace	18. who's
8. piece	19. whose
9. plain	20. witch
10. plane	
11. scents	

What a Card!

Cut out the word cards on this page and make more of your own using the spelling words. Then, place the cards in two stacks. Take turns drawing one card from each stack and using the two words in a silly sentence.

supermarket

knapsack

advice

impractical

enormous

nonsense

Writing and Proofreading Guide

1. Choose a topic to write about.

2. Write your ideas. Don't worry about mistakes.

3. Now organize your writing so that it makes sense.

4. Proofread your work.

   Use these proofreading marks to make changes.

Proofreading Marks

⬭	spelling mistake
≡	capital letter
⊙	add period
⌃	add something
⌄	add apostrophe
℮	take out something
¶	indent paragraph
/	make small letter
⌄⌄	add quotation marks

Isnt a dolfin one of the the most intelligent sea mammals ?

5. Write your final copy.

   Isn't a dolphin one of the most intelligent sea mammals?

6. Share your writing.

Using Your Dictionary

The **Spelling Workout** Dictionary shows you many things about your spelling words.

The **entry word** listed in alphabetical order is the word you are looking up.

The **sound-spelling** or **respelling** tells how to pronounce the word.

The **part of speech** is given as an abbreviation.

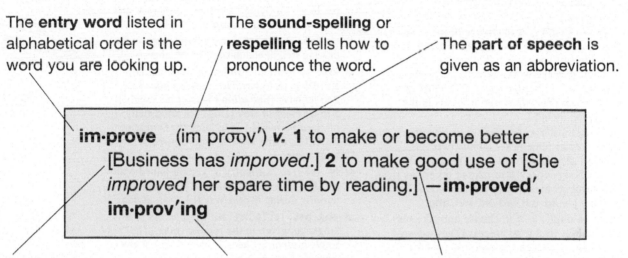

im·prove (im proov′) **v. 1** to make or become better [Business has *improved*.] **2** to make good use of [She *improved* her spare time by reading.] —**im·proved′**, **im·prov′ing**

Sample sentences or **phrases** show how to use the word.

Other **forms** of the word are given.

The **definition** tells what the word means. There may be more than one definition.

Pronunciation Key

SYMBOL	KEY WORDS	SYMBOL	KEY WORDS	SYMBOL	KEY WORDS	SYMBOL	KEY WORDS
a	ask, fat	o͞o	look, pull	b	bed, dub	t	top, hat
ā	ape, date	yo͞o	unite, cure	d	did, had	v	vat, have
ä	car, lot	o͞o	ooze, tool	f	fall, off	w	will, always
		yo͞o	cute, few	g	get, dog	y	yet, yard
e	elf, ten	ou	out, crowd	h	he, ahead	z	zebra, haze
er	berry, care			j	joy, jump		
ē	even, meet	u	up, cut	k	kill, bake	ch	chin, arch
		ʉ	fur, fern	l	let, ball	ŋ	ring, singer
i	is, hit			m	met, trim	sh	she, dash
ir	mirror, here	ə	a in ago	n	not, ton	th	thin, truth
ī	ice, fire		e in agent	p	put, tap	th	then, father
			e in father	r	red, dear	zh	s in pleasure
ō	open, go		i in unity	s	sell, pass		
ô	law, horn		o in collect				
oi	oil, point		u in focus				

An Americanism is a word or usage of a word that was born in this country. An open star (☆) before an entry word or definition means that the word or definition is an Americanism.

Aa

ab·sent (ab′sənt) *adj.* not present; away [No one in the class was *absent* that day.]

a·chieve (ə chēv′) *v.* **1** to do; succeed in doing; accomplish [She *achieved* a lot while she was mayor.] **2** to get or reach by trying hard; gain [He *achieved* his goal of graduating.] —**a·chieved′, a·chiev′ing**

ad·just (ə just′) *v.* **1** to change or move so as to make fit [You can *adjust* the piano bench to suit your size.] **2** to arrange the parts of; to make work correctly; regulate [My watch needs *adjusting*.] **3** to settle or put in order [We *adjust* our accounts at the end of the month.]

ad·mit (ad mit′) *v.* **1** to permit or give the right to enter [One ticket *admits* two people.] **2** to have room for [The hall *admits* 500 people.] **3** to take or accept as being true; confess [Lucy will not *admit* her mistake.] —**ad·mit′ted, ad·mit′ting**

a·dopt (ə däpt′) *v.* **1** to choose and take into one's family by a legal process [They *adopted* their daughter when she was four months old.] **2** to take and use as one's own [He *adopted* her teaching methods for his own classroom.] **3** to choose or follow [We must *adopt* a new plan of action.] —**a·dop′tion** *n.*

ad·vance (ad vans′) *v.* **1** to go or bring forward; move ahead [On first down they *advanced* the football two yards.] **2** to cause to happen earlier [The test date was *advanced* from May 10 to May 5.] —**ad·vanced′, ad·vanc′ing** ◆*n.* a moving forward or ahead; progress [new *advances* in science]

ad·van·tage (ad van′tij) *n.* a more favorable position; better chance [My speed gave me an *advantage* over them.]

ad·ven·ture (ad ven′chər) *n.* **1** an exciting and dangerous happening [He told of his *adventure* in the jungle.] **2** an unusual experience that is remembered [Going to a circus is an *adventure* for a child.]

ad·verb (ad′vurb) *n.* a word used with a verb, adjective, or another adverb to tell when, where, how, what kind, or how much [In the sentence, "She runs fast," the word "fast" is an *adverb*.]

ad·vice (ad vīs′) *n.* opinion given as to what to do or how to do something [We followed her *advice* in selecting a new home.]

af·fec·tion (ə fek′shən) *n.* fond or tender feeling; warm liking

af·ter (af′tər) *adv.* **1** behind; coming next [You go on ahead, and we'll follow *after*.] **2** following in time; later [They came at noon and left three hours *after*.] ◆*prep.* **1** behind [The soldiers marched one *after* the other.] **2** in search of [What are you *after*?] **3** later than [It's ten minutes *after* four.] **4** as a result of; because of [*After* what has happened, he won't go.]

air·craft (er′kraft) *n.* any machine or machines for flying [Airplanes, dirigibles, and helicopters are all *aircraft*.] —*pl.* **air′craft**

☆ **air·line** (er′līn) *n.* a system or company for moving freight and passengers by aircraft

al·low (ə lou′) *v.* **1** to let be done; permit; let [*Allow* us to pay. No smoking *allowed*.] **2** to let have [She *allows* herself no sweets.] **3** to let enter or stay [Dogs are not usually *allowed* on buses.] **4** to admit to be true or right [His claim for $50 was *allowed*.] —**al·lows′**

al·ly (al′ī) *n.* a country or person joined with another for a special purpose [England was our *ally* during World War II.] —*pl.* **al′lies**

al·pha·bet (al′fə bet) *n.* **1** the letters of a language, given in the regular order [The English *alphabet* goes from A to Z.] **2** any system of symbols used in writing [the Braille *alphabet*]

al·though (ôl thō′) *conj.* in spite of the fact that; even if; though: *sometimes spelled* **altho** [*Although* the sun is shining, it may rain later.]

al·ti·tude (al′tə tood′ *or* al′tə tyood′) *n.* **1** height; especially, the height of a thing above the earth's surface or above sea level **2** a high place

a·mount (ə mount′) *v.* to add up; total [The bill *amounts* to $4.50.] ◆*n.* **1** the sum; total [The bill was $50, but he paid only half that *amount*.] **2** a quantity [a small *amount* of rain]

am·pli·fy (am′plə fī′) *v.* to make larger, stronger, louder, etc. —**am′pli·fies′, am′pli·fied′, am′pli·fy′ing**

an·cient (ān′chənt *or* ān′shənt) *adj.* **1** of times long past; belonging to the early history of people, before about 500 A.D. **2** having lasted a long time; very old [their *ancient* quarrel]

An·go·ra (aŋ gôr′ə) *n.* **1** a kind of cat with long, silky fur **2** a kind of goat with long, silky hair: this hair, called **Angora wool**, is used in making mohair **3** a long-eared rabbit (**Angora rabbit**) with long, silky hair: this hair is used to make a soft yarn which is woven into sweaters, mittens, etc.

an·gry (aŋ′grē) *adj.* **1** feeling or showing anger [*angry* words; an *angry* crowd] **2** wild and stormy [an *angry* sea] —**an′gri·er, an′gri·est**

aircraft

a	ask, fat
ā	ape, date
ä	car, lot
e	elf, ten
ē	even, meet
i	is, hit
ī	ice, fire
ō	open, go
ô	law, horn
oi	oil, point
o͝o	look, pull
o͞o	ooze, tool
ou	out, crowd
u	up, cut
u	fur, fern
ə	a in ago
	e in agent
	e in father
	i in unity
	o in collect
	u in focus
ch	chin, arch
ŋ	ring, singer
sh	she, dash
th	thin, truth
th	then, father
zh	s in pleasure

an·swer (an'sər) *n.* **1** something said, written, or done in return to a question, argument, letter, action, etc.; reply; response [The only *answers* required for the test were "true" or "false." His *answer* to the insult was to turn his back.] **2** a solution to a problem, as in arithmetic ◆*v.* **1** to give an answer; reply or react, as to a question or action **2** to be responsible [You must *answer* for the children's conduct.]

Ant·arc·ti·ca (ant ärk'ti kə *or* ant är'ti kə) a large area of land, completely covered with ice, around the South Pole: *also called* **Antarctic Continent**

an·to·nym (an'tə nim) *n.* a word opposite in meaning to another word ["Sad" is an *antonym* of "happy."]

a·part·ment (ə pärt'mənt) *n.* a group of rooms, or a single large room, to live in: usually a single suite in a building (called an **apartment house**) of several or many suites

ap·pe·tiz·er (ap'ə tīz'ər) *n.* a small bit of a tasty food or a drink for giving one a bigger appetite at the beginning of a meal [Olives, tomato juice, etc. are used as *appetizers*.]

ap·ply (ə plī') *v.* **1** to put or spread on [*Apply* glue to the surface.] **2** to put into use [*Apply* your knowledge to this problem.] **3** to work hard and steadily [He *applied* himself to his studies.] **4** to have to do with or be suitable to [This rule *applies* to all of us.] —**ap·plied', ap·ply'ing**

ap·point (ə point') *v.* **1** to fix or set; decide upon [Let's *appoint* a time for our meeting.] **2** to name or choose for an office or position [Federal judges are *appointed* by the President.] —**ap·point'ed**

ap·proach (ə prōch') *v.* **1** to come closer or draw nearer [We saw three riders *approaching*. Vacation time *approaches*.] **2** to go to someone with a plan or request [Have you *approached* the bank about a loan?] ◆*n.* a coming closer or drawing nearer [The first robin marks the *approach* of spring.]

A·pril (ā'prəl) *n.* the fourth month of the year, which has 30 days: abbreviated **Apr.**

a·rith·me·tic (ə rith'mə tik') *n.* the science or skill of using numbers, especially in adding, subtracting, multiplying, and dividing

Ar·i·zo·na (ar'ə zō'nə) a state in the southwestern part of the U.S.: abbreviated **Ariz., AZ**

ar·mor (är'mər) *n.* **1** covering worn to protect the body against weapons [The knight's suit of *armor* was made of metal plates.] **2** any covering that protects, as the shell of a turtle or the metal plates on a warship

ar·my (är'mē) *n.* **1** a large group of soldiers trained for war, especially on land; all the soldiers of a country **2** a large group of persons organized to work for some cause [the Salvation *Army*] **3** any large group of persons or animals [An *army* of workers was building the bridge.] —*pl.* **ar'mies**

ar·riv·al (ə rī'vəl) *n.* **1** the act of arriving [to welcome the *arrival* of spring] **2** a person or thing that has arrived [They are recent *arrivals* to the U.S. from South America.]

ar·rive (ə rīv') *v.* **1** to come to a place after a journey [When does the bus from Chicago *arrive* here?] **2** to come [The time has *arrived* to say goodbye.] —**ar·rived', ar·riv'ing**

art·ist (ärt'ist) *n.* **1** a person who works in any of the fine arts, especially in painting, drawing, sculpting, etc. **2** a person who does anything very well

ash·es (ash'əz) *pl.n.* the grayish powder or fine dust that is left after something has been burned

A·sia (ā'zhə) the largest continent, about 17,000,000 square miles in area: the Pacific Ocean is on its east and it is separated from northern Europe by the Ural Mountains

as·tro·naut (as'trə nôt *or* as'trə nät) *n.* a person trained to make rocket flights in outer space

as·tron·o·my (ə strän'ə mē) *n.* the science that studies the motion, size, and makeup of the stars, planets, comets, etc.

au·di·ence (ô'dē əns *or* ä'dē əns) *n.* **1** a group of people gathered together to hear and see a speaker, a play, a concert, etc. **2** all those people who are tuned in to a radio or TV program

aunt (ant *or* änt) *n.* **1** a sister of one's mother or father **2** the wife of one's uncle

Aus·tral·ia (ô strāl'yə *or* ä strāl'yə) **1** an island continent in the Southern Hemisphere, southeast of Asia **2** a country made up of this continent and Tasmania

au·thor (ôthər *or* ä'ther) *n.* a person who writes something, as a book or story [She is the *author* of many mystery stories.]

au·to·graph (ôt'ə graf) *n.* something written in a person's own handwriting, especially that person's name ◆*v.* to write one's name on [Please *autograph* this baseball.]

au·to·mat·ic (ôt'ə mat'ik *or* ät'ə mat'ik) *adj.* **1** done without thinking about it, as if mechanically or from force of habit; unconscious [Breathing is usually *automatic*.] **2** moving or working by itself [*automatic* machinery]

a·vi·a·tor (ā'vē āt'ər) *n.* a person who flies airplanes; pilot

a·while (ə hwīl' *or* ə wīl') *adv.* for a while; for a short time [Sit down and rest *awhile*.]

awk·ward (ôk′wərd *or* äk′wərd) *adj.* **1** not having grace or skill; clumsy; bungling [an *awkward* dancer; an *awkward* writing style] **2** hard to use or manage; not convenient [an *awkward* tool] **3** uncomfortable; cramped [sitting in an *awkward* position] **4** embarrassed or embarrassing [an *awkward* remark] —**awk′ward·ly** *adv.*

ax or **axe** (aks) *n.* a tool for chopping or splitting wood: it has a long wooden handle and a metal head with a sharp blade —*pl.* **ax′es**

Bb

bag·gage (bag′ij) *n.* the trunks, suitcases, etc. that a person takes on a trip; luggage

bait (bāt) *n.* **1** food put on a hook or trap to attract and catch fish or animals **2** anything used to tempt or attract a person ◆*v.* **1** to put bait on a hook or trap **2** to torment or tease by saying annoying or cruel things [They *baited* me by calling me "Fatty."]

bal·co·ny (bal′kə nē) *n.* **1** a platform with a low wall or railing, that juts out from the side of a building **2** an upper floor of rows of seats, as in a theater: it often juts out over the main floor —*pl.* **bal′co·nies**

bal·lot (bal′ət) *n.* **1** a piece of paper on which a person marks a choice in voting **2** the act or a way of voting

band·age (ban′dij) *n.* a strip of cloth, gauze, etc. used to cover a sore or wound ◆*v.* to bind or cover with a bandage; to bind up an injured part of the body —**band′aged, band′ag·ing**

☆ **ban·jo** (ban′jō) *n.* a stringed musical instrument with a long neck and a round body covered on top with tightly stretched skins: it has, usually, four or five strings that are plucked with the fingers or a pick —*pl.* **ban′jos** or **ban′joes**

ban·ner (ban′ər) *n.* **1** a piece of cloth with an emblem or words on it [The *banner* behind the President's desk bears the seal of the United States] **2** a flag [the Star-Spangled *Banner*] **3** a headline across a newspaper page ◆*adj.* top; leading [Our company had a *banner* year in sales.]

barge (bärj) *n.* a large boat with a flat bottom, for carrying goods on rivers or canals ◆*v.* to enter in a clumsy or rude way [They *barged* in without knocking.] —**barged, barg′ing**

ba·rom·e·ter (bə räm′ə tər) *n.* **1** an instrument that measures the pressure of the air around us: it is used in forecasting changes in the weather and finding the height above sea level **2** anything that shows changes in conditions [The stock market is a *barometer* of business.] —**bar·o·met·ric** (bar′ə met′rik) *adj.*

bar·rel (bar′əl) *n.* **1** a large, round container that has bulging sides and a flat top and bottom: usually made of wooden slats bound together by metal hoops **2** the amount a barrel will hold: the standard barrel in the U.S. holds 31 1/2 gallons (119.2275 liters) ◆*v.* to put in barrels —**bar′reled** or **bar′relled, bar′rel·ing** or **bar′rel·ling**

bask (bask) *v.* to warm oneself pleasantly [to *bask* in the sun]

bass (bas) *n.* a fish with spiny fins, found in both fresh and salt water and used for food —*pl.* **bass** or **bass′es**

bat·ter·y (bat′ər ē) *n.* an electric cell or a group of connected cells that furnishes an electric current [*Batteries* are used in automobiles and flashlights.] —*pl.* **bat′ter·ies**

be·gin (bē gin′) *v.* to start being, doing, acting, etc.; get under way [Work *begins* at 8:00 A.M. My cold *began* with a sore throat.] —**be·gan′, be·gun′, be·gin′ning**

be·gin·ning (bē gin′iŋ) *n.* a start or starting; first part or first action [We came in just after the *beginning* of the movie. Going to the dance together was the *beginning* of our friendship.]

be·lief (bē lēf′) *n.* a feeling that something is true or real; faith [You cannot destroy my *belief* in the honesty of most people.] —*pl.* **be·liefs**

be·lieve (bē lēv′) *v.* **1** to accept as true or real [Can we *believe* that story?] **2** to have trust or confidence [I know you will win; I *believe* in you.] **3** to suppose; guess —**be·lieved′, be·liev′ing** —**be·liev′a·ble** *adj.* —**be·liev′er** *n.*

bench (bench) *n.* **1** a long, hard seat for several persons, with or without a back **2** a strong table on which work with tools is done [a carpenter's *bench*] **3** the place where judges sit in a courtroom **4** a seat where sports players sit when not on the field —*pl.* **bench′es**

bend (bend) *v.* **1** to pull or press something hard or stiff into a curve or angle [*Bend* the branch down so we can reach the plums.] **2** to be curved in this way [The trees *bent* under the weight of the snow.] **3** to stoop [*Bend* over and touch your toes.] —**bent, bend′ing** ◆*n.* **1** the act of bending **2** a bent or curving part

ax

a	ask, fat
ä	ape, date
ä	car, lot
e	elf, ten
ē	even, meet
i	is, hit
ī	ice, fire
ō	open, go
ô	law, horn
oi	oil, point
σο	look, pull
ᴏᴏ	ooze, tool
ou	out, crowd
u	up, cut
ʉ	fur, fern
ə	a in ago
	e in agent
	e in father
	i in unity
	o in collect
	u in focus
ch	chin, arch
ŋ	ring, singer
sh	she, dash
th	thin, truth
ih	then, father
zh	s in pleasure

bicycle

be·tween (bē twēn') *prep.* **1** in the space, time, or degree that separates [a lake *between* the United States and Canada; office hours *between* one and five o'clock; a color *between* blue and green] **2** having to do with; involving [the war *between* the North and the South] **3** that connects [a road *between* Reno and Yuma; a bond *between* friends]

bev·er·age (bev'ər ij *or* bev'rij) *n.* any kind of drink (except water), as milk, coffee, or lemonade

bi·cy·cle (bī'si kəl) *n.* a vehicle to ride on that has two wheels, one behind the other: it is moved by foot pedals and steered by a handlebar ◆*v.* to ride a bicycle —**bi′cy·cled, bi′cy·cling**

birth·day (burth'dā) *n.* **1** the day on which a person is born or something is begun **2** the anniversary of this day

bi·son (bī'sən) *n.* a wild animal of the ox family, with a shaggy mane, short, curved horns, and a humped back: the American bison is often called a *buffalo* —*pl.* **bi′son**

blend (blend) *v.* **1** to mix different kinds together in order to get a certain flavor, color, etc. [to *blend* tea or paint] **2** to come together or mix so that the parts are no longer distinct [The sky *blended* with the sea at the horizon.] **3** to go well together; be in harmony [Her blue sweater *blends* well with her gray skirt.] ◆*n.* a mixture of different kinds [a *blend* of coffee] —**blend′ed, blend′ing**

☆ **bliz·zard** (bliz'ərd) *n.* a heavy snowstorm with very strong, cold winds

board (bôrd) *n.* **1** a long, flat, broad piece of sawed wood, used in building **2** a flat piece of wood or other hard material made for a special use [a checker*board*; a bulletin *board*; an ironing *board*] **3** a group of people who manage or control a business, school, department, etc. [*board* of education] ◆*v.* **1** to cover up with boards [The windows of the old house were *boarded* up.] **2** to get on a ship, airplane, bus, etc.

boast (bōst) *v.* **1** to talk about with too much pride and pleasure; praise too highly; brag [We tired of hearing him *boast* of his bravery.] **2** to be proud of having [Our city *boasts* a fine new zoo.] —**boast′ed**

bob (bäb) *v.* **1** to move with short, jerky motions [Our heads *bobbed* up and down as our car bounced over the ruts.] **2** to cut off short [to *bob* a dog's tail] —**bobbed, bob′bing** ◆*n.* **1** a short, jerky movement [She greeted us with a *bob* of her head.] **2** a style of short haircut for women or girls **3** a hanging weight at the end of a plumb line **4** a cork on a fishing line

bod·y (bäd'ē) *n.* **1** the whole physical part of a person or animal [Athletes have strong *bodies*.] **2** the main part of a person or animal, not including the head, legs, and arms [The boxer received many blows to the *body*.] **3** the main or central part of anything, as the trunk of a tree or the part of a car that holds the passengers —*pl.* **bod′ies**

boil (boil) *v.* **1** to bubble up and become steam or vapor by being heated [Water *boils* at 100°C.] **2** to heat a liquid until it bubbles up in this way [to *boil* water] **3** to cook in a boiling liquid [to *boil* potatoes] **4** to be stirred up, as with rage ◆*n.* the condition of boiling [Bring the soup to a *boil*.]

bomb (bäm) *n.* a hollow case filled with an explosive or a poisonous gas: bombs are blown up by a fuse or timing device or by being dropped or thrown against something with force

☆ **boss** (bôs *or* bäs) *n.* **1** a person who is in charge of workers, as an employer, a manager, or a supervisor **2** a person who controls a political group, as in a county —*pl.* **bosses** ◆*v.* to act as boss of

both·er (bäth'ər) *v.* **1** to annoy; cause worry or trouble to; pester [Does the noise *bother* you?] **2** to take the time or trouble [Don't *bother* to answer this letter.] ◆*n.* something that annoys or causes worry or trouble [Flies are a *bother*.]

bot·tle (bät'l) *n.* **1** a container, especially for liquids, usually made of glass or plastic: bottles generally have a narrow neck and no handles **2** the amount that a bottle holds [The baby drank a *bottle* of milk.] ◆*v.* **1** to put into a bottle or into bottles **2** to store under pressure in a tank [*bottled* gas] —**bot′tled, bot′tling**

bounce (bouns) *v.* **1** to hit against a surface so as to spring back; bound or rebound [to *bounce* a ball against a wall; to *bounce* up and down on a sofa] **2** to move suddenly; jump; leap [I *bounced* out of bed when the alarm went off.] —**bounced, bounc′ing** ◆*n.* **1** a springing or bounding; leap **2** the ability to bound or rebound [This ball has lost its *bounce*.]

bounc·ing (boun'siŋ) *adj.* big, healthy, strong, etc. [It's a *bouncing* baby boy.]

bou·quet (boo kā' *or* bō kā') *n.* **1** a bunch of flowers **2** (boo kā') a fragrant smell

☆ **box·car** (bäks'kär') *n.* a railroad car for carrying freight, with a roof and closed sides

brain (brān) *n.* **1** the gray and white tissue inside the skull of a person or of any animal with a backbone: it is the main part of the nervous system, by which one thinks and feels **2** *often* **brains**, *pl.* intelligence; understanding

brake (brāk) *n.* a device used to slow down or stop a car, machine, etc.: it is often a block or band that is pressed against a wheel or other moving part ◆*v.* to slow down or stop with a brake —**braked, brak′ing**

branch (branch) *n.* any part of a tree growing from the trunk or from a main limb

break (brāk) *v.* 1 to come or make come apart by force; split or crack sharply into pieces [*Break* an egg into the bowl. The rusty hinge *broke.*] 2 to force one's way [A firefighter *broke* through the door.] 3 to get out of working order; make or become useless [You can *break* your watch by winding it too tightly.] 4 to fail to carry out or follow [to *break* an agreement; to *break* the law] —**broke, bro′ken, break′ing** ◆*n.* 1 a broken place [The X-ray showed a *break* in the bone.] 2 an interruption [Recess is a relaxing *break* in our school day.]

break·down (brāk′doun) *n.* a failure to work properly [*breakdown* of a machine]

break·fast (brek′fəst) *n.* the first meal of the day ◆*v.* to eat breakfast

breeze (brēz) *n.* 1 a light and gentle wind 2 a thing easy to do; *used only in everyday talk* [The test was a *breeze.*] ◆*v.* to move or go quickly, briskly, etc.: *slang in this meaning* —**breezed, breez′ing**

brief (brēf) *adj.* 1 not lasting very long; short in time [a *brief* visit] 2 using just a few words; not wordy; concise [a *brief* news report] ◆*v.* to give the main points or necessary facts to [to *brief* pilots before a flight] —**brief′ly** *adv.* —**brief′ness** *n.*

bril·liant (bril′yənt) *adj.* 1 very bright; glittering or sparkling [the *brilliant* sun on the water] 2 outstanding or distinguished [a *brilliant* performance]

bring (briŋ) *v.* 1 to carry or lead here or to the place where the speaker will be [*Bring* it to my house tomorrow.] 2 to cause to happen or come [War *brings* death and hunger.]

broc·co·li (bräk′ə lē) *n.* a plant whose tender shoots and loose heads of tiny green buds are eaten as a vegetable

broil (broil) *v.* 1 to cook or be cooked close to a flame or other high heat [to *broil* steaks over charcoal] 2 to make or be very hot [a *broiling* summer day] ◆*n.* the act or state of broiling —**broil′ing**

broth·er (bru*th*′ər) *n.* 1 a boy or man as he is related to the other children of his parents 2 a person who is close to one in some way; especially, a fellow member of the same race, religion, club, etc. —*pl.* **broth′ers**

brought (brôt *or* brät) *past tense and past participle of* **bring**

buf·fa·lo (buf′ə lō′) *n.* a wild ox, sometimes tamed as a work animal, as the water buffalo of India: the American bison is also commonly called a *buffalo* —*pl.* **buf′fa·loes′** or **buf′fa·los′** or **buf′fa·lo′**

bump (bump) *v.* 1 to knock against something; hit with a jolt [The bus *bumped* the car ahead of it. Don't *bump* into the wall.] 2 to move with jerks or jumps; jolt [The car *bumped* over the railroad tracks.] ◆*n.* 1 a knock or blow; light jolt 2 a part that bulges out, causing an uneven surface 3 a swelling caused by a blow

bur·y (ber′ē) *v.* 1 to put a dead body into the earth, a tomb, or the sea [The Egyptians *buried* the pharaohs in pyramids.] 2 to cover up so as to hide [He *buried* his face in his hands.] 3 to put away and forget [Let's *bury* our feud.] 4 to put oneself deeply into [She *buried* herself in her work.] —**bur′ies, bur′ied, bur′y·ing**

busi·ness (biz′nəs) *n.* 1 what one does for a living; one's work or occupation [Shakespeare's *business* was writing plays.] 2 what one has a right or duty to do [You had no *business* telling her I was here.] 3 the buying and selling of goods and services; commerce; trade 4 a place where things are made or sold; store or factory [Nino owns three *businesses.*] —*pl.* **bus′i·ness·es**

but·ter·milk (but′ər milk) *n.* the sour liquid left after churning butter from milk

buy (bī) *v.* to get by paying money or something else [The Dutch *bought* Manhattan Island for about $24.] —**bought, buy′ing**

byte (bīt) *n.* a series of computer bits, usually eight, used as a single piece of information

cab·in (kab′in) *n.* 1 a small house built in a simple, rough way, usually of wood [Lincoln was born in a log *cabin.*] 2 a room on a ship, especially one with berths for sleeping 3 the space in an airplane where the passengers ride

☆**ca·boose** (kə bōōs′) *n.* a car for the crew on a freight train: it is usually the last car

cac·tus (kak′təs) *n.* a plant with fleshy stems that bear spines or scales instead of leaves: cactuses grow in hot, dry places and often have showy flowers —*pl.* **cac′tus·es** or **cac·ti** (kak′tī)

a	ask, fat
ā	ape, date
ä	car, lot
e	elf, ten
ē	even, meet
i	is, hit
ī	ice, fire
ō	open, go
ô	law, horn
oi	oil, point
oo	look, pull
o͞o	ooze, tool
ou	out, crowd
u	up, cut
u	fur, fern
ə	a in ago
	e in agent
	e in father
	i in unity
	o in collect
	u in focus
ch	chin, arch
ŋ	ring, singer
sh	she, dash
th	thin, truth
th	then, father
zh	s in pleasure

chain

cal·cu·la·tor (kal'kyōō lāt'ər) *n.* **1** a person who calculates **2** a machine that adds, subtracts, etc. rapidly, now often by electronic means

calf¹ (kaf) *n.* **1** a young cow or bull **2** a young elephant, whale, hippopotamus, seal, etc. **3** *a shorter word for* **calfskin** —*pl.* **calves**

calf² (kaf) *n.* the fleshy back part of the leg between the knee and the ankle —*pl.* **calves**

cam·el (kam'əl) *n.* a large, cud-chewing animal with a humped back, that is commonly used for riding and for carrying goods in Asian and North African deserts: when food and drink are scarce, it can keep going for a few days on the fat and water stored in its body tissue: the **Arabian camel** has one hump and the **Bac·tri·an** (bak'trē ən) **camel** has two

can·di·date (kan'di dāt') *n.* a person who seeks, or who has been suggested for, an office or award [a *candidate* for mayor]

car·di·nal (kärd'n əl) *adj.* **1** of most importance; chief [The *cardinal* points of the compass are north, south, east, and west.] **2** bright red ◆☆*n.* an American songbird that is bright red and has a black face

car·go (kär'gō) *n.* the load of goods carried by a ship, airplane, truck, etc. —*pl.* **car'goes** *or* **car'gos**

car·ry (ker'ē) *v.* **1** to take from one place to another; transport or conduct [Please help me *carry* these books home. The large pipe *carries* water. Air *carries* sounds.] **2** to cause to go; lead [A love of travel *carried* them around the world.] **3** to bring over a figure from one column to the next in adding a row of figures —**car'ried, car'ry·ing**

car·ton (kärt'n) *n.* a box or other container made of cardboard, plastic, etc.

cast (kast) *v.* **1** to throw out or down; toss; fling; hurl [to *cast* stones into the water; to *cast* a line in fishing] **2** to deposit a ballot or vote ◆*n.* a stiff plaster form for keeping a broken arm or leg in place while it is healing —**cast, cast'ing**

catch·er (kach'ər *or* kech'ər) *n.* **1** one who catches ☆**2** in baseball, the player behind home plate, who catches pitched balls that are not hit away by the batter

cat·e·go·ry (kat'ə gôr'ē) *n.* a division of a main subject or group; class [Biology is divided into two *categories*, zoology and botany.] —*pl.* **cat'e·go'ries**

cause (kôz *or* käz) *n.* **1** a person or thing that brings about some action or result [A spark from the wire was the *cause* of the fire.] **2** a reason for some action, feeling, etc. [We had *cause* to admire the coach.] ◆*v.* to be the cause of; make happen; bring about [The icy streets *caused* some accidents.] —**caused, caus'ing** —**cause'less** *adj.*

cau·tious (kô'shəs *or* kä'shəs) *adj.* careful not to get into danger or make mistakes [a *cautious* chess player] —**cau'tious·ly** *adv.*

ceil·ing (sēl'iŋ) *n.* the inside top part of a room, opposite the floor

cel·e·ry (sel'ər ē) *n.* a plant whose crisp, long stalks are eaten as a vegetable

ce·ment (sə ment') *n.* **1** a powder made of lime and clay, mixed with water and sand to make mortar or with water, sand, and gravel to make concrete: it hardens like stone when it dries **2** any soft substance that fastens things together when it hardens, as paste or glue ◆*v.* to fasten together or cover with cement [to *cement* the pieces of a broken cup]

cen·ter (sen'tər) *n.* **1** a point inside a circle or sphere that is the same distance from all points on the circumference or surface **2** the middle point or part; place at the middle [A vase of flowers stood at the *center* of the table.] ◆*v.* to place in or at the center [Try to *center* the design on the page.]

chain (chān) *n.* **1** a number of links or loops joined together in a line that can be bent [a *chain* of steel; a *chain* of daisies] **2 chains,** *pl.* anything that binds or holds someone prisoner, as bonds or shackles **3** a series of things joined together [a mountain *chain*; a *chain* of events] ◆*v.* **1** to fasten or bind with chains [The prisoner was *chained* to the wall.] **2** to hold down; bind [I was *chained* to my job.]

cham·pi·on (cham'pē ən') *n.* a person, animal, or thing that wins first place or is judged to be best in a contest or sport [a tennis *champion*]

change (chānj) *v.* **1** to make or become different in some way; alter [Time *changes* all things. His voice began to *change* at the age of thirteen.] **2** to put or take one thing in place of another; substitute [to *change* one's clothes; to *change* jobs] **3** to give or take one thing in return for another; substitute [Let's *change* seats. Can you *change* this dollar bill for four quarters?] —**changed, chang'ing** ◆*n.* **1** the act of changing in some way [There will be a *change* in the weather tomorrow.] **2** something put in place of something else [a fresh *change* of clothing] **3** the money returned when one has paid more than the amount owed [If it costs 70 cents and you pay with a dollar, you get back 30 cents as *change*.]

charge (chärj) **v. 1** to load or fill [to *charge* a gun with ammunition] ☆**2** to supply with electrical energy [to *charge* a battery] **3** to give a task, duty, etc. to; make responsible for [The nurse was *charged* with the care of the child.] **4** to set as a price; ask for payment [Barbers once *charged* a quarter for a haircut. We do not *charge* for gift wrappings.] —**charged, charg'ing**

chat (chat) **v.** to talk in an easy, relaxed way —**chat'ted, chat'ting ◆n.** an easy, relaxed talk or conversation

cheat (chēt) **v.** to act in a dishonest or unfair way in order to get what one wants [to *cheat* on a test]

check (chek) **n. 1** a test to find out if something is as it should be [Add the column of numbers again as a *check* on your answer.] **2** the mark √, used to show that something is right, or to call attention to something **3** a piece of paper telling how much one owes, as for a meal at a restaurant **4** a written order to a bank to pay a certain amount of money from one's account to a certain person **5** a pattern of small squares like a checkerboard; also, any of the squares in such a pattern ◆**v.** to prove to be right or find what is wanted by examining, comparing, etc. [These figures *check* with mine. *Check* the records for this information.] —**checked, check'ing**

cheer·ful (chir'fəl) **adj. 1** full of cheer; glad; joyful [a *cheerful* smile] **2** bright and gay [a *cheerful* room] **3** willing; glad to help [a *cheerful* worker] —**cheer'ful·ly adv.** —**cheer'ful·ness n.**

chee·tah (chēt'ə) **n.** an animal found in Africa and southern Asia that is like the leopard but smaller: it can be trained to hunt

cher·ry (cher'ē) **n. 1** a small, round fruit with sweet flesh covering a smooth, hard seed: cherries are bright red, dark red, or yellow **2** the tree that this fruit grows on **3** bright red —*pl.* **cher'ries**

Chi·ca·go (shi kä'gō) a city in northeastern Illinois

chick·en (chik'ən) **n. 1** a common farm bird raised for its eggs and flesh; hen or rooster, especially a young one **2** the flesh of a chicken

chief (chēf) **n.** the leader or head of some group [an Indian *chief*; the *chief* of a hospital staff] —*pl.* **chiefs ◆adj. 1** having the highest position [the *chief* foreman] **2** main; most important [Jill's *chief* interest is golf.]

chief·ly (chēf'lē) **adv.** most of all; mainly; mostly [A watermelon is *chiefly* water.]

child (chīld) **n. 1** a baby; infant **2** a young boy or girl **3** a son or daughter [Their *children* are all grown up.] —*pl.* **chil'dren**

chil·dren (chīl'drən) **n.** *plural* of **child**

chim·ney (chim'nē) **n. 1** a pipe or shaft going up through a roof to carry off smoke from a furnace, fireplace, or stove: chimneys are usually enclosed with brick or stone **2** a glass tube around the flame of a lamp —*pl.* **chim'neys**

Chi·na (chī'nə) a country in eastern Asia: it has the most people of any country in the world

☆**chow·der** (chou'dər) **n.** a thick soup made of fish or clams with onions, potatoes, milk, or tomatoes, etc.

church (church) **n. 1** a building for holding religious services, especially one for Christian worship **2** religious services [*Church* will be at 11 a.m. on Sunday.] —*pl.* **church'es**

cir·cle (sur'kəl) **n. 1** a closed curved line forming a perfectly round, flat figure: every point on this line is the same distance from a point inside called the center **2** the figure formed by such a line **3** anything round like a circle or ring [a *circle* of children playing a game]

clap (klap) **v. 1** to make the sudden, loud sound of two flat surfaces being struck together **2** to strike the palms of the hands together, as in applauding —**clapped, clap'ping ◆n. 1** the sudden, loud sound of clapping [a *clap* of thunder] **2** a sharp blow; slap

clash (klash) **n. 1** a loud, harsh noise, as of metal striking against metal with great force [the *clash* of a sword on a shield] **2** a sharp disagreement; conflict [a *clash* of ideas] —*pl.* **clash'es ◆v.** to strike with a clash [He *clashed* the cymbals together.]

clasp (klasp) **n. 1** a fastening, as a hook or catch, for holding two things or parts together [The *clasp* on my pocketbook is loose.] **2** a holding in the arms; embrace **3** a holding with the hand; grip ◆**v.** to fasten with a clasp

class (klas) ☆a group of students meeting together to be taught [Half the *class* missed school today.] —*pl.* **clas·ses**

claw (klô *or* klä) **n. 1** a sharp, curved nail on the foot of an animal or bird **2** a foot with such nails [The eagle holds its victims in its *claws*.] **3** the grasping part on each front leg of a lobster, crab, or scorpion

clean (klēn) **adj. 1** without dirt or impure matter [*clean* dishes; *clean* oil] **2** without evil or wrongdoing [to lead a *clean* life] **3** neat and tidy [to keep a *clean* desk] ◆**v.** to make clean [Please *clean* the oven.] —**cleaned, clean'ing**

clerk (klurk) **n. 1** an office worker who keeps records, types letters, etc. [Some *clerks*, as a *clerk* of courts or a city *clerk*, have special duties.] ☆**2** a person who sells in a store; salesperson

cherries

a	ask, fat
ā	ape, date
ä	car, lot
e	elf, ten
ē	even, meet
i	is, hit
ī	ice, fire
ō	open, go
ô	law, horn
oi	oil, point
oo	look, pull
ōō	ooze, tool
ou	out, crowd
u	up, cut
ʉ	fur, fern
ə	a in ago
	e in agent
	e in father
	i in unity
	o in collect
	u in focus
ch	chin, arch
ŋ	ring, singer
sh	she, dash
th	thin, truth
th	then, father
zh	s in pleasure

Cleve·land (klēv'lənd) a city in northeastern Ohio

cli·mate (klī'mət) *n.* **1** the average weather conditions of a place over a period of years [Arizona has a mild, dry *climate*, but its weather last week was stormy.] **2** a region with particular weather conditions [They went south to a warmer *climate*.]

clo·ver (klō'vər) *n.* a low-growing plant with leaves in three parts and small, sweet-smelling flowers. Red *clover* is grown for fodder; white *clover* is often found in lawns

clue (kloo) *n.* a fact or thing that helps to solve a puzzle or mystery [Muddy footprints were a *clue* to the man's guilt.]

clum·sy (klum'zē) *adj.* not having good control in moving the hands or feet; awkward [The *clumsy* waiter dropped the dish.] —**clum'si·er, clum'si·est**

cock·pit (käk'pit) *n.* in a small airplane, the space where the pilot and passengers sit: in a large plane, it is the space for the pilot and copilot

col·an·der (kul'ən dər *or* käl'ən dər) *n.* a pan with holes in the bottom for draining off liquids, as in washing vegetables

cold (kōld) *adj.* **1** having a temperature much lower than that of the human body; very chilly; frigid [a *cold* day; a *cold* drink] **2** without the proper heat or warmth [Your bath will get *cold*.] **3** feeling chilled [If you are *cold*, put on your coat.] **4** without any feeling; unkind, unfriendly, or gloomy [a *cold* welcome; a *cold* stare] —**cold'er, cold'est**

col·lege (käl'ij) *n.* a school that one can go to after high school for higher studies

Co·lum·bus (kə lum'bəs) the capital of Ohio

comb (kōm) *n.* a thin strip of hard rubber, plastic, metal, etc. with teeth: a comb is passed through the hair to arrange or clean it, or is put in the hair to hold it in place ◆*v.* **1** to smooth, arrange, or clean with a comb **2** to search carefully through [I *combed* the house for that book.]

come (kum) *v.* **1** to move from "there" to "here" [*Come* to me. Will you *come* to our party?] **2** to arrive or appear [Help will *come* soon.] —**came, com'ing**

com·ing (kum'iŋ) *adj.* that will come; approaching; on the way [Let's go this *coming* Friday.] ◆*n.* arrival; approach [Cold mornings warn of the *coming* of winter.]

com·mon (käm'ən) *adj.* **1** belonging equally to each or all [The science club members share a *common* interest.] **2** belonging to all the people; public [a *common* park] **3** of, from, by, or to all [the *common* good] **4** often seen or heard; widespread; usual [Squirrels are *common* in these woods. That's a *common* saying.]

com·mu·ni·ty (kə myoo'ni tē) *n.* **1** all the people who live in a particular district, city, etc. [The new swimming pool is for the use of the entire *community*.] **2** a group of people living together and having similar interests and work [a college *community*] —*pl.* **com·mu·ni·ties**

☆**com·mut·er** (kə myoot'ər) *n.* a person who travels daily by train, bus, car, etc. between home and work or school

com·pare (kəm per') *v.* **1** to describe as being the same; liken [The sound of thunder can be *compared* to the roll of drums.] **2** to examine certain things in order to find out how they are alike or different [How do the two cars *compare* in size and price?] **3** to equal or come close to by comparison [Few dogs can *compare* with the Great Dane in size.] —**com·pared', com·par'ing**

com·put·er (kəm pyoot'ər) *n.* **1** a person who computes **2** an electronic device used as a calculator or to store and select data

con·duct (kän'dukt) *n.* the way one acts or behaves; behavior [The teacher praised the students for their good *conduct* in class.] ◆*v.* (kən dukt') **1** to manage; direct; be the leader of [to *conduct* a meeting; to *conduct* an orchestra] **2** to behave [They *conducted* themselves like adults.] **3** to be a means for carrying; transmit [Copper *conducts* electricity.]

cone (kōn) *n.* a solid object that narrows evenly from a flat circle at one end to a point at the other

con·stel·la·tion (kän'stə lā'shən) *n.* a group of stars, usually named after something that it is supposed to suggest [Orion is a *constellation* seen in the winter sky.]

con·struct (kən strukt') *v.* to make or build with a plan [to *construct* a house or a theory]

con·tact (kän'takt) *v.* to get in touch with; communicate with [*Contact* my cousin as soon as possible.]

con·test (kən test') *v.* **1** to try to prove that something is not true, right, or lawful; dispute [to *contest* a will] **2** to fight for; struggle to win or keep [to *contest* a prize] ◆*n.* (kän'test) **1** a fight, struggle, or argument **2** a race, game, etc. in which there is a struggle to be the winner

con·ti·nent (kän'ti nənt) *n.* any of the main large land areas of the earth: the continents are Africa, Asia, Australia, Europe, North America, South America, and, sometimes, Antarctica —**the Continent**, all of Europe except the British Isles

con·tin·ue (kən tin′yoo) *v.* **1** to keep on being or doing [The rain *continued* for five days.] **2** to stay in the same place or position [The chairman will *continue* in office for another year.] **3** to go on or start again after a stop; resume [After a sip of water, the speaker *continued*.] **4** to go on or extend; stretch —**con·tin′ued, con·tin′u·ing**

con·trol (kən trōl′) *v.* **1** to have the power of ruling, guiding, or managing [A thermostat *controls* the heat.] **2** to hold back; curb [*Control* your temper!] —**con·trolled′, con·trol′ling** ◆*n.* power to direct or manage [He's a poor coach, with little *control* over the team.]

con·vince (kən vins′) *v.* to make feel sure; persuade [I'm *convinced* they are telling the truth.] —**con·vinced′, con·vinc′ing**

con·voy (kän′voi) *n.* a group of ships or vehicles traveling together in order to protect one another

cop·y (käp′ē) *n.* **1** a thing made just like another; imitation or likeness [four carbon *copies* of a letter] **2** any one of a number of books, magazines, pictures, etc. with the same printed matter [a library with six *copies* of *Tom Sawyer*] **3** a piece of writing that is to be set in type for printing [Reporters must write clear *copy*.] —*pl.* **cop′ies** ◆*v.* **1** to make a copy or copies of [*Copy* the questions that are on the chalkboard.] **2** to act or be the same as; imitate —**cop′ied, cop′y·ing**

cor·al (kôr′əl) *n.* **1** a hard, stony substance made up of the skeletons of many tiny sea animals: reefs of coral are found in tropical seas **2** piece of coral ◆*adj.* **1** made of coral **2** yellowish-red in color

cor·ner (kôr′nər) *n.* **1** the place where two lines or surfaces come together to form an angle **2** the space between such lines or surfaces [a lamp in the *corner* of a room] **3** the place where two streets meet **4** a place or region; quarter [every *corner* of America]

cos·tume (käs′toom *or* käs′tyoom) *n.* **1** the way or style of dressing of a certain place or time or for a certain purpose [a Japanese *costume*; an eighteenth-century *costume*; a riding *costume*] **2** clothing worn by an actor in a play or by a person at a masquerade [a pirate *costume*]

cot·tage (kät′ij) *n.* a small house [a peasant's *cottage*; a summer *cottage* at the beach]

cou·gar (koo′gər) *n.* a large animal of the cat family, with a slender, tan body and a long tail

cough (kôf *or* käf) *v.* **1** to force air from the lungs with a sudden, loud noise, as to clear the throat **2** to get out of the throat by coughing [to *cough* up phlegm] ◆*n.* **1** the act or sound of coughing **2** a condition of coughing often [I have a bad *cough*.]

coun·ty (koun′tē) *n.* ☆**1** in the United States, any of the sections into which a state is divided: each county has its own officials **2** any of the districts into which Great Britain and Ireland are divided —*pl.* **coun′ties**

cou·ple (kup′əl) *n.* two things of the same kind that go together; pair [a *couple* of bookends]

cour·age (kur′ij) *n.* the quality of being able to control one's fear and so to face danger, pain, or trouble willingly; bravery

cous·in (kuz′ən) *n.* **1** the son or daughter of one's uncle or aunt: *also called* **first cousin**. You are a *second cousin* to the children of your parents' first cousins, and you are a *first cousin once removed* to the children of your first cousins. **2** a distant relation

crack (krak) *v.* **1** to make or cause to make a sudden, sharp noise, as of something breaking [The lion tamer *cracked* his whip.] **2** to break or split, with or without the parts falling apart [The snowball *cracked* the window. *Crack* the coconut open.] **3** to become harsh or change pitch suddenly [Her voice *cracked* when she sang the highest note.]

craft (kraft) *n.* **1** special skill or ability **2** work that takes special skill, especially with the hands [the *craft* of weaving] **3** the members of a skilled trade **4** skill in fooling or tricking others; slyness

crash (krash) *v.* **1** to fall, hit, or break with force and with a loud, smashing noise **2** to fall to the earth so as to be damaged or smashed [The airplane *crashed*.] ◆*n.* **1** a loud, smashing noise **2** the crashing of a car, airplane, etc.

cray·on (krā′ən *or* krā′än) *n.* a small stick of chalk, charcoal, or colored wax, used for drawing or writing ◆*v.* to draw with crayons

cra·zy (krā′zē) *adj.* mentally ill; insane —**cra′zi·er, cra′zi·est**

cream (krēm) *n.* **1** the oily, yellowish part of milk that rises to the top and contains the butterfat **2** any food that is made of cream or is like cream [ice *cream*] **3** a smooth, oily substance used to clean and soften the skin

creep (krēp) *v.* **1** to move along with the body close to the ground, as a baby on hands and knees **2** to move in a slow or sneaking way [The cars *crept* along in the heavy traffic. The thieves *crept* into the store at night.] **3** to come on almost without being noticed [Old age *crept* up on her.] —**crept, creep′ing**

crept (krept) *v.* *past tense and past participle of* **creep**

cries (krīz) **1** *the form of the verb* **cry** *used in the present with* he, she, *or* it **2** *the plural of the noun* **cry**

a	ask, fat
ā	ape, date
ä	car, lot
e	elf, ten
ē	even, meet
i	is, hit
ī	ice, fire
ō	open, go
ô	law, horn
oi	oil, point
oo	look, pull
oo	ooze, tool
ou	out, crowd
u	up, cut
u	fur, fern
ə	a in ago
	e in agent
	e in father
	i in unity
	o in collect
	u in focus
ch	chin, arch
ŋ	ring, singer
sh	she, dash
th	thin, truth
th	then, father
zh	s in pleasure

crime (krīm) *n.* **1** the doing of something that is against the law; serious wrongdoing that breaks the law **2** an evil or foolish act; sin [It would be a *crime* to waste this food.]

cruise (krōōz) *v.* **1** to sail or drive about from place to place, as for pleasure or in searching for something **2** to move smoothly at a speed that is not strained [The airplane *cruised* at 300 miles per hour.] —**cruised, cruis'ing** ✦*n.* a ship voyage from place to place for pleasure

crumb (krum) *n.* **1** a tiny piece broken off, as of bread or cake **2** any bit or scrap [*crumbs* of knowledge]

crunch (krunch) *v.* **1** to chew with a noisy, crackling sound [to *crunch* raw carrots] **2** to grind or move over with a noisy, crushing sound [The wheels *crunched* the pebbles in the driveway.]

crush (krush) *v.* **1** to press or squeeze with force so as to break, hurt, or put out of shape [She *crushed* the flower in her hand. His hat was *crushed* when he sat on it.] **2** to grind or pound into bits [This machine *crushes* rocks.] **3** to bring to an end by force; subdue; suppress [The government *crushed* the revolt.] ✦*n.* a crushing or squeezing; strong pressure

cry (krī) *v.* **1** to make a loud sound with the voice; call out or shout [Lou *cried* out in fright when a face appeared at the window.] **2** to show sorrow, pain, etc. by sobbing or shedding tears **3** to say loudly; shout; exclaim ["Help! Help!" the victim *cried*.] —**cried, cry'ing** ✦*n.* **1** a loud sound made by the voice; shout or call [I heard your *cry* for help.] **2** a fit of sobbing and weeping [I had a good *cry* and fell asleep.] **3** the sound an animal makes [the *cry* of a lost sheep] —*pl.* **cries**

cry

cube (kyōōb) *n.* **1** a solid with six square sides, all the same size **2** anything with more or less this shape [an ice *cube*] **3** the result got by multiplying a number by itself and then multiplying the product by the same number [The *cube* of 3 is 27 (3 × 3 × 3 = 27).] ✦*v.* to cut into cubes [I *cubed* the fruit for salad.] —**cubed, cub'ing**

curb (kurb) *n.* **1** a chain or strap passed around a horse's jaw and attached to the bit: it holds back the horse when the reins are pulled **2** anything that checks or holds back [Fear of punishment is often a *curb* to wrongdoing.] **3** the stone or concrete edging along a street ✦*v.* to hold back; keep in check [to *curb* one's appetite]

curl·y (kur'lē) *adj.* full of curls [*curly* hair] —**curl'i·er, curl'i·est**

cur·rent (kur'ənt) *adj.* **1** of the present time; now going on; most recent [the *current* decade; *current* events] **2** commonly known, used, or accepted [*current* gossip; a belief *current* in earlier times] ✦*n.* **1** a flow of water or air in a definite direction; stream **2** the flow of electricity in a wire or other conductor **3** the general movement or drift, as of opinion —**cur'rent·ly** *adv.*

dair·y (der'ē) *n.* **1** a building where milk and cream are kept and butter and cheese are made **2** a farm (**dairy farm**) on which milk, butter, cheese, etc. are produced **3** a store that sells milk, butter, cheese, etc. —*pl.* **dair'ies**

dai·sy (dā'zē) *n.* ☆**1** a common plant with flowers that have white or pink petals around a yellow center **2** such a flower —*pl.* **dai'sies**

dam·age (dam'ij) *n.* injury or harm to a person or thing that results in a loss of health, value, and so on [A poor diet can cause *damage* to your heart.]

danc·er (dan'sər) *n.* a person who dances

daugh·ter (dôt'ər *or* dät'ər) *n.* a girl or woman as she is related to a parent or to both parents

dawn (dôn *or* dän) *v.* **1** to begin to grow light as the sun rises [Day is *dawning*.] **2** to come into being; begin to develop [With the discovery of electricity, a new age *dawned*.] **3** to begin to be understood or felt [The meaning suddenly *dawned* on me.] ✦*n.* **1** the beginning of day; daybreak **2** the beginning of anything [the *dawn* of the space age]

de·ceive (dē sēv') *v.* to make someone believe what is not true; fool or trick; mislead [The queen *deceived* Snow White by pretending to be her friend.]

de·cide (dē sīd') *v.* **1** to choose after some thought; make up one's mind [I can't *decide* what suit to wear.] **2** to end a contest or argument by giving one side the victory; settle [A jury will *decide* the case.] —**de·cid'ed, de·cid'ing**

deer (dir) *n.* a swift-running, hoofed animal —*pl.* **deer** *or* **deers**

de·fend (dē fend') *v.* **1** to keep safe from harm or danger; guard; protect [She learned karate to *defend* herself.] **2** to uphold something that is under attack; especially, to be the lawyer for a person accused or sued in a law court

de·fine (dē fīn') *v.* to tell the meaning or meanings of; explain [The dictionary *defines* "deficient" as "not having enough."]

de·lay (dē lā′) *v.* to put off to a later time; postpone [The bride's illness will *delay* the wedding.]

de·liv·er·y (dē liv′ər ē) *n.* the act of transferring or distributing [daily *deliveries* to customers] —*pl.* **de·liv′er·ies**

den·tist (den′tist) *n.* a doctor whose work is preventing and taking care of diseased or crooked teeth, or replacing them with artificial teeth

de·ny (dē nī′) *v.* 1 to say that something is not true or right; contradict [They *denied* that they had broken the window.] 2 to refuse to grant or give [We were *denied* permission to see the movie.] —**de·nies′, de·nied′, de·ny′ing**

de·scend (dē send′) *v.* 1 to move down to a lower place [to *descend* from a hilltop; to *descend* a staircase] 2 to become lesser or smaller [Prices have *descended* during the past month.] 3 to come from a certain source [They are *descended* from pioneers.]

des·ert (dez′ərt) *n.* a dry sandy region with little or no plant life ◆*adj.* 1 of or like a desert 2 wild and not lived in [a *desert* island]

de·sign (dē zīn′) *v.* 1 to think up and draw plans for [to *design* a new model of a car] 2 to arrange the parts, colors, etc. of [Who *designed* this book?] 3 to set apart for a certain use; intend [This chair was not *designed* for hard use.] ◆*n.* 1 a drawing or plan to be followed in making something [the *designs* for a house] 2 the arrangement of parts, colors, etc.; pattern or decoration [the *design* in a rug] 3 a plan or purpose [It was my *design* to study law.]

de·stroy (dē stroi′) *v.* to put an end to by breaking up, tearing down, ruining, or spoiling [The flood *destroyed* 300 homes.] —**de·stroyed′, de·stroy′ing**

di·a·ry (dī′ə rē) *n.* a record written day by day of some of the things done, seen, or thought by the writer —*pl.* **di′a·ries**

die (dī) *v.* 1 to stop living; become dead 2 to stop going, moving, acting, etc. [The motor sputtered and *died*.] 3 to lose force; become weak, faint, etc. [The sound of music *died* away.] 4 to want greatly: *used only in everyday talk* [She's *dying* to know my secret.] —**died, dy′ing**

di·et (dī′ət) *n.* 1 what a person or animal usually eats or drinks; usual food [Rice is a basic food in the *diet* of many Asian people.] 2 a special choice as to kinds and amounts of food eaten, as for one's health or to gain or lose weight [a sugar-free *diet*; a reducing *diet*] ◆*v.* to eat certain kinds and amounts of food, especially in order to lose weight

dif·fer·ent (dif′ər ənt *or* dif′rənt) *adj.* 1 not alike; unlike [Cottage cheese is quite *different* from Swiss cheese.] 2 not the same; separate; distinct [There are three *different* colleges in the city.] 3 not like most others; unusual [Their house is really *different*.] —**dif′fer·ent·ly** *adv.*

dif·fi·cult (dif′i kult) *adj.* 1 hard to do, make, or understand; that takes much trouble, thought, or skill [This arithmetic problem is *difficult*.] 2 hard to please; not easy to get along with [a *difficult* employer]

dim (dim) *v.* to make or grow somewhat dark [Cars approaching each other should *dim* their headlights.] —**dimmed, dim′ming**

dirt·y (durt′ē) *adj.* 1 having dirt on or in it; not clean; soiled 2 foul or indecent; not nice; mean [a *dirty* trick] —**dirt′i·er, dirt′i·est** ◆*v.* to make or become dirty; soil —**dirt′ied, dirt′y·ing** —**dirt′i·ness** *n.*

dis·a·gree (dis′ə grē′) *v.* 1 to differ in opinion; often, to quarrel or argue [to *disagree* on politics] 2 to be different; differ [His story of the accident *disagreed* with hers.] —**dis·a·greed′, dis·a·gree′ing**

dis·ap·point (dis′ə point′) *v.* to fail to give or do what is wanted, expected, or promised; leave unsatisfied [I am *disappointed* in the weather. You promised to come, but *disappointed* us.]

dis·be·lief (dis′bə lēf′) *n.* the state of not believing; lack of belief [The guide stared at me in *disbelief*.]

dis·close (dis klōz′) *v.* 1 to bring into view; uncover [I opened my hand and *disclosed* the new penny.] 2 to make known; reveal [to *disclose* a secret] —**dis·closed′, dis·clos′ing**

dis·grace (dis grās′) *n.* loss of favor, respect, or honor; dishonor; shame [in *disgrace* for cheating]

dis·hon·est (dis än′əst) *adj.* not honest; lying, cheating, stealing, etc. —**dis·hon′est·ly** *adv.* —**dis·hon′es·ty** *n.*

dis·in·ter·est·ed (dis in′trəs təd) *adj.* 1 not having a selfish interest in the matter; impartial [A *disinterested* judge picked the winner.] 2 not interested; uninterested: *an older meaning that is being used again*

dis·loy·al (dis loi′əl) *adj.* not loyal or faithful; faithless —**dis·loy′al·ty** *n.*

dis·play (di splā′) *v.* 1 to put or spread out so as to be seen; exhibit [to *display* a collection of stamps] 2 to do something that is a sign or example of; show; reveal [to *display* one's courage] ◆*n.* a displaying or showing; exhibition [a *display* of jewelry; a *display* of strength]

ditch (dich) *n.* a long, narrow opening dug in the earth, as for carrying off water; trench [a *ditch* along the road] —*pl.* **ditch′es** ◆*v.* 1 to dig a ditch in or around 2 to throw into a ditch

a	ask, fat
ā	ape, date
ä	car, lot
e	elf, ten
ē	even, meet
i	is, hit
ī	ice, fire
ō	open, go
ô	law, horn
oi	oil, point
䧞	look, pull
ᵒᵒ	ooze, tool
ou	out, crowd
u	up, cut
ʉ	fur, fern
ə	a in ago
	e in agent
	e in father
	i in unity
	o in collect
	u in focus
ch	chin, arch
ŋ	ring, singer
sh	she, dash
th	thin, truth
ᵗʰ	then, father
zh	s in pleasure

eagle

doc·tor (däk′tər) *n.* **1** a person trained to heal the sick; especially, a physician or surgeon **2** a person who has received the highest degree given by a university [*Doctor* of Philosophy] ✦*v.* to try to heal [to *doctor* oneself]

does·n't (duz′ənt) *contraction* does not

dol·lar (däl′ər) *n.* ☆**1** a U.S. coin or piece of paper money, equal to 100 cents: the dollar is our basic unit of money; its symbol is $ **2** a unit of money in certain other countries, as Canada

dol·phin (dôl′fin) *n.* a water animal related to the whale but smaller: the common dolphin has a long snout and many teeth

☆**down·town** (doun′toun) *adj., adv.* in or toward the lower part or the main business section of a city or town ✦*n.* this section of a city or town

drag (drag) *v.* **1** to pull in a slow, hard way, especially along the ground; haul [He *dragged* the sled up the hill.] **2** to be pulled along the ground, floor, etc. [Her skirt *dragged* in the mud.] **3** to move or pass too slowly [Time *dragged* as we waited for recess.] **4** to search for something in a river, lake, etc. by dragging a net or hooks along the bottom —**dragged, drag′ging**

draw (drô *or* drä) *v.* to make a picture or design with a pencil, pen, or chalk —**drew** (drōō), **draw′ing**

draw·ing (drô′iŋ *or* drä′iŋ) *n.* **1** the making of pictures, designs, etc., as with a pencil or pen **2** such a picture, design, etc. **3** a lottery

drawn (drôn *or* drän) *past participle of* **draw**

dream (drēm) *n.* **1** a series of thoughts, pictures, or feelings that passes through the mind of a sleeping person **2** a pleasant idea that one imagines or hopes for; daydream [to have *dreams* of glory] ✦*v.* **1** to have a dream or dreams **2** to imagine as possible; have any idea of [I wouldn't *dream* of going without you.] —**dreamed** or **dreamt** (dremt), **dream′ing** —**dream′er** *n.*

dress (dres) *n.* **1** the common outer garment worn by girls and women: it is usually of one piece with a skirt **2** clothes in general [native *dress*; formal *dress*] —*pl.* **dress′es** ✦*v.* **1** to put clothes on; clothe **2** to put medicine and bandages on a wound or sore **3** to make ready for use; prepare [to *dress* a chicken; to *dress* leather] ✦*adj.* worn on formal occasions [a *dress* suit]

drive (drīv) *v.* to control the movement of an automobile, horse and wagon, bus, or other vehicle [She *drives* a school bus.] —**drove, driv′ing**

drop (dräp) *n.* **1** a bit of liquid that is rounded in shape, as when falling [*drops* of rain] **2** anything like this in shape [a chocolate *drop*] **3** a very small amount [He hasn't a *drop* of courage.] ✦*v.* **1** to fall or let fall in drops [Tears *dropped* from the actor's eyes.] **2** to fall or let fall [Ripe fruit *dropped* from the trees. He *dropped* his lunch in the mud.] —**dropped** or *sometimes* **dropt, drop′ping**

drown (droun) *v.* to die from being under water, where the lungs can get no air [to fall overboard and *drown*] —**drowned, drown′ing**

drow·sy (drou′zē) *adj.* **1** sleepy or half asleep **2** making one feel sleepy [*drowsy* music] —**drow′si·er, drow′si·est** —**drow′si·ly** *adv.* —**drow′si·ness** *n.*

dry (drī) *adj.* **1** not under water [*dry* land] **2** not wet or damp; without moisture **3** having little or no rain or water [a *dry* summer] **4** with all its water or other liquid gone [a *dry* fountain pen; *dry* bread; a *dry* well] —**dri′er, dri′est** —**dried, dry′ing** —**dry′ly** *adv.* —**dry′ness** *n.*

dues (dōōz *or* dyōōz) *n.* money paid regularly for being a member of a club or institution [The *dues* are $25 per month.]

dusk (dusk) *n.* the dim part of twilight that comes before the dark of night

du·ty (dōōt′ē *or* dyōōt′ē) *n.* **1** what a person should do because it is thought to be right, just, or moral [It is the *duty* of every citizen to vote.] **2** any of the things that are done as part of a person's work [the *duties* of a secretary] —*pl.* **du′ties**

Ee

ea·gle (ē′gəl) *n.* a large, strong bird that captures and eats other birds and animals and has sharp eyesight: the **bald eagle** is the symbol of the United States

ear·ly (ur′lē) *adv., adj.* **1** near the beginning; soon after the start [in the *early* afternoon; *early* in his career] **2** before the usual or expected time [The bus arrived *early*.] —**ear′li·er, ear′li·est** —**ear′li·ness** *n.*

ear·muffs (ir′mufs) *pl.n.* cloth or fur coverings worn over the ears to keep them warm in cold weather

east·ern (ēs′tərn) *adj.* **1** in, of, or toward the east [the *eastern* sky] **2** from the east [an *eastern* wind] **3 Eastern,** of the East

eas·y (ē′zē) *adj.* **1** not hard to do, learn, get, etc. [an *easy* job; an *easy* book] **2** without worry, pain, or trouble [an *easy* life] **3** restful or comfortable [an *easy* chair] —**eas′i·er, eas′i·est**

eas·y·go·ing (ē′zē gō′iŋ) *adj.* not worried, rushed, or strict about things

edge (ej) *n.* **1** the sharp, cutting part [the *edge* of a knife] **2** the line or part where something begins or ends; border or margin [the *edge* of a plate; the *edge* of the forest] **3** the brink [on the *edge* of disaster] —**edged, edg'ing**

ed·i·tor (ed'it ər) *n.* **1** a person who edits ☆**2** the head of a department of a newspaper, magazine, etc.

eight·een (ā'tēn') *n., adj.* eight more than ten; the number 18

el·e·phant (el'ə fənt) *n.* a huge animal with a thick skin, two ivory tusks, and a long snout, or trunk: it is found in Africa and India and is the largest of the four-legged animals

e·lev·en (ē lev'ən) *n., adj.* one more than ten; the number 11

em·broi·der (em broi'dər) *v.* to stitch designs on cloth with a needle and thread [Hal *embroidered* his initials on his shirt.]

e·mer·gen·cy (ē mur'jən sē) *n.* a sudden happening that needs action or attention right away [the *emergency* created by a hurricane] —*pl.* **e·mer'gen·cies**

em·ploy (em ploi') *v.* **1** to hire and pay for the work or services of; have working for one [That company *employs* 50 people.] **2** to use [The baby *employed* clever tricks to get attention.] ◆*n.* the condition of being employed [Chan is no longer in our *employ*.]

emp·ty (emp'tē) *adj.* **1** having nothing or no one in it; not occupied; vacant [an *empty* jar; an *empty* house] —**emp'ti·er, emp'ti·est** ◆*v.* **1** to make or become empty [The auditorium was *emptied* in ten minutes.] **2** to take out or pour out [*Empty* the dirty water in the sink.] **3** to flow out; discharge [The Amazon *empties* into the Atlantic.] —**emp'tied, emp'ty·ing** —**emp'ti·ly** *adv.* —**emp'ti·ness** *n.*

en·e·my (en'ə mē) *n.* a person, group, or country that hates another or fights against another; foe —*pl.* **en'e·mies**

en·er·gy (en'ər jē) *n.* **1** power to work or be active; force; vigor [Eleanor Roosevelt was a woman of great *energy*.] **2** the power of certain forces in nature to do work [Electricity and heat are forms of *energy*.] **3** resources, as coal, oil, etc., used to produce such power; also, the supply of such resources that can be got [an *energy* shortage] —*pl.* **en'er·gies**

e·nor·mous (ē nôr'məs) *adj.* much larger than usual; huge [an *enormous* stadium] —**e·nor'mous·ly** *adv.* —**e·nor'mous·ness** *n.*

e·nough (ē nuf') *adj.* as much or as many as needed or wanted; sufficient [There is *enough* food for all.] ◆*n.* the amount needed or wanted [I have heard *enough* of that music.] ◆*adv.* **1** as much as needed; to the right amount [Is your steak cooked *enough*?] **2** fully; quite [Oddly *enough*, she never asked me.]

en·ter·tain (en tər tān') *v.* to keep interested and give pleasure to [She *entertained* us by playing the organ.]

e·qual (ē'kwəl) *adj.* **1** of the same amount, size, or value [The horses were of *equal* height.] **2** having the same rights, ability, or position [All persons are *equal* in a court of law in a just society.] ◆*n.* any person or thing that is equal [As a sculptor, she has few *equals*.] ◆*v.* to be equal to; match [His long jump *equaled* the school record. Six minus two *equals* four.] —**e'qualed** or **e'qualled, e'qual·ing** or **e'qual·ling** —**e'qual·ly** *adv.*

e·qua·tor (ē kwāt'ər) *n.* an imaginary circle around the middle of the earth, at an equal distance from the North Pole and South Pole

er·ror (er'ər) *n.* **1** a belief, answer, act, etc. that is untrue, incorrect, or wrong mistake [an *error* in multiplication] **2** a play by a baseball fielder which is poorly made, but which would have resulted in an out if it had been properly made

es·say (es'ā) *n.* a short piece of writing on some subject, giving the writer's personal ideas

Eu·rope (yoor'əp) the continent between Asia and the Atlantic Ocean

ev·er·y·bod·y (ev'rē bäd'ē *or* ev'rē bud'ē) *pron.* every person; everyone [*Everybody* loves a good story.]

ex·change (eks chānj') *v.* to give in return for something else; trade [She *exchanged* the bicycle for a larger one.] —**ex·changed', ex·chang'ing**

ex·cuse (ek skyooz') *v.* **1** to be a proper reason or explanation for [That was a selfish act that nothing will *excuse*.] **2** to think of a fault or wrongdoing as not important; overlook; forgive; pardon [Please *excuse* this interruption.] **3** to allow to leave or go [You may be *excused* from the table.] —**ex·cused', ex·cus'ing** ◆*n.* (ek skyoos') a reason given to explain some action or behavior; apology [Ignorance of the law is no *excuse* for wrongdoing.]

ex·er·cise (ek'sər sīz) *n.* **1** active use of the body in order to make it stronger or healthier [Long walks are good outdoor *exercise*.] **2** *usually* **exercises**, *pl.* a series of movements done regularly to make some part of the body stronger or to develop some skill [These *exercises* will strengthen your legs.] **3** a problem to be studied and worked on by a student in order to get more skill [piano *exercises*] ◆*v.* to put into use or do certain regular movements, in order to develop or train [*Exercise* your weak ankle. I *exercise* every morning.] —**ex'er·cised, ex'er·cis·ing**

a	ask, fat
ā	ape, date
ä	car, lot
e	elf, ten
ē	even, meet
i	is, hit
ī	ice, fire
ō	open, go
ô	law, horn
oi	oil, point
oo	look, pull
oo	ooze, tool
ou	out, crowd
u	up, cut
u	fur, fern
ə	a in ago
	e in agent
	e in father
	i in unity
	o in collect
	u in focus
ch	chin, arch
ŋ	ring, singer
sh	she, dash
th	thin, truth
th	then, father
zh	s in pleasure

ex·pen·sive (ek spen'siv) *adj.* costing much; having a high price [She wears *expensive* clothes.] —**ex·pen'sive·ly** *adv.*

ex·plore (ek splôr') *v.* **1** to travel in a region that is unknown or not well known, in order to find out more about it [to *explore* a wild jungle] **2** to look into or examine carefully [to *explore* a problem] —**ex·plored'**, **ex·plor'ing** —**ex·plo·ra'tion** *n.* —**ex·plor'er** *n.*

ex·press (ek spres') *v.* **1** to put into words; state [It is hard to *express* my feelings.] **2** to give or be a sign of; show [a frown that *expressed* doubt] ☆**3** to send goods by a fast way ◆*adj.* taking the shortest and fastest route; not making many stops [an *express* train or bus]

ex·tend (ek stend') *v.* to make longer; stretch out [Careful cleaning *extends* the life of a rug.]

ex·tinct (ek stiŋkt') *adj.* **1** no longer living; having died out [Dinosaurs are *extinct*.] **2** no longer burning or active [an *extinct* volcano]

ex·tin·guish·er (ek stiŋ'gwish ər) *n.* a person or thing that extinguishes; especially, a device for putting out a fire by spraying a liquid or gas on it

eye·lash (ī'lash) *n.* **1** any of the hairs that grow along the edge of the eyelid **2** a fringe of these hairs —*pl.* **eye'lash·es**

Ff

fa·ble (fā'bəl) *n.* **1** a very short story that teaches a lesson: it is usually about animals who act and talk like people [Aesop's *fable* "The Grasshopper and the Ant" teaches the need to work hard and be thrifty.]

fac·to·ry (fak'tər ē *or* fak'trē) *n.* a building or group of buildings where products are made by machinery —*pl.* **fac'to·ries**

fair (fer) *adj.* **1** beautiful [your *fair* city] **2** light in color; blond [*fair* hair; *fair* skin] **3** clear and sunny [*fair* weather] **4** just and honest; according to what is right [a *fair* price; *fair* play] —**fair'ness** *n.*

fame (fām) *n.* the condition of being well known or much talked about; great reputation [Marie Curie's scientific research brought her much *fame*.]

fa·mil·iar (fə mil'yər) *adj.* friendly; intimate; well-acquainted [a *familiar* face in the crowd]

fam·i·ly (fam'ə lē) *n.* **1** a group made up of two parents and all of their children **2** the children alone [a widow who raised a large family] **3** a group of people who are related by marriage or a common ancestor; relatives; clan —*pl.* **fam'i·lies**

fan·cy (fan'sē) *n.* the power of picturing in the mind things that are not real, especially in a light and playful way; imagination ["Alice's Adventures in Wonderland" is the product of Lewis Carroll's *fancy*.] —*pl.* **fan'cies** ◆*adj.* **1** having much design and decoration; not plain; elaborate [a *fancy* tie] **2** of better quality than the usual; special [a *fancy* grade of canned pears] —**fan'ci·er, fan'ci·est** ◆*v.* to have a liking for [He *fancies* Swiss chocolate.] —**fan'cied, fan'cy·ing**

far·ther (fär thɔr) *the comparative of* **far** ◆*adj.* more distant [My home is *farther* from school than yours.] ◆*adv.* at or to a greater distance [I can swim *farther* than you can.]

fault (fôlt) *n.* **1** a thing that keeps something from being perfect; defect; flaw [His main *fault* is that he's lazy.] **2** an error; mistake **3** blame; responsibility [It isn't my *fault* that we're late.]

fawn (fôn *or* fän) *n.* a young deer, less than one year old

fear·less (fir'ləs) *adj.* having no fear; not afraid; brave —**fear'less·ly** *adv.*

feath·er (feth'ər) *n.* any of the parts that grow out of the skin of birds, covering the body and filling out the wings and tail: feathers are soft and light —**feath'er·y** *adj.*

fend·er (fen'dər) *n.* ☆**1** a metal piece over the wheel of a car to keep off splashing mud **2** a metal piece at the front of a locomotive to throw off things that are hit

field (fēld) *n.* **1** a wide piece of open land without many trees; especially, a piece of land for growing crops, grazing animals, etc. **2** a piece of land having a special use or producing a certain thing [a landing *field*; an oil *field*] **3** an area where games or athletic events are held; also, the part of such an area where such events as high jump, long jump, pole vault, shot put, etc. are held ◆*v.* to stop or catch and return a batted ball

fight (fīt) *v.* to use fists, weapons, or other force in trying to beat or overcome someone or something [to *fight* a war] —**fought, fight'ing**

film (film) *n.* **1** a thin skin or coating [a *film* of ice on the pond] **2** a sheet or roll of material covered with a chemical substance that is changed by light, used for taking photographs or making movies **3** a movie

fin·ish (fin′ish) v. **1** to bring or come to an end; complete or become completed [Did you *finish* your work? The game *finished* early.] **2** to give final touches to; perfect [We *finished* the room by putting up molding.] **3** to use up; consume completely [*Finish* your milk.] ◆n. the kind of surface a thing has [an oil *finish* on wood] —**fin′ish·ing**

fish (fish) n. an animal that lives in water and has a backbone, fins, and gills for breathing [The aquarium exhibits many *fishes*.] —pl. **fish** (or when different kinds are meant **fish′es**)

fla·min·go (flə miŋ′gō) n. a wading bird that has a very long neck and legs, and pink or red feathers: it lives in tropical regions —pl. **fla·min′gos** or **fla·min′goes**

flash (flash) v. **1** to send out a short and bright burst of light [Electric signs *flashed* all along the street.] **2** to sparkle or gleam [Her eyes *flashed* with anger.] **3** to come, move, or send swiftly or suddenly [The train *flashed* by. The news was *flashed* to Paris by radio.] ◆n. a short burst of light or of something bright [a *flash* of lightning; a *flash* of wit, hope, etc.] —pl. **flash′es**

fleet¹ (flēt) n. **1** a group of warships under one command [our Pacific *fleet*] **2** any group of ships, trucks, buses, etc. moving together or under one control

fleet² (flēt) adj. moving swiftly; swift

flew (flo͞o) past tense of **fly¹**

flies (flīz) **1** the form of the verb *fly¹*, used in the present with he, she, or it **2** the plural of *fly¹* and *fly²*

flight (flīt) n. **1** the act or way of flying or moving through space **2** a trip through the air, as by an airplane, bird, etc. [a 500-mile *flight*] **3** a group of things flying together [a *flight* of wild swans]

Flor·i·da (flôr′i də) a state in the southeastern part of the United States: abbreviated **Fla., FL**

flu (flo͞o) n. a disease caused by a virus, like a bad cold only more serious

flue (flo͞o) n. a tube, pipe, or shaft through which smoke, steam, or hot air can escape [the *flue* in a chimney]

fly¹ (flī) v. **1** to move through the air by using wings, as a bird **2** to travel or carry through the air, as in an aircraft **3** to pilot an aircraft **4** to wave or float in the air, or cause to float in the air, as a flag or kite **5** to move swiftly [The door *flew* open. Time *flies*.] —**flew, flown, fly′ing** ◆n. a baseball batted high in the air inside the foul lines —pl. **flies**

fly² (flī) n. **1** a flying insect having one pair of wings, as the housefly and gnat: some insects with two pairs of wings are called flies, as the mayfly **2** an object used in fishing, made of bright feathers, silk, etc. tied to a fishhook to look like a fly —pl. **flies**

folk (fōk) n. people or persons [The farmer disliked city *folk*. *Folks* differ in customs.] —pl. **folk** or **folks** ◆adj. of the common people [a *folk* saying]

folk tale a story made and handed down by word of mouth among the common people: also **folk story**

fol·low·ing (fä′lō iŋ) adj. going or coming after; next after [the *following* week] ◆n. people who follow; followers ◆prep. after [*Following* dinner we played cards.]

fond (fänd) v. loving and tender; affectionate [*fond* parents]

fool·ish (fo͞ol′ish) adj. without good sense; silly —**fool′ish·ly** adv. —**fool′ish·ness** n.

force (fôrs) n. **1** power or energy that can do or make something [Electricity is a powerful natural *force*. The *force* of the high winds broke the windows.] **2** power or strength used against a person or thing [The police used *force* to scatter the crowd.] **3** the power to cause motion or to stop or change motion [the *force* of gravity] ◆v. **1** to make or do something by using strength or power of some kind [You shouldn't *force* a child to eat. The blizzard *forced* us to stay home.] **2** to break open or through by using strength [He *forced* the lock with a pick.] —**forced, forc′ing**

fore·head (fôr′hed or fär′hed) n. the part of the face above the eyebrows

forth (fôrth) adv. **1** forward or onward [She never left the house from that day *forth*.] **2** out, into view [The bears came *forth* from their den.]

fought (fôt or fät) past tense and past participle of **fight**

fox (fäks) n. **1** a wild animal of the dog family, with pointed ears, a bushy tail, and usually, reddish-brown fur —pl. **fox** or **fox′es**

France (frans) a country in western Europe

fraud (frôd or fräd) n. **1** a cheat, trick, or lie; dishonesty **2** a person who cheats or is not what he or she pretends to be

fray (frā) v. to wear down so as to become ragged and have loose threads showing [a coat *frayed* at the elbows]

free·dom (frē′dəm) n. **1** the condition of being free; liberty; independent **2** a being able to use or move about as one wishes [Has your dog been given *freedom* of the house?]

freight·er (frāt′ər) n. a ship for freight

front (frunt) n. **1** the part that faces forward; most important side [The *front* of a house usually faces the street.] **2** the part ahead of the rest; first part; beginning [That chapter is toward the *front* of the book.] **3** outward look or behavior [I put on a bold *front* in spite of my fear.] **4** the land alongside a lake, ocean, street, etc. [docks on the water*front*]

fox

a	ask, fat
ā	ape, date
ä	car, lot
e	elf, ten
ē	even, meet
i	is, hit
ī	ice, fire
ō	open, go
ô	law, horn
oi	oil, point
o͝o	look, pull
o͞o	ooze, tool
ou	out, crowd
u	up, cut
ʉ	fur, fern
ə	a in ago
	e in agent
	e in father
	i in unity
	o in collect
	u in focus
ch	chin, arch
ŋ	ring, singer
sh	she, dash
th	thin, truth
th	then, father
zh	s in pleasure

fron·der (frun'tir') *n.* **1** the line or border between two countries ☆**2** the part of a settled country that lies next to a region that is still a wilderness **3** any new field of learning or any part of it still to be explored [the *frontiers* of medicine]

fry (frī) *v.* to cook in hot fat over direct heat —**fried, fry'ing** ◆*n.* ☆**1** a kind of picnic at which food is fried and eaten [a fish *fry*] **2 fries,** *pl.* things fried, as potatoes —*pl.* **fries**

fun·ny (fun'ē) *adj.* **1** causing smiles or laughter; amusing; comical **2** odd or unusual; *used only in everyday talk* [It's *funny* that he's late.] —**fun'ni·er, fun'ni·est** ◆☆*n.* usually **funnies,** *pl.* comic strips; *used only in everyday talk* —*pl.* **fun'nies** —**fun'ni·ness** *n.*

glove

gal·ax·y (gal'ək sē) *often* **Galaxy,** *another name for* **Milky Way** ◆*n.* **1** any vast group of stars **2** a group of very famous people —*pl.* **gal'ax·ies**

gal·ley (gal'ē) *n.* **1** large, low ship of long ago, having both sails and many oars: the oars were usually rowed by slaves or prisoners in chains **2** the kitchen of a ship —*pl.* **gal'leys**

gal·lon (gal'ən) *n.* a measure of liquids, equal to four quarts or eight pints: one gallon equals 3.785 liters

gar·bage (gär'bij) *n.* spoiled food or food waste that is thrown away

gasp (gasp) *v.* to breathe in suddenly [She *gasped* in sudden surprise.]

gath·er (ga*th*'ər) *v.* **1** to bring or come together in one place or group [The child *gathered* her toys together. The families *gathered* for a reunion.] **2** to get or collect gradually; accumulate [to *gather* wealth; to *gather* one's strength; to *gather* news for a paper] **3** to pick or glean [to *gather* crops]. —**gath'er·er** *n.*

gaunt (gônt *or* gänt) *adj.* **1** so thin that the bones show; worn and lean, as from hunger or illness **2** looking gloomy and deserted [the *gaunt,* rocky coast of the island] —**gaunt'ly** *adv.* —**gaunt'ness** *n.*

geese (gēs) *n.* *plural of* **goose**

gen·tle (jent'l) *adj.* **1** mild, soft, or easy; not rough [a *gentle* touch; a *gentle* scolding] **2** tame; easy to handle [a *gentle* horse] **3** gradual; not sudden [a *gentle* slope] —**gen'tler, gen'tlest** —**gen'tle·ness** *n.*

ge·og·ra·phy (jē òg'rə fē *or* jē ä'grə fē) *n.* **1** the study of the surface of the earth and how it is divided into continents, countries, seas, etc.: geography also deals with the climates, plants, animals, minerals, etc. of the earth **2** the natural features of a certain part of the earth [the *geography* of Ohio] —**ge·og'ra·pher** *n.*

ger·bil *or* **ger·bille** (jur'bəl) *n.* an animal like a mouse but with very long hind legs: it is found in Africa and Asia

ghost (gōst) *n.* **1** a pale, shadowy form that some people think they can see and that is supposed to be the spirit of a dead person **2** a mere shadow or slight trace [not a *ghost* of a chance]

gift (gift) *n.* **1** something given to show friendship, thanks, support, etc.; a present [Christmas *gifts;* a *gift* of $5,000 to a museum] **2** a natural ability; talent [a *gift* for writing catchy tunes]

gi·raffe (ji raf') *n.* a large animal of Africa that chews its cud: it has a very long neck and legs and a spotted coat, and is the tallest animal alive

give (giv) *v.* **1** to pass or hand over to another [*Give* me your coat and I'll hang it up.] **2** to hand over to another to keep; make a gift of [My uncle *gave* a book to me for my birthday.] **3** to cause to have [Music *gives* me pleasure.] **4** to be the source of; supply [Cows *give* milk.] —**gave, giv'en, giv'ing**

gla·cier (glā'shər) *n.* a large mass of ice and snow that moves very slowly down a mountain or across land until it melts: icebergs are pieces of a glacier that have broken away into the sea

glove (gluv) *n.* **1** a covering to protect the hand, with a separate part for each finger and the thumb [Surgeons wear rubber *gloves.* Padded *gloves* are worn in playing baseball.] **2** a padded mitt worn in boxing: *also* **boxing glove** ◆*v.* to put gloves on —**gloved, glov'ing**

glow (glō) *v.* **1** to give off light because of great heat; be red-hot or white-hot [embers *glowing* in a fire] **2** to give out light without flame or heat [Fireflies *glow* in the dark.]

glue (glo͞o) *n.* **1** a thick, sticky substance made by boiling animal hoofs and bones, used for sticking things together **2** any sticky substance like this ◆*v.* **1** to stick together with glue **2** to keep or hold without moving [The exciting movie kept us *glued* to our seats.] —**glued, glu'ing** —**glue'y** *adj.*

gnaw (nô *or* nä) *v.* to bite and wear away bit by bit with the teeth [The rat *gnawed* the rope in two. The dog *gnawed* on the bone.]

gob·ble (gäb′əl) *v.* to eat quickly and greedily [She *gobbled* half the pizza before I finished a single piece.] —**gob′bled, gob′bling**

goose (gōōs) *n.* a waterfowl that is like a duck but has a larger body and a longer neck; especially, the female of this bird: the male is called a *gander* —*pl.* **geese**

gov·ern·ment (guv′ərn mənt) *n.* **1** control or rule, as over a country, city, etc. **2** a system of ruling or controlling [a centralized *government*; democratic *governments*] **3** all the people who control the affairs of a country, city, etc. [The French *government* moved to Vichy during World War II.] —☆**gov′ern·men′tal adj.**

grab (grab) *v.* **1** to seize or snatch suddenly **2** to take by force or in a selfish way —**grabbed, grab′bing** ◆*n.* **1** the act of grabbing [He made a *grab* for the handle.] **2** something grabbed

grace·ful (grās′fəl) *adj.* having grace, or beauty of form or movement —**grace′ful·ly adv.** —**grace′ful·ness n.**

gram (gram) *n.* the basic unit of weight in the metric system: it is the weight of one cubic centimeter of distilled water at 4°C; one gram equals about 1/28 of an ounce

graph (graf) *n.* a chart or diagram that shows the changes taking place in something, by the use of connected lines, a curve, etc. [a *graph* showing how sales figures vary during the year]

Greece (grēs) a country in southeastern Europe, on the Mediterranean

greed·y (grēd′ē) *adj.* wanting or taking all that one can get with no thought of what others need [The *greedy* girl ate all the cookies.] —**greed′i·er, greed′i·est** —**greed′i·ly adv.** —**greed′i·ness n.**

grid·dle (grid′əl) *n.* a heavy, flat, metal plate or pan for cooking pancakes, etc.

griz·zly (griz′lē) *n.* a large, ferocious bear found in western North America —*pl.* **griz′zlies**

groan (grōn) *v.* to make a deep sound showing sorrow, pain, annoyance, or disapproval [We *groaned* when our team lost.]

gro·cer·y (grō′sər ē) *n.* ☆**1** a store selling food and household supplies **2 groceries**, *pl.* the goods sold by a grocer —*pl.* **gro′cer·ies**

guess (ges) *v.* **1** to judge or decide about something without having enough facts to know for certain [Can you *guess* how old he is?] **2** to judge correctly by doing this [She *guessed* the exact number of beans in the jar.] **3** to think or suppose [I *guess* you're right.] ◆*n.* a judgment formed by guessing; surmise [Your *guess* is as good as mine.]—**guess′er n., guessed**

gulp (gulp) *v.* to swallow in a hurried or greedy way [She *gulped* her breakfast and ran to school.] —**gulped, gulp′ing**

Hh

hair (her) *n.* **1** any of the thin growths, like threads, that come from the skin of animals and human beings **2** the whole number of these growths that cover a person's head, the skin of an animal, etc. [I must comb my *hair*.]

half (haf) *n.* **1** either of the two equal parts of something [Five is *half* of ten.] **2** either of two almost equal parts: *thought by some people to be not a proper use* [Take the smaller *half* of the pie.] **3** a half hour [It is *half* past two.]—*pl.* **halves** ◆*adj.* being either of the two equal parts [a *half* gallon.]

half·way (haf′wā′) *adj.* **1** at the middle between two points or limits [to reach the *halfway* mark] **2** not complete; partial [to take *halfway* measures] ◆*adv.* **1** to the midway point; half the distance [They had gone *halfway* home.] **2** partially [The house is *halfway* built.]

halt (hôlt) *n., v.* stop [I worked all morning without a *halt*. Rain *halted* the game.]

halves (havz) *n. plural of* **half**

ham·mer (ham′ər) *n.* **1** a tool for driving in nails, breaking stones, shaping metal, etc.: it usually has a metal head and a handle **2** a thing like this in shape or use, as the part that strikes against the firing pin of a gun or any of the parts that strike the strings of a piano ◆*v.* to hit with many blows [They *hammered* on the door with their fists.]

hand (hand) *n.* **1** the end of the arm beyond the wrist, including the palm, fingers, and thumb **2** any of the pointers on a clock or watch **3** a person hired to work with the hands [a farm *hand*; dock *hand*] **4** help [Give me a *hand* with this job.] **5** a clapping of hands; applause [Give the dancer a big *hand*.] ◆*v.* to give with the hand; pass [*Hand* me the book, please.]

hand·ker·chief (haŋ′kər chif) *n.* a small piece of cloth for wiping the nose, eyes, or face, or worn as a decoration —*pl.* **hand′ker·chiefs**

hand

a	ask, fat
ā	ape, date
ä	car, lot
e	elf, ten
ē	even, meet
i	is, hit
ī	ice, fire
ō	open, go
ô	law, horn
oi	oil, point
͞oo	look, pull
͞oo	ooze, tool
ou	out, crowd
u	up, cut
ʉ	fur, fern
ə	a in ago
	e in agent
	e in father
	i in unity
	o in collect
	u in focus
ch	chin, arch
ŋ	ring, singer
sh	she, dash
th	thin, truth
th	then, father
zh	s in pleasure

hap·py (hap′ē) *adj.* **1** feeling or showing pleasure or joy; glad; contented [a *happy* child; a *happy* song] **2** lucky; fortunate [The story has a *happy* ending.] —**hap′pi·er, hap′pi·est** —**hap′pi·ly** *adv.* —**hap′pi·ness** *n.*

har·bor (här′bɔr) *n.* **1** a place where ships may anchor and be safe from storms; port; haven **2** any place where one is safe; shelter ◆*v.* to shelter or hide [to *harbor* an outlaw]

hare (her) *n.* a swift animal with long ears, a split upper lip, large front teeth used for gnawing, and long, powerful hind legs: hares are related to rabbits but are usually larger

har·vest (här′vəst) *n.* the act or process of gathering a crop of grain, fruit, or vegetables when it becomes ripe

has·n't (haz′ənt) *contraction* has not

haunt (hônt *or* hänt) *v.* **1** to spend much time at; visit often [We like to *haunt* bookstores. A *haunted* house is one that is supposed to be visited by a ghost.] **2** to keep coming back to the mind [Memories *haunt* her.] ◆*n.* a place often visited [They made the library their *haunt*.]

heal (hēl) *v.* to get or bring back to good health or a sound condition; cure or mend [The wound *healed* slowly. Time *heals* grief.]

heart (härt) *n.* **1** the hollow muscle that gets blood from the veins and sends it through the arteries by squeezing together and expanding **2** the part at the center [*hearts* of celery; the *heart* of the jungle] **3** the main or most important part [Get to the *heart* of the matter.] **4** the human heart thought of as the part that feels love, kindness, pity, sadness, etc. [a tender *heart*; a heavy *heart*]

hearth (härth) *n.* the stone or brick floor of a fireplace

heav·y (hev′ē) *adj.* **1** hard to lift or move because of its weight; weighing very much [a *heavy* load] **2** weighing more than is usual for its kind [Lead is a *heavy* metal.] **3** larger, deeper, greater, etc. than usual [a *heavy* vote; a *heavy* sleep; a *heavy* blow] —**heav′i·er, heav′i·est** ◆*adv.* in a heavy manner [*heavy*-laden]

heel (hēl) *n.* **1** the back part of the foot, below the ankle and behind the arch **2** that part of a stocking or sock which covers the heel **3** the part of a shoe that is built up to support the heel

herd (hurd) *n.* a number of cattle or other large animals feeding or living together [a *herd* of cows; a *herd* of elephants] ◆*v.* **1** to form into a herd, group, or crowd **2** to take care of a herd of animals

heel

her·on (her′ən) *n.* a wading bird with long legs, a long neck, and a long, pointed bill: herons live in marshes or along river banks

hes·i·tate (hez′i tāt′) *v.* **1** to stop or hold back, as because of feeling unsure [Never *hesitate* to speak the truth. He *hesitated* at the door before entering.] **2** to feel unwilling [I *hesitate* to ask you for money.] —**hes′i·tat·ed, hes′i·tat·ing**

high·way (hī′wā) *n.* a main road

hob·by (häb′ē) *n.* something that one likes to do, study, etc. for pleasure in one's spare time [Her *hobby* is collecting coins.] —*pl.* **hob′bies**

hoe (hō) *n.* a garden tool with a thin, flat blade on a long handle: it is used for removing weeds, loosening the soil, etc. ◆*v.* to dig, loosen soil, etc. with a hoe —**hoed, hoe′ing**

hol·i·day (häl′ə dā) *n.* **1** a day on which most people do not have to work, often one set aside by law [Thanksgiving is a *holiday* in all states.] **2** a religious festival; holy day [Easter is a Christian *holiday*.]

hol·low (häl′ō) *adj.* **1** having an empty space on the inside; not solid [a *hollow* log] **2** shaped like a bowl; concave **3** sunken in [*hollow* cheeks] —**hol′low·ness** *n.*

home·work (hōm′wurk) *n.* **1** lessons to be studied or schoolwork to be done outside the classroom **2** any work to be done at home

hom·o·nym (häm′ə nim) *n.* a word that is pronounced like another word, but has a different meaning and is usually spelled differently ["Bore" and "boar" are *homonyms*.]

hon·est (än′əst) *adj.* **1** that does not steal, cheat, or lie; upright or trustworthy [an *honest* person] **2** got in a fair way, not by stealing, cheating, or lying [to earn an *honest* living] **3** sincere or genuine [He made an *honest* effort.]

hoof (hoof *or* hoof) *n.* **1** the horny covering on the feet of cows, horses, deer, pigs, etc. **2** the whole foot of such an animal —*pl.* **hoofs** or **hooves**

hor·ri·fy (hôr′ə fī) *v.* to fill with horror [He was *horrified* at the sight of the victims.] —**hor′ri·fied, hor′ri·fy·ing**

horse·shoe (hôrs′shoo) *n.* **1** a flat metal plate shaped like a U, nailed to a horse's hoof to protect it **2** anything shaped like this **3** **horseshoes**, *pl.* a game in which the players toss horseshoes at a stake in the ground

host·ess (hōs′təs) *n.* **1** a woman who has guests in her own home, or who pays for their entertainment away from home **2** a woman hired by a restaurant to welcome people and show them to their tables —*pl.* **host′ess·es**

hour (our) *n.* **1** any of the 24 equal parts of a day; 60 minutes **2** a particular time [At what *hour* shall we meet?] **3** *often* hours, *pl.* a particular period of time [the dinner *hour*; the doctor's office *hours*]

how (hou) *adv.* **1** in what way [*How* do you start the motor? She taught him *how* to dance.] **2** in what condition [*How* is your mother today?] **3** for what reason; why [*How* is it that you don't know?]

how's (houz) *contraction* **1** how is **2** how has **3** how does

hum (hum) *v.* **1** to make a low, steady, buzzing sound like that of a bee or a motor **2** to sing with the lips closed, not saying the words —**hummed, hum′ming**

☆**hum·ming·bird** (hum′iŋ burd′) *n.* a tiny bird with a long, thin bill that it uses to suck nectar from flowers: its wings move very fast, with a humming sound, and it can hover in the air

hun·dred (hun′drəd) *n., adj.* ten times ten; the number 100

hur·ri·cane (hur′ə kān) *n.* a very strong windstorm, often with heavy rain, in which the wind blows in a circle at 73 or more miles per hour: hurricanes usually start in the West Indies and move northward

hur·ry (hur′ē) *v.* **1** to move, send, or carry quickly or too quickly [You fell because you *hurried*. A taxi *hurried* us home.] **2** to make happen or be done more quickly [Please try to *hurry* those letters.] **3** to try to make move or act faster [Don't *hurry* me when I'm eating.] —**hur′ried, hur′ry·ing**

hy·giene (hī′jēn) *n.* the practice of keeping clean [good personal *hygiene*]

i·de·a (ī dē′ə) *n.* **1** something one thinks, knows, imagines, feels, etc.; belief or thought **2** a plan or purpose [an *idea* for making money]

im·mov·a·ble (im moov′ə bəl) *adj.* **1** that cannot be moved; firmly fixed [The ancients thought the earth *immovable*.] **2** not changing; steadfast [an *immovable* purpose]

im·pa·tient (im pā′shənt) *adj.* not patient; not willing to put up with delay or annoyance [*impatient* customers standing in line]

im·per·fect (im pur′fikt) *adj.* **1** not perfect; having some fault or flaw **2** lacking in something; not complete; unfinished [an *imperfect* knowledge of Russian] —**im·per′fect·ly** *adv.*

im·per·son·al (im′pur′sən əl) *adj.* not referring to any particular person [The teacher's remarks about cheating were *impersonal* and meant for all the students.] —**im′per′son·al·ly** *adv.*

im·prac·ti·cal (im′prak′ti kəl) *adj.* not practical; not useful, efficient, etc.

im·pure (im pyoor′) *adj.* **1** not clean; dirty [Smoke made the air *impure*.] **2** mixed with things that do not belong [*impure* gold] **3** not decent or proper [*impure* thoughts]

in·de·pend·ent (in′dē pen′dənt) *adj.* **1** not ruled or controlled by another; self-governing [Many colonies became *independent* countries after World War II.] **2** not connected with others; separate [an *independent* grocer] **3** not influenced by others; thinking for oneself [an *independent* voter] —**in′de·pend′ent·ly** *adv.*

In·di·a (in′dē ə) **1** a large peninsula of southern Asia **2** a country in the central and southern part of this peninsula

in·ju·ry (in′jər ē) *n.* harm or damage done to a person or thing [*injuries* received in a fall; *injury* to one's good name] —*pl.* **in′ju·ries**

in·stant (in′stənt) *n.* a very short time; moment [Wait just an *instant*.]

in·stead (in sted′) *adv.* in place of the other; as a substitute [If you have no cream, use milk *instead*.]

in·tel·li·gent (in tel′ə jənt) *adj.* having or showing intelligence, especially high intelligence —**in·tel′li·gent·ly** *adv.*

is·land (ī′lənd) *n.* **1** a piece of land smaller than a continent and surrounded by water **2** any place set apart from what surrounds it [The oasis was an *island* of green in the desert.]

It·a·ly (it′'l ē) a country in southern Europe, including the islands of Sicily and Sardinia

jag·uar (jag′wär) *n.* a large wildcat that looks like a large leopard: it is yellowish with black spots and is found from the southwestern U.S. to Argentina

Jan·u·ar·y (jan′yoo er′ē) *n.* the first month of the year, which has 31 days: abbreviated **Jan.**

Ja·pan (jə pan′) a country east of Korea, made up of many islands

jaw (jô *or* jä) *n.* **1** either of the two bony parts that form the frame of the mouth and that hold the teeth **2** either of two parts that close to grip or crush something

a	ask, fat
ā	ape, date
ä	car, lot
e	elf, ten
ē	even, meet
i	is, hit
ī	ice, fire
ō	open, go
ô	law, horn
oi	oil, point
σο	look, pull
ōō	ooze, tool
ou	out, crowd
u	up, cut
ʉ	fur, fern
ə	a in ago
	e in agent
	e in father
	i in unity
	o in collect
	u in focus
ch	chin, arch
ŋ	ring, singer
sh	she, dash
th	thin, truth
th	then, father
zh	s in pleasure

[A vise and a pair of pliers have *jaws*.]
3 jaws, the mouth; also, the entrance of a canyon, valley, etc.

jog (jäg) *v.* **1** to give a little shake to; jostle or nudge [*Jog* him to see if he's awake.] **2** to shake up or rouse, as the memory or the mind —**jogged, jog´ging** *n.* **1** a little shake or nudge **2** a jogging pace; trot —**jog´ger**

jog

jour·nal (jur´nəl) *n.* **1** a daily record of what happens, such as a diary [She kept a *journal* of her trip.] **2** a written record of what happens at the meetings of a legislature, club, etc. **3** a newspaper or magazine

jour·ney (jur´nē) *n.* a traveling from one place to another; trip —*pl.* **jour´neys** *v.* to go on a trip; travel —**jour´neyed, jour´ney·ing**

judge (juj) *n.* **1** a public official with power to hear cases in a law court and decide what laws apply to them **2** a person chosen to decide the winner in a contest or to settle an argument *v.* **1** to decide the winner of a contest or settle an argument [to *judge* a beauty contest] **2** to form an opinion on something [Don't *judge* by first impressions.] —**judged, judg´ing** —**judg´ship´** *n.*

juic·y (jōō´sē) *adj.* full of juice [a *juicy* plum] —**juic´i·er, juic´i·est**

Ju·ly (jōō lī´) *n.* the seventh month of the year, which has 31 days; abbreviated **Jul.**

June (jōōn) *n.* the sixth month of the year, which has 30 days; abbreviated **Jun.**

Kk

kay·ak (kī´ak) *n.* an Eskimo canoe made of a wooden frame covered with skins all around, except for an opening for the paddler

kelp (kelp) *n.* a brown seaweed that is large and coarse

kil·o·gram (kil´ə gram) *n.* a unit of weight, equal to 1,000 grams

kil·o·li·ter (kil´ə lēt´ər) *n.* a unit of volume, equal to 1,000 liters or one cubic meter

kiss (kis) *v.* **1** to touch with the lips as a way of showing love, respect, etc. or as a greeting **2** to touch lightly [Her bowling ball just *kissed* the last pin.] *n.* a touch or caress with the lips —*pl.* **kiss´es**

knap·sack (nap´sak) *n.* a leather or canvas bag worn on the back, as by hikers, for carrying supplies

knead (nēd) *v.* to keep pressing and squeezing dough or clay to make it ready for use [to *knead* bread dough]

knife (nīf) *n.* **1** a tool having a flat, sharp blade set in a handle, used for cutting **2** a cutting blade that is part of a machine —*pl.* **knives** *v.* to cut or stab with a knife —**knifed, knif´ing**

knives (nīvz) *n. plural of* **knife**

know (nō) *v.* **1** to be sure of or have the facts about [Do you *know* why grass is green? She *knows* the law.] **2** to be aware of; realize [He suddenly *knew* he would be late.] **3** to have in one's mind or memory [The actress *knows* her lines.] **4** to be acquainted with [I *know* your brother well.] —**knew, known, know´ing**

knowl·edge (nä´lij) *n.* the fact or condition of knowing [*Knowledge* of the crime spread through the town.]

known (nōn) *past participle of* **know**

knuck·le (nuk´əl) *n.* **1** a joint of the finger; especially, a joint connecting a finger to the rest of the hand **2** the knee or hock joint of a pig, calf, etc., used as food — *v.* **knuckle down**, to work hard —**knuckle under**, to give in

kook·a·bur·ra (kook´ə bur ə) *n.* an Australian bird related to the kingfisher; its cry sounds like someone laughing loudly

Ll

la·dy (lā´dē) *n.* **1** a woman, especially one who is polite and refined and has a sense of honor **2** a woman belonging to a family of high social standing, as the wife of a lord —*pl.* **la´dies**

land·ing (lan´diŋ) *n.* **1** a coming to shore or a putting on shore [the *landing* of troops] **2** a place where a ship can land; pier or dock **3** a platform at the end of a flight of stairs **4** a coming down after flying, jumping, or falling

late (lāt) *adj., n.* **1** happening or coming after the usual or expected time; tardy [*late* for school; a *late* train] **2** happening or appearing just before now; recent [a *late* news broadcast] —**lat´er** or **lat´ter, lat´est** or **last** *adv.* **1** after the usual or expected time [Roses bloomed *late* last year.] **2** toward the end of some period [They came *late* in the day.] —**lat´er, lat´est** —**late´ness** *n.*

lat·i·tude (lat´ə tōōd *or* lat´ə tyōōd) *n.* **1** freedom from strict rules; freedom to do as one wishes [Our school allows some *latitude* in choosing courses.] **2** distance north or south of the equator, measured in degrees [Minneapolis is at 45 degrees north *latitude*.]

laugh (laf) *v.* **1** to make a series of quick sounds with the voice that show one is amused or happy or, sometimes, that show scorn: one usually smiles or grins when laughing ◆*n.* the act or sound of laughing

launch (lônch *or* länch) *v.* **1** to throw, hurl, or send off into space [to *launch* a rocket] **2** to cause to slide into the water; set afloat [to *launch* a new ship] **3** to start or begin [to *launch* an attack]

law·yer (lô′yər *or* lä′yər) *n.* a person whose profession is giving advice on law or acting for others in lawsuits

lead (lēd) *v.* **1** to show the way for; guide [*Lead* us along the path. The lights *led* me to the house.] **2** to go or make go in some direction [This path *leads* to the lake. Drainpipes *lead* the water away.] **3** to be at the head of or be first [He *leads* the band. Their team was *leading* at the half.] —**led** (led), **lead′ing** ◆*n.* **1** the first place or position [The bay horse is in the *lead*.] **2** a clue [The police followed up every *lead*.]

lead·ing (lē′diŋ) *adj.* **1** that leads; guiding [A *leading* question guides one toward a certain answer.] **2** most important; playing a chief role [She played a *leading* part in our campaign.]

leaf (lēf) *n.* **1** any of the flat, green parts growing from the stem of a plant or tree **2** a petal [a rose *leaf*] **3** a sheet of paper in a book [Each side of a *leaf* is a page.] —*pl.* **leaves**

learn (lurn) *v.* **1** to get some knowledge or skill, as by studying or being taught [I have *learned* to knit. Some people never *learn* from experience.] **2** to find out about something; come to know [When did you *learn* of his illness?] **3** to fix in the mind; memorize [*Learn* this poem by tomorrow.] —**learned** (lurnd) *or* **learnt** (lurnt), **learn′ing** —**learn′er** *n.*

leash (lēsh) *n.* a strap or chain by which a dog, etc. is led or held —*pl.* **leash′es** ◆*v.* to put a leash on

leaves (lēvz) *n. plural of* **leaf**

leg·end (lej′ənd) *n.* **1** a story handed down through the years and connected with some real events, but probably not true in itself [The story of King Arthur is a British *legend*.] **2** all such stories as a group [famous in Irish *legend*]

☆**length·y** (leŋkth′ē) *adj.* long or too long [a *lengthy* speech] —**length′i·er**, **length′i·est** —**length′i·ly** *adv.*

leop·ard (lep′ərd) *n.* **1** a large, fierce animal of the cat family, having a tan coat with black spots: it is found in Africa and Asia **2** *another name for* **jaguar**

let's (lets) *contraction* let us

let·ter (let′ər) *n.* **1** any of the marks used in writing or printing to stand for a sound of speech; character of an alphabet **2** a written message, usually sent by mail ◆*v.* to print letters by hand [Will you *letter* this poster?]

li·brar·y (lī′brer′ē) *n.* **1** a place where a collection of books is kept for reading or borrowing **2** a collection of books —*pl.* **li′brar′ies**

life (līf) *n.* **1** the quality of plants and animals that makes it possible for them to take in food, grow, produce others of their kind, etc. and that makes them different from rocks, water, etc. [Death is the loss of *life*.] **2** a living thing; especially, a human being [The crash took six *lives*.] —*pl.* **lives**

life·boat (līf′bōt) *n.* **1** any of the small boats carried by a ship for use if the ship must be abandoned **2** a sturdy boat kept on a shore, for use in rescuing people in danger of drowning

lift (lift) *v.* **1** to bring up to a higher place; raise [Please *lift* that box onto the truck.] **2** to rise or go up [Our spirits *lifted* when spring came.] ◆*n.* **1** a ride in the direction one is going **2** a device for carrying people up or down a slope [a ski *lift*]

lis·ten (lis′ən) *v.* to pay attention in order to hear; try to hear [*Listen* to the rain. *Listen* when the counselor speaks.] —**lis′ten·er** *n.*

li·ter (lēt′ər) *n.* the basic unit of capacity in the metric system, equal to 1 cubic decimeter: a liter is equal to a little more than a quart in liquid measure and to a little less than a quart in dry measure

lives (līvz) *n. plural of* **life**

loaf (lōf) *n.* **1** a portion of bread baked in one piece, usually oblong in shape **2** any food baked in this shape [a meat *loaf*] —*pl.* **loaves**

loan (lōn) *n.* **1** the act of lending [Thanks for the *loan* of your pen.] **2** something lent, especially a sum of money ◆*v.* to lend, especially a sum of money or something to be returned —**loaned, loan′ing**

loaves (lōvz) *n. plural of* **loaf**

lo·cate (lō′kāt *or* lō kāt′) *v.* **1** to set up or place; situate [Their shop is *located* in the new mall.] **2** to find out where something is [Have you *located* the gloves that you lost?] —**lo′cat·ed, lo′cat·ing**

lock (läk) *n.* **1** a device for fastening a door, safe, etc. by means of a bolt: a lock can usually be opened only by a special key, etc. **2** an enclosed part of a canal, river, etc. with gates at each end: water can be let in or out of it to raise or lower ships from one level to another ◆*v.* to fasten or become fastened with a lock [I *locked* the door.] —**locked, lock′ing**

lock

a	ask, fat
ā	ape, date
ä	car, lot
e	elf, ten
ē	even, meet
i	is, hit
ī	ice, fire
ō	open, go
ô	law, horn
oi	oil, point
oo	look, pull
o͞o	ooze, tool
ou	out, crowd
u	up, cut
u	fur, fern
ə	a in ago
	e in agent
	e in father
	i in unity
	o in collect
	u in focus
ch	chin, arch
ŋ	ring, singer
sh	she, dash
th	thin, truth
th	then, father
zh	s in pleasure

lo·co·mo·tive (lō'kə mō'tiv) *n.* a steam, electric, or diesel engine on wheels, that pulls or pushes railroad trains ◆*adj.* moving or able to move from one place to another

lodge (läj) *n.* **1** a place to live in; especially a small house for some special purpose [a hunting *lodge*] **2** the hut or tent of an American Indian ◆*v.* **1** to provide with a place to live or sleep in for a time [She agreed to *lodge* the strangers overnight.] **2** to come to rest and stick firmly [A fish bone *lodged* in her throat.] —**lodged, lodg'ing**

lone·ly (lōn'lē) *adj.* **1** unhappy because one is alone or away from friends or family [Billy was *lonely* his first day at camp.] **2** without others nearby; alone [a *lonely* cottage] **3** with few or no people [a *lonely* island] —**lone'li·er, lone'li·est** —**lone'li·ness** *n.*

love (luv) *n.* **1** a deep and tender feeling of fondness and devotion [parents' *love* for their children; the *love* of Romeo and Juliet] **2** a strong liking [a *love* of books] **3** a person that one loves [my own true *love*] ◆*v.* to feel love for [to *love* one's parents; to *love* all people] —**loved, lov'ing**

love·ly (luv'lē) *adj.* very pleasing in looks or character; beautiful [a *lovely* person] —**love'li·er, love'li·est**

loy·al (loi'əl) *adj.* **1** faithful to one's country [a *loyal* citizen] **2** faithful to one's family, duty, or beliefs [a *loyal* friend]

luck·y (luk'ē) *adj.* having good luck [She is *lucky* to go to Rome.] —**luck'i·er, luck'i·est**

lug·gage (lug'ij) *n.* the suitcases, trunks, etc. of a traveler; baggage

locomotive

Mm

mag·ni·fy (mag'nə fī') *v.* to make look or seem larger than is really so [to *magnify* an object with a lens] —**mag'ni·fied', mag'ni·fy'ing**

mam·mal (mam'əl) *n.* any warm-blooded animal with a backbone; female mammals have glands that produce milk for feeding their young —**mam·ma'li·an** (mə mā'lē ən) *adj., n.*

mam·moth (mam'əth) *n.* a type of large elephant that lived long ago: mammoths had a hairy skin and long tusks that curved upward ◆*adj.* very big; huge

man (man) *n.* an adult male human being **2** any human being; person ["that all *men* are created equal"] —*pl.* **men**

man·ag·er (man'ij ər) *n.* a person who manages a business, baseball team, etc.

man·a·tee (man'ə tē) *n.* a large animal that lives in shallow tropical waters and feeds on plants: it has flippers and a broad, flat tail; sea cow

March (märch) *n.* the third month of the year, which has 31 days: abbreviated **Mar.**

marsh·mal·low (märsh'mel'ō *or* märsh'mal'ō) *n.* a soft, white, spongy candy coated with powdered sugar

mas·cot (mas'kät) *n.* a person, animal, or thing thought to bring good luck by being present [Our team's *mascot* is the lion.]

match[1] (mach) *n.* **1** a slender piece of wood or cardboard having a tip coated with a chemical that catches fire when rubbed on a certain surface **2** a slowly burning cord or wick once used for firing a gun or cannon —*pl.* **match'es**

match[2] (mach) *n.* **1** two or more people or things that go well together [That suit and tie are a good *match.*] **2** a game or contest between two persons or teams [a tennis *match*]

mead·ow (med'ō) *n.* **1** a piece of land where grass is grown for hay **2** low, level grassland near a stream or lake

mean·ing (mēn'iŋ) *n.* what is meant; what is supposed to be understood; significance [She repeated her words to make her *meaning* clear. What is the *meaning* of this poem?] —**mean'ing·ful** *adj.*

meas·ure (mezh'ər) *v.* **1** to find out the size, amount, or extent of, as by comparing with something else [*Measure* the child's height with a yardstick. How do you *measure* a person's worth?] **2** to set apart or mark off a certain amount or length of [*Measure* out three pounds of sugar.] **3** to be of a certain size, amount, or extent [The table *measures* five feet on each side.] —**meas'ured, meas'ur·ing** ◆*n.* the size, amount, or extent of something, found out by measuring [The *measure* of the bucket is 15 liters.] **2** the notes or rests between two bars on a staff of music **3** rhythm or meter, as of a poem or song

meat (mēt) *n.* **1** the flesh of animals used as food: meat usually does not include fish and often does not include poultry **2** the part that can be eaten [the *meat* of a nut]

med·i·cine (med'ə sən) *n.* **1** any substance used in or on the body to treat disease, lessen pain, heal, etc. **2** the science of treating and preventing disease **3** the branch of this science that makes use of drugs, diet, etc., especially as separate from surgery

mel·o·dy (mel′ə dē) *n.* **1** an arrangement of musical tones in a series so as to form a tune; often, the main tune in the harmony of a musical piece [The *melody* is played by the oboes.] **2** any pleasing series of sounds [a *melody* sung by birds] —*pl.* **mel′o·dies**

mem·ber (mem′bər) *n.* **1** any of the persons who make up a church, club, political party, or other group **2** a leg, arm, or other part of the body

mem·o·ry (mem′ər ē) *n.* **1** the act or power of remembering [to have a good *memory*] **2** all that one remembers **3** something remembered [The music brought back many *memories*.] **4** the part of a computer that stores information —*pl.* **mem′o·ries**

men (men) *n. plural of* **man**

mend (mend) *v.* to put back in good condition; repair; fix [to *mend* a torn shirt] —**mend′ed, mend′ing**

men·u (men′yo͞o) *n.* a list of the foods served at a meal [a restaurant's dinner *menu*]

me·ter (mēt′ər) *n.* **1** a measure of length that is the basic unit in the metric system: one meter is equal to 39.37 inches **2** rhythm in poetry; regular arrangement of accented and unaccented syllables in each line **3** rhythm in music; arrangement of beats in each measure [Marches are often in 4/4 *meter*, with four equal beats in each measure.]

Mi·am·i (mī am′ē) a city on the southeastern coast of Florida

mice (mīs) *n. plural of* **mouse**

mi·cro·wave (mī′krō wāv′) *n.* any radio wave within a certain range, usually between 300,000 and 300 megahertz: those of a certain wavelength create great heat when they pass through substances such as food. A **microwave oven** uses these waves for fast cooking: others are used to transmit signals to and from communications satellites

mi·grate (mī′grāt) *v.* **1** to move from one place or country to another, especially in order to make a new home **2** to move from one region to another when the season changes, as some birds do in the spring and fall —**mi′grat·ed, mi′grat·ing** —**mi·gra′tion** *n.*

milk (milk) *n.* a white liquid formed in special glands of female mammals for suckling their young: the milk that is a common food comes from cows ◆*v.* to squeeze milk out from a cow, goat, etc. —**milk′er** *n.* —**milk′ing** *n.*

mil·li·gram (mil′i gram) *n.* a unit of weight, equal to one thousandth of a gram

mil·li·li·ter (mil′i lēt′ər) *n.* a unit of volume, equal to one thousandth of a liter

mil·li·me·ter (mil′i mēt′ər) *n.* a unit of measure, equal to one thousandth of a meter (.03937 inch)

min·er·al (min′ər əl) *n.* **1** a substance formed in the earth by nature; especially, a solid substance that was never animal or vegetable [Iron, granite, and salt are *minerals*. Coal is sometimes called a *mineral*, too.] **2** any of certain elements, as iron or phosphorus, needed by plants and animals

miss (mis) *v.* **1** to fail to hit, meet, reach, get, catch, see, hear, etc. [The arrow *missed* the target. We *missed* our plane. I *missed* you at the play last night.] **2** to let go by; fail to take [You *missed* your turn.] **3** to escape; avoid [He just *missed* being hit.] —**missed**

mol·lusk or **mol·lusc** (mäl′əsk) *n.* an animal with a soft body that is usually protected by a shell, as the oyster, clam, snail, etc.

☆**moose** (mo͞os) *n.* a large animal related to the deer, of the northern U.S. and Canada: the male has broad antlers with many points —*pl.* **moose**

moun·tain (mount′n) *n.* **1** a part of the earth's surface that rises high into the air; very high hill **2 mountains**, *pl.* a chain or group of such high hills

mouse (mous) *n.* **1** a small, gnawing animal found in houses and fields throughout the world —*pl.* **mice** (mīs) ☆**2** a small device moved by the hand, as on a flat surface, so as to make the cursor move on a computer terminal —*pl.* **mouses**

mov·er (mo͞ov′ər) *n.* a person or thing that moves; especially, ☆one whose work is moving people's furniture from one home to another

mug·ger (mug′ər) *n.* a person who assaults others, usually in order to rob them

mul·ti·ply (mul′tə plī) *v.* **1** to become more, greater, etc.; increase [Our troubles *multiplied*.] **2** to repeat a certain figure a certain number of times [If you *multiply* 10 by 4, or repeat 10 four times, you get the product 40.] —**mul′ti·plied, mul′ti·ply·ing**

mus·cle (mus′l) *n.* **1** the tissue in an animal's body that makes up the fleshy parts: muscle can be stretched or tightened to move the parts of the body **2** any single part or band of this tissue [The biceps is a *muscle* in the upper arm.] **3** strength that comes from muscles that are developed; brawn

mu·si·cal (myo͞o′zi kəl) *adj.* **1** of music or for making music [a *musical* score; a *musical* instrument] **2** like music; full of melody, harmony, etc. [Wind has a *musical* sound.] **3** fond of music or skilled in music —**mu′si·cal·ly** *adv.*

milk

a	ask, fat
ā	ape, date
ä	car, lot
e	elf, ten
ē	even, meet
i	is, hit
ī	ice, fire
ō	open, go
ô	law, horn
oi	oil, point
o͝o	look, pull
o͞o	ooze, tool
ou	out, crowd
u	up, cut
ʉ	fur, fern
ə	a in ago
	e in agent
	e in father
	i in unity
	o in collect
	u in focus
ch	chin, arch
ŋ	ring, singer
sh	she, dash
th	thin, truth
th	then, father
zh	s in pleasure

☆musk·rat (musk'rat) *n.* 1 a North American animal that is like a large rat: it lives in water and has glossy brown fur

mys·ter·y (mis'tər ē *or* mis'trə) *n.* 1 any event or thing that remains unexplained or is so secret that it makes people curious [That murder is still a *mystery.*] 2 a story or play about such an event [She read a murder *mystery.*] —*pl.* mys'ter·ies

Nn

need (nēd) *v.* to require; want [She *needs* a car.]

neigh·bor (nā'bər) *n.* 1 a person who lives near another 2 a person or thing that is near another [France and Spain are *neighbors.*] 3 another human being; fellow person ["Love thy *neighbor.*"]

neph·ew (nef'yōō) *n.* 1 the son of one's brother or sister 2 the son of one's brother-in-law or sister-in-law

nerv·ous (nur'vəs) *adj.* feeling fear or expecting trouble [He is *nervous* about seeing the dentist.]

night·in·gale (nīt'n gāl) *n.* a small European thrush: the male is known for its sweet singing

noise (noiz) *n.* sound, especially a loud, harsh, or confused sound [the *noise* of fireworks; *noises* of a city street] —*pl.* nois'es ◆*v.* to make public by telling; spread [to *noise* a rumor about] —noised, nois'ing

nom·i·nate (näm'ə nāt) *v.* 1 to name as a candidate for an election [Each political party *nominates* a person to run for president.] 2 to appoint to a position [The president *nominates* the members of the Cabinet.] —nom'i·nat·ed, nom'i·nat·ing

non·fic·tion (nän'fik'shən) *n.* a piece of writing about the real world, real people, or true events, as a biography or history

non·prof·it (nän präf'it) *adj.* not intending to make a profit [a *nonprofit* hospital]

non·sense (nän'sens) *n.* 1 speech or writing that is foolish or has no meaning [I read the letter but it just sounded like *nonsense* to me.] 2 silly or annoying behavior [She is a teacher who will put up with no *nonsense* in the classroom.] ◆*interj.* how silly! how foolish! indeed not!

non·stop (nän'stäp') *adj., adv.* without making a stop [to fly *nonstop* from New York to Seattle]

North America the northern continent in the Western Hemisphere: Canada, the United States, Mexico, and the countries of Central America are in North America

north·west (nôrth west' *or* nôr west') *n.* 1 the direction halfway between north and west 2 a place or region in or toward this direction ◆*adj.* 1 in, of, or toward the northwest [the *northwest* part of the county] 2 from the northwest [a *northwest* wind] ◆*adv.* in or toward the northwest [to sail *northwest*]

numb (num) *adj.* not able to feel, or feeling very little; deadened [My toes were *numb* with cold. He sat *numb* with grief.] ◆*v.* to make numb —numb'ly *adv.* numb'ness *n.*

nurse (nurs) *n.* a person who has been trained to take care of sick people and help doctors

nu·tri·ent (nōō'trē ənt *or* nyōō'trē ənt) *adj.* nourishing ◆*n.* any of the substances in food that are needed for health, such as proteins, minerals, vitamins, etc.

Oo

o·cean·og·ra·phy (ō'shən äg'rə fē) *n.* the science that studies the oceans and the animals and plants that live in them —o'cean·og'ra·pher

of·ten (ôfən *or* ôf'tən) *adv.* many times; frequently

o·pen (ō'pən) *adj.* not closed, shut, covered, or stopped up [*open* eyes; *open* doors; an *open* jar; an *open* drain] ◆*v.* 1 to make or become open, or no longer closed [Please *open* that trunk. The door suddenly *opened.*] 2 to begin or start [We *opened* the program with a song.] 3 to start operating [She *opened* a new store. School will *open* in September.] —o'pened —o'pen·ly *adv.* —o'pen·ness *n.*

op·er·a·tor (äp'ər āt ər) *n.* ☆1 a person who operates a machine or device [a telephone *operator*] 2 an owner or manager of a factory, mine, etc.

or·gan (ôr'gən) *n.* 1 a musical instrument having sets of pipes that make sounds when keys or pedals are pressed to send air through the pipes; *also called* pipe organ 2 a part of an animal or plant that has some special purpose [The heart, lungs, and eyes are *organs* of the body.]

or·gan·i·za·tion (ôr'gə ni zā'shən) *n.* 1 the act of organizing or arranging 2 a group of persons organized for some purpose

or·gan·ize (ôr′gə nīz) *v.* to arrange or place according to a system [The library books are *organized* according to their subjects.] —**or′gan·ized, or′gan·iz·ing** —**or′gan·iz′er** *n.*

or·phan (ôr′fən) *n.* a child whose parents are dead or, sometimes, one of whose parents is dead ◆*adj.* **1** being an orphan [an *orphan* child] **2** of or for orphans [an *orphan* home] ◆*v.* to cause to become an orphan [children *orphaned* by war]

os·trich (äs′trich) *n.* a very large bird of Africa and southwestern Asia, with a long neck and long legs: it cannot fly, but runs swiftly

ot·ter (ät′ər) *n.* **1** a furry animal related to the weasel: it has webbed feet used in swimming and a long tail, and it eats small animals and fish

☆**out·doors** (out′dôrz′) *adv.* in or into the open; outside [We went *outdoors* to play.] ◆*n.* (out dôrz′) the world outside of buildings; the open air

out·fit (out′fit) *n.* the clothing or equipment used in some work, activity, etc. [a hiking *outfit*] ◆*v.* to supply with what is needed [Their store *outfits* campers.] —**out′fit·ted, out′fit·ting**

out·stand·ing (out′stan′diŋ) *adj.* that stands out as very good or important [an *outstanding* lawyer]

☆**o·ver·coat** (ō′vər kōt) *n.* a heavy coat worn outdoors in cold weather

ox (äks) *n.* **1** a castrated male of the cattle family, used for pulling heavy loads **2** any animal of a group that chew their cud and have cloven hoofs, including the buffalo, bison, etc. —*pl.* **ox·en** (äk′s'n)

Pp

pace (pās) *n.* **1** a step in walking or running **2** the length of a step or stride, thought of as about 30 to 40 inches **3** the rate of speed at which something moves or develops [The scoutmaster set the *pace* in the hike. Science goes forward at a rapid *pace*.] ◆*v.* **1** to walk back and forth across [While waiting for the verdict, I *paced* the floor nervously.] **2** to measure by paces [*Pace* off 30 yards.] —**paced, pac′ing** —**pac′er** *n.*

pad (pad) *n.* **1** anything made of or stuffed with soft material, and used to protect against blows, to give comfort, etc.; cushion [a shoulder *pad*; seat *pad*] **2** the under part of the foot of some animals, as the wolf, lion, etc. ◆*v.* to stuff or cover with soft material [*padded* the chair] —**pad′ded, pad′ding**

par·don (pärd′n) *n.* the act of forgiving or excusing —*pl.* **par′dons**

par·ty (pär′tē) *n.* **1** a gathering of people to have a good time [a birthday *party*] **2** a group of people who share the same political opinions and work together to elect certain people, to promote certain policies, etc. [the Republican *Party*] **3** a group of people working or acting together [a hunting *party*] —*pl.* **par′ties**

pas·sen·ger (pas′ən jər) *n.* a person traveling in a car, bus, plane, ship, etc., but not driving or helping to operate it

☆**pa·ti·o** (pat′ē ō *or* pät′ē ō) *n.* **1** in Spain and Spanish America, a courtyard around which a house is built **2** a paved area near a house, with chairs, tables, etc. for outdoor lounging, dining, etc. —*pl.* **pa′ti·os**

pa·trol (pə trōl′) *v.* to make regular trips around a place in order to guard it [The watchman *patrolled* the area all night.] —**pa·trolled′, pa·trol′ling**

peace (pēs) *n.* **1** freedom from war or fighting [a nation that lives in *peace* with all other nations] **2** law and order [The rioters were disturbing the *peace*.] **3** calm or quiet [to find *peace* of mind]

pen·cil (pen′səl) *n.* a long, thin piece of wood, metal, etc. with a center stick of graphite or crayon that is sharpened to a point for writing or drawing ◆*v.* to mark, write, or draw with a pencil —**pen′ciled** or **pen′cilled, pen′cil·ing** or **pen′cil·ling**

pen·guin (peŋ′gwin) *n.* a sea bird mainly of the antarctic region, with webbed feet and flippers for swimming and diving: penguins cannot fly

pen·in·su·la (pə nin′sə lə) *n.* a long piece of land almost completely surrounded by water [Italy is a *peninsula*.] —**pen·in′su·lar** *adj.*

per·ceive (pər sēv′) *v.* **1** to become aware of through one of the senses, especially through seeing [to *perceive* the difference between two shades of red] **2** to take in through the mind [I quickly *perceived* the joke.] —**per·ceived′, per·ceiv′ing**

perch (purch) *n.* **1** a small fish living in lakes and streams: it is used for food **2** a similar saltwater fish —*pl.* **perch** or **perch′es**

per·fect (pur′fəkt) *adj.* complete in every way and having no faults or errors [a *perfect* test paper]

per·form·er (pər fôrm′ər) *n.* one who does something to entertain an audience [The *performer* sang and danced.]

per·fume (pur′fyoom *or* pər fyoom′) *n.* **1** a sweet smell; pleasing odor; fragrance [the *perfume* of roses] **2** a liquid with a

overcoat

a	ask, fat
ā	ape, date
ä	car, lot
e	elf, ten
ē	even, meet
i	is, hit
ī	ice, fire
ō	open, go
ô	law, horn
oi	oil, point
ၺ	look, pull
ഓ	ooze, tool
ou	out, crowd
u	up, cut
u	fur, fern
ə	a in ago
	e in agent
	e in father
	i in unity
	o in collect
	u in focus
ch	chin, arch
ŋ	ring, singer
sh	she, dash
th	thin, truth
th	then, father
zh	s in pleasure

piano

pleasing smell, for use on the body, clothing, etc. ➛v. (pər fyōōm′) to give a pleasing smell to, as with perfume —**per·fumed′, per·fum′ing**

per·son (pur′sən) *n.* a human being; man, woman, or child [every *person* in this room]

pet·ri·fy (pe′tri fī) *v.* **1** to change into a substance like stone by replacing the normal cells with minerals [Trees buried under lava for a great many years can become *petrified.*] **2** to make unable to move or act, as because of fear or surprise —**pet′ri·fied, pet′ri·fy·ing**

phase (fāz) *n.* **1** any of the sides or views of a subject by which it may be looked at, thought about, or shown [We discussed the many *phases* of the problem.] **2** any stage in a series of changes [Adolescence is a *phase* we all go through.] ➛v. —**phased, phas′ing**

☆**pho·ny** or **pho·ney** (fō′nē) *adj.* not real or genuine; fake; false —**pho′ni·er, pho′ni·est** ➛n. a person or thing that is not really what it is supposed to be —*pl.* **pho′nies** *this is a slang word*

pho·to (fōt′ō) *n.* a shorter name for **photograph**: *used only in everyday talk* —*pl.* **pho′tos**

pho·to·graph (fōt′ə graf) *n.* a picture made with a camera ➛v. **1** to take a photograph of **2** to look a certain way in photographs [She *photographs* taller than she is.]

pho·tog·ra·pher (fə täg′rə fər) *n.* a person who takes photographs, especially for a living

phrase (frāz) *n.* a group of words that is not a complete sentence, but that gives a single idea, usually as a separate part of a sentence

pi·an·o (pē ä′nō) *n.* a large musical instrument with many wire strings in a case and a keyboard: when a key is struck, it makes a small hammer hit a string to produce a tone; **grand piano** *and* **upright** —*pl.* **pi·an′os**

pic·ture (pik′chər) *n.* a likeness of a person, thing, scene, etc. made by drawing, painting, or photography; also, a printed copy of this ➛v. **1** to make a picture of **2** to show; make clear [Joy was *pictured* in her face.] **3** to describe or explain [Dickens *pictured* life in England.] **4** to form an idea or picture in the mind; imagine [You can *picture* how pleased I was!] —**pic′tured, pic′tur·ing**

pie (pī) *n.* a dish with a filling made of fruit, meat, etc., baked in a pastry crust

piece (pēs) *n.* **1** a part broken or separated from a whole thing [The glass shattered and I swept up the *pieces.*] **2** a part or section of a whole, thought of as complete by itself [a *piece* of meat; a *piece* of land] **3** any one of a set or group of things [a dinner set of 52 *pieces*; a chess *piece*] ➛v. to join the pieces of, as in mending [to *piece* together a broken jug]

pine·ap·ple (pīn′ap′əl) *n.* **1** a juicy tropical fruit that looks a little like a large pine cone **2** the plant it grows on, having a short stem and curved leaves with prickly edges

pi·o·neer (pī′ə nir′) *n.* ☆a person who goes before, opening up the way for others to follow, as an early settler or a scientist doing original work [Daniel Boone was a *pioneer* in Kentucky. Marie Curie was a *pioneer* in the study of radium.] ➛v. to act as a pioneer; open up the way for others [The Wright brothers *pioneered* in air travel.]

Pitts·burgh (pits′burg) a city in southwestern Pennsylvania

pit·y (pit′ē) *v.* to feel sorrow for another's suffering or trouble [to *pity* someone's misfortune] —**pit′ied, pit′y·ing**

plain (plān) *adj.* **1** open; clear; not blocked [in *plain* view] **2** easy to understand; clear to the mind [The meaning is *plain.*] **3** simple; easy [I can do a little *plain* cooking.] —**plain′ly** *adv.* —**plain′ness** *n.*

plane[1] (plān) *adj.* **1** flat; level; even ➛n. **2** a shorter form of **airplane**

plane[2] (plān) *n.* a tool used by carpenters for shaving wood in order to make it smooth or level ➛v. to make smooth or level with a plane —**planed, plan′ing**

plat·form (plat′fôrm) *n.* a flat surface or stage higher than the ground or floor around it [a *platform* at a railroad station; a speaker's *platform*]

po·et·ry (pō′ə trē) *n.* **1** the art of writing poems **2** poems [the *poetry* of Keats]

po·lit·i·cal (pə lit′i kəl) *adj.* **1** having to do with government, politics, etc. [*political* parties] **2** of or like political parties or politicians [a *political* speech] —**po·lit′i·cal·ly** *adv.*

poll (pōl) *n.* **1** a voting or listing of opinions by persons; also, the counting of these votes or opinions [A *poll* of our class shows that most of us want a party.] **2** the number of votes cast **3** a list of voters ☆**4 polls,** *pl.* a place where people go to vote

porch (pôrch) *n.* **1** a covered entrance to a building, usually with a roof that is held up by posts **2** a room on the outside of a building, either open or enclosed by screens, etc.

por·poise (pôr′pəs) *n.* **1** a water animal that is like a small whale: it is dark above and white below and has a blunt snout **2** *another name for* **dolphin**

port·hole (pôrt′hōl) *n.* a small opening in a ship's side, as for letting in light and air

pow·er·ful (pou′ər fəl) *adj.* having much power; strong or influential [a *powerful* hand; a *powerful* leader] —**pow′er·ful·ly** *adv.*

prac·tice (prak′tis) *v.* **1** to do or carry out regularly; make a habit of [to *practice* what one preaches; to *practice* charity] **2** to do something over and over again in order to become skilled at it [She *practices* two hours a day on the piano.] **3** to work at as a profession or occupation [to *practice* medicine] —**prac′ticed, prac′tic·ing**

☆ **prai·rie** (prer′ē) *n.* a large area of level or rolling grassy land without many trees

praise (prāz) *v.* **1** to say good things about; give a good opinion of [to *praise* someone's work] **2** to worship, as in song [to *praise* God] —**praised, prais′ing**

pre·cau·tion (prē kô′shən or prē kä′shən) *n.* care taken ahead of time, as against danger, failure, etc. [She took the *precaution* of locking the door before she left.] —**pre·cau′tion·ar′y** *adj.*

pre·cip·i·ta·tion (prē sip′ə tā′shən) *n.* **1** a sudden bringing about of something [the *precipitation* of a cold by getting chilled] **2** sudden or reckless haste **3** rain, snow, etc. or the amount of this

pre·dict (prē dikt′) *v.* to tell what one thinks will happen in the future [I *predict* that you will win.] —**pre·dict′a·ble** *adj.* —**pre·dict′a·bil·i·ty** *adv.*

pre·fix (prē′fiks) *n.* a syllable or group of syllables joined to the beginning of a word to change its meaning: some common prefixes are *un-, non-, re-, anti-,* and *in-*

pre·paid (prē pād′) *past tense and past participle of* **prepay**

pre·pay (prē pā′) *v.* to pay for ahead of time [Postage is normally *prepaid.*] —**pre·paid′, pre·pay′ing**

pre·set (prē set′) *v.* to set or adjust ahead of time [He *presets* the oven so it will be ready for the cake.] —**pre·set′, pre·set′ting**

pret·ty (prit′ē) *adj.* **1** pleasant to look at or hear, especially in a delicate, dainty, or graceful way [a *pretty* girl; a *pretty* voice; a *pretty* garden] **2** fine; good; nice —**pret′ti·er, pret′ti·est**

pre·view (prē′vyoo) *n.* ☆a view or showing ahead of time; especially, a private showing of a movie before showing it to the public ◆*v.* to give a preview of

price (prīs) *n.* **1** the amount of money asked or paid for something; cost [What is the *price* of that coat?] **2** value or worth [a painting of great *price*] ◆*v.* to set the price of [The rug was *priced* at $40.] —**priced, pric′ing**

pride (prīd) *n.* **1** an opinion of oneself that is too high; vanity [Her *pride* blinded her to her own faults.] **2** proper respect for oneself; dignity; self-respect [He has too much *pride* to go begging.] **3** pleasure or satisfaction in something done, owned, etc. [We take *pride* in our garden.] **4** a person or thing that makes one proud [She is her father's *pride* and joy.] —**prid′ed, prid′ing**

prince (prins) *n.* a son or grandson of a king or queen

prin·ci·pal (prin′sə pəl) *n.* the head of a school

print·ing (print′iŋ) *n.* **1** the act of one that prints **2** the making of printed material, as books, newspapers, etc. **3** printed words —**print′er**

pro·ceed (prō sēd′) *v.* **1** to go on, especially after stopping for a while [After eating, we *proceeded* to the next town.] **2** to begin and go on doing something [I *proceeded* to build a fire.]

prod·uct (präd′əkt) *n.* **1** something produced by nature or by human beings [Wood is a natural *product.* A desk is a manufactured *product.*] **2** result [The story is a *product* of her imagination.] **3** a number that is the result of multiplying [28 is the *product* of 7 multiplied by 4.]

pro·gram (prō′gram) *n.* **1** the acts, speeches, or musical pieces that make up a ceremony or entertainment [a commencement *program*] **2** a scheduled broadcast on radio or TV

prom·ise (präm′is) *n.* **1** an agreement to do or not to do something; vow [to make and keep a *promise*] **2** a sign that gives reason for expecting success; cause for hope [She shows *promise* as a singer.] ◆*v.* to make a promise to [I *promised* them I'd arrive at ten.] —**prom′ised, prom′is·ing**

prompt (prämpt) *adj.* **1** quick in doing what should be done; on time [He is *prompt* in paying his bills.] **2** done, spoken, etc. without waiting [We would like a *prompt* reply.] ◆*v.* to urge or stir into action [Tyranny *prompted* them to revolt.] —**prompt′ly** *adv.* —**prompt′ness** *n.*

prop·er (präp′ər) *adj.* **1** right, correct, or suitable [the *proper* tool for this job; the *proper* clothes for a party] **2** not to be ashamed of; decent; respectable [*proper* manners] —**prop′er·ly** *adv.*

pro·tect (prō tekt′) *v.* to guard or defend against harm or danger; shield [armor to *protect* the knight's body] —**pro·tec′tor** *n.*

prince

a	ask, fat
ā	ape, date
ä	car, lot
e	elf, ten
ē	even, meet
i	is, hit
ī	ice, fire
ō	open, go
ô	law, horn
oi	oil, point
oo	look, pull
oo	ooze, tool
ou	out, crowd
u	up, cut
u	fur, fern
ə	a in ago
	e in agent
	e in father
	i in unity
	o in collect
	u in focus
ch	chin, arch
ŋ	ring, singer
sh	she, dash
th	thin, truth
th	then, father
zh	s in pleasure

pro·te·in (prō′tēn) *n.* a substance containing nitrogen and other elements, found in all living things and in such foods as cheese, meat, eggs, beans, etc.: it is a necessary part of an animal's diet

pro·test (prō test′ *or* prō′test) *v.* **1** to speak out against; object [They joined the march to *protest* against injustice.] **2** to say in a positive way; insist [Bill *protested* that he would be glad to help.] ◆*n.* (prō′test) the act of protesting; objection [They ignored my *protest* and continued hammering.] —**pro·test′er** or **pro·tes′tor**

prove (prōōv) *v.* **1** to show that something is true or correct [She showed us the method of *proving* our arithmetic problems.] **2** to put to a test or trial; find out about through experiments [A *proving* ground is a place for testing new equipment, as aircraft.] **3** to turn out to be [Your guess *proved* right.] —**proved, proved** or **prov′en, prov′ing**

pub·lic (pub′lik) *adj.* of or having to do with the people as a whole [*public* opinion] ◆*n.* the people as a whole [what the *public* wants]

punc·tu·a·tion (puŋk′chōō ā′shən) *n.* **1** the use of commas, periods, etc. in writing [rules of *punctuation*] **2** punctuation marks [What *punctuation* is used to end sentences?]

purse (pʉrs) *n.* a bag of leather or cloth used for carrying money, cosmetics, keys, and so on —*pl.* **purs′es**

☆**quit·ter** (kwit′ər) *n.* a person who quits or gives up too easily

Rr

rail·road (rāl′rōd) *n.* **1** a road on which there is a track made up of parallel steel rails along which trains run **2** a series of such roads managed as a unit, together with the cars, engines, stations, etc. that belong to it

rai·sin (rā′zən) *n.* a sweet grape dried for eating

rake (rāk) *n.* a tool with a long handle having a set of teeth or prongs at one end: it is used for gathering loose grass, leaves, etc. or for smoothing broken ground ◆*v.* to gather together or smooth as with a rake [to *rake* leaves; to *rake* a gravel path] —**raked, rak′ing**

☆**ranch** (ranch) *n.* a large farm, especially in the Western part of the United States, where cattle, horses, or sheep are raised —*pl.* **ranch′es** —**ranch′er** *n.* ◆*v.* to work on or manage a ranch

rap·id (rap′id) *adj.* very swift or quick [a *rapid* journey] ◆☆*n. usually* **rapids,** *pl.* a part of a river where the water moves swiftly —**rap′id·ly** *adv.*

reach (rēch) *v.* **1** to stretch out one's hand, arm, etc. [He *reached* up and shook the branch.] **2** to touch, as by stretching out [Can you *reach* the top shelf?] **3** to stretch out in time, space, amount, etc. [Her fame *reaches* into all parts of the world.] —**reach′es**

re·ac·tion (rē ak′shən) *n.* an action, happening, etc. in return or in response to some other action, happening, force, etc. [What was their *reaction* to your suggestion? A rubber ball bounces as a *reaction* to hitting the ground.]

rea·son (rē′zən) *n.* **1** something said to explain or try to explain an act, idea, etc. [Write the *reasons* for your answer.] **2** a cause for some action, feeling, etc.; motive [Noisy neighbors were our *reason* for moving.] **3** the power to think, get ideas, decide things, etc. [Human beings are the only creatures that truly have *reason*.]

re·ceipt (rē sēt′) *n.* **1** a receiving or being received [Upon *receipt* of the gift, she thanked him.] **2** a written statement that something has been received [My landlord gave me a *receipt* when I paid my rent.] **3 receipts,** *pl.* the amount of money taken in, as in a business

re·ceive (rē sēv′) *v.* **1** to take or get what has been given or sent to one [to *receive* a letter] **2** to meet with; be given; undergo [to *receive* punishment; to *receive* applause] **3** to find out about; learn [He *received* the news calmly.] **4** to greet guests and let them come in [Our hostess *received* us at the door.] —**re·ceived′, re·ceiv′ing**

re·count (rē kount′) *v.* to count again [You had better *recount* your change just to make sure.]

re·duce (rē dōōs′ *or* rē dyōōs′) *v.* **1** to make smaller, less, fewer, etc.; decrease [to *reduce* speed; to *reduce* taxes] **2** to loose weight, as by dieting **3** to make lower, as in rank or condition; bring down [to *reduce* a major to rank of captain; a family *reduced* to poverty] —**re·duced′, re·duc′ing** —**re·duc′er** *n.* —**re·duc′i·ble** *adj.*

reel (rēl) *n.* **1** a frame or spool on which film, fishing line, wire, etc. is wound **2** the amount of movie film, wire, etc. usually wound on one reel ◆*v.* to wind on a reel

re·fill (rē fil′) *v.* to fill again ◆*n.* (rē′fil) **1** something to replace the contents of a special container [a *refill* for a ball point pen] **2** any extra filling of a prescription for medicine —**re·fill′a·ble** *adj.*

re·frig·er·a·tor (ri frij′ər āt′ər) *n.* a box or room in which the air is kept cool to keep food, etc. from spoiling

re·fund (rē fund′) *v.* to give back money, etc.; repay [We will *refund* the full price if you are not satisfied.] ◆*n.* (rē′fund) the act of refunding or the amount refunded —**re·fund′a·ble** *adj.*

reg·is·ter (rej′is tər) *n.* **1** a record or list of names, events, or things; also, a book in which such a record is kept [a hotel *register*, *register* of accounts] **2** a device for counting and keeping a record of [a cash *register*] ◆*v.* ☆**1** to keep a record of in a register [to *register* a birth] **2** to put one's name in a register, as of voters

reg·u·lar (reg′yə lər) *adj.* formed or arranged in an orderly way; balanced [a face with *regular* features]

rein·deer (rān′dir) *n.* a large deer found in northern regions, where it is tamed and used for work or as food: both the male and female have antlers —*pl.* **rein′deer**

re·lief (rē lēf′) *n.* **1** a lessening of pain, discomfort, worry, etc. [This salve will give *relief* from itching.] **2** anything that lessens pain, worry, etc. or gives a pleasing change [It's a *relief* to get out of that stuffy hall.] **3** help given to poor people, to victims of a flood, etc.

re·ly (rē lī′) *v.* to trust or depend [You can *rely* on me to be on time.] —**re·lied′, re·ly′ing**

re·mem·ber (rē mem′bər) *v.* **1** to think of again [I suddenly *remembered* I was supposed to mow the lawn.] **2** to bring back to mind by trying; recall [I just can't *remember* your name.] **3** to be careful not to forget [*Remember* to look both ways before crossing.] —**re·mem′bered**

re·move (rē mōōv′) *v.* to move to another place; take away or take off [They *removed* their coats.]

re·pair (rē per′) *v.* **1** to put into good condition again; fix, mend [to *repair* a broken toy] **2** to set right; correct [to *repair* a mistake; to *repair* an injustice] ◆*n.* **1** the act of repairing **2** *usually* **repairs** *pl.* work done in repairing [to make *repairs* on a house] —**re·pair′a·ble** *adj.*

re·ply (rē plī′) *v.* to answer by saying or doing something [to *reply* to a question; to *reply* to the enemy's fire with a counterattack] —**re·plied′, re·ply′ing** ◆*n.* an answer —*pl.* **re·plies′**

re·port (rē pôrt′) *v.* **1** to tell about; give an account of [I *reported* on my trip to the Falls.] **2** to tell as news [the papers *reported* little damage as a result of the storm.] ◆*n.* an account of something, often one in written or printed form [a financial *report*]

☆**res·tau·rant** (res′tər änt *or* res′tränt) *n.* a place where meals can be bought and eaten

re·turn (rē turn′) *v.* **1** to go or come back [When did you *return* from your trip?] **2** to bring, send, carry, or put back [Our neighbor *returned* the ladder.] **3** to pay back by doing the same [to *return* a visit; to *return* a favor] **4** to report back [The jury *returned* a verdict of "not guilty."]

rid·er (rīd′ər) *n.* a person who rides

rise (rīz) *v.* **1** to stand up or get up from a lying or sitting position [*rise* to greet the guests] **2** to get up after sleeping [She *rises* early.] —**rose** (rōz), **ris′en** (riz′ən), **ris′ing**

risk (risk) *n.* the chance of getting hurt, or of losing, failing, etc.; danger [He ran into the burning house at the *risk* of his life.] ◆*v.* to take the chance of [Are you willing to *risk* a fight for your beliefs?]

roast (rōst) *v.* **1** to cook with little or no liquid, as in an oven or over an open fire [to *roast* a chicken or a whole ox] **2** to dry or brown with great heat [to *roast* coffee] ◆*n.* a piece of roasted meat —**roast′ed**

ro·dent (rōd′nt) *n.* an animal having sharp front teeth for gnawing: rats, mice, rabbits, squirrels, woodchucks, and beavers are rodents

rough·ly (ruf′lē) *adv.* **1** in a rough manner **2** more or less; about [*Roughly* 50 people came to the party.]

roy·al·ty (roi′əl tē) *n.* **1** a royal person, or royal persons as a group [a member of British *royalty*] **2** the rank or power of a king or queen **3** royal quality or nature; nobility, splendor, etc. —*pl.* **roy′al·ties**

rude (rōōd) *adj.* without respect for others; impolite [It was *rude* of them not to thank you.] —**rud′er, rud′est**

rule (rōōl) *n.* **1** a statement or law that is meant to guide or control the way one acts or does something [the *rules* of grammar; baseball *rules*] **2** a usual way of doing something, behaving, etc. [to make it a *rule* never to rush] **3** government or reign [the *rule* of Elizabeth I]

rodent

a	ask, fat
ā	ape, date
ä	car, lot
e	elf, ten
ē	even, meet
i	is, hit
ī	ice, fire
ō	open, go
ô	law, horn
oi	oil, point
ᴏᴏ	look, pull
ᴏᴏ	ooze, tool
ou	out, crowd
u	up, cut
ʉ	fur, fern
ə	a in ago
	e in agent
	e in father
	i in unity
	o in collect
	u in focus
ch	chin, arch
ŋ	ring, singer
sh	she, dash
th	thin, truth
th	then, father
zh	s in pleasure

☆**run·way** (run′wā) *n.* a track or path on which something moves, as a paved strip on an airfield used by airplanes in taking off and landing

Ss

sauce pan

safe (sāf) *adj.* **1** free from harm or danger; secure [a *safe* hiding place; *safe* in bed] **2** not hurt or harmed [We emerged *safe* from the wreck.] **3** that can be trusted [a *safe* investment] —**saf′er, saf′est** —**safe′ly** *adv.*

sal·ad (sal′əd) *n.* any mixture of vegetables, fruits, fish, eggs, etc., with a dressing of oil, vinegar, spices, etc.: it is usually served cold, often on lettuce leaves

sand·wich (san′dwich *or* san′wich) *n.* slices of bread with a filling of meat, cheese, etc. between them —*pl.* **sand′wich·es** ◆*v.* to squeeze in [a shed *sandwiched* between two houses]

San Fran·cis·co (san′ fran sis′kō) a city on the coast of central California

sar·dine (sär dēn′) *n.* a small fish, as a young herring, preserved in oil and packed in cans

sash (sash) *n.* a band, ribbon, or scarf worn over the shoulder or around the waist —*pl.* **sash′es**

sat·el·lite (sat′l īt) *n.* **1** a heavenly body that revolves around another, larger one [The moon is a *satellite* of the earth.] **2** an artificial object put into orbit around the earth, the moon, or some other heavenly body

sat·is·fy (sat′is fī) *v.* **1** to meet the needs or wishes of; content; please [Only first prize will *satisfy* him.] **2** to make feel sure; convince [The jury was *satisfied* that he was innocent.] —**sat′is·fied, sat′is·fy·ing**

sauce (sôs *or* säs) *n.* **1** a liquid or soft dressing served with food to make it tastier [spaghetti with tomato *sauce*] ☆**2** fruit that has been stewed [apple*sauce*]

sauce·pan (sôs′pan *or* s′äs′pan) *n.* a small metal pot with a long handle, used for cooking

sau·cer (sô′sər *or* sä′sər) *n.* a small, shallow dish, especially one for a cup to rest on

save (sāv) *v.* **1** to rescue or keep from harm or danger [He was *saved* from drowning.] **2** to keep or store up for future use [She *saved* her money for a vacation.] **3** to keep from being lost or wasted [Traveling by plane *saved* many hours.] —**saved, sav′ing** —**sav′er** *n.*

scale¹ (skāl) *n.* **1** a series of marks along a line, with regular spaces in between, used for measuring [A Celsius thermometer has a basic *scale* of 100 degrees.] **2** the way that the size of a map, model, or drawing compares with the size of the thing that it stands for [One inch on a map of this *scale* equals 100 miles of real distance.] **3** a series of steps or degrees based on size, amount, rank, etc. [A passing grade on this *scale* is 70.]

scale² (skāl) *n.* **1** any of the thin, flat, hard plates that cover and protect certain fish and reptiles **2** a thin piece or layer; flake [*scales* of rust in a water pipe] ◆*v.* to scrape scales from [to *scale* a fish] —**scaled, scal′ing**

scale³ (skāl) *n.* **1** either of the shallow pans of a balance **2** *often* **scales,** *pl.* the balance itself; also, any device or machine for weighing ◆*v.* to weigh —**scaled, scal′ing**

scare (sker) *v.* to make or become afraid; frighten —**scared, scar′ing** ◆*n.* a sudden fear; fright [The loud noise gave me quite a *scare.*]

scarf (skärf) *n.* **1** a long or broad piece of cloth worn about the head, neck, or shoulders for warmth or decoration **2** a long, narrow piece of cloth used as a covering on top of a table, bureau, etc. —*pl.* **scarfs** *or* **scarves** (skärvz)

scent (sent) *n.* **1** a smell; odor [the *scent* of apple blossoms] **2** the sense of smell [Lions hunt partly by *scent.*] **3** a smell left by an animal [The dogs lost the fox's *scent* at the river.]

school·house (skool′hous) *n.* a building used as a school

scout (skout) *n.* a soldier, ship, or plane sent to spy out the strength or movements of the enemy

scram·ble (skram′bəl) *v.* to climb or crawl in a quick, rough way [The children *scrambled* up the steep hill.] —**scram′bled, scram′bling**

scratch (skrach) *n.* **1** a mark or cut made in a surface by something sharp **2** a slight wound —*pl.* **scratch′es**

scrawl (skrôl) *v.* to write or draw in a hasty, careless way ◆*n.* careless or poor handwriting that is hard to read

screech (skrēch) *v.* to give a harsh, high shriek ◆*n.* a harsh, high shriek

screen (skrēn) *n.* **1** a mesh woven loosely of wires so as to leave small openings between them: screens are used in windows, doors, etc. to keep insects out. **2** a covered frame or curtain used to hide, separate, or protect **3** anything that hides, separates, or protects [a smoke *screen*; a *screen* of trees]

scrub (skrub) *v.* to clean or wash by rubbing hard [to *scrub* floors] —**scrubbed, scrub'bing** ◆*n.* the act of cleaning by rubbing hard

scur·ry (skur'ē) *v.* to run quickly; scamper —**scur'ried, scur'ry·ing** ◆*n.* the act or sound of running quickly

sea·son (sē'zən) *n.* **1** any of the four parts into which the year is divided: spring, summer, fall, or winter **2** a special time of the year [the Easter *season*; the hunting *season*] **3** a period of time [the busy *season* at a factory] ◆*v.* to add to or change the flavor of [to *season* meat with herbs]

Se·at·tle (sē at'l) a city in Washington

sea·weed (sē'wēd) *n.* any plant or plants growing in the sea, especially algae: there are some plants like these that grow in fresh water and are also called seaweed

seek (sēk) *v.* **1** to try to find; search for [to *seek* gold] **2** to try to get; aim at [to *seek* a prize] —**sought, seek'ing**

seize (sēz) *v.* **1** to take hold of in a sudden, strong, or eager way; grasp [to *seize* a weapon and fight; to *seize* an opportunity] **2** to capture or arrest, as a criminal **3** to take over as by force [The troops *seized* the fort. The city *seized* the property for nonpayment of taxes.] —**seized, seiz'ing**

sense (sens) *n.* **1** any of the special powers of the body and mind that let one see, hear, feel, taste, smell, etc. **2** a feeling or sensation [a *sense* of warmth; a *sense* of guilt] **3** an understanding or appreciation; special awareness [a *sense* of honor; a *sense* of beauty; a *sense* of rhythm; a *sense* of humor] **4** judgment or intelligence; reasoning [He showed good *sense* in his decision. There's no *sense* in going there late.]

serve (surv) *v.* **1** to work for someone as a servant [I *served* in their household for ten years.] **2** to do services for; aid; help [She *served* her country well.] **3** to hold a certain office [She *served* as mayor for two terms.] **4** to offer or pass food, drink, etc. to [May I *serve* you some chicken?] —**served, serv'ing**

sev·en (sev'ən) *n., adj.* one more than six; the number 7

shake (shāk) *v.* to move quickly up and down, back and forth, or from side to side [She *shook* her head in disapproval.]. —**shook, shak'en, shak'ing**

share (sher) *n.* a part that each one of a group gets or has [your *share* of the cake; my *share* of the blame] ◆*v.* **1** to divide and give out in shares [The owners *shared* the profits with their employees.] **2** to have a share of with others; have or use together [The three of you will *share* the back seat.] —**shared, shar'ing**

sharp (shärp) *adj.* **1** having a thin edge for cutting, or a fine point for piercing [a *sharp* knife; a *sharp* needle] **2** not gradual; abrupt [a *sharp* turn] **3** severe or harsh [a *sharp* reply] ◆*adv.* in a sharp manner; keenly, alertly, briskly, etc. [Look *sharp* when crossing streets.] —**sharp'ly** —**sharp'ness** *n.*

shawl (shôl) *n.* a large piece of cloth worn, especially by women, over the shoulders or head

sheep (shēp) *n.* an animal that chews its cud and is related to the goat: its body is covered with heavy wool and its flesh is used as food, called mutton —*pl.* **sheep**

shelf (shelf) *n.* a thin, flat length of wood, metal, etc. fastened against a wall or built into a frame so as to hold things [the top *shelf* of a bookcase] —*pl.* **shelves**

she'll (shēl) *contraction* **1** she will **2** she shall

shel·ter (shel'tər) *n.* a place or thing that covers or protects from the weather or danger [The *shelter* protected us from the rain.]

sher·bet (shur'bət) *n.* a frozen dessert of fruit juice, sugar, and water, milk, etc.

ship·ment (ship'mənt) *n.* **1** the shipping of goods by any means **2** the goods shipped

shoe (shoo) *n.* an outdoor covering for the foot, usually of leather ◆*v.* to furnish with shoes; put shoes on [to *shoe* a horse]

shore (shôr) *n.* **1** land at the edge of a sea or lake **2** land, not water [The retired sailor lives on *shore*.]

short·en (shôrt'n) *v.* to make or become short or shorter [to *shorten* a skirt]

should·n't (shood'nt) *contraction* should not

shov·el (shuv'əl) *n.* **1** a tool with a broad scoop and a handle, for lifting and moving loose material **2** a machine with a part like a shovel, used for digging or moving large amounts of loose material [a steam *shovel*] ◆*v.* to lift and move with a shovel [to *shovel* coal] —**shov'eled** or **shov'elled, shov'el·ing** or **shov'el·ling**

show·er (shou'ər) *n.* **1** a short fall of rain or hail **2** a sudden, very full fall or flow, as of sparks, praise, etc. ☆**3** a bath in which the body is sprayed with fine streams of water: *the full name is* **shower bath**

shriek (shrēk) *n.* a loud, sharp, shrill cry; screech; scream ◆*v.* to cry out with a shrill cry [to *shriek* in terror]

shrimp (shrimp) *n.* a small shellfish with a long tail, used as food —*pl.* **shrimp** or **shrimps**

shut·tle (shut'əl) *n.* **1** a device in weaving that carries a thread back and forth between the threads that go up and down ☆**2** a bus, train, or airplane that makes frequent trips back and forth over a short route ◆*v.* to move rapidly to and fro —**shut'tled, shut'tling**

a	ask, fat
ā	ape, date
ä	car, lot
e	elf, ten
ē	even, meet
i	is, hit
ī	ice, fire
ō	open, go
ô	law, horn
oi	oil, point
oo	look, pull
ōo	ooze, tool
ou	out, crowd
u	up, cut
u	fur, fern
ə	a in ago
	e in agent
	e in father
	i in unity
	o in collect
	u in focus
ch	chin, arch
ŋ	ring, singer
sh	she, dash
th	thin, truth
th	then, father
zh	s in pleasure

☆ **side·walk** (sīd'wôk) *n.* a path for walking, usually paved, along the side of a street

si·lent (sī'lənt) *adj.* **1** not speaking or not talking much **2** with no sound or noise; noiseless [Find a *silent* place to study. We went to a *silent* movie.] **3** not spoken or told [*silent* grief; the *silent* "b" in "debt"] —**si'lent·ly** *adv.*

sing·er (siŋ'ər) *n.* **1** a person that sings **2** a bird that sings

sink (siŋk) *v.* to go or put down below the surface [The boat is *sinking*] —**sank** or **sunk, sink'ing**

sink·er (siŋk'ər) *n.* something that sinks, as a lead weight put on the end of a fishing line

sis·ter (sis'tər) *n.* **1** a girl or woman as she is related to the other children of her parents **2** a girl or woman who is close to one in some way; especially, a fellow member of the same race, religion, club, etc. **3** a nun

sit (sit) *v.* **1** to rest the weight of the body upon the buttocks or haunches [She is *sitting* on a bench. The dog *sat* still.] **2** to perch, rest, lie, etc. [A bird *sat* on the fence. Cares *sit* lightly on him.] —**sat, sit'ting**

sit·ting (sit'iŋ) *n.* **1** the act or position of one that sits, as for a picture **2** a meeting, as of a court or a council **3** a period of being seated [I read the book in one *sitting*.]

skat·er (skāt'ər) *n.* one who moves along on skates [The *skater* twirled on the ice.]

skill (skil) *n.* **1** ability that comes from training, practice, etc. [He plays the violin with *skill*.] **2** an art, craft, or science, especially one that calls for use of the hands or body [Weaving is a *skill* often taught to the blind.]

skim (skim) *v.* **1** to take off floating matter from the top of a liquid [to *skim* cream from milk; to *skim* molten lead] **2** to look through a book, magazine, etc. quickly without reading carefully **3** to glide lightly, as over a surface [bugs *skimming* over the water] —**skimmed, skim'ming**

☆ **skunk** (skuŋk) *n.* **1** an animal having a bushy tail and black fur with white stripes down its back: it sprays out a very bad-smelling liquid when frightened or attacked

☆ **sleigh** (slā) *n.* a carriage with runners instead of wheels, for travel over snow or ice ◆ *v.* to ride in or drive a sleigh

slen·der (slen'dər) *adj.* small in width as compared with the length or height; long and thin [a *slender* woman]

slice (slīs) *n.* a thin, broad piece cut from something [a *slice* of cheese; a *slice* of bread] ◆ *v.* **1** to cut into slices [to *slice* a cake] **2** to cut as with a knife [The plow *sliced* through the soft earth.] —**sliced, slic'ing** —**slic'er** *n.*

slice

slip (slip) *v.* **1** to go or pass quietly or without being noticed; escape [We *slipped* out the door. It *slipped* my mind. Time *slipped* by.] **2** to pass slowly into a certain condition [to *slip* into bad habits] **3** to move, shift, or drop, as by accident [The plate *slipped* from my hand.] **4** to slid by accident [He *slipped* on the ice.] —**slipped, slip'ping**

slip·per (slip'ər) *n.* a light, low shoe that is usually worn while a person is relaxing at home

smooth (smooth) *adj.* having an even or level surface, with no bumps or rough spots [*smooth* water on the lake]

snap (snap) *v.* to bite, grasp, or snatch suddenly [The frog *snapped* at the fly.] —**snapped, snap'ping**

sneeze (snēz) *v.* to blow out breath from the mouth and nose in a sudden way that cannot be controlled [My cold made me *sneeze*.] —**sneezed, sneez'ing**

soar (sôr) *v.* to rise or fly high into the air [The plane *soared* out of sight.]

soft·en (sôf'ən *or* säf'ən) *v.* to make or become soft or softer —**soft'en·er** *n.*

soft·ware (sôft'wer' *or* säft'wer) *n.* the special instructions, information, etc. that make a computer operate

sol·id (säl'id) *adj.* **1** keeping its shape instead of flowing or spreading out like a liquid or gas; quite firm or hard [Ice is water in a *solid* form.] **2** filled with matter throughout; not hollow [a *solid* block of wood] **3** that has length, width, and thickness [A prism is a *solid* figure.] **4** strong, firm, sound, dependable, etc. [*solid* thinking; a *solid* building] —**sol'id·ly** *adv.*

sor·row (sär'ō) *n.* **1** a sad or troubled feeling; sadness; grief **2** a loss, death, or trouble causing such a feeling [Our grandmother's illness is a great *sorrow* to us.] ◆ *v.* to feel or show sorrow [We are *sorrowing* over his loss.]

sort (sôrt) *n.* **1** a group of things that are alike in some way; kind; class [various *sorts* of toys] **2** quality or type [phrases of a noble *sort*] ◆ *v.* to separate or arrange according to class or kind [*Sort* out the clothes that need mending.] —**sort'ed**

sought (sôt *or* sät) *v.* past tense and past participle of **seek**

sound (sound) *n.* **1** the form of energy that acts on the ears so that one can hear: sound consists of waves of vibrations carried in the air, water, etc. [In air, *sound* travels at a speed of about 332 meters per second, or 1,088 feet per second.] **2** anything that can be heard; noise, tone, etc. [the *sound* of bells] **3** any of the noises made in speaking [a vowel *sound*] ◆ *v.* to make a sound [Your voice *sounds* hoarse.]

soup (so͞op) *n.* a liquid food made by cooking meat, vegetables, etc. as in water or milk

South America the southern continent in the Western Hemisphere —**South American** *adj., n*

south·east (sou͞th ēst' *or* sou ēst') *n.* **1** the direction halfway between south and east **2** a place or region in or toward this direction ◆*adj.* **1** in, of, or toward the southeast [the *southeast* part of the county] **2** from the southeast [a *southeast* wind] ◆*adv.* in or toward the southeast [to sail *southeast*]

south·ern (su*th*'ərn) *adj.* **1** in, of, or toward the south [the *southern* sky] **2** from the south [a *southern* wind]. **3 Southern**, of the South

soy·bean (soi'bēn) *n.* **1** the seed, or bean, of a plant of Asia, now grown throughout the world: the beans are ground into flour, pressed for oil, etc. **2** the plant itself

space (spās) *n.* **1** the area that stretches in all directions, has no limits, and contains all things in the universe [The earth, the sun, and all the stars exist in *space*.] **2** the distance or area between things or inside of something, especially as used for some purpose [a closet with much *space*; parking *space*] **3** *a shorter name for* **outer space** ◆*v.* to arrange with spaces in between [The trees are evenly *spaced*.] —**spaced, spac'ing**

space·craft (spās'kraft') *n.* any spaceship or satellite designed for use in outer space —*pl.* **space'craft'**

spare (sper) *v.* **1** to save or free from something [*Spare* us the trouble of listening to that story again.] **2** to get along without; give up [We can't *spare* the money or the time for a vacation trip.] —**spared, spar'ing** ◆*adj.* **1** kept for use when needed [a *spare* room; a *spare* tire] **2** not taken up by regular work or duties; free [*spare* time] —**spar'er, spar'est** ◆*n.* **1** an extra part or thing ☆**2** in bowling, the act of knocking down all ten pins with two rolls of the ball —**spare'ly** *adv.*

spark (spärk) *n.* **1** a small bit of burning matter, as one thrown off by a fire **2** any flash of light like this [the *spark* of a firefly] **3** the small flash of light that takes place when an electric current jumps across an open space, as in a spark plug

spar·row (sper'ō) *n.* a small gray and brown songbird with a short beak: the common sparrow seen on city streets is the **English sparrow**

spe·cies (spē'shēz *or* spē'sēz) *n.* a group of plants or animals that are alike in certain ways [The lion and tiger are two different *species* of cat.] —*pl.* **spe'cies**

speed (spēd) *n.* **1** fast motion; swiftness **2** rate of motion; velocity [a *speed* of 10 miles per hour] **3** swiftness of any action [reading *speed*] ◆*v.* **1** to go or move fast or too fast [The arrow *sped* to its mark.] **2** to make go or move fast [He *sped* the letter on its way.] —**sped** or **speed'ed, speed'ing**

spend (spend) *v.* **1** to pay out or give up, as money, time, or effort [He *spent* $50 for food. Try to *spend* some time with me.] **2** to pass [She *spent* the summer at camp.] —**spent, spend'ing** —**spend'er** *n.*

spent (spent) *past tense and past participle of* **spend** ◆*adj.* tired out; used up

spice (spīs) *n.* any one of several vegetable substances used to give a special flavor or smell to food [Cinnamon, nutmeg, and pepper are kinds of *spices*.]

splash (splash) *v.* **1** to make a liquid scatter and fall in drops [to *splash* water or mud about] **2** to dash a liquid on, so as to wet or soil [The car *splashed* my coat.] ◆*n.* the act or sound of splashing —*pl.* **splash'es** —**splash'y** *adj.*

splen·did (splen'did) *adj.* very bright, brilliant, showy, or magnificent [a *splendid* gown]

splin·ter (splin'tər) *v.* to break or split into thin, sharp pieces [Soft pine *splinters* easily.] ◆*n.* a thin, sharp piece of wood, bone, etc. broken off

spoil (spoil) *v.* **1** to make or become useless, worthless, rotten, etc.; damage; ruin [Ink stains *spoiled* the paper. Illness *spoiled* my attendance record. Meat *spoils* fast in warm weather.] **2** to cause a person to ask for or expect too much by giving in to all of that person's wishes [to *spoil* a child] —**spoiled** or **spoilt, spoil'ing**

sponge (spunj) *n.* **1** a sea animal that is like a plant and grows fixed to surfaces under water **2** the light, elastic skeleton of such an animal, that is full of holes and can soak up much water: sponges are used for washing, bathing, etc. **3** any artificial substance like this, as of plastic or rubber, used in the same way ◆*v.* to wipe, clean, make wet, or soak up as with a sponge [to *sponge* up gravy with a crust of bread] —**sponged, spong'ing**

sport (spôrt) *n.* **1** active play, a game, etc. taken up for exercise or pleasure and, sometimes, as a profession [Football, golf, bowling, swimming, diving, etc. are *sports*.] **2** fun or play [They thought it was great *sport* to fool others on the telephone.]

sprain (sprān) *v.* to twist a muscle or ligament in a joint without putting the bones out of place [to *sprain* one's wrist] ◆*n.* an injury caused by this

sport

a	ask, fat
â	ape, date
ä	car, lot
e	elf, ten
ē	even, meet
i	is, hit
ī	ice, fire
ō	open, go
ô	law, horn
oi	oil, point
o͝o	look, pull
o͞o	ooze, tool
ou	out, crowd
u	up, cut
u	fur, fern
ə	a in ago
	e in agent
	e in father
	i in unity
	o in collect
	u in focus
ch	chin, arch
ŋ	ring, singer
sh	she, dash
th	thin, truth
th	then, father
zh	s in pleasure

sprin·kle (spriŋ'kəl) *v.* 1 to scatter in drops or bits [to *sprinkle* salt on an egg] 2 to scatter drops or bits on [to *sprinkle* a lawn with water] 3 to rain light — **sprin'kled, sprin'kling** ◆*n.* 1 the act of sprinkling 2 a light rain —**sprin'kler**

spy (spī) *n.* a person who watches others secretly and carefully —*pl.* **spies**

squall (skwôl) *n.* a short, violent windstorm, usually with rain or snow ◆*v.* to storm for a short time —**squall'y** *adj.*

stage (stāj) *n.* 1 a raised platform or other area on which plays, speeches, etc. are given 2 the profession of acting; the theater [He left the *stage* to write.] 3 *a shorter name for* **stagecoach** 4 a period or step in growth or development [She has reached a new *stage* in her career.] ◆*v.* to present on a stage, as a play —**staged, stag'ing**

stamp (stamp) *v.* 1 to bring one's foot down with force ["No!" she cried, *stamping* on the floor.] 2 to beat, press, or crush as with the foot [to *stamp* out a fire; to *stamp* out a revolt] 3 to press or print marks, letters, a design, etc. on something [He *stamped* his initials on all his books.] ◆*n.* 1 a machine, tool, or die used for stamping 2 a small piece of paper printed and sold by a government for sticking on letters, packages, etc. as proof that postage or taxes were paid

stand (stand) *v.* 1 to be or get in an upright position on one's feet [*Stand* by your desk.] 2 to be or place in an upright position on its base, bottom, etc. [Our trophy *stands* on the shelf. *Stand* the broom in the corner.] 3 to put up with; endure; bear [The boss can't *stand* noise.] —**stood, stand'ing** ◆*n.* 1 an opinion, belief, or attitude [What is the senator's *stand* on higher taxes?] 2 *often* **stands,** *pl.* seats in rising rows, as in a stadium, from which to watch games, races, etc. 3 a booth or counter where goods are sold [a popcorn *stand*] 4 a rack, framework, etc. for holding something [a music *stand*]

stare (ster) *v.* to look steadily with the eyes wide open [to *stare* in curiosity] —**stared, star'ing**

starve (stärv) *v.* to die or suffer from lack of food [Many pioneers *starved* during the long winter.] —**starved, starv'ing**

sta·tion (stā'shən) *n.* 1 the place where a person or thing stands or is located, as one's post when on duty, a building for a special purpose, etc. [a sentry's *station*; a police *station*] 2 a regular stopping place, as for a bus or train; also, a building at such a place

☆**steam·boat** (stēm'bōt) *n.* a steamship, especially a small one

step (step) *v.* to move by taking a step or steps [We *stepped* into the car.] —**stepped, step'ping**

stern¹ (sturn) *adj.* strict or harsh; not gentle, tender, easy, etc. [*stern* parents; *stern* treatment] —**stern'ly** *adv.* —**stern'ness** *n.*

stern² (sturn) *n.* the rear end of a ship or boat

stick (stik) *n.* 1 a twig or branch broken or cut off 2 any long, thin piece of wood, with a special shape for use as a cane, club, etc. [a walking *stick*; a hockey *stick*] 3 a long, thin piece [a *stick* of celery; a *stick* of chewing gum] ◆*v.* 1 to press a sharp point into; pierce; stab [He *stuck* his finger with a needle.] 2 to fasten or be fastened as by pinning or gluing [I *stuck* my name tag on my coat. The stamp *sticks* to the paper.] —**stuck, stick'ing**

stiff (stif) *adj.* 1 that does not bend easily; firm [*stiff* cardboard] 2 not able to move easily [*stiff* muscles] 3 not relaxed; tense or formal [a *stiff* smile] —**stiff'ly** *adv.* —**stiff'ness** *n.*

stitch (stich) *n.* 1 one complete movement of a needle and thread into and out of the material in sewing 2 one complete movement done in various ways in knitting, crocheting, etc. 3 a loop made by stitching [Tight *stitches* pucker the cloth.] —*pl.* **stitches**

sto·ry¹ (stôr'ē) *n.* 1 a telling of some happening, whether true or made-up [the *story* of the first Thanksgiving] 2 a made-up tale, written down, that is shorter than a novel [the *stories* of Poe] —*pl.* **sto'ries**

sto·ry² (stôr'ē) *n.* the space or rooms making up one level of a building, from a floor to the ceiling above it [a building with ten *stories*] —*pl.* **sto'ries**

stove (stōv) *n.* a device for cooking or heating by the use of gas, oil, electricity, etc.

straight (strāt) *adj.* 1 having the same direction all the way; not crooked, curved, wavy, etc. [a *straight* line; *straight* hair] 2 upright or erect [*straight* posture] 3 level or even [a *straight* hemline] 4 direct; staying right to the point, direction, etc. [a *straight* course; a *straight* answer]

strange (strānj) *adj.* 1 not known, seen, or heard before; not familiar [I saw a *strange* person at the door.] 2 different from what is usual; peculiar; odd [wearing a *strange* costume] 3 not familiar; without experience [She is *strange* to this job.] —**strang'er, strang'est** —**strange'ly** *adv.*

straw (strô *or* strä) *n.* 1 hollow stalks, as of wheat or rye, after the grain has been threshed out; straw is used as stuffing or is woven into hats, etc. 2 a tube, as of plastic, used for sucking a drink

strength (streŋkth *or* streŋth) *n.* the quality of being strong; force; power [the *strength* of a blow]

stretch (strech) *v.* **1** to reach out or hold out, as a hand, object, etc. **2** to draw out to full length, to a greater size, to a certain distance, etc.; extend [She *stretched* out on the sofa. Will this material *stretch*? Stretch the rope between two trees. The road *stretches* for miles through the hills.] **3** to pull or draw tight; strain [to *stretch* a muscle]

strict (strikt) *adj.* **1** keeping to rules in a careful, exact way [a *strict* supervisor] **2** never changing; rigid [a *strict* rule] —**strict′ly** *adv.* —**strict′ness** *n.*

stuff (stuf) *n.* **1** what anything is made of; material; substance **2** a collection of objects, belongings, etc. [I emptied the *stuff* from my bag.] ◆*v.* **1** to fill or pack [pockets *stuffed* with candy] **2** to fill with seasoning, bread crumbs, etc. before roasting [to *stuff* a turkey] **3** to force or push [I *stuffed* the money in my wallet.]

stum·ble (stum′bəl) *v.* to trip or almost fall while walking or running [to *stumble* over a curb] —**stum′bled, stum′bling**

stur·dy (stur′dē) *adj.* strong and hardy [a *sturdy* oak] —**stur′di·er, stur′di·est** —**stur′di·ly** *adv.* —**stur′di·ness** *n.*

sub·trac·tion (səb trak′shən) *n.* the act of subtracting one part, number, etc. from another

☆**su·per·mar·ket** (sōō′pər mär′kət) *n.* a large food store in which shoppers serve themselves from open shelves and pay at the exit

sup·ply (sə plī′) *v.* **1** to give what is needed; furnish [The camp *supplies* sheets and towels. The book *supplied* us with the facts.] **2** to take care of the needs of [to *supply* workers with tools] —**sup·plied′, sup·ply′ing** ◆*n.* **1** the amount at hand; store; stock [I have a small *supply* of money but a large *supply* of books.] **2 supplies**, *pl.* things needed; materials; provisions [school *supplies*] —*pl.* **sup·plies**

sur·prise (sər prīz′) *v.* to cause to feel wonder by being unexpected [Her sudden anger *surprised* us.] —**sur·prised′, sur·pris′ing**

sur·pris·ing (sər prīz′iŋ) *adj.* causing surprise; strange —**sur·pris′ing·ly** *adv.*

sur·vey (sər vā′) *v.* **1** to look over in a careful way; examine; inspect [The lookout *surveyed* the horizon.] **2** to measure the size, shape, boundaries, etc. of a piece of land by the use of special instruments [to *survey* a farm] ◆*n.* (sur′vā) a general study covering the main facts or points [The *survey* shows that we need more schools. This book is a *survey* of American poetry.] —*pl.* **sur′veys**

sur·viv·al (sər vī′vəl) *n.* the act or fact of surviving, or continuing to exist [Nuclear war threatens the *survival* of all nations.]

swal·low (swä′lō) *v.* **1** to let food, drink, etc. go through the throat into the stomach **2** to move the muscles of the throat as in swallowing something [I *swallowed* hard to keep from crying.] **3** to take in; engulf [The waters of the lake *swallowed* him up.] —**swal·lowed′**

swamp (swämp) *n.* a piece of wet, spongy land; marsh; bog; *also called* ☆**swamp′land** —**swamp′y** *adj.*

sway (swā) *v.* **1** to swing or bend back and forth or from side to side [The flowers *swayed* in the breeze.] **2** to lean or go to one side; veer [The car *swayed* to the right on the curve.] **3** to change the thinking or actions of; influence [We will not be *swayed* by their promises.] —**sway′ing**

sweat (swet) *v.* **1** to give out a salty liquid through the pores of the skin; perspire [Running fast made me *sweat*.] —**sweat** *or* **sweat′ed, sweat′ing** ◆*n.* **1** the salty liquid given out through the pores of the skin

sweat shirt (swet shurt) *n.* a heavy, loose cotton shirt with long or short sleeves

swift (swift) *adj.* **1** moving or able to move very fast [a *swift* runner] **2** coming, happening, or done quickly [a *swift* reply] **3** acting quickly; prompt [They were *swift* to help us.] —**swift′ly** *adv.* —**swift′ness** *n.*

sword (sôrd) *n.* a weapon having a long, sharp blade, with a handle, or hilt, at one end

syl·la·ble (sil′ə bəl) *n.* **1** a word or part of a word spoken with a single sounding of the voice ["Moon" is a word of one *syllable.* "Moonlight" is a word of two *syllables.*] **2** any of the parts into which a written word is divided to show where it may be broken at the end of a line [The *syllables* of the entry words in this dictionary are divided by tiny dots.]

syn·o·nym (sin′ə nim) *n.* a word having the same or almost the same meaning as another ["Big" and "large" are *synonyms.*]

tail (tāl) *n.* **1** the part at the rear of an animal's body that sticks out beyond the backbone **2** any thing or part like this [the *tail* of a shirt; a pig*tail*] **3** the hind or last part [the *tail* of a parade] —*pl.* **tails** —**tail′less** *adj.*

tai·lor (tā′lər) *n.* a person who makes or repairs suits, coats, etc. ◆*v.* **1** to work as a tailor or make as a tailor does [suits *tailored* for stout people] **2** to make or change so as to fit a certain need [That movie was *tailored* to please children.]

a	ask, fat
ā	ape, date
ä	car, lot
e	elf, ten
ē	even, meet
i	is, hit
ī	ice, fire
ō	open, go
ô	law, horn
oi	oil, point
oo	look, pull
ōo	ooze, tool
ou	out, crowd
u	up, cut
ʉ	fur, fern
ə	a in ago
	e in agent
	e in father
	i in unity
	o in collect
	u in focus
ch	chin, arch
ŋ	ring, singer
sh	she, dash
th	thin, truth
th	then, father
zh	s in pleasure

tale (tāl) *n.* a story, especially about things that are imagined or made up [The sitter read the child both folk *tales* and fairy *tales*.]

tar·dy (tär′dē) *adj.* not on time; late; delayed [to be *tardy* for class] —**tar′di·er**, **tar′di·est** —**tar′di·ly** *adv.* —**tar′di·ness** *n.*

tast·y (tās′tē) *adj.* tasting good; full of flavor [a *tasty* meal] —**tast′i·er**, **tast′i·est**

tax (taks) *n.* money that citizens and businesses must pay to help support a government —*pl.* **tax′es**

tax·pay·er (taks′pā ər) *n.* a person who pays a tax or taxes

teach·er (tēch′ər) *n.* a person who teaches, especially in a school or college

tea·spoon (tē′spōōn) *n.* **1** a spoon for stirring tea, coffee, etc. and eating some soft foods **2** *a shorter form of* **teaspoonful**

teeth (tēth) *n. plural of* **tooth**

tel·e·scope (tel′ə skōp) *n.* a device for making far-off things seem closer and larger, used especially in astronomy: it consists of one or more tubes containing lenses and, often, mirrors

tel·e·vi·sion (tel′ə vizhən) *n.* **1** a way of sending pictures through space by changing the light rays into electric waves which are picked up by a receiver that changes them back to light rays shown on a screen: the sound that goes with the picture is sent by radio at the same time **2** such a receiver, usually in a cabinet

tem·per·ate (tem′pər ət *or* tem′prət) *adj.* **1** using or showing temperance in one's actions, appetites, etc.; moderate [Although she was angry, she made a *temperate* reply.] **2** neither very hot nor very cold [a *temperate* climate] —**tem′per·ate·ly** *adv.*

ten·der (ten′dər) *adj.* **1** soft or delicate and easily chewed, cut, etc. [*tender* meat; *tender* blades of grass] **2** that is hurt or feels pain easily; sensitive [My sprained ankle still feels *tender*.] —**ten′der·ly** *adv.* —**ten′der·ness** *n.*

tense[1] (tens) *adj.* **1** stretched tight, taut [a *tense* rope; *tense* muscles] **2** feeling or showing nervous strain, anxious [a *tense* silence] **3** causing a nervous feeling [a *tense* situation] —**tens′er, tens′est** *v.* to make or become tense; tighten, as muscles —**tensed, tens′ing** —**tense′ly** *adv.*

tense[2] (tens) *n.* any of the forms of a verb that show the time of the action or condition [Present, past, and future *tenses* of "sail" are "sail" or "sails," "sailed," and "will sail."]

☆**te·pee** (tē′pē) *n.* a tent made of animal skins and shaped like a cone, used by some Native Americans

ter·ri·to·ry (ter′ə tôr′ē) *n.* **1** the land ruled by a nation or state **2** **Territory**, a large division of a country or empire, that does not have the full rights of a province or state, as in Canada or Australia [the Northwest *Territories*] **3** any large stretch of land; region **4** the particular area chosen as its own by an animal or group of animals —*pl.* **ter′ri·to′ries**

thank·ful (thaŋk′fəl) *adj.* feeling or showing thanks; grateful

their (ther) *adj.* of them or done by them: this possessive form of **they** *is used before a noun and thought of as an adjective* [*their* house; *their* work]

there (ther) *adv.* **1** at or in that place [Who lives *there*?] **2** to, toward, or into that place [Go *there*.]

there·fore (ther′fôr) *adv.* for this or that reason; as a result of this or that; hence: *this word is often used as a conjunction* [We missed the bus; *therefore*, we were late.]

there's (therz) *contraction* there is

these (thēz) *pron., adj. plural of* **this**

they'll (thāl) *contraction* **1** they will **2** they shall

thief (thēf) *n.* a person who steals, especially secretly *pl.* **thieves** (thēvz)

think (thiŋk) *v.* to use the mind; reason [*Think* before you act.] —**thought**, **think′ing**

this (this) *pron.* **1** the person or thing mentioned or understood [*This* is Juan. *This* tastes good.] **2** the thing that is present or nearer [*This* is prettier than that.] **3** the fact, idea, etc. about to be told [Now hear *this*!] —*pl.* **these** (thēz) *adj.* **1** being the one that is mentioned or understood [Copy down *this* rule.] **2** being the one that is present or nearer [*This* house is newer than that one.] *adv.* to such a degree; so [It was *this* big.]

thought[1] (thôt *or* thät) *n.* **1** the act or process of thinking [When deep in *thought*, he doesn't hear.] **2** what one thinks; idea, opinion, plan, etc. [a penny for your *thoughts*]

thought[2] (thôt *or* thät) *past tense and past participle of* **think**

thou·sand (thou′zənd) *n., adj.* ten times one hundred; the number 1,000

thumb (thum) *n.* the short, thick finger nearest the wrist

thun·der (thun′dər) *n.* **1** the loud noise that comes after a flash of lightning: it is caused when the discharge of electricity disturbs the air **2** any loud, rumbling noise like this [We heard the *thunder* of stampeding cattle.]

Thurs·day (thurz′dē) *n.* the fifth day of the week

tight (tīt) *adj.* **1** put together firmly or closely [a *tight* knot] **2** fitting too closely [a *tight* shirt] **3** stretched and strained; taut [a *tight* wire; *tight* nerves] —**tight′ly** *adv.* —**tight′ness** *n.*

tim·id (tim′id) *adj.* feeling or showing fear or shyness

tip·toe (tip′tō) *n.* the tip of a toe ◆*v.* to walk on one's tiptoes in a quiet or careful way —**tip′toed, tip′toe·ing**

to·ma·to (tə māt′ō *or* tə mät′ō) *n.* a red or yellow, round fruit with a juicy pulp —*pl.* **to·ma′toes**

tooth (tōōth) *n.* **1** any of the white, bony parts growing from the jaws and used for biting and chewing **2** any part more or less like a tooth, as on a saw, comb, gearwheel, etc. —*pl.* **teeth** (tēth) —**tooth′less** *adj.*

tooth·ache (tōōth′āk) *n.* pain in or near a tooth

tooth·brush (tōōth′brush) *n.* a small brush for cleaning the teeth —*pl.* **tooth′brush·es**

tor·na·do (tôr nā′dō) *n.* a high, narrow column of air that is whirling very fast: it is often seen as a slender cloud shaped like a funnel, that usually destroys everything in its narrow path —*pl.* **tor·na′does** or **tor·na′dos**

toss (tôs *or* täs) *v.* **1** to throw from the hand in a light, easy way [to *toss* a ball] **2** to throw about; fling here and there [The waves *tossed* the boat.] —**tossed**

tough (tuf) *adj.* **1** able to bend or twist without tearing or breaking [*tough* rubber] **2** not able to be cut or chewed easily [*tough* meat] **3** very difficult or hard [a *tough* job]

town (toun) *n.* **1** a place where there are a large number of houses and other buildings, larger than a village but smaller than a city **2** *another name for* **city 3** the business center of a city or town

trace (trās) *n.* **1** a mark, track, sign, etc. left by someone or something [no human *trace* on the island] **2** a very small amount [a *trace* of garlic in the dressing] ◆*v.* **1** to follow the trail of; track [The hunter *traced* the lions to their den.] **2** to follow or study the course of [We *traced* the history of Rome back to Caesar.] **3** to copy a picture, drawing, etc. by following its lines on a thin piece of paper placed over it —**traced, trac′ing**

trade (trād) *n.* **1** any work done with the hands that needs special skill got by training [the plumber's *trade*] **2** all those in a certain business or kind of work [the book *trade*] **3** the act of giving one thing for another; exchange [an even *trade* of my comic books for your football] ◆*v.* **1** to carry on a business; buy and sell [This company *trades* in tea. Our country *trades* with other countries.] **2** to exchange [I *traded* my stamp collection for a camera.] —**trad′ed, trad′ing**

traf·fic (traf′ik) *n.* the movement or number of automobiles, persons, ships, etc. along a road or route of travel [to direct *traffic* on city streets; the heavy *traffic* on weekends] —**traf′ficked, traf′fick·ing**

trail·er (trā′lər) *n.* a wagon, van, cart, etc. made to be pulled by an automobile, truck, or tractor: some trailers are outfitted as homes

treat (trēt) *v.* **1** to deal with or act toward in a certain way [We were *treated* with respect. Don't *treat* this matter lightly.] **2** to try to cure or heal, as with medicine [The doctor *treated* my cuts.] **3** to act upon, as by adding something [The water is *treated* with chlorine.] —**treat′ed, treat′ing**

tribe (trīb) *n.* a group of people or families living together under a leader or chief [a North American Indian *tribe*; the *tribes* of ancient Israel] —**trib′al** *adj.*

trim (trim) *v.* **1** to make neat or tidy, especially by clipping, smoothing, etc. [She had her hair *trimmed*.] **2** to cut, clip, etc. [He *trimmed* dead branches off the tree.] —**trimmed, trim′ming** ◆*n.* good condition or order [An athlete must keep in *trim*.] —**trim′mer, trim′mest** *adj.* —**trim′ly** *adv.* —**trim′ness** *n.*

trip (trip) *v.* to stumble or make stumble [She *tripped* over the rug. Bill put out his foot and *tripped* me.] —**tripped, trip′ping**

tro·phy (trō′fē) *n.* anything kept as a token of victory or success, as a deer's head from a hunting trip, a silver cup from a sports contest, or a sword from a battle —*pl.* **tro′phies**

trop·i·cal (träp′i kəl) *adj.* of, in, or like the tropics [heavy *tropical* rains; *tropical* heat]

trou·ble (trub′əl) **1** worry, care, annoyance, suffering, etc. [My mind is free of *trouble*.] **2** a difficult or unhappy situation; disturbance [We've had no *trouble* with our neighbors.] —**trou′bled, trou′bling**

trust (trust) *n.* a strong belief that some person or thing is honest or can be depended on; faith [You can put your *trust* in that bank.] ◆*v.* **1** to have or put trust in; rely; depend [I *trust* him to be on time. Don't *trust* that rickety ladder.] **2** to put something in the care of [Her mother *trusted* her with the car.] **3** to believe [I *trust* her story.]

try (trī) *v.* **1** to make an effort; attempt [We must *try* to help them.] **2** to seek to find out about, as by experimenting; test [Please *try* my recipe. *Try* the other window, which may not be locked.] **3** to put to a severe test or strain [Such exercise *tried* my strength.] —**tries, tried, try′ing** ◆*n.* an effort; attempt; trial [He made a successful jump on his third *try*.] —*pl.* **tries**

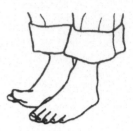

tiptoe

a	ask, fat
ā	ape, date
ä	car, lot
e	elf, ten
ē	even, meet
i	is, hit
ī	ice, fire
ō	open, go
ô	law, horn
oi	oil, point
००*	look, pull
००	ooze, tool
ou	out, crowd
u	up, cut
u	fur, fern
ə	a in ago
	e in agent
	e in father
	i in unity
	o in collect
	u in focus
ch	chin, arch
ŋ	ring, singer
sh	she, dash
th	thin, truth
th	then, father
zh	s in pleasure

tu·ba (tōō′bə *or* tyōō′bə) *n.* a large brass instrument with a full, deep tone

tun·dra (tun′drə *or* tōōn′drə) *n.* a large, flat plain without trees in the arctic regions

turn (turn) *v.* **1** to move around a center point or axis; revolve; rotate [The wheels *turn. Turn* the key.] **2** to do by moving in a circle [*Turn* a somersault.] **3** to change in position or direction [*Turn* your chair around. *Turn* to the left. The tide has *turned.*] —**turned, turn′ing**

twelve (twelv) *n., adj.* two more than ten: the number 12

twist·er (twis′tər) *n.* **1** a person or thing that twists ☆**2** a tornado or cyclone

type·writ·er (tīp′rīt ər) *n.* a machine with a keyboard for making printed letters or figures on paper

vessel

Uu

um·pire (um′pīr) *n.* **1** a person who rules on the plays of a game, as in baseball **2** a person chosen to settle an argument ◆*v.* to be an umpire in a game or dispute —**um′pired, um′pir·ing**

un·cle (uŋ′kəl) *n.* **1** the brother of one's father or mother **2** the husband of one's aunt

un·clear (un klir′) *adj.* not clear; hard to see or understand

un·fold (un fōld′) *v.* **1** to open and spread out something that has been folded [to *unfold* a map] **2** to make or become known [to *unfold* one's plans]

u·ni·verse (yōōn′ə vurs) *n.* all space and everything in it; earth, the sun, stars, and all things that exist

u·ni·ver·si·ty (yōōn′ə vur′sə tē) *n.* a school of higher education, made up of a college or colleges —*pl.* **u′ni·ver′si·ties**

un·known (un nōn′) *adj.* **1** not known, seen, or heard before [a song *unknown* to me] **2** not discovered, identified, etc. [an *unknown* writer] ◆*n.* an unknown person or thing

un·pleas·ant (un plez′ənt) *adj.* not pleasant or agreeable; offensive; disagreeable [an *unpleasant* taste] —**un·pleas′ant·ly adv.** —**un·pleas′ant·ness n.**

un·pre·pared (un′prē perd′) *adj.* not prepared or ready [We are still *unprepared* for the visitors.]

un·re·al (un rēl′) *adj.* not real; imaginary or made up —**un·re·al·i·ty** (un′rē al′ə tē) *n.*

un·re·lat·ed (un′rē lāt′əd) *adj.* not of the same family or kind

un·til (un til′) *prep.* **1** up to the time of; till [Wait *until* noon.] **2** before [Don't leave *until* tomorrow.] ◆*conj.* **1** up to the time when [He was lonely *until* he met her.] **2** to the point, degree, or place that [She ate *until* she was full.] **3** before [Don't stop *until* he does.]

un·wise (un wīz′) *adj.* not wise; not showing good sense; foolish —**un·wise′ly adv.**

ur·gent (ur′jənt) *adj.* **1** needing quick action [an *urgent* situation] **2** demanding in a strong and serious way; insistent [an *urgent* call for help] —**ur′gent·ly adv.**

Vv

vague (vāg) *adj.* not clear, definite, or distinct, as in form, meaning, or purpose [*vague* figures in the fog; a *vague* answer] —**va′guer, va′guest** —**vague′ly adv.** —**vague′ness n.**

val·ley (val′ē) *n.* **1** low land lying between hills or mountains **2** the land that is drained or watered by a large river and its branches [the Mississippi *valley*] —*pl.* **val′leys**

veil (vāl) *n.* a piece of thin cloth, such as net or gauze, worn especially by women over the face or head [a bride's *veil*]

ves·sel (ves′əl) *n.* a ship or large boat

Vi·et·nam (vē′ət näm′) a country in southeastern Asia —**Vi·et·nam·ese** (vē′et nə mēz′ *or* vē′et nə mēs′) *adj., n.*

vi·ta·min (vīt′ə min) *n.* any of certain substances needed by the body to keep healthy: vitamin A is found in fish-liver oil, yellow vegetables, egg yolk, etc.; one kind of vitamin B, called vitamin B₁, is found in cereals, green peas, beans, liver, etc.; vitamin C is found in citrus fruits, tomatoes, etc.; vitamin D is found in fish-liver oil, milk, eggs, etc.; lack of these vitamins or others can cause certain diseases

voice (vois) *n.* **1** sound made through the mouth, especially by human beings in talking, singing, etc. **2** anything thought of as like speech or the human voice [the voice of the sea; the *voice* of one's conscience] **3** the right to say what one wants, thinks, or feels [Each voter has a *voice* in the government.] ◆*v.* to put into words, as an idea, feeling, etc.; utter —**voiced, voic′ing** —**voice′less adj.**

vote (vōt) *n.* one's decision on some plan or idea, or one's choice between persons running for office, shown on a ballot, by raising one's hand, etc. ◆*v.* **1** to give or cast a vote [For whom did you *vote*?] **2** to decide, elect, or bring about by vote [Congress *voted* new taxes.] —**vot´ed, vot´ing**

Ww

waist (wāst) *n.* **1** the part of the body between the ribs and the hips **2** the part of a garment that covers the body from the shoulders to the waistline

wait·er (wāt´ər) *n.* **1** a man who waits on tables, as in a restaurant **2** one who waits

wait·ress (wā´trəs) *n.* a woman who waits on tables, as in a restaurant

walk·er (wôk´ər) *n.* **1** a person or animal that walks ☆**2** a frame with or without wheels for use by babies in learning to walk or by people who have trouble walking because of injuries or disease

wal·rus (wôl´rəs) *n.* a large sea animal like the seal, found in northern oceans: it has two tusks and a thick layer of blubber

Wash·ing·ton, DC (wòsh´iŋ tən *or* wäsh´iŋ tən) the capital of the United States, in the District of Columbia

watch (wäch *or* wôch) *v.* **1** to keep one's sight on; look at [We *watched* the parade.] **2** to pay attention to; observe [I've *watched* her career with interest.] **3** to take care of; look after; guard [The shepherd *watched* his flock.] —**watch´ing**

wa·ter·fall (wôt´ər fôl *or* wät´ər fôl) *n.* a steep fall of water, as from a high cliff

wax (waks) *n.* **1** a yellow substance that bees make and use for building honeycombs; beeswax **2** any substance like this, as paraffin: wax is used to make candles, polishes, etc. ◆*v.* to put wax or polish on

wea·ry (wir´ē) *adj.* **1** tired; worn out [*weary* after a day's work] **2** having little or no patience or interest left; bored [I grew *weary* of listening to them.] —**wea´ri·er, wea´ri·est** —**wea´ried, wea´ry·ing** —**wea´ri·ly** *adv.* **wea´ri·ness** *n.*

Wednes·day (wenz´dē) *n.* the fourth day of the week

weigh (wā) *v.* **1** to use a scale, balance, etc. to find out how heavy a thing is [to *weigh* oneself] **2** to have a certain weight [The suitcase *weighs* six pounds.]

we're (wir) *contraction* we are

west·ward (west´wərd) *adv., adj.* in the direction of the west

wheat (hwēt *or* wēt) *n.* **1** the cereal grass whose grain is used in making the most common type of flour **2** this grain

where (hwer *or* wer) *adv.* **1** in or at what place? [*Where* is the car?] **2** in what way? how? [*Where* is she at fault?]

where's (hwerz *or* werz) *contraction* **1** where is **2** where has

wheth·er (hwe*th*´ər *or* we*th*´ər) *conj.* **1** if it is true or likely that [I don't know *whether* I can go.] **2** in either case that [It makes no difference *whether* he comes or not.]

which (hwich *or* wich) *pron.* **1** what one or what ones of those being talked about or suggested [*which* will you choose?] **2** the one or the ones that [I know *which* I like best.] **3** that [the story *which* we all know] ◆*adj.* what one or ones [*Which* apples are the best for baking?]

whisk·er (hwis´kər *or* wis´kər) *n.* **1 whiskers**, *pl.* the hair growing on a man's face, especially the beard on the cheeks **2** a single hair of a man's beard **3** any of the long, stiff hairs on the upper lip of a cat, rat, etc. —**whisk´ered**, *adj.*

whis·tle (hwis´əl *or* wis´əl) *n.* a device for making high, shrill sounds

who's (hōōz) *contraction* **1** who is **2** who has

whose (hōōz) *pron.* the one or the ones belonging to whom [*Whose* are these books?]

wife (wīf) *n.* the woman to whom a man is married —*pl.* **wives**

wild (wīld) *adj.* **1** living or growing in nature; not tamed or cultivated by human beings [*wild* animals; *wild* flowers] **2** not civilized; savage [*wild* tribes] **3** not controlled; unruly, rough, noisy, etc. [*wild* children] —**wild´ly** *adv.* —**wild´ness** *n.*

win·ner (win´ər) *n.* **1** one that wins **2** a person who seems very likely to win or be successful; *used only in everyday talk*

wish (wish) *v.* **1** to have a longing for; want; desire [You may have whatever you *wish*.] **2** to have or express a desire about [I *wish* you were here. We *wished* her good luck.] ◆*n.* something wanted or hoped for [He got his *wish*.] —*pl.* **wish´es** —**wish´ing**

witch (wich) *n.* **1** a person, now especially a woman, who is imagined to have magic power **2** an ugly and mean old woman

with·out (wi*th* ᴐut´ *or* with ᴐut´) *prep.* free from; not having [a person *without* a worry; a cup *without* a saucer]

wit·ness (wit´nəs) *n.* a person who saw or heard something that happened [A *witness* saw the fire start.] —*pl.* **wit´nes·ses**

wives (wīvz) *n.* *plural of* **wife**

wom·an (wōōm´ən) *n.* an adult, female human being —*pl.* **wom´en**

whiskers

a	ask, fat
ā	ape, date
ä	car, lot
e	elf, ten
ē	even, meet
i	is, hit
ī	ice, fire
ō	open, go
ô	law, horn
oi	oil, point
ōō	look, pull
ōō	ooze, tool
ᴐu	out, crowd
u	up, cut
u	fur, fern
ə	a in ago
	e in agent
	e in father
	i in unity
	o in collect
	u in focus
ch	chin, arch
ŋ	ring, singer
sh	she, dash
th	thin, truth
th	then, father
zh	s in pleasure

wom·en (wim'ən) *n.* *plural of* woman

wor·ry (wur'ē) *v.* 1 to be or make troubled in mind; feel or make uneasy or anxious [Don't *worry.* Her absence *worried* us.] 2 to annoy, bother, etc. [Stop *worrying* me with such unimportant matters.] —wor'ried, wor'ry·ing ◆*n.* 1 a troubled feeling; anxiety; care [sick with *worry*] 2 a cause of this [He has many *worries.*] —*pl.* wor'ries

would·n't (wood'nt) *contraction* would not

wrap (rap) *v.* 1 to wind or fold around something [She *wrapped* a scarf around her head.] 2 to cover in this way [They *wrapped* the baby in a blanket.] 3 to cover with paper, etc. [to *wrap* a present] —wrapped or wrapt (rapt), wrap'ping

yacht

wreck (rek) *n.* 1 the loss of a ship, or of a building, car, and so on, through storm, accident, etc. 2 the remains of something that has been destroyed or badly damaged [an old *wreck* stranded on the reef] ◆*v.* 1 to destroy or damage badly; ruin [to *wreck* a car in an accident; to *wreck* one's plans for a picnic] 2 to tear down; raze [to *wreck* an old house] —*pl.* wrecks

wrench (rench) *n.* 1 a sudden, sharp twist or pull [With one *wrench,* he loosened the lid.] 2 an injury, as to the back or an arm, caused by a twist 3 a sudden feeling of sadness, as at parting with someone 4 a tool for holding and turning nuts, bolts, pipes, etc.

wrin·kle (riŋ'kəl) *n.* a small or uneven crease or fold [*wrinkles* in a blouse]

wrist (rist) *n.* the joint or part of the arm between the hand and forearm

writ·ing (rīt'iŋ) *n.* 1 the act of one who writes 2 something written, as a letter, article, poem, book, etc. [the *writings* of Thomas Jefferson] 3 written form [to put a request in *writing*] 4 handwriting [Can you read her *writing*?]

yacht (yät) *n.* a large boat or small ship for racing, taking pleasure cruises, etc. ◆*v.* to sail in a yacht —yacht'ing *n.*

yak (yak) *n.* an ox with long hair, found wild or raised in Tibet and central Asia

yawn (yòn *or* yän) *v.* to open the mouth wide and breathe in deeply in a way that is not controlled, as when one is sleepy or tired

your·self (yoor self') *pron.* 1 your own self: *this form of* you *is used when the object is the same as the subject of the verb* [Did you cut *yourself*?] 2 your usual or true self [You are not *yourself* today.] Yourself *is also used to give force to the subject* [You *yourself* told me so.] —*pl.* your·selves (yoor selvz')

Level D Student Record Chart

Name _____

			Pretest	Final Test
Lesson	1	Consonant Sounds		
Lesson	2	Short-Vowel Sounds		
Lesson	3	Long-Vowel Sounds		
Lesson	4	Hard and Soft **c** and **g**		
Lesson	5	Beginning Consonant Blends		
Lesson	6	Lessons 1–5 • Review	██████████	
Lesson	7	Consonant Blends		
Lesson	8	Vowels with **r**		
Lesson	9	Consonant Digraphs		
Lesson	10	Words with the Sound of **f**		
Lesson	11	Silent Letters		
Lesson	12	Lessons 7–11 • Review	██████████	
Lesson	13	Adding **ed**, **er**, and **ing** to Words		
Lesson	14	Dropping the Final **e**		
Lesson	15	Doubling Final Consonants		
Lesson	16	Words Ending with **y**: Adding **ed**, **es**, **ing**		
Lesson	17	Words Ending with **y**: Adding **er**, **est**		
Lesson	18	Lessons 13–17 • Review	██████████	
Lesson	19	Vowel Pairs and Digraphs		
Lesson	20	Words with **ie** and **ei**		
Lesson	21	Vowel Digraphs **au** and **aw**		
Lesson	22	Vowel Pairs **ai**, **ay**; Diphthongs **oi**, **oy**		
Lesson	23	Words with **ou** and **ow**		
Lesson	24	Lessons 19–23 • Review	██████████	
Lesson	25	Plurals		
Lesson	26	Plurals of Words That End in **y**		
Lesson	27	Irregular Plurals		
Lesson	28	Possessives and Contractions		
Lesson	29	Plural Possessives		
Lesson	30	Lessons 25–29 • Review	██████████	
Lesson	31	Prefixes **pre**, **re**, **im**, **non**, and **con**		
Lesson	32	Prefixes **ex**, **de**, **dis**, **un**, and **ad**		
Lesson	33	Compound Words		
Lesson	34	Synonyms and Antonyms		
Lesson	35	Homonyms		
Lesson	36	Lessons 31–35 • Review	██████████	

Lesson	6	12	18	24	30	36
Standardized Review Test						

Review Test
Answer Key

Lesson 6

1. d	11. c
2. c	12. b
3. a	13. c
4. d	14. a
5. b	15. d
6. b	16. b
7. c	17. d
8. a	18. a
9. d	19. b
10. a	20. c

Lesson 12

1. b	11. c
2. c	12. a
3. b	13. d
4. d	14. a
5. b	15. d
6. c	16. c
7. c	17. b
8. d	18. d
9. b	19. d
10. a	20. a

Lesson 18

1. a	11. c
2. c	12. c
3. b	13. b
4. b	14. a
5. d	15. d
6. c	
7. a	
8. d	
9. c	
10. b	

Lesson 24

1. d	11. b
2. b	12. c
3. a	13. d
4. c	14. d
5. b	15. a
6. a	16. b
7. d	17. d
8. b	18. a
9. a	19. c
10. c	20. b

Lesson 30

1. b	11. b
2. d	12. b
3. a	13. d
4. c	14. a
5. d	15. b
6. b	16. b
7. d	17. d
8. a	18. a
9. c	19. b
10. a	20. d

Lesson 36

1. a	11. c
2. c	12. d
3. b	13. d
4. d	14. c
5. d	15. b
6. b	
7. a	
8. a	
9. d	
10. b	

List Words

Word	Lesson	Word	Lesson	Word	Lesson	Word	Lesson
absent	7	bodies'	29	claws	21	diet	20
admit	32	boiling	22	cleaned	13	different	7
adopt	2	bosses	25	clover	3	difficult	34
advance	32	bother	9	clues	19	dirty	8
adventure	32	bottles	1	colder	7	disagree	32
adverb	32	bouncing	14	comb	11	disappoint	22
advice	32	bouquet	23	coming	14	disbelief	34
after	10	brains	5	common	4	disclose	32
aircraft	33	brake	35	communities	26	dishonest	32
airlines'	29	break	35	comparing	14	disinterested	32
allows	23	breakfast	33	conduct	31	disloyal	22
alphabet	10	breeze	19	construct	31	displays	22
although	23	brief	20	contest	2	ditches	25
amount	23	broiling	22	control	31	doctor's	28
amplifies	20	brother	9	convince	31	dollar	1
ancient	34	brought	23	copied	16	dolphin	10
angrier	17	buffaloes	27	copies	26	downtown	33
angriest	17	bumps	2	corner	4	dragging	15
answer	11	buries	16	costume	3	drawings	21
applied	16	businesses'	29	cough	10	dream	5
appointed	22	buying	16	counties	26	dresses'	29
approach	19	cactus	4	courage	34	dropped	15
Arizona's	28	calves	27	cousin's	28	drowsy	34
armies'	29	carried	16	crack	2	drying	16
arrive	3	carton	8	craft	5	dusk	7
artist	8	catcher	13	crashes	25	duties	26
ashes	25	category	4	crayon	22	eagle	19
audience	21	causing	21	crept	7	earlier	17
aunt's	28	cautious	34	cries	16	earliest	17
autograph	10	celery	4	crime	3	easier	17
awhile	9	cement	4	crumb	11	easiest	17
awkward	21	center	4	crunch	7	eastern	19
axes	25	chains	25	crush	9	edge	4
baggage	4	charge	9	cubes	3	eighteen	20
banjos'	29	chatting	15	curb	8	elephants	10
banner	1	checking	13	current	34	eleven	1
barrel	1	cheerfully	8	daisies'	29	employ	22
batteries	26	cherries	26	dancer	14	emptied	16
beginning	15	chicken	9	dawn	21	energy	4
believe	20	chiefly	20	deceive	20	enormous	34
benches'	29	chiefs	27	decide	4	enough	10
bending	13	children's	29	defend	32	equal	3
between	19	child's	28	denies	16	error	8
bicycle's	28	chimney	9	dentist	2	everybody	33
birthdays	26	chowder	23	deny	3	excuse	32
bison	27	churches	25	descend	34	expensive	34
blended	7	circle	4	desert's	28	explore	32
boards	8	clapping	15	design	32	express	32
boasted	19	clashes	25	destroyed	22	eyelashes	25
bobbing	15	clasp	2	died	20	fair	8

List Words

Word	Lesson	Word	Lesson	Word	Lesson	Word	Lesson
fame	1	greedy	5	judge	2	nonsense	31
families'	29	groceries	26	juicier	17	nonstop	31
fancier	17	guessed	13	juiciest	17	northwest	33
fanciest	17	hair	35	kisses	25	numb	11
farther	9	halfway	11	knapsack	33	often	11
fault	21	halt	7	knives	27	opened	3
fawns	21	halves	27	known	11	organ	8
fearless	8	hammer	1	knuckle	11	orphan	10
feathers	9	handkerchiefs	27	ladies	26	outdoors	33
fender	2	hands	2	landing	13	outfitted	15
fields	20	happier	17	later	1	outstanding	33
film	1	happiest	17	laughs	10	overcoat	33
finishing	13	harbor	8	launch	21	oxen	27
flashes	25	hare	35	leading	13	paces	25
fleet	19	hasn't	28	learner	13	padded	15
flies	26	haunt	21	leash	9	parties	26
flight	11	heal	35	leaves	27	passengers'	29
Florida's	28	heart	8	lengthy	34	peace	35
folks	11	heavier	17	let's	28	pencil	2
following	13	heaviest	17	letters	1	perceive	20
foolish	9	heel	35	libraries	26	perfume	8
force	4	highways	26	lifted	2	person's	28
foxes	25	hobbies	26	listen	11	petrified	16
fraud	21	hoed	19	lives	27	phase	10
fray	22	holidays	26	loaned	19	phony	10
freedom	19	hollow	23	loaves	27	photo	10
freighter	20	homework	33	locate	3	pianos'	29
front	5	honest	11	locked	2	pictured	14
frying	16	hoofs	27	lonelier	17	piece	35
funnier	17	horseshoes	33	loneliest	17	pies	20
funniest	17	hostesses'	29	loved	14	pineapple	1
gallon	1	hours	23	matches	25	plain	35
garbage	8	how's	28	meadow	19	plane	35
gather	9	humming	15	meaning	19	powerful	23
gaunt	21	hundred	1	measure	19	practice	2
geese	27	hurrying	16	melodies	26	praised	22
gentle	4	idea	3	members'	29	precaution	31
geography	10	immovable	31	men's	29	predict	31
gerbil	4	imperfect	31	mice	27	prepaid	31
ghost	11	impersonal	31	milk	7	prettier	17
gifts	4	impractical	31	missed	13	prettiest	17
giraffe	10	impure	31	moose	27	preview	31
giving	14	independent	7	mountain	23	prices	4
gloves	5	injuries	26	mover	14	pride	3
glued	19	instead	19	multiplied	16	printing	7
gnaw	21	island	11	musical	3	product	7
governments'	29	jaw	21	neighbors	20	promised	14
grabbing	15	joggers	15	nephew	10	proper	5
graceful	4	journal	8	noises	22	protect	5
graphs	10	journey	34	nonprofit	31	protesting	7

List Words

Word	Lesson	Word	Lesson	Word	Lesson	Word	Lesson
proved	14	sharing	14	stiff	10	trouble	23
quitter	15	sharply	9	stories	26	trust	2
railroad	22	shawl	21	stove	3	tuba	3
raking	14	sheep	27	straight	5	turning	13
ranches'	29	shelf	10	strange	4	twelve	1
rapidly	34	she'll	28	straw	21	twister	7
reaches	9	sherbet	8	stretch	7	typewriter	33
reaction	31	shipment	9	strict	5	umpires'	29
reason	19	shoes	25	stuff	5	uncle's	28
receipt	20	shore	8	sturdy	34	unclear	32
receive	20	shovel	9	supermarket	33	unfold	7
reduced	14	shower	23	supplied	16	unknown	32
refills	31	shriek	20	surprising	14	unpleasant	32
refund	7	shrimp	2	surveys	26	unprepared	32
relief	20	sidewalk	33	swallowed	23	unreal	32
relying	16	silent	1	swaying	22	until	1
remembered	13	singer	13	swift	1	unwise	32
repaired	34	sister's	28	tail	35	vague	34
replies	16	sitting	15	tale	35	valleys	26
report	31	skill	5	teacher	13	voices	22
restaurant	21	skimming	15	teaspoon	33	waist	22
returned	31	skunk	7	teeth	27	walker	13
rider	14	sleigh	20	televisions'	29	watching	13
risk	7	sliced	14	tender	34	waterfall	33
roasted	19	slipping	15	tense	34	waxes	25
rodent	3	soften	11	their	35	weary	34
roughly	10	solid	2	there	35	Wednesday	11
royalty	22	sorrow	34	therefore	33	weigh	20
rules	3	sorted	13	these	3	we're	28
safely	3	sought	23	they'll	28	wheat	9
sandwiches	25	sounds	7	thieves'	29	where's	28
sashes	25	southeast	33	thought	23	which	35
satisfied	16	southern	23	thousand	23	whiskers	9
sauce	21	soybean	22	thumb	11	who's	35
saved	14	spaces	5	thunder	9	whose	35
scale	3	spare	8	Thursday	9	wild	1
scared	5	sparks	8	tight	3	winners	15
scarves	27	sparrows	23	tiptoes	19	wishing	13
scents	35	speed	5	toothache	33	witch	35
schoolhouse	33	spent	2	toothbrushes	25	without	23
scrawl	21	splashes	25	tossed	13	women	27
screech	5	splinter	5	towns	23	worries	16
screens	5	spoiled	22	trace	5	wouldn't	28
scrubbing	15	sports	8	traded	14	wrapped	15
scurrying	16	sprain	22	traffic	1	wrecks	11
season's	28	sprinkle	5	treating	19	wrench	11
seize	20	stage	4	tries	16	wrist	11
sense	35	stamp	2	trimmer	15	writing	14
served	14	stand	2	tripped	15	yawn	21
seven	1	sticks	2	trophy	10	yourselves	27

Bonus Words

Word	Lesson	Word	Lesson	Word	Lesson	Word	Lesson
achieve	20	embroider	22	nonfiction	31	strength	5
advantage	32	enemy	1	nurse	8	stumble	7
affection	10	entertain	22	pardons	25	sweatshirt	33
allies	20	essays	26	patios	27	tastier	17
arithmetic	9	exchange	32	patrolling	15	taxes	25
author	21	extend	2	perfect	10	taxpayer	33
automatic	21	factory's	28	performer	13	thankful	9
bask	7	familiar	34	phrase	10	there's	28
beliefs	27	fish's	29	pitying	16	timid	2
bomb	11	flew	35	preset	31	tomato	3
branch	7	flu	35	prince	4	tough	10
breakdown	33	flue	35	principal's	28	universities	26
brilliant	34	fond	2	program	5	unrelated	32
broccoli	27	forehead	19	public	2	veil	20
ceiling	20	forth	8	purses	25	vessel	1
champion	9	fought	23	raisin	22	westward	33
cheat	19	gasp	4	recount	31	whether	9
classes'	29	glow	5	regular	34	whistle	11
clumsier	17	gobble	4	remove	3	witnesses	25
college	4	grizzlies	26	rising	14	wives	27
cone	3	groan	19	rude	3	wrinkle	11
contact	31	gulped	13	saucer	21		
convoys	26	harvest	7	scouts	23		
couple	23	hearth	8	scramble	5		
crazy	5	horrified	16	scratches	25		
curlier	17	hygiene	20	shaking	14		
dairies	16	impatient	31	shelter	9		
damage	4	instant	1	shouldn't	28		
daughter	11	intelligent	34	sinking	13		
deer	27	knead	35	skater	14		
define	32	knowledge	11	slender	7		
delay	22	lawyer	21	slipper	1		
deliveries	26	loveliest	17	smooth	34		
diaries'	29	loyal	22	snapping	15		
dimmed	15	luckiest	17	sneeze	19		
disgrace	32	magnifying	16	soared	13		
doesn't	28	marshmallow	23	species'	29		
drawn	21	mascot	2	spice	3		
driving	14	mending	13	spies'	29		
drowned	23	mugger	15	splendid	1		
dues	19	mysteries	16	stared	14		
earmuffs	10	need	35	starve	8		
easygoing	33	nervous	8	stepped	15		

Spelling Enrichment

Bulletin Board Suggestion

Eggs-pert Spellers Display a picture of a large hen sitting near a nest. Make large eggs out of white construction paper. Encourage students to write words on the eggs that are similar in structure to the words in the week's spelling list. Post the eggs on the nest.

You may also want to display a chart showing the number of eggs each student has posted to the bulletin board during the year. It might then be fun to keep a basket in the classroom that contains plastic eggs with little surprises in them. The surprise might be a note telling them they can skip an assignment or have extra minutes of free time, or it could be a small trinket. Students could then pick an egg from the basket after they have posted a predetermined number of eggs on the bulletin board.

Group Practice

Fill-In Write spelling words on the board. Omit some of the letters and replace them with dashes. Have the first student in Row One come to the board to fill in one of the missing letters in any of the words. Then, have the first student in Row Two continue the procedure. Continue having students in each row take turns coming up to the board to fill in letters until all the words are completed. Any student who is able to correctly fill in a word earns a point for his or her row. The row with the most points at the end of the game wins.

Erase Write list words on the board. Then, ask the class to put their heads down while you call on a student to come to the board and erase one of the words. This student then calls on a class member to identify the erased word. The identified word is then restored and the student who correctly identified the erasure can be the person who erases next.

Crossword Relay First draw a large grid on the board. Then, divide the class into several teams. Teams compete against each other to form separate crossword puzzles on the board. Individuals on each team take turns racing against members of the other teams to join list words until all possibilities have been exhausted. A list word may appear on each crossword puzzle only once. The winning team is the team whose crossword puzzle contains the greatest number of correctly spelled list words or the team who finishes first.

Scramble Prepare letter cards sufficient to spell all the list words. Distribute letter cards to all students. Some students may be given more than one letter card. The teacher then calls out a list word. Students holding the letters contained in the word race to the front of the class to form the word by standing in the appropriate sequence with their letter cards.

Proofreading Relay Write two columns of misspelled list words on the board. Although the errors can differ, be sure that each list has the same number of errors. Divide the class into two teams and assign each team to a different column. Teams then compete against each other to correct their assigned lists by team members taking turns erasing and replacing an appropriate letter. Each member may correct only one letter per turn. The team that corrects its entire word list first wins.

Detective Call on a student to be a detective. The detective must choose a spelling word from the list and think of a structural clue, definition, or synonym that will help classmates identify it. The detective then states the clue using the format, "I spy a word that. . . " Students are called on to guess and spell the mystery word. Whoever answers correctly gets to take a turn being the detective.

Spelling Tic-Tac-Toe Draw a tic-tac-toe square on the board. Divide the class into X and O teams. Take turns dictating spelling words to members of each team. If the word is spelled correctly, allow the team member to place an X or O on the square. The first team to place three X's or O's in a row wins.

Words of Fortune Have students put their heads down while you write a spelling word on the board in large letters. Then, cover each letter with a sheet of sturdy paper. The paper can be fastened to the board with magnets. Call on a student to guess any letter of the alphabet the student thinks may be hidden. If that particular letter is hidden, then reveal the letter in every place where it appears in the word by removing the paper.

The student continues to guess letters until an incorrect guess is made or the word is revealed. In the event that an incorrect guess is made, a different student continues the game. Continue the game until every list word has been hidden and then revealed.

Dictionary Activities

Around the World Designate the first person in the first row to be the traveler. The traveler must stand next to the student seated behind him or her. Then, dictate

Spelling Enrichment

any letter of the alphabet at random. Instruct the two students to quickly name the letter of the alphabet that precedes the given letter. The student who is first to respond with the correct answer becomes the traveler while the other student sits at that desk. The traveler then moves to compete with the next person in the row. The game continues with the traveler moving up and down the rows as the teacher dictates various alphabet letters. See who can be the traveler who has moved the farthest around the classroom. For variety, you may want to require students to state the letter that follows the given letter. You may also want to dictate pairs of list words and have students name which word comes first.

Stand-Up While the teacher pronounces a word from the spelling dictionary, students look up the entry word and point to it. Tell students to stand up when they have located the word. See who is the first student to stand up.

This game can be played using the following variations:

1. Have students stand when they have located the guide words for a given word.

2. Have students stand when they are able to tell on what page a given list word appears in the dictionary.

Guide Word Scramble Prepare tagboard cards with spelling words written on them in large letters. Distribute the cards to students. Call on two students to come to the front of the room to serve as guide words. Then, call one student at a time to hold their word card either in front of, in between, or behind the guide words so that the three words are in alphabetical order. You may want to vary the guide words occasionally.

Cut-Off Distribute a strip of paper to each student. Instruct students to write any four spelling words on the strip. All but one of the words should be in alphabetical order. Then, have students exchange their strip with a partner. Students use scissors to cut off the word that is not in alphabetical sequence and tape the remaining word strips together. If students find this activity too difficult, you might have them cut all four words off the strip and arrange them alphabetically on their desks.

Applied Spelling

Journal Allow time each day for students to write in a journal. A spiral bound notebook can be used for this purpose. Encourage students to express their feelings about events that are happening in their lives at home or at school, or they could write about what their plans are for the day. To get them started, you may have to provide starter phrases. Allow them to use "invented" spelling for words they can't spell.

Collect the journals periodically to write comments that echo what the student has written. For example, a student's entry might read, "I'm hape I gt to plae bazball todae." The teacher's response could be "Baseball is my favorite game, too. I'd be happy to watch you play baseball today at recess." This method allows students to learn correct spelling and sentence structure without emphasizing their errors in a negative way.

Letter to the Teacher On a regular basis, invite students to write a note to you. At first you may have to suggest topics or provide a starter sentence. It may be possible to suggest a topic that includes words from the spelling list. Write a response at the bottom of each letter that provides the student with a model of any spelling or sentence structure that apparently needs improvement.

Daily Edit Each day, provide a brief writing sample on the board that contains errors in spelling, capitalization, or punctuation. Have students rewrite the sample correctly. Provide time later in the day to have the class correct the errors on the board. Discuss why the spelling is as it is while students self-correct their work.

Acrostic Poems Have students write a word from the spelling list vertically. Then, instruct them to join a word horizontally to each letter of the list word. The horizontal words must begin with the letters in the list word. They also should be words that describe or relate feelings about the list word. Encourage students to refer to a dictionary for help in finding appropriate words. Here is a sample acrostic poem:

Zebras
Otters
Ostriches

Words-in-a-Row Distribute strips of writing paper to each student. Ask students to write three spelling words in a row. Tell them to misspell two of the words. Then, have students take turns writing their row of words on the board. They can call on a classmate to identify and underline the correctly spelled word in the row. Continue until all students have had a chance to write their row of words.

Spelling Enrichment

Partner Spelling Assign spelling buddies. Allow partners to alternate dictating or writing sentences that contain words from the spelling list. The sentences can be provided by the teacher or generated by students. Have students check their own work as their partner provides the correct spelling for each sentence.

Scrap Words Provide each student with several sheets of tagboard, scraps of fabric or wallpaper, and some glue. Ask students to cut letters out of the scrap materials and glue them to the tagboard to form words from the spelling list. Display the colorful scrap words around the classroom.

Punch Words Set up a work center in the classroom with a supply of construction paper strips, a hole puncher, sheets of thin paper, and crayons. Demonstrate to students how the hole puncher can be used to create spelling words out of the construction paper. Permit students to take turns working at the center in their free time. Students may also enjoy placing a thin sheet of paper over the punch words and rubbing them with a crayon to make colorful word designs. You can then display their punch word and crayon creations.

Word Cut-Outs Distribute scissors, glue, a sheet of dark-colored construction paper, and a supply of old newspapers and magazines to the class. Have students look through the papers and magazines for list words. Tell them to cut out any list words they find and glue them on the sheet of construction paper. See who can find the most list words. This technique may also be used to have students construct sentences or cut out individual letters to form words.

Word Sorts Invite students to write each list word on a separate card. Then, ask them how many different ways the words can be organized (such as animate vs. inanimate, past-tense or vowel patterns, similarity or contrast in meaning). As students sort the words into each category, have them put words that don't belong in a category into an exception pile.

Spelling Notebook

Spelling Notebook

Definitions and Rules

The alphabet has two kinds of letters—**vowels** and **consonants**. The **vowels** are **a**, **e**, **i**, **o**, and **u** (and sometimes **y**). All the rest of the letters are **consonants**.

Each **syllable** in a word must have a vowel sound. If a word or syllable has only one vowel and it comes at the beginning or between two consonants, the vowel usually stands for a **short-vowel** sound.

> cat   sit   cup

A **long-vowel** sound usually has the same sound as its letter name.

When **y** comes at the end of a word with one syllable, the **y** at the end usually has the sound of long **i**, as in *dry* and *try*. When **y** comes at the end of a word with more than one syllable, it usually has the sound of long **e**, as in *city* and *funny*.

When two or more **consonants** come together in a word, their sounds may blend together. In a **consonant blend**, you can hear the sound of each letter.

> smile   slide   friend

A **consonant digraph** consists of two consonants that go together to make one sound.

> sharp   fourth   each

A **consonant cluster** consists of three consonants together in one syllable.

> thrills   patch   splash

A **vowel pair** consists of two vowels together where the first vowel stands for the long sound and the second vowel is silent.

> teacher   fail   soak

A **vowel digraph** consists of two vowels that together make a long-vowel sound, a short-vowel sound or a special sound of their own.

> bread   sooner   auto

A **diphthong** consists of two vowels that blend together to make one sound.

> boy   oil   cloud

A **base word** is a word to which a prefix or suffix may be added to change its meaning.

> unlawful   replace   shyness

A **root** is a word part to which a prefix or suffix may be added to change its meaning.

> induction   repel   conduct

An **ending** is a letter or group of letters added to the end of a base word to make the word singular or plural or to tell when an action happened.

> hats   foxes   runs   rained   helping

A **prefix** is a word part that is added to the beginning of a base word or a root. A prefix changes the meaning of the base word.

> **un**happy   **dis**trust   **re**pel   **con**duct

A **suffix** is a word part that is added to the end of a base word or root to make a new word.

> cheer**ful**   agree**able**   dic**tion**   port**able**

When you write words in **alphabetical order**, use these rules:

1. If the *first letter* of two words is the same, use the second letter.
2. If the *first two letters* are the same, use the third letter.

There are two **guide words** at the top of each page in the dictionary. The word on the left tells you the first word on the page. The word on the right tells you the last word on the page. All the words in between are in alphabetical order.

The dictionary puts an **accent mark** (´) *after* the syllable with the strong sound.

> pur′sən

There is a vowel sound that can be spelled by any of the vowels. It is often found in a syllable that is not accented, or stressed, in a word. This vowel sound has the sound-symbol /ə/. It is called the **schwa**.

The word *I* is always a **capital** letter.

A **contraction** is a short way of writing two words. It is formed by writing two words together and leaving out one or more letters. Use an **apostrophe** (′) to show where something is left out.

> it is = it's   we will = we'll

A **compound word** is a word made by joining two or more words.

> cannot   anyway   maybe   firehouse

Teacher Notes